Science, Spirituality and Ontological Mysticism

By the same author

- **Buddhist Tantra:** A Philosophical Reflection & Religious Investigation
- **Tantra:** Its Mystic and Scientific Basis

About the Author

Professor Singh spent about two decades as a mendicant in search of truth and salvation. He was awarded D. Litt. Degree from Ranchi University, Ranchi in 1972. He retired as a professor of Philosophy from Magadh University, Bodh Gaya in January 1996 and in February of the same year he became Senior Fellow of the Indian Council of Philosophical Research, Govt. of India for three years. In 2000 A.D. Professor Singh was awarded Fellowship of Indian Institute of Advanced Studies, Shimla for three years. He became a visiting Research Professor in 2004 at the Catholic University of America, Washington D.C. He was also awarded Indo-French Cultural Fellowship in 1994. During his sojourn at Paris, he delivered lectures at the Department of Philosophy, Soubourn University IV, Paris. He also addressed the students and staff members of Nihon and Toyo University, Tokyo in 2006. He delivered a special lecture at the Faculty of Humanities and Social Sciences, Khon Kaen University, Thailand in 2013. He presented several papers at the National and International Conferences and Seminars such World Philosophical Congress 1975, International Congress of Orientalists, Mexico City 1976, First Sanskrit Symposia, Mexico City 1982, World Sanskrit Congress, Lieden, Holland, International Conferences at East China Normal University, Shanghai, Xiaotong University, Xi'an in December 2013. He also presented papers at the School of the Social sciences and the Humanities, East China Normal University and at the School of Social Sciences, Shanghai University, Shanghai, China in 2014. He chaired many International sessions. Twenty one Research Scholars worked under his supervision and were awarded Ph.D. degrees. He has written many books of high academic value, published several papers at the National and International proceedings and Journals of high academic repute. Prof. Singh is a distinguished professor of philosophy and a social activist.

Science, Spirituality and Ontological Mysticism

The Philosophical Enquiry and Reflection

Lalan Prasad Singh M.A.; D. Litt

CONCEPT PUBLISHING COMPANY PVT. LTD.
NEW DELHI-110059

ISBN-13: 978-93-5125-221-4

First Published 2016

Published and Printed by

Concept
Since 1974

Concept Publishing Company Pvt. Ltd.
Regd. Office:
A/15-16, Commercial Block, Mohan Garden,
New Delhi-110059 (INDIA)
Phones : 25351460, 25351794,
Fax : 091-11-25357109
Email : publishing@conceptpub.com
Website: www.conceptpub.com

Editorial Office: H-13, Bali Nagar, New Delhi-110 015, India.

Cataloging in Publication Data—DK Courtesy: D.K. Agencies (P) Ltd. <docinfo@dkagencies.com>

Singh, Lalan Prasad, 1936- **author.**
Science, spirituality and ontological mysticism : the philosophical enquiry and reflection/ Lalan Prasad Singh (M.A.; D. Litt).
pages cm
Includes bibliographical references and index.
ISBN 9789351252214

1. Religion and science. 2. Hinduism and science. 3. Buddhism and science. 4. Ontology. 5. Mysticism. I. Title.

BL240.3.S56 2016 DDC 215 23

To

Shri Digvijay Singh

The Hope and Promise of New India

Preface

This book is the outcome of two decades of my reflection over this subject. I have also been inspired by some unknown force whom I refer as cosmic consciousness which is not only the substratum of all existence but existent itself. The recent developments in science since the publication of Albert Einstein's special theory of relativity and Quantum Mechanics, science is moving away from the classical physics. Neil Bohr, Werner Heisenberg, and Erwin Schrodinger are the founding fathers of Quantum Mechanics who started questioning the very existence of objective, static, physical world of classical physics. Time, Space and Causation have lost their independent existence in the absence of a perceiver. Science, especially the Quantum Mechanics is coming closer to oriental spirituality and ontological mysticism. Not only oriental philosophical tradition is rooted in spirituality and ontological mysticism but the Western Philosophical Schools and systems have been founded on the sound spiritual and ontological mystical ideas and concepts. Spirituality and ontological mysticism are the basis of philosophical and scientific thinking. Apart from analysing, evaluating and examining the different philosophical and scientific concepts, I have introduced some new ideas and concepts in the form of cosmic consciousness as the ultimate reality and the scientific and philosophic importance of subject or perceiver. Subject or perceiver may be accepted as the fifth dimension. We have to examine the philosophical and scientific questions, both from the transcendental and relativistic perspective for the fuller and complete understanding of the scientific issues and problems. The Heisenberg's ground breaking formulation of the theory of uncertainty has opened new issues and vistas which cannot be answered by relativistic, scientific perspective. I have discussed in some detail on these vexed scientific and philosophical issues in chapters Science and Mysticism and Ontological Mysticism. However, I leave it to the world of academia to pass judgements on the originality of this work.

The publication of Einstein's special theory of relativity in 1905 and general theory of relativity in 1916 and Ludwig Wittgenstein's, Tractatus brought a Copernicus revolution in scientific and philosophical world. The theory of relativity may be marked as a transition phase of scientific development from classical physics to Quantum mechanics. The doctrine of non-dual (*advaita*) which is the quintessential teachings of Hinduism, Buddhism and Taoism, is the basis of oriental and occidental scientific and philosophical traditions. "Whereof we cannot sayeth, thereof we must consign to silence", of Wittgenstein's Tractatus validates the Upaniṣadic teachings that reality (*Brahman*) is beyond the reach of senses and mind. According to Wittgenstein, truth is beyond the limit of sayable and unsayable. It is mystical. The doctrines of relativity, the Quantum Mechanics and Tractatus have changed the scientific and philosophical thinking. They have paved the path for the convergence of science and spirituality, philosophy and ontological mysticism. Science and spirituality, myth and reality are inextricably linked. This book is full of paradoxes and contradictions; it is full of allegories and metaphors. They are not truths, but pointer to deeper and profound truth. Sometimes myths and metaphors, fables and allegories speak out greater truth than truth itself as truth is unspeakable.

I owe great deal of indebtedness to Shri U.P. Singh, my friend, philosopher and guide for his constant help and inspiration in the completion of this book. I owe debt of gratitude to my friend Shri Kamal Morarka for his constant help and co-operation in my academic pursuit. I would like to express my indebtedness to my son Amitabh Kumar Singh who lives in Tokyo for funding my visit to U.S.A. to work at the Library of Congress and buying some valuable books for day to day consultation and reference. I would be failing in my duty if I do not acknowledge the help and the encouragement from my foster mother Mrs. Pratima Singh and her loving daughter Anju of Maryland for their warm hospitality. I express my thanks to Ratan and his wife Sunny, Munna and his wife Vatsala (Micky) for making my stay comfortable at McLean, Virginia. I am also thankful to Ninder Singh of Frezno of California State for his hospitality. I am thankful to the members of the staff of Library of Congress, especially to Miss Carter, Head of Science section.

However, without the loving help of Janu and his friend Vipin, this work would not have been completed. I express my loving thanks to Arvind (Bantu) for his help and cooperation in preparing the bibliography. My youngest daughter Varsha and son Raja are the great source of my happiness.

However, my life would have become insipid and worthless without the pure love and affection of my grandsons Kishu, Rishi and Anirvana. I express my sincere thanks and loving gratitude to Ashok Mittal, the owner of Concept Publishing Company (P) Ltd., for publishing my third book. I am very much indebted to my friend Prof. H.S. Gill for his help and cooperation in editing the book. Last but not the least I express my thanks to Mrs Menka Solanki for her help in the correction of Sanskrit verses.

Vasant Panchami **L.P. Singh**
12th February, 2016

Gautam Buddha University
Greater Noida, U.P.-201312

Contents

PART – I

1

Introduction

Since time immemorial philosophical reflection is the basis of existential quest for human identity and destiny. In search of the realization of spiritual reality and religious *summum bonum* of life, Lord Śiva expounded scientific and mystic philosophical system known as Śaivism. Mysticism forms the basis of all religions and provides sound philosophical foundation for science and spirituality.

The Himālayas is *the isle of the blest* where the fertile seed of meditation was sown that engendered various schools of philosophy.

Śiva is the founding father of philosophical and scientific tradition in India. The Harappan Civilization is the gift of Śaivism. The only male God of the Harappan culture is Lord Śiva. He is characterised by a horned headdress, the symbol of great mystic power. A seal showing Śiva seated on a raised throne in the posture of *yoga* was discovered at Mohenjo-Daro (Pl. V. 4). Sir John Marshall says, "The figure represents a prototype of the historic Śiva."[1] The ontological mysticism of Śaivism is the foundation of Indian science and spirituality that becomes the first principle of epistemology. This first principle explains the nature of reality and at the same time it explains itself. In search of the knowledge of ultimate reality we are led to the unfathomable undercurrents of ontological mysticism.

Western rationalism and Oriental mysticism laid down the foundation of the modern doctrine of Relativity, Quantum Mechanics and Monism. The doctrine of Relativity and Quantum Mechanics is based on ontological mysticism. This is evident from the recent researches made by Einstein, Heisenberg and Schrodinger.

Hinduism, Buddhism and Taoism reached the pinnacle of spiritual glory and sublimity in transcendentalism. The Śiva, the Buddha and the Lao Tse realised their spiritual sublimity and unreality of personal God of religion. According to Oriental philosophical system, time, space and causation are relativistic in nature. The Hindu seers, Buddhist patriarchs and Taoist had the awareness and understanding of relativistic nature of reality and hence instead of paying undue attention to ephemeral truths and worldly achievements, they kept themselves engrossed in the pursuits of enlightenment. I shall examine and analyse the origin and development of modern scientific doctrine of Relativity and Quantum Mechanics and the growth and evolution of spiritual monastic and mystical tradition of Hinduism, Buddhism and Taoism for their proper and fuller understanding and their impact on humanity in subsequent chapters.

Spirituality has been the basis of all knowledge. Philosophy is conceived as *Brahma Vidyā* in *Muṇḍaka Upaniṣad. Brahma Vidyā* is the ontological and mystical basis of all sciences. According to Chāṇakya, "Philosophy is the lamp of all sciences, the means of performing all the works, and the support of all the duties."[2]

In India Philosophy is based on ontological mysticism. It has originated in the origin of life. The founding fathers of philosophy in India laid down a sound spiritual and ethical foundation. India has survived the pillage of time and plunder of history because of its strong spiritual and ethical foundation. Radhakrishnan writes, "The idea of Plato that philosophers must be the rulers and directors of society is practised in India. The ultimate truths are truths of spirit, and in the light of them actual life has to be refined. Religion in India is not dogmatic. It is a rational synthesis which goes on gathering into itself new conceptions as philosophy progresses. It is experimental and provisional in its nature, attempting to keep pace with the progress of thought."[3]

In the beginning there was no difference between philosophy, science and logic in Indian and Greek traditions. Subsequently with more and more specialization, they emerged as different approaches to knowledge. To *Know Thy Self* was the basis of philosophical reflection. The facts of the empirical world were analysed and understood with logic and rational thinking.

In the Greek tradition the first rationalist thinker is Thales who considered water as the primordial reality.With Parmenides we have the first serious philosophical reflections who pondered over the existential reality of the Being. For him all reality is in flux. It is transitory. All that is born dies. All that is created withers away. And hence, we cannot have knowledge of reality which is in the state of constant change and becoming. Parmenides wanted to find the permanent and the eternal in the world of change and becoming. For Parmenides the Being alone was real. As such, it was the first principle of the real and the eternal.

The pursuit of philosophy is a rigorous search for unchanging and the eternal in this world where nothing lasts forever and where one is not certain of anything. Heraclitus followed this quest further, and like the Buddhist, considered all reality in flux. The world is constituted of the "central fire which was, ever is, now, and ever shall be, and ever-living Fire". Parmenides was born in Elea, South of Italy. At that time south Italy was rooted in mysticism. Mathematics was an integral form of mysticism. Apart from propagating the philosophy of the Being as the eternal reality, he founded his philosophical doctrine on the basis of metaphysical arguments. He is considered as the father of logic, but his importance lies in the world of philosophy for putting metaphysics on the sound basis of logic. This has been the inspiration for all subsequent philosophers including Hegel.

To Question is to philosophise. With the evolution of *Homo sapiens* man became conscious of self and nature, he started enquiring about the fundamental question; '*Who am I*', and '*What is Nature*'. The first enquiry blossomed in mysticism and second led to scientific rationalism. Mysticism became the hallmark of Eastern philosophy and scientific rationalism became the leading approach of Western tradition. There is evidence in the Indian doctrine of rebirth and salvation in the philosophy of Pythagoreans, Socrates and Plato.

However, there is a happy and harmonious blending of Ontological mysticism and scientific rationalism in the doctrine of Relativity and Quantum Mechanics. Einstein, Heisenberg and Schrodinger speak of the ontological mysticism as the foundation of their ground breaking scientific discoveries of Relativity and Quantum Mechanics.

Their formulation of the doctrines is rooted in the philosophy of oriental mysticism and Western philosophy. The impact of Hinduism, Buddhism on the formulation of Pythagoreans, Heraclitus and Parmenides is evident at the every phase of their writings. Dikaiarchos says that Pythagoras taught "first, that the soul is an immortal thing, that is transformed into other kinds of living things; further, that whatever comes into existence is born again in the revolutions of a certain cycle, nothing being absolutely new; and that all things that are born with life in them ought to be treated as kindred."[4]

Pythagorean society was primarily an ascetic society. Like Hinduism and Buddhism, Pythagorean ascetic society shared with the doctrine of reincarnation and rebirth. Like Hinduism and Buddhism the Pythagoreans believed that release from the cycle of birth and death could be obtained by mystical practices.

Pythagorean's religious perspective and life style were rigorous and ascetic. They believed in the ascetism and the purity of life. Pythagoreans are considered as the inventor of arithmetic which is the science of numbers. It is believed that Copernicus was greatly influenced in formulating his ground breaking theory that it is earth that rotates around the sun, is based on heliocentric hypothesis of Pythagoreans.

While summarizing the teachings of Pythagoreans Burnett says, "We are strangers in this world, and the body is the tomb of the soul, and yet we must not seek to escape by self-murder; for we are chattels of God who is our herdsman, and without his command we have no right to make our escape. In this life, there are three kinds of men, just as there are three sorts of people who come to the Olympic Games. The lowest class is made of those who come to buy and sell, the next above them are those who compete. Best of all, however, are those who come simply to look on. The greatest purification of all is, therefore, disinterested science, and it is the man who devotes himself to that, the true philosopher, who has effectually released himself from the 'wheel of birth.' "[5]

The modern science is rooted in the Greek tradition of sixth century B.C. when science and philosophy were an integral part of the pursuits of knowledge. The word physics owes its origin in Greek. It stands for the human endeavour to understand the basic structure and nature of the world. The monastic and the mystic world view of Indian and Chinese were closer to the Pythagoreans and Parmenides views of universal reality. Though the Western world view, especially of the early Greeks, was closely similar and parallel to that of Oriental philosophical and religious thoughts, the mystical and monastic world view has been the main stream of Oriental culture and civilization. The cultural divides of East and West gave birth to two parallel trends and tendencies both wise and unwise. Aristotle's doctrine of form and matter culminated in Cartesian dualism. Aristotle's dualistic doctrine and world view kept the whole Western scientific thinking captive and in hibernation for two thousand years. It was Einstein's dictum $E = mc^2$ awakened from the dogmatic slumber of Aristotle in 1905 with the publication of revolutionary historic paper on Special Theory of Relativity. This parallel world view blossomed in Oriental and Occidental traditions in the form of spiritual humanism and scientific materialism respectively. India neglected scientific rationalism and its resultant materialism for which India had to pay the heavy and humiliating price of remaining under foreign rule and exploitation for thousands of years. Western scientific materialism resulted in the decline of its culture and civilization by becoming Faustian in nature and goal.

Albert Schweitzer lamenting on the decline and degeneration of Western culture and civilization says, "Our civilization is going through a severe crisis. The disastrous features of our civilization are that it is far more developed materially than spiritually. Through the discoveries which now place the forces of Nature at our disposal in such an unprecedented way, the relations to other individuals, of social groups, and of states have undergone a revolutionary change. We value too highly its material achievements and no longer keep in our mind as vividly as is desirable the importance of the spiritual."[6] Galileo is the founding father of modern science. The scientific temper and vision of Galileo blossomed in most matured form in the theory of Relativity and Quantum Mechanics. He had to undergo great hardship and imprisonment for opposing unscientific and dogmatic belief of the Church. He upheld the findings of Copernicus discovery and revolutionary postulates of earth orbiting the sun. He pronounced that the earth is not the centre of the universe. This went against the basic hypothesis of the Church. He formulated the scientific method of conceptual research, the analysis and examination of facts and objects which are governed by the laws of nature. Galileo's experiment of the falling of bodies from the Leaning Tower of Pisa brought a revolution in modern science. It went against the established view espoused by Aristotle that all moving bodies not acted upon by external forces continue to be in a state of motion.

Before Galileo the geocentric view of Ptolemy was a scientific tool that was used with reasonable accuracy for the prediction of the movement of celestial bodies. Galileo accepted the Copernican heliocentric universe against the opposition of the Church, which not only proved to be a revolutionary change in scientific method to examine and analyse with more accuracy the prediction of celestial phenomena. This laid down the foundation of new science which ushers in the Era of Renaissance and Reformation in the seventeenth century in Europe. Galileo introduced a new tool of experiment to understand the laws of nature that operates on the structure of matter and force responsible for the phenomenal world. This may be acclaimed as Galileo's fundamental method of modern natural science. In Einstein, we find the unification and happy blending of the Buddha's *Śūnyatā* and Spinoza's Substance (God). His unfinished task of finding unified theory which could be the basis of formulation of finding a rational scientific thinking in explaining the birth of universe and its sustenance. His concept of God that doesn't play dice with the world and rejection of personal God and his exposition of doctrine of cosmic religious feeling is in the search of transcendental reality which combine in itself both matter and consciousness: the World and God. Monism of Hinduism, Buddhism and Taoism could be the unified theory according to which world and God are one. Kashmir Śaivism and Vedānta, *Śūnyavāda*, *Vijñānavāda* of Buddhism and Tao of Taoism speak of the same reality and truth in different language. The different language speaks of the different cultural ethos. Schrodinger's revolutionary doctrine which combines Quantum Mechanics with Vedāntic teachings is a step towards formulating a unified theory. I find Schrodinger as an altered ego of the Śaṅkara. He attaches philosophical and scientific importance and significance of Vedāntic teachings in solving some of the age old scientific enigma and ethical questions. His declaration that '*the World is I*' is of great scientific and mystical significance. Heisenberg's formulation of uncertainty principle is another landmark in the search of scientific truth and reality. This has raised many problems than solving the vex question of wave and particles. His honest confession of inability to give an unambiguous account of atom is the confirmation of Wittgenstein's concluding statement of Tractatus, that "*whereof we cannot sayeth thereof we must consign to silence*". Heisenberg admits that "*Truth dwells in deeps*". His quest to reach the central order of things and events whose existence is beyond any doubt leads to the search for spiritual and ethical basis of different civilizations and culture. This spiritual content of culture gets its affirmation in all religious traditions. Science and philosophy have been in quest of truth since time immemorial. Both are comprised of two distinct domains and systems, however, surprisingly they come to the similar conclusion. Both science and philosophy agree in principle that truth is beyond their reach. Heisenberg says that we do not know Nature as such, but as it is exposed to us. Kant stated that we do not know the noumena. Our knowledge is confined and limited to the phenomenal world. Thing in itself is unknown and unknowable. The eastern philosophy agrees with Kant's first part of his assertions that our knowledge is confined to the domain of phenomena, but it doesn't accept Kant's latter declaration that the thing in itself which constitutes the ultimate reality is unknowable. Buddhism and Vedānta are of the opinion that in the state of spiritual sublimity and divinity, truth is experienced in its totality and wholeness. "Though Vedānta also states very clearly that ultimate reality is beyond the reach of mind and senses."[7] Kashmir Śaivism and Vedānta expound that ultimate reality could be experienced through the transcendental system of knowledge (*Parā Jñāna*). Taoism and Buddhism also speak in the same vein. Western world view is embedded in dualism. This dualistic philosophy and scientific tradition have created all the problems for a seeker of truth in comprehending and experiencing ultimate reality in its depth and totality.

Albert Schweitzer writes, "The dualistic world view does not comprehend with reality, for it comprises doctrines about the universe which cannot be made to square with the facts".[8]

The close examination and analysis of scientific and philosophical quest leads to a reality which is spiritual in nature. Science and spirituality are integral form and part of existence and being. Hinduism, Buddhism and Taoism provide the world view which is rooted in monism and mysticism. The Western world view is essentially dualistic and naïve. It doesn't confirm with reality.

Albert Schweitzer writes, "Even the philosophy of Kant's is dualistic. It works with idea derived from Christianity, of an ethical creator of the universe, without making clear to itself how it can succeed in identifying him with the Primal Cause of Being."[9]

The new scientific thought especially that of Quantum Mechanics is in variance with the classical physics of continuous description of facts and truths. The new element of the role of *Subject* has become inevitable in determination and observation of facts. We cannot make any real and rational formulation of natural objects without having any kind of conscious relation with it. Hence, the role of consciousness or a subjective counterpart of reality occupies an important role in formulating the world view. Schrodinger has tried to explain the role of observing subject in his series of lectures which was compiled in a book form titled "Science and Humanism". He tries to clarify that there should not be any misunderstanding about the knowledge of fully determined physical world of existence as explained by Bohr and Heisenberg. He believes that we cannot have any knowledge about the physical world without '*getting in touch*' with it. Here a role of consciousness or we may call it observing mind becomes very important in formulation of any scientific doctrine or theory in the background of Bohr's and Heisenberg's formulation of Quantum Mechanics. Schrodinger writes, that "what they mean that object has no existence independent of the observing subject. They mean that the recent discoveries in physics have pushed forward to the mysterious boundary between the *Subject* and the *Object* which thereby has turned out not to be sharp boundary at all. We are to understand that we never observe an object without its being modified and tinged by our own activity in observing it. We are to understand under the impact of our refined methods of observation, and of thinking about the results of our experiments, that mysterious boundary between the subject and the object has broken down."[10]

Heisenberg also recognises the subjectivity as an important element in the observation of nature. According to him we observe nature not as it is, but as exposed to our tool of observation. He says, "Our scientific work in physics consists in asking questions about nature in the language that we possess and trying to get our answer from experiment by the means that are at our disposal. In this way Quantum theory reminds us, as Bohr has put it, of the old wisdom that when searching for harmony in life one must never forget in the drama of existence we are ourselves both players and spectators. It is understandable in our scientific relation to nature our own activity becomes very important when we have to deal with parts of nature into which we can penetrate only by using the most elaborate tools."[11]

According to Indian tradition there are two types of knowledge, i.e., *Parā Jñāna* (transcendental knowledge or wisdom), *Aparā Jñāna* (relativistic knowledge). Subjectivisation of supreme subjectivity is called *Parā Jñāna* (transcendental or wisdom) and Subjectivisation of external objects is known as *Aparā Jñāna* (relativistic knowledge). Indian philosophical tradition has been aware of the importance and inevitability of consciousness (subject) in the realm of knowledge. No kind of knowledge bereft of subjective elements is possible because it believes that consciousness is the penultimate source of all kinds of knowledge. Schrodinger says, "It is the only the individual peculiarities in any one ontogenesis which become conscious".[12] Thus, all organic and inorganic existence is associated with consciousness.

Consciousness is the very core of all organic and inorganic substance. The modern rational scientific thinking is mystical (According to religion *science is mystical*), but when we accept this view then it goes against the principles of classical physics which believes in the ontology of materialism. We have to examine the philosophical, classical, relativity and quantum mechanics doctrines related with this very important problem. Science is a rational quest for understanding nature. The ontology of materialism has been debated by thinkers of different traditions since the advent of civilizations. The concept of matter has been analysed, examined and evaluated in different philosophical systems. With the advancement of civilization and rational thinking, the concept of matter has gone under scrutiny of different systems and as such it has undergone great change. According to Aristotle matter is a "*potentia*". By "*potentia*" Aristotle means relation between form and matter. It does not exist by itself. It is only a possibility.

The noted French mathematician, Marquis De Laplace says, “Strictly speaking it may even be said that nearly all our knowledge is problematical; and in the small number of things which we are able to know with certainty, even in mathematical sciences themselves, the principle means of ascertaining truth—induction and analogy are based on probabilities.”[13]

Phenomenon is a metaphysical. For the proper understanding of nature we will have to indulge in metaphysical pursuits.

According to Wittgenstein language is a picture of reality. Reality stands for fact. Fact means state of affairs. Objects are not facts as for example pen is not a fact. Pen is lying on the table is a fact, neither pen nor table are facts. They are things. World is a totality of facts not of things. There is an isomorphic relation between language and world. The analysable unit of language is elementary proposition and its counterpart in the world of facts is atomic facts. Elementary proposition is a picture of atomic facts. The atomic fact is a logical possibility. There is a great similarity between Wittgenstein’s atomic fact and Quantum Mechanics concept of ultimate unit of matter. Heisenberg has made a very bold statement about the ultimate unit of matter. He says, “In the experiments about the atomic events we have to do with things and facts, with phenomena that are just real as any phenomena in daily life. But the atoms are elementary. Particles themselves are as real; they form a world of potentialities and probabilities rather than one of things or facts.”[14]

Since Galileo science adopted the method of experiment and observation for understanding the mystery of nature. All the scientific discoveries since Galileo are the outcome of observations and experiments. Whereas philosophy is analytical and reflective. Strangely enough scientific and philosophical quest have culminated in ontological mysticism. Nature is vast and mysterious. Scientists and philosophers have been trying to discover some of the hidden mysteries of nature.

Galileo’s espousal and support for the Copernicus theory of heliocentric universe landed him into prison. His method of experiment and direct observation became the foundation of science. Galileo’s acceptance of Copernican heliocentric world was confirmed by Newton’s theory of gravitation. In science there are always the principles of probability working in any systematic discovery and measurement. Accuracy is an evasive term. Measurements are never accurate and precise. They are always associated with some amount of inaccuracies. Lisa Randall writes, "Measurements themselves have some intrinsic uncertainties necessitating their repetition. Quantum Mechanics tells us that the underlying events do too. Quantum Mechanics implies that no matter how cleverly design our technology, we can compute only the probability that interactions occur. This uncertainty exists, no matter how we make a measurement."[15]

However, scientists lack of infinite certainty does not erode the importance of any discovery or measurement. It only speaks of the relativistic characteristics of our understanding about phenomena. This is why it has been termed in Indian tradition as *Aparā Jñāna*. Lisa Randall further writes, "Science generally settles issues with some degree of probability. Of course we can achieve high confidence in any particular idea or observation and use science to make sound judgements. But only infrequently can anyone absolutely settle an issue—scientific or otherwise—on the basis of evidence. We can collect enough data to trust casual relationships and even to make incredibly precise predictions, but we can generally do it only probabistically."[16]

Karl Popper is of the opinion that all scientific theories are open to falsification. However, science has made tremendous progress and opened new vistas of our knowledge. It has stood the test of application when it came to landing of a man on moon and returning back safely. However, there has been a persistent attack on science by conservative clergy. Especially against Charles Darwin theory of evolution by natural selection. Christopher Toumey writes, "This monkey mythology of Darwin is the cause of permissiveness, promiscuity, pills, prophylactics, perversions, pregnancies, abortions, pornography, pollution, poisoning and proliferation of crimes of all types."[17] However, the founding father of modern science Galileo Galilei stood against the orthodoxy of Church while accepting and propagating the Copernican theory of heliocentric world. He wrote to the dogmatic religious authority: 'To the Discerning Reader' at the beginning of his great Dialogue Concerning Two Chief World System. "Several years ago there was published in Rome a salutary edict which in order to obviate the dangerous tendencies of our age, imposed a seasonable silence upon the Pythagorean (or Copernican), opinion that earth moves. There were those who prudently asserted that this decree had its origin, nor injudicious inquiry, but in passion, more too well informed. Complaints were to be heard that advisors, who were totally unskilled at astronomical observation ought not to clip the wings of reflective intellects by means of rash prohibitions. Upon hearing such curbing insolence, my zeal could not be contained."[18]

The apparent disagreements in classical physics have been debated and discussed in depth in the last century. According to the classical physics phenomenal world exists 'out there'. It believes in absolute objectivity. Nature is objectively real. Classical physics is based on Newton's mechanical model of the Universe. This laid down a strong foundation for all science and it became the fundamental assumptions for philosophy. The Newtonian world view ruled the science and philosophical world for three centuries. Classical physics is deterministic. It was assumed that nature is governed by causation and is deterministic. The theory of causation which was considered as necessary certainty was the tools and the scientific methods for explaining every events of nature having a particular cause which resulted in particular effects. Hence, the future could be predicted on the basis of causation with perfect theory of determinism. Thus, according to classical physics there is an isomorphic relation between fact and scientific concept. Einstein holds the view that every aspects of nature depicts the corresponding elements in scientific theory. The classical view of truth has been associated with the concept of nature as an external independent existence. Einstein's world view is different from Newton's classical mechanistic world view. The theory of relativity which propagates time as the other dimensions and integral part of nature is known as four dimensional continuum. Space-time is interrelated and interdependent. We cannot talk of space without time and *vice versa*. Time doesn't have a linear flow which was the basic assumptions of Newtonian world view. Einstein writes, "I wish to show that space-time is not necessarily something to which one can ascribe a separate existence, independently of the actual objects of physical reality". On the other hand, Quantum Mechanics introduces a new element of subjectivity in the measurement and the observation of nature. Subject becomes the part of measurement and observation. We cannot give any observation and measurement of sub-atomics phenomena with certainty; it is case of probability and not certainty. In the process of observation and measurement, reality is changed and modified. Gary Zukav writes, "Philosophically, however, the implication of quantum mechanics is psychedelic. Not only do we influence our reality, but, in some degree actually *create* it. Because it is the nature of things that we can know either the momentum of a particle or its position, but not both, *we must choose* which of those two properties we want to determine. Metaphysically, this is very close to saying that we *create* certain properties because we choose to measure those properties."[19] Thus, it follows from Quantum Mechanics that pure and independent objectivity is an illusion. Observer is an active partner in the act of observation. Nobel Laureate French physicist, Wolfang Pauli observes that "from an inner centre, the psyche seems to more outward, in the sense of an extra version, into the physical world".

According to the new development and discovery, modern science is becoming a part of psychology in understanding the structure of consciousness. Fritjof Capra writes, "In modern physics, the universe is thus experienced as a dynamic, inseparable whole which always includes the observer in an essential way. In this experience, the traditional concepts of space and time, of isolated objects, and of cause and effect, lose their meaning. Such an experience, however, is very similar to that of the Eastern mystics. The similarity becomes apparent in quantum and relativity theory, and becomes even stronger in the "Quantum-relativistic" models of sub-atomic physics where both these theories combine to produce the most striking parallels to Eastern mysticism."[20]

I think that the concept of consciousness is central to the philosophical and scientific investigation and reflection. Consciousness is discussed in the sense of sensation and thought. Descartes, the father of modern philosophy says, "I think, therefore, I am (*Cogito Ergo Sum*)". In his celebrated work 'Discourse on Method', he tried to provide a sound philosophical foundation on the basis of rational thinking and doubt. He argued that we can doubt the existence of everything but we cannot doubt the thinking doubter. It follows from this that our thinking mind contains more certainty than the phenomenal world. The problem of mind-body relation has been debated in almost all philosophical systems.

Spinoza's Substance (God) contains both thought and extension. Leibniz's doctrine of Monodology contains logical basis of ontological mysticism as the monads are mystical entities.

The concept of consciousness which has been the central thought of philosophy and psychology has become now one of the important scientific inquiry and investigation. Saul-Paul Sirag writes, "Idea that reality is hyper dimensional, is entertained today by the physicist attempting to unify all physical forces in a unified field theory. It is reasonable to suppose that the detailed descriptions of this hyper dimensional reality will yield a theory of consciousness."[21] Werner Heisenberg, Schrodinger and other scientific thinkers are convinced of the role of subject in understanding nature. Subject does play an important role in understanding the phenomenal world. Without giving a proper place and importance to consciousness in rational scientific formulation theory of relativity and quantum mechanics are incomplete. Thus Time, Space, Subject is the proper and rational paradigm for understanding the universe. Thus, apart from four dimensional paradigm of Relativity we must add in the light of the recent researches and observations made by Heisenberg and Schrodinger, "subject" as the fifth dimension. Without accepting subject as the fifth dimension the theory of relativity and Quantum Mechanics lose their signification. Science has not taken into account the role of consciousness (Subject) in providing rational explanation of nature until and the birth and development of Quantum Mechanics. As the subject is transcendental in nature the world view presented by space-time-subject paradigm become multi-dimensional. Subject (mind) doesn't function in a linear way rather it functions in a multi-dimensional way and considering the inevitable working of mind in process of cognition making Nature modified and tinged. I think the universe becomes multi-dimensional. I am of the opinion that in the combine doctrine of Relativity, Quantum Mechanics and Ontological mysticism, the proper and the right picture of the world view becomes multi-dimensional. Saint Augustine's concept that time is an aspect of human cognition played an important role in the formulation of Einstein's theory of Relativity. By accepting time-space-subject as a new paradigm and combined theory of Relativity, Quantum Mechanics and Ontological mysticism would, provide a new doctrine of Einstein's dream of unified theory of the universe. This unified theory has been the kernel of Kashmir's Śaivism, and Vedānta of Hinduism, *Vijñānavāda* and *Śūnyavāda* of Buddhism and Tao of Taoism.

According to Ontological mysticism, Reality is One. It is cosmic consciousness. This manifests itself in and through nature and history. Hegel is probably only the outstanding thinker in the West who could understand and appreciate the idealistic monism of the East and his concept of Absolute has close similarity and approximation with Hinduism, Buddhism and Taoism. The contrast and conflict between philosophy and science gets harmonious and happy blending in spiritual monism propagated by Hinduism, Buddhism and Taoism.

Evolution of psycho-spiritual doctrine is based largely on meditation and mysticism. The irresistible urge for Beyond is the sheet anchor of the religio-philosophical culture in India. The problems of inner life and the mysteries of the world of becoming and the world of spirit are *the raison 'd'ētre'*, a *Philosophical Revolution* and *Spiritual Renaissance*. "The evolution of cult and culture in India is inspired and fed by intuitive vision and subjective realization and not by reason and argument. The orientation to the goal of liberation from the meshes and trammels which connotes total cessation of metempsychosis is both the beginning and the end of the religio-philosophical movement of India."[22] *Śivādvaita* School of Kashmir's Śaivism and *Advaita Vedānta* propagate the philosophy of spiritual monism. According to these schools of Hinduism, Reality is of the nature of pure consciousness self-luminous and all pervading. In Kashmir Śaivism, it is called, *Parama Śiva*, which is both transcendent and imminent. According to Vedānta, the reality is one and absolute monistic in nature. It is described as *Brahman* or *Ātman*. There is complete identity between *Brahman* and Self according to monistic school of Vedānta. Gauḍapāda is the exponent and expounder of *Advaita Vedānta*. The phenomenal world is the manifest nature of the reality (absolute) from which the process of involution emanates which is perceived by the subject as different from itself. The world of appearance is the integral part of the reality, but it does not cognise in its wholeness and totality. Reality is unsubjectivated transcendentality. It is unaffected by the limitation of Time, Space and Causality. It is

Supreme Subjectivity. There is nothing outside and beyond reality according to Kashmirs Śaivism.

The *Advaita Vedānta* is based on the teachings of *Upaniṣads*, *Brahma sūtra* and *Gītā*. According to Vedānta the *Brahman* is one and the only reality. The Self (*Ātman*) and ultimate reality are one, is the essence of *Advaita Vedānta*. According to *Chāndogya Upaniṣad*, *Brahman* is the essence—the whole world has that as its self (*ātman*), i.e. reality. This is described as *ātman*, *Thou art that.* The *Brahman* is conceived as the self of the inner essence and nature of all existence and being. It is infinite and beyond all categories and concept. It is beyond the reach of mind and senses. *Brahman* is beginingless, supreme, eternal, absolute and beyond existence and non-existence. The reality cannot be described in language. Upaniṣadic seers have taken help of allegories and metaphors to communicate in *Twilight language*. However, *Brahman* is free from any mythological concepts and contents. The central objective of philosophical pursuits of Hinduism is to rid the mind from the snares of false subjectivity and take one from the dualism of subject and object to the spiritual transcendence and sublimity. This is called enlightenment or liberation. According to the Vedānta, enlightenment means becoming one with the *Brahman*. Vedānta believes "to know" is "to be".

According to spiritual monism of Hinduism, absolute and reality, God and nature become one. Knowledge and wisdom become one. It combines the mystical with philosophical reality in the spiritual monism. Man and God become one. Buddhism propounds the doctrine of two truths or two realities, a conventional or nominal truth and an ultimate truth. *Śūnyavāda* and *Vijñānavāda* is the kernel of the Buddhism. The Buddha is the one and only historical figure who founded a school of philosophy and a world religious order. His teachings which have been compiled in *Tripiṭaka* is pregnant with profound philosophical imports which have been interpreted by different Āchārya differently in different periods of history out of which grew different schools of thoughts and religious sects. I shall confine myself to *Vijñānavāda* and *Śūnyavāda* schools of Buddhism. To me these two schools of thought are based on ontological mysticism and spiritual monism.

According to Buddhism nothing permanent and unchanging entity exists which is known as ontology of substance. Buddhism advocates process ontology or it may be called as model ontology. It is close to Heraclitus and Henry Bergson. The Buddha may be called as process philosopher.

Buddhism is the philosophy of change and becoming. The central teachings of the Buddha are the doctrine of eternal flux and impermanence. Everything is changing. Thus Buddhism is a process philosophy. The change and impermanence are the fundamental properties of all existence. The doctrine of eternal flux, change and becoming is the basis of the doctrine of dependent origination. This is considered by some as foundation of Buddhism. Every affirmation is negation and every negation is affirmation. According to *Mādhyamikā*, the reality is free from all kinds of affirmation and negation. It is called *Śūnyatā* (emptiness), *Tathatā* (suchness). It is beyond the four categories of existence (*bhāva*), non-existence (*abhāva*), neither nor (*ubhāva*), nor both (*nobhāva*). These four categories of thought have been applied in postulating the theories of causation, substance, self and relation. This notion of reality has been absolute, non-dual, is beyond the reach of mind and senses. This reality could be experienced by enlightened person when he becomes free from the bondage of *Avidyā* and ignorance. *Śūnyatā* can be realized by making mind free from all kinds of reification.

Nāgārjuna employed method of *reductio abasurdum* in analysing the concept of suchness and emptiness. The emptiness is the core of *Mūla Mādhyamikā Kārikā*. According to Nāgārjuna, all phenomena are empty and that emptiness is also empty. Emptiness is the essence of all things. Emptiness itself is empty. When we ask a question about existence we use the word 'exist' sometimes with wrong connotation. If we connote the word, exist, that a substance exists inherently independent of its attributes we are committing a mistake, but if we apply the word, exists, conventionally then it speaks of the Buddhists point of view. According to Buddhism, the phenomenal world exists *nominally* or conventionally. Emptiness forms the basis of all fundamental Buddhist soteriological conceptions. After analysis and evaluation of the above stated position we come to the conclusion that entire world is non-existence. Nāgārjuna says, "Just as grammarian may teach even the first letters, so Buddha taught the *Dharma* to his disciples according to their capacity. Some he instructed in the *Dharma* which would turn them away from sins, some he instructed in the attainment of virtue, some he taught a dualistic doctrine, some he taught the non-dualistic, profound and frightful for the timid, he taught others the means of *Bodhi*, the matrix of emptiness and compassion."[23] I would like to focus and reflect upon the basic problem which has kept the philosophical minds engaged. This is the question of ontology, the essential mode of existence of things and beings. Different philosophical traditions have presented different views. The two different doctrines propagated by philosopher and scientists have some similarity. The ontological nature as has been postulated by traditional philosophical system seems apparently different from the natural sciences. However, this does not mean that different views and theories invalidate one another. The infallibility of classical physics and sensory experiences has been questioned by the theories of Relativity and Quantum Mechanics. It is now accepted that there is an incongruity between the mode of existence and their mode of appearance. Reality as a whole is conceptual designation. The eminent physicist Louis de Broglie says: "May it not be universally true that concepts produced by the human mind, when formulated in slightly vague form, are roughly valid for Reality, but that when extreme precision is aimed at, they became ideal forms whose real content tends to vanish away. It seems to me that such is, in fact, the case."[24] Taoism and Confucianism are two schools of Chinese thought. Confucianism is an ethical system. I, therefore, confine my exposition to Taoism only because it is based on ontological mysticism like Hinduism and Buddhism. Lao-tze (century 6th B.C.) is the founder of Taoism. There is no record of the death of Lao-tze. We get an account of Lao-tze's life by the first great Chinese historian, Sze-ma Khien who has written his biography. "Lao-tze was a curator at the Royal Library of Kau and that one morning over the decadence of the dynasty, he wished to withdraw from the world, and proceeded to the pass of Hsien-Ku leading from China to the west. Then he was recognised by the warden of the pass Yein Hsi, who insisted on his leaving writing before he went into seclusion.

Lao-tze then wrote his views on the Tao and its Characteristics in two parts or sections, containing more than 5,000 characters. He gave the manuscripts to the warden and went his way, nor is it known when he died."[25] Tao Teh King is the canonical literature of Taoism. The whole philosophy of Taoism is written in Twilight language. This has been the practice of Indian mystics and seers to take help of allegories and fables in explaining the inexplicable truth because it is beyond the reach of thought and language. Lao-tze teachings are also based on mysticism. He could be compared with the teachings of Buddhism and other mystic traditions of India. Kabir has also used the allegories and fables to express his Ontological mysticism. The Twilight language is employed to safeguard the highest form of mystical teachings from falling in the hands of the profane. Only the initiates get the clear understanding and awareness of the truth written in Twilight language. The apparent meaning is quite different from the real meaning. Zen Buddhism has also employed the same methods in communicating the highest truth and reality. The *koan* of Zen Buddhism is full of riddles and mystical imports. It was a general practice in oriental traditions of Hinduism, Buddhism and Taoism to communicate the mystic truth only to the seeker of knowledge and wisdom.

According to Taoism to know and yet (think) we do not know is the highest; not to know (and yet think) we do not know is a disease. According to Tao Teh King:

"The Tao does nothing, and so there is nothing it does not do.

The movement of the Tao,
By contraries proceed;
And weakness marks the course,
Of Tao's mighty deeds.
Simplicity without a name,
Is free from all external aim;
With no desire, at rest and still,
All things go right, as of their will."[26]

The life of the mystic is quite different from the life of a lay man. For mystic who has attained the state of moral and spiritual sublimity, all the perspectives of relativity and contradictions are resolved. According to the higher point of mysticism there is no difference between the good and the bad, the virtue and the vice. By recognising the relativity of the good and bad, virtue and vice the follower of Taoism maintains a dynamic and delicate balance between good and bad. The spiritual sublimity lies beyond any kind of dualism like God and nature, good and bad, truth and untruth. Tao Teh King says, "The Tao is (like) emptiness of a vessel; and our employment of it we must be on our guard against all fullness. How deep and unfathomable it is, as if it were the Honoured Ancestors of all Things. 'The fountainless', there is nothing before the Tao; it might seem to have been before God. And yet there is no demonstration by it of its presence and operation. It is like emptiness of a vessel. The practical lesson is that in following the Tao we must try to be like it."[27]

Taoism is both a philosophical system and a mystic search for immortality and liberation. There is a common misunderstanding both among the philosophers and scientists that human mind in its essential nature has intimate relationship with reality. The mystic believes that as the phenomenal world which is in the state of constant flux, how can we have real and absolute knowledge. Hence, there is no knowledge which could be said final and irrefutable. After analysing the structure of language and thought we come to the Taoist conclusion that there is "no one to know, nothing to be known". Herrlee G. Creel while summarizing the teachings of Taoism writes, "This philosophy has not always been studied with the seriousness it deserves, in part because it has often been regarded as a system of mystical incomprehensibilities. Another part of the reason is that it has sometimes been confused with the other kind of Taoism, which I suggest should be known as Hsien Taoism. The doctrines that fall under this heading, aiming at the achievement of immortality by a variety of means, have their roots in ancient Chinese magical practices and an immortality cult. Hsien Taoism also incorporates elements from Confucianism, Moism, and Buddhism. But there is one element that we might expect to find which is completely absent from Hsien Taoism. That is the central insight of philosophical Taoism."[28]

If we summarize the philosophical and the scientific system of thought we are left with no alternative but to accept that the world of plurality is relative and conventional. Consciousness is singular. It is never experienced in multiple dimensions. Only by meditation can we experience the ultimate reality which pervades the whole world. The world is one singular consciousness.

We can speak of science of consciousness with confidence and legitimacy as we speak of science of physics and psychology. When we talk of imminent aspects of God which is the substratum of all existence and being, we don't ascribe any predication other than suchness. We can experience the *Brahman*, the *Śūnyatā* and Tao in their totality and wholeness only in a state of spiritual, mystical sublimity.

Science and spirituality, nature and God become integral form of the whole existence and being. The root of all knowledge is spirituality.While enumerating real truth which science seeks, Werner Heisenberg writes, "Science is esoteric", so it is said, "it is only for the few."[29] Knowledge bereft of mysticism is Pyrrhonism. Knowledge and wisdom become one in Ontological mysticism. This is *Satori*; this is the real *Advaita* and spiritual monism of Hinduism, Buddhism and Taoism. The recent development in science in the form of theory of Relativity and Quantum Mechanics take us towards the same truth. This is true philosophy and it is true science. The knowledge and awareness of reality is the pursuits of science and to experience the reality in its wholeness and totality is the goal of spirituality. The convergence of science and ontological mysticism will herald a new era of spiritual humanism which is the only hope and promise of mankind.

References

1. Sir John Marshall. *Mohenjo-Daro and the Indus Civilization,* Vol. I, p. 52. Arthur Probsthain, 41, Great Russell Street, London, 1931.
2. *Indian Antiquary*, 1988, p. 102.
3. *Indian Philosophy*, S. Radhakrishnan, Oxford University Press, p. 25, Volume I.
4. *From Religion to Philosophy*, Corn ford, p. 201.
5. *Early Greek Philosophy*, p. 108.
6. *Civilization and Ethics: The Philosophy of Civilization*, Part II, p. 2.
7. *Taittirīya Upaniṣad*, Verse II, 4.1.
8. *Indian Thoughts and its Development*. Albert Schweitzer. Hodder and Stranghton Ltd., London, 1936, p. 12.
9. *Ibid.*
10. *Science and Humanism*, Erwin Schrodinger, Cambridge, University Press, 1952, pp. 50-51.
11. *Physics and Philosophy*. Werner Heisenberg, Harper Perennial Modern Thought, New York, 2007, p. 32.
12. *My View of World,* Erwin Schrodinger, p. 51.
13. *A Philosophical Essay on Probabilities*. Marquis De Laplace, Dover Publication, Inc. New York, 1951, p. 2.
14. *Physics and Philosophy*, p. 160.

15. *Knocking on Heaven's Door*, Lisa Randall, Harper Collins Publisher, 2011, New York, p. 209.
16. *Ibid.*, p. 202.
17. *God's Own Scientist: Creationist in a Secular World*, Christopher Toumey, New Brunswick, N.J.: Rutgers University Press, 1994, p. 94.
18. *Dialogue Concerning Two Chief World Systems: Ptolemaic and Copernican*, Galileo Galilei, Berkeley and Los Angeles, University of California Press, 1953, p. 5.
19. *Dancing Wu Li Masters*, Gary Zukav, Perennial Classics, New York, 1979, p. 30.
20. *The Tao of Physics*, Bantam Books, *New York*, 1984, pp. 70-71.
21. *The Roots of Consciousness*, Jeffrey Mishlove, Consciousness: A Hyper Space View (Appendix), Marlow & Company, 1993, p. 375.
22. *Tantra: Its Mystic and Scientific Basis*, Lalan Prasad Singh, Concept Publishing Company Pvt. Ltd., New Delhi, Revised Edition, 2010, p. 16.
23. *Ratnāvalī*, IV. C. 94-97.
24. Louis de Broglie, *Matter and Light: The New Physics*, Trans. W.H. Johnston (New York: Norton, 1939), p. 280.
25. *The Sacred Books of the East.* Edited by F. Max Müller, Vol. XXXIX, Oxford, At the Clarendon Press, 1891, pp. 4-5.
26. *Ibid.*, p. 26.
27. *Ibid.*, p. 49.
28. *What is Taoism? and Other Studies in Chinese Cultural History*, Herrlee G. Creel. The University of Chicago Press, 1970, Chicago and London, p. 24.
29. *Physics and Philosophy, Werner Heisenberg, Harper Perennial Modern Thought*, New York, 2007, p. 115.

2

Western Philosophical Background of Science, Spirituality and Ontological Mysticism

In the history of philosophy, I find two distinct schools of thought: that is monism and dualism. The Oriental school is dominated by monism and mysticism and Western philosophy is predominantly dualistic. Monism and mysticism are the fundamental and basic philosophical thought of East and dualism is the salient feature of Western rationalism. Monism culminated in mysticism and dualism became the basis of Western scientific rationalism. The origin and development of science and spirituality can be traced to these two philosophical schools and traditions. The conquest of nature is the hallmark of science and the conquest of self is the goal of Eastern mystical and spiritual tradition. The scientific materialism became the dominant culture of one school and spiritual humanism became the cornerstone of other school of thought. Man became the author and choreographer of drama of nature in Western culture and nature became living and pulsating poetry of divinity in the other. Nature is all divine in Oriental culture and tradition.

Greece is the birth place of Western philosophy of dualism. Matter and Form became the guiding principles of Aristotle and *Brahman*, *Śūnyatā* and Tao were pronounced as the ultimate reality by Indian and Chinese thinkers. Albert Schweitzer has summarized the Indian philosophy and its world-view as follows: "A distinguishing Indian world-view from ours, there is yet another difference, which lies just as deep as that between world and life affirmation and world life denial. That of India is monastic and mystical, ours is dualistic and doctrinaire. Mysticism is the perfect form of world-view. In this world-view man endeavours to arrive at a spiritual relationship to the infinite Being to which he belongs as a part of Nature. He studies the universe to discover whether he can apprehend and become one with mysterious will which governs it. Only in spiritual unity with infinite Being can he give meaning to his life and find strength to suffer and to act".[1]

Philosophy is a pursuit of truth, knowledge and value. In the beginning science was a part of philosophical enquiry and speculation. With the development of knowledge science acquires an independent status and discipline, while philosophy still remains the basis of all scientific discovery and investigation. The West being dualistic and doctrinaire, science flourished with leaps and bounds. Leucippus and Dermocratus laid down the formulation of scientific atomism. Science is a product of rational thinking. Rational thinking is based on logic. Logic is the greatest gift of Greek philosophy. Hence, all scientific thinking and discoveries have the background of Greek philosophical tradition. We can trace the origin and development of scientific knowledge and thinking in the philosophy of Greece. Western philosophy is a process of ratiocination to understand facts and truth. Bertrand Russell published a paper entitled *Logic is the Essence of Philosophy* in 1914. In his fundamental work with Whitehead titled *Principia Mathematica* asserted that mathematics is a logic. Both Whitehead and Russell were unanimous on one point that "the proper study of philosophers is logic".[2] The Vienna Circle agreed with Russell–Whitehead theory that mathematics can be deduced to logic. Logic had been developed in India even before the Greeks. *Nyāya Philosophy* is rooted in logic. Later Buddhist thinkers developed a sound logical system. But the Hindu and the Buddhist logical pursuit were devoted to pave the path of spiritual enlightenment by showing the limitation of logic and its inability to take man to cross the limit of reason.

Zeno has demonstrated through dialectic the illusion and unreality of infinite space and time. But the philosophers could not get awakened from their dogmatic slumber until Kant. Kant was the first Western thinker who denied and refuted the objective and independent existence of space and time. According to Kant, Time and Space are *a priori* categories of Sensibility. Time and Space are modes of our perception. All our perceptions and cognitions are timed and spaced.

However, Kant's refutation of objectivity of Space and Time does not solve the age old scientific and philosophical problem of signification of truth. St. Augustine formulated for the first time relativistic theory of time. His philosophical work known as Confessions deals with the concept of time. According to St. Augustine, the concept of time came with the concept of the world. Augustine's view is in opposition to the Greek view that world was created out of nothing. St. Augustine tried to explain the creation of world by putting pantheistic concept of God that holds that God and world are integral part of creation. World is not different from God. Everything in the world is an integral part of God. This pantheistic concept of God is fully developed in the philosophy of Spinoza; however, God stands eternally outside the realm of time. According to St. Augustine, there are three streams of time, "a present of things past, a present of things present, and a present of things future" further he says, "the present of things past is memory; the present of things present is sight; and the present things of future is expectation"[3]. Bertrand Russell writes, "I do not myself agree with this theory, insofar as it makes time something mental. But it is clearly a very able theory, deserving to be seriously considered. I should go further, and say that it is great advance on anything to be found on the subject in Greek philosophy. It contains a better and clearer statement than Kant's of the subjective theory of time—a theory which, since Kant, has been widely accepted among philosophers."[4] Further he says, Subjectivism of St. Augustine's paved the path for Kant's concept of time and Descartes *Cogito Ergo Sum* the method through which Descartes brought a revolution in philosophy and he was rightly called the father of modern philosophy. That concept of time has been developed in the philosophy of Protagoras and Socrates and others. The concept of time as an aspect of our thoughts is one of the most revolutionary concept which I think was developed in full form in a full philosophical and a scientific doctrine known as the Einstein's General Theory of Relativity.

Western philosophy originated in Greece. Science considers the existence of the world as certainty. Science takes the existence of matter as real whereas philosophy starts with the questioning of the very existence of world and matter. Philosophy tries to understand the nature of matter and reality. Philosophy tries to understand the reality in totality. Philosophy is not concerned with a particular, but being as such. Philosophy tries to understand the whole cosmos in the light of a single universal principle.

Thales is considered the founding father of all philosophy. He was born about 624 B.C. and died around about 550 B.C. We don't have the correct account of his life. According to Thales water is the ultimate reality. He tried to ascertain the basic principles that govern the multiplicity of the world. He tries to throw a new light on the nature of that first principle from which the whole world emerged. There has been no unanimity on the single principle which governs and has given birth to the cosmos. Thales says, "It is water" Anaximander, indefinite matter, Anaximander's air the Pythagorean number and Parmenides of Elea calls it Being.

I consider Parmenides as the founding father of philosophy because he was the first thinker who stated that ultimate reality is Being. Not-Being is not real in ultimate philosophical analysis. Not being loses its truth and reality. He identifies not being with becoming. The world which is known to us by means of our mind and senses is changing and fleeting. It does not have permanent existence. The world of sense perception is unreal and an illusion. The world of not-being is only an appearance according to Parmenides. Only Being is the ultimate reality.

In philosophy this problem of ultimate reality has kept all the great philosophers occupied with this vex questions. The different philosophers at different periods of time tried to explain the nature of ultimate reality. The profundity and the sublimity of different philosophers depend upon the rationalistic and the mystical understanding of this problem.

Ex nihilo nihil fit is the kernel of philosophy of Parmenides. Being is neither existence nor non-existence, it does not come out of nothing nor something out of nothing, being does not come out of not being. We cannot explain Being in terms of past, present and future. The past, present and future is bound by limitation, hence Being is eternal and timeless. It is undivided, individual and absolute. It is absolutely self-identical. If we analyse the common features of the universe, we come to the strange conclusion that what is common in all is simply "*being*". It is a concept. It is a thought and not a thing. Thus Parmenides can be called the founding father of Western philosophy.

Zeno who is considered a founder of dialectic tried to justify Parmenides's philosophy of Being by destroying the multiplicity of the world. Parmenides stated that the world of multiplicity is false and only an appearance. Parmenides came from Elea which is situated in Southern part of Italy. It is said that Plato's teacher Socrates had an intimate contact with Parmenides. Socrates was greatly influenced by Parmenides. Plato through Socrates also got inspiration from the thought of Parmenides. South Italy and Sicily was beehives of mysticism. Parmenides was also greatly influenced by Pythagoras. Parmenides according to me is a founder of Western philosophy. I do not deny the importance of Thales, who was the first to propound that everything is made of water. To me the importance of Thales lies in the propagation of scientific thinking rather than the philosophical doctrine. There is enough evidence to prove to say that Thales had travelled to Egypt to learn the science of geometry. Credit goes to Thales for the prediction of eclipse which took place in 585 B.C. It seems that the whole Greek philosophy is rooted in ontological mysticism. Pythagoras is another important Greek philosopher who was florist about 532 B.C. He is pioneer in mathematical deductive logic which is rooted in mysticism. It is quite evident from the life and teaching of Pythagoras that he was greatly influenced by Hindu philosophy. He believed in the transmigration of soul which is the *quint essential* teachings of Hinduism. Cornford says, "The school of Pythagoras represents the main current of that mystical tradition which we have set in contrast with scientific tendency." Further he considers, "Parmenides as the discoverer of logic." "An offshoot of Pythagoreans and Plato himself as finding in the Italian philosophy as the chief source of his inspiration." There is no doubt that the basic philosophical teachings of Pythagoras were mystical. He says, "There are men and gods, and beings like Pythagoras." According to Cornford Pythagorean teaching is other worldly, putting all value in unseen unity of God and condemning the visible world as false and illusive, a turbid medium in which the rays of heavenly lights are broken and obscured in mist and darkness. Dikaiarchos says that Pythagoras taught "first, that the soul is an immortal thing, and that it is transformed into other kinds of living things; further, that whatever comes into existence is born again in the revolutions of a certain cycle, nothing being absolutely new; and that all things that are born with life in them ought to be treated as kindered."[5] I find great similarity between the teachings of Pythagoras and the philosophy propounded by Kashmir Śaivism and Vedānta. It could be said with some amount of certainty that Pythagoras was the first founder of a religious and a moral Order. His concept of wheel of things and a spiritual religious endeavour to get released from the wheels of things to escape the transmigration of soul or the rebirth. This is fundamentally and basically the Hindu teaching. Pythagoreans believed in Orphic religious rituals and put emphasis on moral and spiritual pursuits, and meditative contemplation for the release of the soul. Science and philosophy become integral part of Pythagorean doctrines. There is evidence of Hindu influence in the form of Pythagoreans religious doctrines which were based on rigorous and ascetic life style. Pythagoras himself was living a life of a mendicant. He believed that soul is imprisoned in the body. Body is the tomb of the soul. He was against any attempt to get soul liberated from the body by committing suicide. According to him "man is the property of God." W.T. Stace while writing about Pythagoreans says, "It was largely a mystical society. The Pythagoreans developed their own ritual, ceremonial and mysteries. This love of mystery, and their general character as miracle-mongers, largely account for their legends which grew-up around the life of Pythagoras himself. Their scientific activities were also considerable. They enforced moral self-control.

They cultivated arts and crafts, gymnastics, music, medicine, and mathematics. The development of mathematics in early Greece was largely the work of the Pythagoreans. Pythagoras is said to have discovered the 47th Proposition of Euclid, and to have sacrificed an ox in honour thereof. And there is good reason to believe that practically the whole of the substance of the First Book of Euclid is the work of Pythagoras."[6] The kernel of Pythagorean philosophy is the concept of the first principle of things is number. The number is the world's substance out of which the phenomenal world is composed. However, there has been some disagreement amongst the Pythagoreans in identifying different numbers with different things. It is said that musical notes were discovered by Pythagoreans. Difference in musical harmony and note is due to different numbers of waves and vibrations of the instrument. Thus, according to Pythagoreans the world is harmonious and orderly like music. Arithmetic is the basis of scientific thinking and all other mathematical and other branches of science could be deduced from numbers. According to Pythagoreans, number is an important dimension of the world and it is substantial and fundamental. Pythagoreans considered mathematics as the main source of belief in real truth. Bertrand Russell rightly observes as, "that all exact reasoning applies to ideal as opposed to sensible objects; it is natural to go further, and to argue that thought is nobler than sense, and the objects of thoughts more real than those of sense-perception, Mystical doctrines as to the relation of time to eternity are also reinforced by pure mathematics, for fundamental objects, such as numbers, if real at all, are eternal and not in time. Such eternal objects can be conceived as God's thoughts, hence Plato's doctrine that God is a geometer, and Sir James Jeans' belief that He is addicted to arithmetic. Rationalistic as opposed to apocalyptic religion has been, ever since Pythagoras and notably ever since Plato, very completely dominated by mathematics and mathematical method."[7] Pythagoras can be considered as the founder of mathematics and religion, which became the religious philosophy in Greece. This has greatly influenced the thought and philosophy which were essentially based on Hindu mysticism right from Plato, St. Augustine, Descartes, Spinoza and Kant. Bertrand Russell has rightly observed that there has been no parallel in history of philosophy like Pythagoras who has exercised such tremendous impact on the life and philosophy of the Western world. He writes, "I say this because what appears as Platonism is, when analysed, found to be in essence Pythagoreanism. The whole conception of an eternal world, revealed to the intellect, but not to the senses, is derived from him. But from him, Christians would not have thought of Christ as the Word; but for him, theologians would not have sought logical *proofs* of God and immortality."[8] Knowledge is a dialectical process and in the process of development the contradictions and dissent play an important role in the enrichment of our thinking. It could be said with certainty that all the Western great ideas whether scientific or philosophical are rooted in Greek intellectual and mystical traditions. Without the Greek discovery of mathematics modern science would not have attained its profundity and sublimity. There is another great Greek thinker who has played an important role in the formulation of scientific and philosophical thinking of modern times. His name is Heraclitus. He was a mystic. He considered fire as the basic substance. According to him "all things come out of the one and the one out of the all things." However, all other reality is less than God. His doctrine is based on the concept of "perpetual flux". According to him there is a universal change. It could be expressed as "all things are flowing". There is a very famous saying of Heraclitus, "We cannot enter into the same river, we go down and we do not go down; but into the same river no man can enter twice; ever it flows in and flows out." He thus rejects and denies the existence of anything as of permanent nature. He further rejects the relative permanence of things as an illusion. Nothing is permanent. Nothing remains identical from one moment to another. Appearance of any kind of permanence is an illusion. Everything is becoming. Becoming is the identity of being and not being.

The philosophy of Heraclitus has great similarity with Buddhist philosophy of eternal flux. The Buddhist being and not being is of dependent origination. Being is not being. Everything in the universe is bounded by the "harmony of opposite tensions". Harmony embodies in itself, the opposite principles. This opposite principle is the basis of the underlying unity. It is this principle of harmony of opposite that is the basis of the existence of the universe. This is the basic and the kernel principle of Heraclitus. This conflict and harmony of opposites gives and sustains the very existence of the universe. At the centre of existence is conflict and configuration. Without conflict there is no existence. Heraclitus says, "Strife is the father of all things. The one, sundering from itself, coalesces with itself, like harmony of the bow and the lyre. God is day and night, summer and winter, war and peace, satiety and hunger. Join together whole and unwhole, congruous and incongruous, accordant and discordant, then comes from one all and from all one."

Bertrand Russell considers ethics of Heraclitus as a kind of proud asceticism, very similar to Nietzsche's. According to Heraclitus soul is a combination of fire and water. Fire is the nobler and the water is the ignoble part of the soul. The dry soul is the wisest and the best. His asceticism is dependent on self-mastery. He abhors the passion that distracts men from their moral path. However, Heraclitus religion is considered by some as the Bacchii religion. Cornford has been very vociferous in levelling Heraclitus as the follower of Bacchii. However, I don't consider Heraclitus as a Bacchii.

If we examine and evaluate the teachings of Heraclitus, we would come to the conclusion that harmony and unity is more substantial than diversity and strife. I quote to highlight the fundamental unity and harmony of Heraclitus doctrines:

"Good and ill are one."

"To God all things are fair and good and right, but men hold some things wrong and some right."

"The way up and the way down are one and the same."

"God is day and night, winter and summer, war and peace, surfeit and hunger; but he takes various shapes, just as fire, when it is mingled with spices, is named according to the savour of each."

Nevertheless, there would be no unity if there were not opposites to combine: "it is the opposite which is good for us."

Bertrand Russell considers, "Heraclitus doctrine contains the germ of Hegel's philosophy, which proceeds by a synthesis of opposites."

The metaphysics of Heraclitus, like that of Anaximander, is dominated by a conception of cosmic justice, which prevents the strife of opposites from ever issuing in the complete victory of either.

"All things are an exchange for Fire and Fire for all things, even as wares for gold for wares."

"Fire lives the death of air, and air lives the death of fire; water lives the death of earth, earth that of water."

"The sun will not overstep his measures; if he does, the Erinys, the handmaid of justice, will find him out."

"We must know that war is common to all, and strife is justice."

Heraclitus repeatedly speaks of, "God" as distinct from "the gods."

"The way of man has no wisdom, but that of God has..... Man is called a baby by God, even as a child by man.... The wisest man is an ape compared to God, just as the most beautiful ape is ugly compared to man."

Heraclitus is basically a mystical and sceptical, he rejects the vulgar and outward display of rituals. He does not believe in lifeless rituals and dogmas. There is distinction between sense and reason.

Truth can be ascertained and experienced in rational cognition. Senses are the basis of illusion or permanence. It is only with the help of rational thinking and ratiocination, we can understand and appreciate the fundamental law of becoming. With the understanding of law of becoming man becomes enlightened and contented. This throws light on the harmony of opposites, i.e., good and bad are necessary and integral part of happiness. Good and bad together are the fundamental basis of the very existence of the world.

The source of our understanding and knowledge of Heraclitus philosophy is through the criticism and appreciation of Heraclitus philosophy largely made by Plato and Aristotle. Plato has summarised the whole doctrine of Heraclitus as "nothing ever is" and Aristotle put it "nothing steadfastly is". The quest for a universal principle and truth is eternal yearnings of a philosopher from time immemorial. Religion tries to understand the universal principle and truth in forms of God and immortality. Philosopher and scientists, quest for ultimate reality leads him to ontological mysticism. Heraclitus, the pioneer of the doctrine of becoming an eternal flux believes in eternity which is the gift of Parmenides. As in the philosophy of Heraclitus central fire does not die and hence it embodies the conception of eternity as opposed to change and impermanence. Science and philosophy have always strived to dive deep into the world of change and becoming for the underlying principles which govern change, and the becoming within itself is changeless and eternal.

Bertrand Russell writes, "The doctrine of the perpetual flux, as taught by Heraclitus, is painful, and science, as we have seen, can do nothing to refute it. One of the main ambitions of philosophers has been to revive hopes that science seemed to have killed. Philosophers, accordingly, have sought, with great persistence, for something not subject to the empire of Time. This search begins with Parmenides."[9] The critical and the comparative study of Parmenides and Heraclitus is necessary for understanding the origin and development of different Western schools of philosophy. As against Heraclitus doctrine of eternal flux Parmenides placed the reality and truth of the world in thought and concept. This became the basis of all subsequent schools of idealism. The whole idealistic philosophy is based on the dictum that truth lies in reason not in the world of senses. Parmenides became the source of both of materialism and idealism. The two contradictory thoughts remain unreconciled in Parmenides contradicting each other. However, Parmenides was not aware of any contradictions while formulating his concept of Being as the sole reality. Empedocles and Democritus deduced from the doctrines of Parmenides the materialistic aspects of his thoughts. The basic principle of Parmenides was that being cannot come out from not-being and that being neither originates nor destroys. Empedocles and Democritus caught hold of the concept of matter, i.e., based on the "modern doctrine of indestructibility of matter". Matter has neither a beginning nor an end. The apparent origination and passing away of things is simply the combinations and the dissolution of particles of matter which are indestructible. This is the main view of Democritus. And on the basis of that he recreated the doctrine of Parmenides on the basis of his own philosophy that being cannot come out from not being or passed into not being. On the other hand Plato ceased the idealistic aspects of Parmenides doctrine and developed it into a grand philosophical system of idealism. Plato identified the concept and the idea with the being of Parmenides. However, it is a debatable point who is the right and truthful interpreter of Parmenides doctrine of being. Parmenides was a great thinker and a pioneer; he had the honour and the distinction of establishing a system of philosophical thoughts and traditions in the West. But it is also true that the whole philosophy of Plato is based upon the doctrines of Parmenides.

The third and last great thinker of Eleatic school is Zeno. Zeno is acknowledged as the father and the discoverer of dialectic in the West. In support of Parmenides doctrine of Being, Zeno tried to destroy the very basis of the world of becoming. The world of becoming has two essential features—multiplicity and change. The being of Parmenides is absolutely one and it does not recognise and believe in plurality or multiplicity and change. Being is one, individual, eternal and unchangeable. The multiplicity, plurality, change and motions speak of the world of senses which is false and an illusion. To disprove the very basis of multiplicity and motion, Zeno proved through his dialectical reasoning that admission and acceptance of motion and change are illusion and impossibility. He demonstrated through his argument that multiplicity and motions are unreal and contradictory propositions. Two propositions and views which contradict each other cannot both be true on the basis of dialectical arguments. He refuted the very basis of multiplicity and motion. Zeno's dialectic against motion is based upon antinomy of infinite divisibility as for example, the flight of an arrow. Arrow is where it is. It cannot be where it is not, therefore arrow is not moving.

The arrow can be in the movements of motion in one place. It cannot be at two places at the same time. This whole concept is based on the time as being infinitely divisible. There cannot be any absolute moment of pause having no duration that arrow is at rest. This is antinomical in character, in our thinking of space and time. The mathematician is aware of the contradictions and antinomical characters of the concept of infinity. For example, the supposition that parallel straight line will meet at infinity is a contradiction. Likewise the concept of infinite space is also antinomical and a contradiction. It follows from this argument that space is finite. On the other hand, it is impossible to conceptualise a limited space because it entails than beyond the limit there must be more space and, therefore, it follows from this argument that space in infinite. Zeno has demonstrated antinomy in the form of his argument. His argument is as follows: every object exists in space. Space itself exists, therefore, space must be in space and this argument leads to an infinity. This is just to prove that the normal understanding to conceive a limit to space is an impossibility.

Zeno's does not propagate his own philosophy. His dialectic is to defend the thesis of the doctrine of Parmenides. His dialectic is aimed against the acceptability of multiplicity, plurality, change and motion as the very concept of multiplicity and change is embedded in contradictions. Therefore, the multiplicity, plurality, change and motion are unreal and illusive. Zeno upholds the Parmenides doctrine of One Being without any multiplicity and becoming. Kant was aware of antinomical character of reason and he tried to rise above reason and antinomy to conceptualise the concept of time and space which are not real things but mere appearances. Time and space do not belong to the objects rather they are the medium of our perception. Time and space are *a priori* categories of sensibility. According to Kant, space and time are subjective mode of our perception. They are means of our perception. Kant calls time and space as "categories". According to Kant, the phenomenal world consists of sensation which our mental apparatus puts to order this phenomenal world in space and time. Understanding and sensibilities are two apparatus of our synthetic judgements. The whole question of the concept of the phenomena and noumena is the main doctrine of *The Critique of Pure Reason*. Kant in a preface to the second edition thinks that he has brought a Copernican revolution in philosophy. According to him criticism itself is philosophy.

Parmenides propagated the philosophy of being which is one, infinite and individual. Parmenides is the first philosopher who is said to have discovered metaphysics. Bertrand Russell writes "Parmenides was influenced by Pythagoras, but the extent of his influence was conjectural. What makes Parmenides historically important is that he invented a form of metaphysical argument that, in one form or another, is to be found in most subsequent metaphysicians down to and including Hegel. He is often said to have invented logic, but what he really invented was metaphysics based on logic."[10] The philosophy of Heraclitus is the antithesis of Parmenides. According to Parmenides, being and becoming is unreal, all change and becoming are mere illusions. In opposition to this philosophy of Parmenides, Heraclitus says that permanence and identity are mere illusions. Only reality is becoming. The whole philosophy of both Parmenides and Heraclitus is based on ontological mysticism. Heraclitus considered basic substance at a higher level. He says, "mortals are immortals, and immortals are mortals, the one living the others death and dying the others life". The apparent unity and cohesion is a blending of the opposites. "All things come out of the one and the one out of all things". He says, "You cannot step twice into the same river; for fresh water is ever flowing in upon you, the sun is new everyday". His belief in universal change and eternal flux is the greatest contribution to the world of philosophy. According to him, unity and cohesion is more fundamental than diversity, "good and ill are one", "To God all things are fair and good and right, but men hold something wrong and something right". However, we cannot think of unity and harmony in the absence of opposites. This combination of opposites which is the fundamental basis of unity contains the germ of Hegelian dialectic which is based on the synthesis of opposites. The philosophy of Heraclitus gets developed and matured in Plato and Hegel.

However, the quest for eternal and permanent is one of the greatest search of man's yearnings which has led to the formulation of philosophy. God and immortality are the basis of origin of religion and search for truth and reality is the basis of the origin and development of philosophy, but both the philosophical and religious pursuits are embedded in mysticism. In spite of Heraclitus emphasis on eternal flux and change, he believed in something which does not change. Though Heraclitus does not believe in eternity and permanence but his concept of fire which never dies gives rise to the concept of something everlasting. Bertrand Russell observes, "The doctrine of the perpetual flux, as taught by Heraclitus, is painful, and science, as we have seen, can do nothing to refuse it. One of the main ambitions of the philosophers has been to revive hope that science seemed to have killed. Philosophers, accordingly, have sought, with great persistence, for something not subject to the empire of Time. This search begins with Parmenides."[11] The philosophy of Heraclitus created some problem for science which tried to find a way out from the doctrine of perpetual flux. Science tried to take refuge in some permanent substratum in the midst of change and becoming. Science especially physics discovered some particles known as electrons and protons which are considered as the composed form of atoms and atoms were thought to be indestructible. The new researches in science replaced matter with energy. Energy is sometimes equated with Heraclitian fire. In spite of all the achievements of scientific discoveries and inventions, doctrine of Heraclitus stands as a beacon light. The Greek philosophers, Leucippus and Democritus posited the first existence of atoms. However, the physical theories that have been propagated are so counter intuitive that it would be difficult for the scientific fraternity to accept that the component of atoms operate according to physical laws which are governed by properties so different that it appears that they are part of a completely different world. However, the contribution of Greek atomist is the basis of modern atomic doctrines. Leucippus existence is dated about 440 B.C. There has been great impact of Parmenides and Zeno on the life and thoughts of Leucippus. However, there has been great controversy and debate about the existence of Leucippus. Democritus is a historical figure; he was a citizen of Avdera. He was a man of learning and wisdom. His hunger for knowledge and wisdom made him a wanderer in search of truth. He visited Egypt and Babylonia. There is some controversy about his death, but he enjoyed a long life. Democritus developed the philosophy of Leucippus and is responsible for giving it a form of systematic doctrine. Democritus says that everything is atom. Atoms are physical entities. However, they are not geometrically indivisible. There is empty space between the atoms. Atoms are indestructible. They are always being, in motion. They are infinite in numbers. Democritus says, "The more any individual exceeds the heavier it is". The Greek atomist were determinist, they believed that everything was governed by natural laws. Democritus does not believe in chance. However, there is some controversy between Leucippus and Democritus on the question of chance and determination. Leucippus has stated: "Naught happens for nothing, but everything from a ground and of necessity." Leucippus has not explained the origin of the world. According to some, the world might have been originated by chance. But he does accept that after the origination of the world, it is governed by some natural laws which are fixed and mechanical. It goes without doubt that Leucippus and Democritus laid down the foundation of modern science. The doctrine of atomism as propounded by Leucippus and Democritus is closer to modern science. The concept of their causation is considered as a great contribution in explaining some of the mysteries of creation. Causation might have some beginning in something. However, the uncaused cause, the initial datum may be attributed to God. This is why some religious thinkers considered uncaused cause of the universe as God. However, this theory has been the point of great controversy amongst the scientist, philosophers and religious thinkers. Democritus does not think of any purpose and final cause in explaining the existence of the world. Socrates, Plato and Aristotle tried to explain the world with the help of motion and purpose and final cause, which are the antithesis of Greek atomists. Atomists believed in mechanistic scientific explanation whereas Socrates, Plato and Aristotle took recourse to teleological explanations.

The debate of chance and determinism has been the source of philosophical reflection and scientific formulations. A noted French mathematician, Marquis de Laplace (1749-1827), is of the opinion that all our knowledge is problematic. He writes "Strictly speaking it may even be said that nearly all our knowledge is problematic; and in the small number of things which we are able to know with certainty, even in mathematical science themselves, the principal means for ascertaining truth, induction and analogy are based on probabilities; so that, the entire system of human knowledge is connected with the theory set forth in this essay. Doubtless it will be seen here with interest that in considering, even in the eternal principles of reason, justice and humanity, only the favourable chances which are constantly attached to them. There is a good advantage in following their principles and serious inconvenience in departing from them; their chances like those favourable to lotteries, always end by prevailing in the midst of the vacillations of hazard. I hope that the reflections given in this essay may merit the attention of the philosophers and direct it, the subject so worthy of engaging their mind."[12]

There has been an attempt to harmonize and reconcile the arguments of Parmenides and Heraclitus. Parmenides believed against not being is based on logic. We may state Parmenides's doctrine in the following words, "You say there is the void: therefore, the void is not nothing: therefore, it is not the void". This problem of void and motion kept the modern scientific mind engaged for centuries. They have tried to resolve the problem by accepting the distinction between matter and space. As per this theory, space is not anything. Aristotle says (*Physics*, 208 b) "the theory that the void exists involves the existence of place; for one would define void as place bereft of body." This view has been accepted by Newton. According to Newton, the existence of absolute space distinguishes absolute from relative motion. However, if we accept that all motion is relative and space is not substantial, we are forced to accept Parmenides doctrine of void.

We now have to believe that the germ of Albert Einstein theory could be traced in Leucippus and Democritus doctrines. Albert Einstein writes in his Note to the preface of his monumental work Relativity *The Special and General Theory*; "physical objects are not in space, but these objects are spatially extended. In this way, the concept of *empty space* loses its meaning." Thus, the Newtonian theory of absolute space has been refuted by Einstein. Modern physics posits that matter in some sense is atomic, it does not accept the existence of empty space. Matter loses its glorious status through the doctrine of Parmenides. It is no more the unchanging and permanent substance. Parmenides doctrine of substance was accepted as irrefutable doctrine until the advent of general and special theory of Relativity and Quantum Mechanics. It is now closer to Heraclitus doctrine of eternal flux and change. Bertrand Russell says, "As regards space, the modern view is that it is neither a substance, as Newton maintained, and as Leucippus and Democritus ought to have said, nor an adjective of extended bodies, as Descartes thought, but a system of relations, as Leibniz held. It is not by any means clear whether this view is compatible with the existence of the void. Perhaps, as the matter of abstract logic, it can be reconciled with the void. We might say that, between any two things, there is a certain greater or smaller *distance*, and that distance does not imply the existence of intermediate things. Such a point of view, however, would be impossible to utilize in modern physics. Since Einstein, distance is between *events,* not between *things,* it involves time as well as space. It is essentially a causal conception, and in modern physics there is no action at a distance. All this, however, is based upon empirical rather than logical grounds. Moreover, the modern view cannot be stated in terms of differential equations, and would, therefore, be unintelligible to the philosophers of antiquity."[13]

There are some atomists who believed that the motion is product of the force of necessity. Anaxagoras believed that intelligence or reason is the source of motion. Democritus does not accept any doctrine of necessity, he rejects the view that reason or intelligence is the origin of motion.

According to him, the universe is guided and controlled by blind mechanical principles. This gave rise to the polemic against the belief in God and religion. According to Democritus, God is a creation of human fear of astronomical occurrences like volcano and comets. Democritus laid down certain epistemological and ethical doctrines. According to Democritus, epistemology projects itself into space images, themselves composed of atoms. These images are the cause of our sense perception. The quality of objects such as smell, taste and colour do not exists in objects themselves. We perceive things in the way in which they strike our senses and, therefore, our perception of objects is relative. On the ethical doctrines, Democritus is of the opinion that happiness and satisfaction of man is not related and dependent on material possessions. It is a state of the soul. He is of the view that the man of wisdom maintains equanimity and cheerfulness. Equanimity and happiness is result of living a life of simplicity and moderation. Democritus occupies an important place in the history of Western philosophy. He tried to explain the world in scientific and philosophical terminology.

Socrates is one of the greatest philosophers that the world has produced. His impact on philosophy is monumental. I consider him one of the greatest thinkers who have brought revolution in thinking and living as an ethical life. He was a mystic. It is a historical fact that Socrates was guided by some mystic experiences. Some writers have wrongly identified the mystical experiences or oracle or a supernatural voice which Socrates calls daemon with common form of insanity. Sometimes this has been explained as cataleptic trances which Socrates experienced while he was in military service:

> One morning he was thinking about something which he could not resolve; he would not give up, but continued thinking from early dawn until noon, there he stood fixed in thought; and at noon attention was drawn to him, and the rumour ran through the wondering crowd that Socrates has been standing and thinking about something ever since the break of the day. At last, in the evening after supper, some Ionians out of curiosity, brought out their mats and slept in the open air that they might watch him and see whether he would stand all night. There he stood until the following morning; and with the return of light he offered a prayer to the sun, and went his way.[14]

This mystic experience was a guiding principle of Socrates life. The Western mind does not have the proper understanding of the deeper and the profound meaning and richness of such spiritual experiences, because it is antithesis to Western mechanistic and materialistic Western tradition. In Symposium, the unusual transcendental mystical experience of Socrates has been explained in historical details. Socrates was going to attend a dinner with Aristodemus when went into a mystical trance.

Agathan who had hosted the dinner inquired from Aristodemus about the cause of the non-arrival of Socrates who had accompanied him. A slave was ordered to find out the lost guest and to his utter astonishment, the slave informed Agathan that Socrates was in a supernatural state. Socrates was found in the portico of the neighbouring house in the state of ecstasy, he couldn't respond to the slave's call. This had been the recurrent experience of Socrates which has been explained as "he has a way of stopping anywhere and loosing himself without reason." He was living a life of a mystic. He was always dressed in shabby old clothes and used to walk bare foot. He was oblivious of heat and cold, hunger and thirst which is one of the conditions laid down by Vedānta teachings for the attainment of enlightenment. It is termed as *Titikṣā*.

Alcibiades gives a graphical description of Socrates of this kind of mystical experience in the Symposium while on military service in the following words: "His endurance was simply marvellous when, being cut off from our supplies, we were compelled to go without food, on such occasions, which often happen in time of war, he was superior not only to me, but to everybody: there was no one to be compared to him.... His fortitude in enduring cold was surprising. There was a severe frost, for the winter in that region is really tremendous, and everybody else either remained indoors, or if they went out had on an amazing quantity of clothes, and were well shod, and had their feet swathed in felt and fleeces: in the midst of this, Socrates with his bare feet on the ice and in his ordinary dress marched better than the other soldiers who had shoes, and they looked daggers at him because he seemed to despise them." From the life and teachings of Socrates it is evident that he was a mystic rather than an intellectual. He considered knowledge as a virtue. According to the Stoics, God is virtue. The teachings of the Cynics condemned and despised the world of sensuous pleasures. The germs of the teachings of Stoics and the Cynics are found in the teachings of Socrates. Socrates lived a virtuous and spiritual life. He practised what he believed. His life was a message like that of Mahatma Gandhi. Bertrand Russell has made a proper and real estimation and observation of Socrates life and teachings in following words: "He was the perfect Orphic saint: in the dualism of heavenly soul and earthly body, he had achieved the complete mastery of the soul over the body. His indifference to death at the end is the final proof of this mastery. At the same time, he is not an orthodox Orphic; it is only the fundamental doctrines that he accepts, not the superstitions and ceremonies of purification."

It is very difficult to give a proper account of life and teachings of Socrates. Socrates was born about 470 B.C. in Athens. His father was a sculpture. There is not enough information about his boyhood days and education. He accepted his father's occupation as a sculpture. But he intensely pursued a life of philosophy and in search of truth and reality. He deserted his father's occupation. He lived in Athens till the time he was condemned to death through the drinking of hemlock. In 399 B.C. at about the age of 70, he tried his level best to restore and resuscitate the values of truth and morality which were destroyed by the Sophists. He brought sanity and dignity in the chaotic intellectual life of the Athenians. He spent his whole life in Athens in dissemination of philosophical truth. He did not believe in monologue. He was a firm believer in dialogue. He believed that knowledge is a dialectical process and the enrichment of knowledge and thought could be achieved only through dialogue. He served in military expedition in Athenian army for some time. He was ugly looking; short, bald, flat, thumb nosed. He did not care for the life of luxury and pretensions. He was charged with denying the national God and corrupting the youth. All these charges were baseless and frivolous. He did not deny the national God, he always had veneration and respect towards the gods. He always appealed to his friends, disciples and the youths to honour and show respect to gods according to their beliefs and tradition. A charge was also levelled against him for creating his own gods. This might be because of the misguided experience of the people who could not understand the supernatural and mystical inner voice which used to guide his life and destiny.

Socrates became a threat to Athenian democracy because of his upholding of free thinking. He believed in the freedom of thought. He was of course against mobocracy which was the name of democracy at that time. He was against State being governed by incompetent and men of untrained minds. He wanted that State should be run by the men of wisdom and learning. He always believed that the fear of death is not wisdom. Since no one knows, death may not be a greater good. There is a detailed account of Socrates life at the time of his death in *Apology*. He says, "God orders me to fulfil the philosopher's mission of searching to myself and other men."

"Men of Athens, I honour and love you: but I shall obey God rather than you and while I have life and strength I shall never cease from the practice and teaching of philosophy, exhorting, anyone whom I meet... For now, that this is the command of God, I believe that no greater good has ever happened in the State, than my service to God." He always maintained equanimity of mind that whatever has happened is good for him and he always thought that those who think death is an evil are in error. He considered death as a dreamless sleep or the state of soul migrating to another world. Socrates would say, "the hour of departure has arrived, we go our ways, I to die, and you to live, which is better, God only knows." It entails that Socrates believed in immortality and freedom. The moment of his life speaks of his belief in ontological mysticism. He believed that death is a deliverer; it is a state of enlightenment when attained with the unification of God.

Socrates identification of knowledge with virtue is monastic and mystical, not dualistic and doctrinaire. On a close examination and evaluation of the life and teachings of Socrates, I come to the conclusion that he was a lone philosopher who believed in monism and mysticism.

Socrates like an oriental mystic always maintained that he knew nothing. He considered himself wiser than others, in his awareness that he is aware that he knows nothing. His whole philosophy is based on the dictum "know thyself". This is analogous to Vedāntic teachings of to know "who am I?" The teachings of Socrates could be compared with the Vedāntic teachings of *Mahāvākya* "thou art that" (*tattvamasi*).

Socrates always pleaded that he did not commit any sin against God and any crime against society and thus, the capital punishment imposed upon him was wrong and malicious. There was a normal practice in those days for the persons were awarded capital punishment to take recourse to flattering the judges and begging for compassion and pity by presenting their wives and children in the court. Socrates did not take recourse of any such thing. There was other recourse also to escape from the punishment. There was enough time to get away in the thirty days he spent in prison before execution. Some of his well-wishers and friends had a free entry and they urged him to escape. These things were quite prevalent in those days in Athens. Anaxagoras had escaped from the prison with the help of Pericles. A few silver coins of bribe to jail guards could have been enough to get him out. But Socrates refused to escape from the prison. He considered that the escape from death would be cowardly and against his whole philosophy. He always believed to obey the laws. As he had been awarded capital punishment, hence he must obey. This speaks of his conviction and belief that Socrates was a firm believer in the decree of God and not in the decree of the state. He drank the poison which was given by Archons. Even at the last phase of his life he was courteous and discussed the truth and virtue. There is a very revealing conversation of Socrates with Crito. He talked to Crito that let someone bring the hemlock properly pounded. Then Crito said, "but I think Socrates that sun is still on the mountains and has not yet set. Besides I know that others have drunk the poison very late, after it had been announced to them, and had supped and drunk freely, and some had even enjoyed the objects of their love. Do not hasten them, for there is yet time." Upon this Socrates replied, "these men whom you mention, Crito, do these things with good reason, for they think they shall gain by doing, and I too with good reason, shall not do so; for I think I shall gain nothing by drinking a little later, except to become ridiculous to myself, in being so fond of life, and sparing of it when none any longer remains. Go then," he said, "obey, and do not resist." Socrates drank the poison with the equanimity of mind. Crito was in tears. Applaudorous had even been weeping, he was overtaken by the agony of grief. Socrates asked them, "What are you doing my admirable friends, I indeed for this reason chiefly sent away the women, so that, they might not commit folly of this kind, for I have heard, it is right to die with good omens. They all felt ashamed and tried to restrain themselves. We derive our information about the life and teachings about Socrates from Plato and Xenophon. Plato in his dialogues has made Socrates the mouth piece of his own teachings. It would be difficult for anybody to separate the original teachings of Socrates from that of Plato. With these limitations we have no other recourse than to depend upon Plato's dialogue and Xenophon's memorabilia. Plato's dialogue and Xenophon's memorabilia are the only source of our knowledge about the life and teachings of Socrates.

Nietzsche says, "The time will come when in order to perfect ourselves morally and rationally, we will prefer to have recourse to Xenophon's memorabilia rather than the Bible, and we will use Montaigne and Horace's guides along the path which leads to the understanding of the sage, and of Socrates the most imperishable of them all."[15]

The greatest contribution of Socrates is his use of dialectic for understanding the problem of knowledge through the method of question and answer. There is some controversy regarding the discoverer of dialectics. There is a common belief that it was Zeno disciple Parmenides who discovered the dialectical method for seeking knowledge. According to T.R.V. Murthy, it was the Buddha who was the first to discover the dialectic because he was aware of the antinomical character of reason and he was right that the truth could be experienced only by transcending the limits of reason.

But credit goes to Socrates for making it a philosophical method for understanding knowledge and truth. We get confirmation from Socrates last utterances when he was condemned to death to attain immortality. He would practise dialectic because there was no fear of death. Socrates had helped in promoting logical consistency by the use of dialectic. If there would not have been Socrates there would not have been Plato who has the honour and distinction of being the founding father of a school of philosophy, in the Western tradition. There is a very intimate relation between virtue and knowledge in Socrates doctrine which became the guideline for Plato.

Plato was born in 428 B.C. He was a disciple of Socrates. Plato had profound love and respect for his teacher. Apart from Socrates he was greatly influenced by Pythagoras, Parmenides and Heraclitus. Plato derived mystical elements in philosophy from Pythagoras. This is clear from Plato's simile of myth of a cave in which there is an evident reference to the distinction between appearance and reality. Plato had made use of allegories, fables and stories to understand the distinction between appearance and reality. Plato's allegories, fables and stories may be classed under Platonic myths. They speak of Plato's great literary beauty and grace. W.T. Stace has wrongly charged Plato for use of myth as a defect.

He writes, "Plato slips so easily from scientific exposition into myth, that it is often not easy matter to decide whether his statements are meant literally or allegorically. Moreover, the myths usually signify a defect in his thought itself. The fact is that the combination of a poet and a philosopher in one man is an exceedingly dangerous combination. I have explained before that the object of philosophy is, not merely to feel the truth, as the poet and mystic feel it, but intellectually to comprehend it, not merely to give us a series of pictures and metaphors, but a reasoned explanation of things upon scientific principles."[16] I think W.T. Stace does not have the full understanding of Plato's philosophy. Plato's philosophy is based on the distinction between reality and appearance. Plato like other mystic thinker was aware that reality cannot be described in linguistic form, while charging Plato for his dangerous combination of poet and philosopher in him. W.T. Stace also find the same defects and shortcomings in the seers of *Upaniṣads* who believed that only *Brahman* is real and the world is only an appearance. Like *Upaniṣadic* seers, Plato had been left with no alternative but to take refuge in metaphors, allegories and fables to explain the world of intelligentsia and common man, the profound philosophical doctrine of ontological mysticism.

The doctrine of Parmenides had exercised great influence on Plato's philosophy, particularly the Parmenides concept of absolute, eternal and immutable being as the one and the only reality. Parmenides created a philosophical background by introducing to Plato, the concept of eternal and timeless reality which became the logical grounds of Plato's philosophy for rejecting the appearance and change as illusion.

Plato introduced in his philosophy the Heraclitus theory of eternal flux and formulated that knowledge is not to be attained with the senses. I consider that the whole philosophical system of Plato is based on ontological mysticism. Bertrand Russell writes, "In the first place: Goodness and Reality being timeless, the best state will be the one which most nearly copies the heavenly model, by having a minimum of change and a maximum of static perfection, and its rulers should be those who best understand the eternal Good. In the second place: Plato, like all mystics, has, in his beliefs, a core of certainty which is essentially incommunicable except by a way of life. The Pythagoreans had endeavoured to set up a rule of the initiate, and this is, at bottom, what Plato desires. If a man is to be a good statesman, he must know the Good; this can only do by a combination of intellectual and moral discipline."[17]

Plato's monumental work the *Republic* deals with both the political philosophy and philosophy as such. The first part of Plato's *Republic* is known as Utopia. His Political philosophy as propounded in the *Republic* is definitely Utopian. In Plato's state, man doesn't have any legal father. He believes that the women shall be without exception, the common wives of the guardians.

He doesn't approve of anybody having his own legal wife. His concept of philosopher king is definitely an imaginative thinking, divorced from political and historical reality. In *Republic*, he writes, "Until philosophers are kings, or the kings and princes of this world have the spirit and the power of philosophy, and political greatness and wisdom meet in one, and those commoner nature who pursue either to the exclusion of the other are compelled to stand aside, cities will never have rest from these evils—no, nor the human race, as I believe—then only will this our state have a possibility of life and behold the light of day." I am not much concerned right now with Plato's Political philosophy. My concern is with his metaphysical, ethical and logical systems which are the kernel of Plato's philosophical system. Plato is essentially a mystic, and he weaves whole philosophical system to understand the problem of reality and appearance. Philosophy for Plato is a pursuit of reality and the "vision of truth". Philosophy is not for Plato an intellectual pursuits alone. He makes a distinction between knowledge and wisdom. His concept of wisdom is closer to the Hindu concept of *Parājñāna*, (transcendental knowledge). It is very close to Spinoza's profound Love of God. It is very difficult for normal Western minds that are deeply rooted in dry intellectualism to understand the transcendental and the mystical dimension of the philosophy of Socrates and Plato.

In the latter part of *Republic* Plato formulates his philosophy. Plato makes a difference between knowledge and opinion. According to him knowledge is certain and infallible, opinion suffers from mistakes and error. Opinion is both *is* or *is not*, because the things posit the opposite characters. A thing could be cognised as both beautiful and ugly. According to Plato, opinion is related to the phenomenal world and knowledge is related to the transcendental. I find great similarity between Plato and Kant. For Kant, *thing in itself* is unknown and unknowable. Kant makes a distinction between *phenomena* and *noumena* the only difference between Plato and Kant theory is that according to Kant *thing in itself* is beyond the reach of human knowledge and understanding, but according to Plato knowledge of reality is a possibility. Opinion is related to particular things, knowledge is concerned with the universal. This is the basis of Plato's theory of Ideas.

Plato's dialectic or theory of Idea is related with the nature of eternal reality.

His theory of Ideas is dependent on his concept of knowledge and truth. Plato initiates the discussions with the refutation and rejections of wrong theories and doctrines. After refuting the false theories of knowledge he formulates his own doctrine of ideas and knowledge. According to Plato, perception provides contradictory knowledge as for example an object appears large when we are near and small from a distance. As the object has many dimensions, perception does not provide complete knowledge as such. Perception does not provide the proper knowledge because it is bereft of the objectivity of truth. If we accept the objectivity of truth as a criterion of knowledge then the distinction between truth and falsehood becomes a meaningless proposition. Perception does not provide the ideas of identity and difference; it is only through reasoning and intellect that we can have real knowledge.

The whole theory of knowledge as perception of Protagoras and the sophists has been rejected by Plato. To know a thing is not just to know that a thing is so, but why it is so, one must know the reasons. Knowledge is proper understanding and rational comprehension. Knowledge cannot be merely an instinctive belief. Knowledge is based on reason. It is based on concepts. Reason is a pursuit of understanding knowledge through the faculty of conceptualising. If we closely examine the Socratic subject matter of dialectic, we come to the conclusion that Plato's concept of knowledge and his theory of ideas is based on the teachings of Socrates. Plato transformed the Socrates's subject matter of dialectic into his grand metaphysical system. Thus, Plato is indebted to Socrates. Plato transformed Socratic thought and ideas into theory of objectivity of concepts and knowledge. The concept of Socrates according to Plato is not merely an idea rooted in mind, but it has an objective existence in the form of reality. This is the quintessence of Plato's metaphysics. He considered that truth has some intimate relation with the objects of existence. Knowledge is the understanding of concepts. Thus reality is a concept. Knowledge of concept is real knowledge. Sensation does not provide the proper background of true knowledge and understanding of facts in existence.

Plato makes a distinction between the world of intellect and the world of senses. He further divides the reason and sense perceptions into two kinds. There is a higher kind of reason which is related with pure ideas and thoughts. It could be understood through the dialectic method. Other kind of reason, he calls it understanding. This kind of intellect is employed in mathematical formulation. It is inferior to reason because it is based on hypothesis as for example we always use in geometry as "let ABC be a triangle", it is based on hypothesis. Thus, the knowledge which is derived from mathematics is hypothetical, not real. The mathematical truths cannot be derived from hypothetical truth or derivation of mathematical truth and reality we have to take the recourse to a super sensible world. We cannot have knowledge of super sensible objects which exist in super sensible world by understanding. Thus, geometrical propositions can be known through reason and not through sense perception.

Plato compares eye with soul. We have knowledge of ideas only when the object is illuminated by the soul. We cannot have the knowledge and understanding of facts of existence without this illumination. Plato says, "the soul is like an eye: when resting upon that on which truth and being shine, the soul perceives and understands, and is radiant with intelligence; but when trusted towards the twilight of becoming and perishing, she has opinion only, and goes blinking about, and is first of one opinion and then of another, and seems to have no intelligence...., Now, what imparts truth to the known and the power of knowing to the knower is what I would have termed the idea of good, and this you will deem to be the cause of science."

Plato concepts are realities. His objective concepts are known as ideas. The main problem of philosophy has been the quest for reality which is the basis of appearances and the unrealities of facts of existence. Philosophy has been engaged in answering these eternal questions of the nature of absolute and ultimate reality. According to Plato, idea is absolute and ultimate reality. It is known as substance. Substance in philosophical parlance stands for reality in itself. Substance is reality which has its whole being in its self. Substance is reality that does not depend on anything else which is the ultimate source and basis of its own reality. Plato's ideas can be compared by Spinoza's concept of substance. Spinoza in his celebrated work *Ethics* begins with the definition of substance as follows:

"First Part
Concerning God
Definitions"

I. By cause of itself.
II. That thing is said to be finite in its kind which can be limited by another thing of the same kind.
III. By Substance—I understand that which is itself conceived through itself.
IV. By God (Dues)—I understand a being absolutely infinite, that is, a substance consisting of infinite attributes, each of which express eternal and infinite essence.
V. By Attribute—I understand that which the intellect perceives of a substance as constituting its essence.
VI. By Mode—I understand the modification of a substance; as that which is in something else through which it is also conceived.

The comparison is made with Plato's idea of the good with Spinoza's substance or God. God is a substance and the world is not. However, both the Plato's idea of the good and Spinoza God is quite different from the God of Christianity and Judaism. The God of Christianity and Judaism is theistic whereas Spinoza's concept of God is pantheistic. Spinoza does not believe in personal God.

As a mystic, Plato was aware of the limitation of reason in understanding and comprehending the ultimate reality which is absolutely infallible and eternal. This pushed him to his famous myth of a cave according to which we are all compared with prisoners in a cave because we have limitations. In knowing the reality, we are bound by the limitation of reason. The myth of cave has beautifully explained the limitation of not only the perception but also of reason. The prisoners in a cave can look only in one direction because it is covered and bounded by fire behind and the wall in front. Between the prisoners and the wall there is nothing. The prisoners have no option, they can only satisfy with the shadow of themselves and the objects behind them which are reflected on the wall by the illumination of a fire behind them. The prisoners consider the shadow as real because they are denied of knowledge of the objects of which the shadows are reflected on the wall. Some man succeeded in coming out of the prison of the cave to the light of sun and gets the glimpse and sees the real things and becomes conscious that until now, he had had completely wrong understanding and knowledge of the real things.

The myth of the cave throws light on the predicament and the misfortune of a philosopher and an intellectual, because without the mystical experience one cannot have the real knowledge and experience of reality which is transcendental in nature. Williams James rightly observes that the mystic alone has excess to reality. He says, "In psychology, physiology and medicine whenever there is a debate between the mystics and the scientists mystics have usually been proved to be right about the facts, which the scientists had the better of it in respect to the theories."[18]

Plato's spirituality is evident in his metaphysical formulation of the theory of Ideas. There has been a great controversy regarding the mystical element of Plato's philosophy. W.T. Stace rejects out rightly the elements of mysticism in the philosophy of Plato. However, he admits that towards the end of his life Plato became victim of mathematical mysticism and he considers that the Pythagoreans impact on Plato was disastrous. He writes, "The ideas are rational, that is to say, they are apprehended through reason. The finding of the common element in the manifold is the work of inductive reason and through this alone is knowledge of the ideas possible. This should be noted by those persons who imagine that Plato was some sort of benevolent mystic. The imperishable one, the absolute reality, is apprehended, not by intuition, or in any kind of mystic ecstasy, but only by rational cognition and laborious thought. Lastly, towards the end of his life, Plato identified the ideas with the Pythagorean numbers. We know this from Aristotle, but it is not mentioned in the dialogue of Plato himself. It appears to have been a theory adopted in old age, and set forth in the lectures which Aristotle attended. It is retrograde step, and tends to degrade the great and lucid idealism of Plato into a mathematical mysticism. In this, as in other respects, the influence of the Pythagoreans upon Plato was harmful."[19]

I consider the accusation of W.T. Stace that under the influence of Pythagoras Plato's idealism lost its metaphysical sublimity, profundity and flavour by grounding himself in mathematical mysticism is wrong and frivolous. To me this was the Plato's greatest and grandeur metaphysical enumeration of reality which is beyond any categories of rationalism. The myth of the cave has enough evident of Plato's orientation to mysticism. He was aware and convinced through the analysis of reason that it has its own limitation and hence he resorted to myth, parables and allegories to express which is inexpressible, the formulation of absolute as, "neither an abstract to one nor multiple abstract". There cannot be many aims in one. This idea of many in one speaks of the bankruptcy of dry and insipid intellectualism. I consider W.T. Stace evaluation and understanding of Plato incomplete and dogmatic. Stace lacks in understanding the spirituality of Plato's metaphysics.

Plato is very clear on the spirituality of the soul. Soul according to Plato is eternal.

Soul loses its essences and spirituality when it comes in contact with the sense perception. Soul loses its true nature and spirituality in contemplation and comprehension of the phenomenal world of change and becoming. Plato writes, "The soul when using the body as an instrument of perception that is to say, when using the sense of sight or hearing or some other sense (for the meaning of perceiving through the body is perceiving through the sense).... Is then dragged by the body into the region of the changeable, and wanders and is confused; the world spins around her, and she is like a drunkard, when she touches change... But when returning into herself she reflects, and then she passes into the other world, the region of purity, and eternity, and immortality, and unchangeableness, which are her kindred, and with them she ever lies, when she is by herself, and is not let or hindered; then she ceases from her erring ways, and being in communion with the unchanging is unchanging. And this state of the soul is called wisdom."

Plato contemplated that only a philosopher goes to heaven and enters into the company of God, but he puts a condition that only the philosopher who has attained wisdom, i.e., Lover of wisdom is entitled to enjoy the divine companionship and unity with God. He has explained it in no uncertain terms that the soul is liberated from the thraldom of the worldly desires when he becomes a philosopher that is when he considers the attainment of the wisdom as the ultimate goal and purpose of life. The pure soul must abstain from the lust of flesh and worldly possessions. A true philosopher and a pure soul does not fear poverty or disgrace because the philosopher is aware that the lust for mundane possessions fastens the soul with body. Lust is the cause of souls own captivity and bondage. This is to my mind is similar to that of Vedāntic teachings. It is more akin to spirituality than to dry intellectualism. Bertrand Russell's criticism of the Socrates farewell address to Crito is unwanted and frivolous. He has completely misunderstood and misconstrued Socrates teachings. His perception and understanding of Plato is incomplete and hollow. He tries to evaluate and examine Socrates and Plato's philosophy from the prisms of misguided scientific lens and perception. Russell's ethical evaluation of Plato and Socrates is unjust and unwarranted and it speaks of the lack of deeper understanding of spiritual and mystical elements of philosophy which enriches and sublimates the metaphysics of Plato and Socrates. In the concluding observation in *Phaedo,* Socrates highest tributes have been paid in most eloquent and lofty words—"of all the men of his times he was the wisest and the justest and bestest". In this background Bertrand Russell's criticism and condemnation of Socrates sayings that after his final departure he was going to enjoy eternal bliss in the company of God is unjustified and unwarranted.

Bertrand Russell remarks that, "There is something smug and unctuous about him, which reminds one of a bad type of cleric. His courage in the face of death would have been more remarkable if he had not believed that he was going to enjoy eternal bliss in the company of the gods. Unlike some of his predecessors, he was not scientific in his thinking, but was determined to prove the universe agreeable to his ethical standards. This is treachery to truth, and the worst of philosophic sins. As a man, we may believe him admitted to the communion of saints, but as a philosopher he needs a long residence in a scientific purgatory."[20]

Bertrand Russell misses Plato's concept of a good in its metaphysical formulations. The concept of good occupies the most sublime position in Plato's philosophy. The dialectic leads to the understanding of the absolute good. It is with the help of the idea of good that Plato's dialectic get rids itself from the hypothesis of mathematics. The good of Plato is the substance of Spinoza. To perceive the idea of the good is to know the reality. Russell does admit that "throughout Plato's philosophy there is the same fusion of intellect and mysticism as in Pythagoreanism, but at this final culmination mysticism clearly has the upper hand."[21]

If someone admits that Plato's philosophy is a culmination of mysticism then he or she should try to first understand what is mysticism and why Plato has been so much influenced by Pythagoreanism. The lack of this understanding of mysticism and Pythagoreanism does not justify Bertrand Russell's unwarranted criticism of Plato's mysticism occupying an upper hand as worst of philosophic sins.

The problem of distinction between reality and appearance has been the perennial source of philosophical debates. This is the problem of Hindu, Buddhist and even the Western philosophy. Even the modern idealist like F.S. Bradley in his book *Appearance and Reality*, tried to resolve this problem from the perspective of the empiricist. He is of the opinion that truth can be known only through intuition. It goes against the established norms of dry intellectualism.

Plato was aware that one can have the proper knowledge and understanding of reality only through transcending the bondage of intellect. One can have real knowledge only by getting liberated from the thraldom of sensuous world. Intellectuals are living in the cave among those who have never seen the truth in the light of sun. Plato would like to emphasize that our life is prisoned in the cave of existence. We could be liberated and see and experience the truth and reality after getting out of the bondage of cave dwellings. This is the essence and the kernel of Hinduism and Buddhism. I find here that Plato and Socrates in the mystical assessment of truth and reality are closer to Hinduism, Buddhism than Einstein and Schrodinger. I would discuss in detail in subsequent chapters about Einstein's and Schrodinger's concept of science and spirituality.

Socrates admits, "I seem to hear in my ears, like the sound of the flute in the ears of the mystic". During the last hours of his life, Socrates was allowed to converse freely. He asks his weeping wife to go away, so that, there should not be any disturbance in discussions and dialogues with his friends. He talks about death and he says that the man of philosophy and knowledge will not fear death, rather he would embrace it with grace and dignity. According to Socrates, death is separation of soul from body. However, it would be preposterous to think and evaluate Plato's philosophy of distinction between reality and appearance, ideas and sensible objects, reason and sense perception and soul and body on the Socrates parable of death as separation of soul and body. Ascetic, virtue does not come from the philosophy of dualism. Ascetic morality is the result of one's conviction and firm belief in monism and mysticism. Socrates postulates the ethical ideal of philosophers as the dissever of the soul from the attachment of body contrary to common man who thinks life is not worth living without the sensuous pleasure. According to Socrates, one should always try to return back to the elemental and real home of soul by getting away from the bondage of flesh and sense.

Bertrand Russell does admit that Socrates was an ascetic. He writes, "Socrates, in Phaedo, proceeds at once to develop the ascetic implications of his doctrine, but his asceticism is of a moderate and gentlemanly sort. He does not say that the philosopher should wholly abstain from ordinary pleasures, but only that he should not be a slave to them. The philosopher should not care about eating and drinking, but of course he should eat as much as is necessary; there is no suggestion of fasting..... In like manner, the philosopher must not care for the pleasures of love, or for costly raiment, or sandal, or other adornments of the person. He must be entirely concerned with the soul, and not with body."

There is a great comparison between the Buddhist and Hindu concept of spirituality which pervades the whole life of a man and that of Socrates and Plato's view on moralism. According to Socrates and Plato, wisdom alone brings liberation of soul from the thraldom of the body. Soul is eternal and only in contemplation of the transcendental in which its essence becomes harmony in life and thought, soul when it is used as an instrument of sense perception, gets rooted in the world of change and becoming. Soul attains the eternal bliss in the company of gods when it is liberated from the attachment of senses. Plato does believe in the rebirth, this is the clear and unquestionable impact of Hinduism on the philosophy of

Plato. Like a mystic, Plato advocates for keeping oneself away from the life of lust and cravings in which the soul becomes attached and glued to body. According to him, a philosopher "is conscious that the soul is simply fastened or glued to the body—until philosophy received her, she could only view real existence through the bars of the prison, not in and through herself... and by reason of lust had become the principal accomplice in her own captivity." The man of wisdom is aware that "each pleasure and pain is a sort of nail which nails and rivets the soul to the body, until she becomes like the body, and believes that to be true which the body affirms to be true." There is happy and harmonious blending of the precept of Virtue and Transcendence in the philosophy of Plato.

Plato's concept of heaven is different from the Christian Anthromorphic concept of heaven. Plato and Socrates both consider the life of the puckish delight in living a life of sense pleasure as the greatest impediment in living with God for the attainment of wisdom. This is a life of a wallow in despair when a man uses the soul as an instrument of enjoying puckish delight. Soul loses its divine essences when it is used for enjoyment, lust and worldly pleasures.

The soul when using the body as an instrument of perception, that is to say, when using the sense of sight or hearing or some other sense (for the meaning of perceiving through the body is perceiving through the senses)....is then dragged by the body into the region of the changeable, and wanders and is confused; the world spins around her, and she is like a drunkard, when she touches change... But when returning into herself, she reflects, then she passes into the other world, the region of purity, and eternity, and immortality, and unchangeableness, which are her kindred, and with them she ever lives, when she is by herself, and is not let or hindered; then she ceases from her erring ways, and being in communion with the unchanging is unchanging. And this state of the soul is called wisdom.

According to Plato, morality is not pleasure. Knowledge is not perception. Knowledge is not a proper or right opinion likewise morality cannot be identified with right action. Morality is action due to rational and proper understanding of real values. Plato propagates two kinds of morality: philosophical values and customary values. The true moral values is derived from the true knowledge of the nature of the *summum bonum* of life. If we summarize the philosophy of Plato then we come to the conclusion that his philosophy is closer to Buddhism and Hinduism. W.T. Stace observes about Plato's kernel of philosophy as such, "What, in all probability, he did believe, however, may be summarized as follows. The soul is pre-existent as well as immortal. Its natural home is the world of ideas, where at first it existed, without a body, in the pure and blissful contemplation of ideas. But because it has affinities with the world of sense, it sinks down into a body. After death, if a man has lived a good life, and especially if he has cultivated the knowledge of ideas, philosophy, the soul returns to its blissful abode in the world of ideas, and after a long period it again returns to earth in a body. Those who do evil suffer after death severe penalties, and are reincarnated in the body of some being lower than themselves. A man may become a woman. Men may even, if their lives have been utterly sensual, pass into the bodies of animals."[22]

Plato's conception of soul as immortal and eternal is the foundation of his philosophy. According to Plato, soul in a pre-existent state is transcendental and immortal. But when he comes in contact with body he loses its transcendental nature. In the world of senses, soul gets attached to body. Plato considers customary virtue which springs from custom, habit, traditional culture milieu is not sufficient to rid the soul, it takes it to the company of eternal bliss after death. The customary virtue and moral values is like the virtue of bees and ants. Such people after death are reborn as bees and ants. Even the best of statesmen and politicians lack philosophical virtue like masses. Socrates and Plato put emphasis on the life of the real philosopher whose soul is liberated from cravings and desires. If we examine carefully and critically the philosophy of Socrates and Plato, I think that there is no trace of Bacchii enthusiasm in the enumeration of the concept of ideal life of philosopher. I don't agree with Bertrand Russell's observation about Socrates. I believe what is the best and the *quint essential* elements of Socrates philosophy is being condemned and criticised by Russell. This is not only unwarranted, but it speaks of Russell's lack of understanding of Socrates. I consider that whole philosophical edifice of Socrates is based on Ontological mysticism. Bertrand Russell's abhorrence for spirituality and ontological mysticism is known to everybody, but while enumerating the teachings of any philosopher one should not be guided by one's own prejudices and misgivings. Bertrand Russell is the victim of this misconception and misunderstanding. While examining the teachings and thought of any thinker one should not evaluate the contribution of a thinker from one's own misguided, misconstrued prism or perspective. He writes, "There is something smug and unctuous about him, which reminds one of a bad type of a cleric. His courage in the face of death would have been more remarkable if he had not believed that he was going to enjoy eternal bliss in the company of the gods. Unlike some of his predecessors, he was not scientific in his thinking, but was determined to prove the universe agreeable to his ethical standards.

This is a treachery to truth, and the worst of philosophic sins. As a man, we may believe him admitted to the communion of saints; but as a philosopher he needs a long residence in a scientific purgatory."[23]

Bertrand Russell's bias for science forces him to write such derogatory remarks against Socrates. I think philosopher does not need to live in the residence of scientific purgatory for the propagation of truth and wisdom, rather the scientist need a long residence in philosophical and mystic purgatory to comprehend the truth in its totality.

The business of philosophy is to comprehend truth in its totality. The philosophers have been trying to explain the phenomenal world from the perspective of the first principle. The first principle is conceived as ideas, concepts, reason, and substance and God as reality. The success of any philosophical evaluation depends upon the proper account of the first principles. The first principle must be capable of explaining the world of existence and being. Our analysis of the philosophy of East and the West leads to Ontological mysticism as the basis of explaining the concept of existence and being. I shall deal with this concept of Ontological mysticism in the subsequent chapters.

Aristotle occupies unique position in the history of Western philosophy. He was born in 384 B.C. at Stagyra in Thrace. He became disciple of Plato and he spent nearly 20 years at the academy established by Plato. He founded his own school at Athens and completed most of his writings at his school. Aristotle's writings are systematic and creative. His philosophy is free from the mystic elements of Plato. The doctrine of matter and form is the foundation of Aristotle's philosophy. The form in its essence is primary substance. He makes a difference between substance and universal. According to him *form* is a substance which the universal lacks. Aristotle's metaphysical doctrine has grown out of his polemic against Plato's doctrine of ideas. According to Aristotle, matter and form are inseparable. We cannot think of form without matter or matter without form. Every object is composed of matter and form.

Most of Western philosophers introduce the concept of God as the first principle to explain the world. Aristotle's first principle is also God, thus God or absolute is the ultimate cause and the world as its effect. However, God is not related to the world as cause to effect. The relation of cause and effect in the context of God does not depend on time; it is rather a logical relation. According to Aristotle, God is a logical premise from which the world is deduced just like the syllogistic reasoning. In Aristotelian logic the conclusion is deduced from the first premise. However, the concept of premise is not in time, but it is in thought. God is a thought, God is spirit, and He is the form of form. Aristotle defines God as "the thought of thought". No dualism of subject and object exists in God. Aristotle while enumerating the concept of God as He is essentially self-consciousness. God embodies in himself the principle of form that contains formal, final and the efficient causes. God is the totality of all these. While propagating the theory of causation, Aristotle, it seems landed himself in the pitfalls of mechanism. W.T. Stace while summarizing Aristotle's doctrine of causation writes, "This last agreement sounds as if Aristotle is now thinking in terms of mechanism. It sounds as if he meant that the first mover is something at the beginning of time, which, so to speak, gave things a push to start them off. This is not what Aristotle means. For the true efficient cause is the final cause. And God is the first mover only His character as the absolute end. As far as time is concerned, neither the universe, nor the motion in it, ever had any beginning. Every mechanical cause has its cause in turn, and so *ad infinitum.* God is not a first cause, in our sense, that is, a first mechanical cause which existed before the world, and created it. He is a teleological cause working from the end."[24] However, Aristotle's theory of causation and concept of God do not explain the concept of motion. Even Newton's explanation of motion is not sufficient to explain the real nature of matter. We will see in the subsequent chapter while dealing with the motion and the concept of reality which has been the central theme of Einstein's doctrine of relativity and Heisenberg's and Schrodinger's doctrine of Quantum Mechanics which culminates in Ontological Mysticism.

However, Aristotle's concept of God is not Anthromorphic as his God lives in eternal blessedness. God is absolute form and the form is universal. Thus, God of Aristotle is a form without matter. His God is absolutely real, but not existent. Therefore, God is neither nor existent. Aristotle does not believe in a personal God as conceived in all sematic religions. Zeller while dealing with Aristotle's doctrines of form and matter writes, "The final explanation of Aristotle's want of clearness on this subject is, however, to be found in the fact that he *had* only half emancipated himself, as we shall see, from Plato's tendency to hypostatise ideas. The 'Forms' had for him, as the 'Ideas' had for Plato, a metaphysical existence of their own, as conditioning all individual things. As keenly as he followed the growth of ideas out of experience, it is nonetheless true that these ideas, especially at the point where they are farthest removed from experience and immediate perception, are metamorphosed in the end from a logical product of human thought into an immediate presentment of a supersensible world, and the object, in that sense, of an intellectual intuition."[25]

Whatever may be the shortcomings of Aristotle's metaphysics, he has raised some philosophical issues which subsequent generations have been trying to solve. Here lies the greatness and the originality of Aristotle's philosophy. The God of Aristotle is not a subjective thought, but a pure thought which is objective and real. Here Aristotle makes a radical departure from the Plato's theory of Ideas. For Plato thought is real and objective only when it is an existent. Absolute thought is absolutely real for Aristotle, but he does not ascribe existent status to God. Here Aristotle's metaphysics ends with the concept of God.

The ancient Greek philosophers such as Socrates, Epicurus and Plato lived up to the idea of the doctrine that they preached. Once Plato inquired from an old man who was attending classes on virtue that "When will you finally begin to live virtuously". These ancient thinkers were conscious that philosophy is not merely a pursuit to speculate, but ultimately to live according to the ideal of ethical life, that is to apply the knowledge acquired by speculation to living according to the principles of wisdom and virtue.

Friedrich Nietzsche's monumental work *Thus Spoke Zarathustra* created a great debate in the world of philosophy and religion by declaring that, "God is dead". There is a saint who talks about songs that he composes and sings which makes him to laugh and cry. The whole song is devoted to the praise of God. After hearing the saint's narration about God Zarathustra made a farewell to the saint "What should I have to give you? But let me go quickly lest I take something from you!" and thus they separated, the old one and the man, laughing as two boys laugh. But when Zarathustra was alone he spoke thus to his heart: "Could it be possible? This old saint in the forest has not yet heard anything of this, that *God is dead!*"[26]

He rejected the God of religion which is the basis of the meaning and values of Western civilization. Joachim Kohler says, "God is dead!—Nietzsche's most famous aphorism. There is no higher purpose to life, merely eternal chaos, and we transient mortals are only deceiving ourselves with our religions and our intellectual constructs. "Where are we going?" he asks in *La gaia scienza*. "Away from all the suns? Are we not always falling—backwards, sideways, forwards, in all directions? Is there still a top and a bottom? Are we not wandering through an endless maze? Do we not feel the chill breath of an empty universe"?"[27]

Nietzsche put on himself the mask of the Persian prophet Zoroaster. The life of Zoroaster has been of suffering in a sublime form of wisdom and enlightenment. I find similarity between the Buddhist concept of rebirth and eternal flux with Nietzsche doctrine of Eternal Recurrence. His concept of Eternal Recurrence provides a new foundation to the existence of mankind.

We need not fear death because life is eternal and hence we can enjoy and rejoice in the thought of divinity. Nietzsche declared himself as a disciple of the unknown God and a "free spirit", born out of his time. In 1889 he writes that, "In India I was Buddha and in Greece I was Dionysus." Joachim Kohler writes, "The death of his revered father was not the only trauma experienced by Fritz in his early childhood. Six months later he had a dream in which he saw his father, draped in a white shroud, rise from his grave and then return to the depths with a small child clasped to his breast. The following day, the dream came true—his younger brother Joseph also died. From that time onwards he was credited with having the gift of prophecy, and he himself appeared to believe that he had mystical links with the kingdom of the dead."[28]

I personally feel that Friedrich Nietzsche's philosophy which dominated the entire philosophical world of nineteenth century has been misinterpreted and misunderstood. He introduced three main doctrines in *Thus Spoke Zarathustra,* i.e., the doctrine of God is dead, Superman and Eternal Recurrence. We have to take into account these three basic concepts of Nietzsche while evaluating and understanding his philosophy. He declared the God of religion as dead. There has been historical religious and cultural milieu prevalent at that time that created a great misunderstanding and notion about God. Moreover, it is the accepted view that the concept of personal God, as has been propagated in most of the sematic religions does not satisfy the rational mind of modern times. The God of theistic religion have outlived its utility. People are in search of a real God which could satisfy both the rationality and the spirituality of modern man. While enumerating the teachings of Friedrich Nietzsche, Graham Parkes who has translated: Thus, Spoke Zarathustra into English enumerates the teachings of Nietzsche in the following words:

"Since, it seems that a condition for the possibility of the appearance of the Overhuman is 'the death of God', it is often assumed that this advent heralds the disappearance of the Divine. The book's First Part does indeed end with the resounding cry, '*Dead are all Gods: now we want the Overhuman to live'*—but this is only a provisional teaching of Zarathustra's that will soon be superseded. At this early stage he would rather his disciples rid themselves of all belief in supernatural beings than move too soon to a more salutary polytheism from which they might relapse into some other form of 'monotonotheism'. A careful reading of the last three parts of the book reveals that for Zarathustra the world, seen clearly and rightly understood, is 'a dance-floor for divine accidents' and 'a Gods' table for divine dice and dice-throwers' (3.4). There is a new kind of religion here—what has been aptly called Nietzsche's 'Dionysian Pantheism' ".[29] Graham Parkes had made a detailed comparison between Mahāyāna Buddhist impact on *Thus Spoke Zarathustra* in his essay published in John Lippitt and James Urpeth (eds.) Nietzsche and the Divine, and he is of the opinion that Nietzsche's concept of Dionysian Pantheism has been wrongly understood by the Western minds.[30]

Nietzsche's famous statement that "dead are all gods: now, he wants Overhuman to lives speaks of the decline of the Christian religious belief and teachings". Nietzsche's declaration of the death of God was not against the real and the transcendental divine being, but it was against the prevalent corruptions that were being exercised in the name of God by the then Christian world. The proper reading and understanding of last part of the *Thus Spoke Zarathustra* enumerates a new form of monotonotheism. *Thus Spoke Zarathustra* is Nietzsche's whole oeuvre over the years and it has exercised a great impact on the life and the philosophy of both Western and Eastern world. *Thus Spoke Zarathustra* was received in Asia with great enthusiasm. It goes without saying that some of the ideas of Nietzsche's philosophies have great similarities with Hindu, Buddhist , and Chinese philosophy. It has made great impact on Japanese culture also. It is evident that Nietzsche was greatly influenced by oriental philosophy. His perspective of philosophy is definitely trans-European and even an Asiatic and trans-Asiatic eye that brought him success.[31]

Western philosophy is littered with the problem of God and reality.

Rene Descartes is considered as the father of modern Western philosophy. After Aristotle, Rene Descartes is the first eminent philosopher who developed a system of philosophy. Apart from his contribution to philosophy he was a mathematician and man of science. His greatest contribution to science was the discovery of co-ordinate geometry. His concept of *Cogito ergo sum, I think therefore I exist is the basis and foundation of his whole philosophical superstructure.* After discovering a strong foundation in the form of *Cogito ergo sum* from which he deduced the concept of God and the soul. Descartes says, "'God is positively infinite, that is, he exists everywhere, etc.' 'I do not agree with this 'everywhere'.' For here you seem to locate God's infinity in the fact that he exists everywhere; I do not agree with this view but I think that God is everywhere by reason of his power. He has no relation at all to any place by reason of His essence. Since power and essence are not distinguished in God, I think it is more satisfactory to reason about such things in the case of our mind or the angels, as realities that are more suited to our perception, rather than in the case of God."[32] I think 'therefore I am' with this aphorism, Descartes tried to establish a single indubitable truth in certainty. Descartes views have been refuted by many. Hume's arguments against the certainty of relation have been of great philosophical importance. However, Descartes diffusion of his doctrine of God as transcendental reality occupies an important position in the history of philosophy and religion. He says "the feebleness of human understanding and the arrogance that masks, it is most apparent when we try to reduce the transcendent reality of God to the limits of Human concept, but the uncertainty of human knowledge is not limited to speculation about God. Our senses frequently deceive us."[33]

Our sense does not provide the basis of certainty of relations. "Anybody can provide as many examples as he pleases of the ways our senses deceive or cheat us, since so many of their faults or deceptions are quite banal."[34]

Spinoza is one of the most respected and lovable philosophers that the world has produced. His whole philosophy is based on the doctrine of pantheism. Ethics is the monumental work of Spinoza. He writes "By God (Deus) I understand a being absolutely infinite, that is, a substance constituting of infinite attributes, each of which expresses eternal and infinite essence. By Attribute, I understand that which the intellect perceives of substance by constituting its essence. By mode—I understand the modifications of a substance; as that which is in something else through which it is also conceived."

Spinoza's concept of God is analogous to the theistic concept of personal God. He was one of the most misunderstood philosophers of his time. He was born as a Jew but he was excommunicated by Jews brotherhood. In spite of Spinoza's firm faith in God and divinity, the orthodox Christians accused him of atheism. Spinoza's concept of God is closer to Hindu concept of *Brahman*. According to Spinoza, everything is manifestation of God's inscrutable nature. He believes in absolute logical necessity. God being the absolute and real, there is no possibility of any negation. This has created a great debate among the philosophers and the religious thinkers.

According to Spinoza there is no such thing as evil or sins as evil and sins are part of the divinity. Bertrand Russell rightly observed that the doctrine of Spinoza's God is based on his deep ontological mysticism. Bertrand Russell writes, "This doctrine, though, in one form or another, has been held by most mystics, cannot, obviously, be reconciled with the orthodox doctrine of sin and damnation. It is bound up with Spinoza's complete rejection of free will. Although not at all polemical, Spinoza was too honest to conceal his opinion, however, shocking to contemporaries; the abhorrence of his teachings is, therefore, not surprising."[35]

Our examination and evaluation of Spinoza's Ethics leads to the fact he was very much aware of the importance and rationality of science of his time. Bible as an authoritative that speaks of his deep faith which becomes a fundamental basis of philosophical and scientific postulation based on the principles of supremacy of mysticism.

The prevalent religion of his time was littered with lifeless rituals and dogmas and this was the basis of opposition between science and religion. G.H.R. Parkinson in his introduction to *Ethics* by Spinoza observes "What has just been said about Spinoza and religion provides an answer to another question raised earlier (p. xvii): namely, whether Spinoza is one of those who see science and religion as in conflict. The answer is that he would not recognise such a conflict, provided that 'religion' is taken in his sense of the term. We have seen that, for Spinoza, to speak of religion is to speak of those desires and actions that spring from the knowledge of God. Similarly, he would say that a scientific knowledge of the world depends in the last analysis on the knowledge of God, the ultimate explanation of all things. Spinoza would say, then, that in his sense of the term, 'religion', there is no conflict between religion and science. However, he also believed that false views about God had been a major obstacle to understanding, and to those false views he was firmly opposed."[36]

Spinoza's philosophy is based on *monism*. He believes in one substance from which all parts are dependent for their existence. He doesnot believe in any other reality apart from God or Substance. The relation and plurality are illusions.

Leibniz is another great philosopher of Germany. His father was a professor of moral philosophy. Leibniz is a discoverer of infinitesimal calculus. Leibniz's philosophy is based on the doctrine of Monodolgy and the principles of nature and of grace. He was inspired by Descartes and Spinoza. However, he didn't believe in the Cartesian dualism of matter and mind. Descartes' propounded the existence of three substances, i.e., God, mind and matter. According to Descartes, extension is the integral part of a matter. Spinoza rejected Descartes concept of mind and matter and accepted only God as the supreme substance. According to Spinoza extension and thought are attributes of God which was rejected by Leibniz. Leibniz replaced the doctrine of substance by the doctrine of monads. Monads are windowless. According to Leibniz, every monad's mirror is an inverse because of God who has provided the monads with this inherent power:

According to Leibniz, the existence of God is based on the following four logical principles:

1. The ontological argument,
2. The cosmological argument,
3. The argument from the eternal truths, and
4. The argument from the pre-established harmony.

Bertrand Russell while dealing with Leibniz has come to the conclusion that Leibniz philosophy is based on mysticism. However, he wrongly considers that all the inconsistency and incoherence that exist in metaphysical system of Leibniz because of his esoteric philosophy.

Bertrand Russell writes, "I come now to Leibniz esoteric philosophy, in which we find reasons for much that seems arbitrary or fantastic in his popular expositions, as well as an interpretation of his doctrines which, if it had become generally known, would have made them much less acceptable.....

Most of the texts upon which we must rely for an understanding of his esoteric doctrine were first published in 1901 or 1903, in two works by Louis Couturat. One of these was even headed by Leibniz with the remark: "Here I have made enormous progress. But in spite of this, no editor thought it worth printing until Leibniz had been dead for nearly two centuries."[37] This is wrong contention that doctrine of substance of Descartes, Spinoza and Leibniz is derived from logical necessity of subjects and objects. The substance and God are not a logical category *subjects and objects*. So, the whole analysis of Bertrand Russell is based on the misunderstanding of concept of God and substance which is based on esotericism and Ontological mysticism. David Hume is one of the most original British thinkers. His *Treatise* of *Human Nature* is a great work of philosophical originality. In this book the philosophical question that David Hume raised are still unanswered. Here lies the greatness of Hume. The empirical philosophy of Locke and Berkeley was culminated in Hume's scepticism and solipsism."Of Knowledge and Probability" which form the important section of Hume's treatise is kernel of Hume's philosophy. Bertrand Russell writes, "What Hume is concerned with is uncertain knowledge, such as is obtained from empirical data by inferences that are not demonstrative. This includes all our knowledge as to the future, and as to be unobserved portions of the past and present. In fact, it includes everything, except, on the one hand direct observation, and, on the other, logic and mathematics. The analysis of such "probable" knowledge led Hume and to certain sceptical conclusions, which are equally difficult to refute and to accept. The result was a challenge to philosophers, which, in my opinion, has still not been adequately met."[38] Hume's rejection of causation is based on his rejections of "necessary connection". According to Hume our observation doesn't prove the necessary connection between cause and effects. It is based on our habit and impression. The impression is not an impression of necessary connection. His rejection of concept of causation still remains one of the unanswered problems of philosophy.

There is great similarity between the Buddhist and the Hume's concept of self. I know that I exist. The existence of I that he finds that is based on the many particular impressions and ideas. Hume argues that no specific impression or idea of self-corresponds to the 'I' that have any independent and permanent existence. My feeling or idea of what I am is nothing, but totality of isolated impressions and particular ideas. Hume employed the same argument which Berkley has used against Locke's theory of physical world. So, there is no permanent mental substance which is considered wrongly as self. Buddhism makes comparison of the concept of self with the burning of a candle which happens in such quick succession in the burning of the candle that it creates illusion of identity. The basic property of the burning of the candle is change and flux.

According to Hume "all our ideas are copied from our impressions". In Cartesian philosophy cause and effect is considered as logical necessity. Hume argues that cause and effects do not have logical connections based on necessity. Our knowledge of cause and effects is based on experience and not from reasoning and reflection. According to him "Objects have no discoverable connection together: nor is it from any other principle, but custom operating upon the imagination that we can draw any inference from the appearance of one to the experience of another". What appears before us as necessary connection in the objects is based on customs. His concept of "necessity is something that exists in the mind, not in the objects". If we analyse the Hume's conception of causation we come to this view that causation is a concept of sequence. It is not an independent doctrine. Hume's sceptism is based on the refutation of doctrine of induction. Hume's refutation of principles of induction has created a great problem before the scientific community. We will find in subsequent chapters while dealing with Einstein's theory of Relativity and Heisenberg's and Schrodinger's doctrine of Quantum Mechanics, that they have deeper understanding of Hume's Scepticism and his rejection of principle of induction. Hume's postulated that all, "our reasoning's concerning causes and effects derived from nothing, but customs: and that belief is more properly an act of sensation, than of the causative part of our natures". This is the basis of Hume's scepticism.

Hume has raised both philosophical and scientific issues which have kept all the subsequent philosophers and scientists baffled with no finality.

Immanuel Kant (1724-1804) is the founder of German Idealism. He is one of the greatest and the most original thinker that Germany has produced. It is said that Kant was awakened by Hume's dogmatic slumbers. The *Critique of Pure Reason* is the metaphysical treatise of Kant. He dealt in this book the problem of *analytic* and *synthetic* propositions. The analytic proposition is in which predicate is part of the subject. On the other hand synthetic proposition is not analytic. The source of synthetic proposition is experienced. Analytical proposition is considered as universal and necessary. However, analytical proposition does not throw any new information. It lacks newness whereas synthetic propositions based on experience provide some new information. The basis of empirical proposition is sense perception.

An "*a priori*" proposition is the basis of our mathematical knowledge. All mathematical propositions are *a priori.* Hume's rejection of law of causality is based on the postulation that it is not universal and necessary like the *a priori* proposition. Kant has tried to bring some kind of reconciliation between the Empiricism and the Rationalism. Kant's acceptance of arithmetical and geometrical proposition as synthetic and *a priori* has created a new metaphysics known as "Criticism".

The main theme of the *Critique of Pure Reason* is to prove that synthetic judgement *a priori* is possible.

Kant made a distinction between sensibility and understanding. According to him *time* and *space* are not objective entities, but they are *a priori* categories of sensibility. All our perceptions are timed and spaced. As our knowledge about the world is coloured by *a priori* categories of *time* and *space*, we have no access to the *things in itself.* Thus, Kant makes for the first time a distinction between the phenomena and neumena. According to Kant *thing in itself* is unknown and unknowable.

Kant rejected the Berkeley's transcendental idealism as form of empirical realism. Kantian exegesis has been a source of great debate and discussion. His refutation of transcendental idealism has posed some difficult questions for Kant. Kant believed that source of our knowledge is through the synthesis of concept and intuition. Kant's doctrine of synthetic judgement *a priori* and his rejection of Hume's Scepticism are to establish the reality of the phenomenal world.

Transcendental idealism is the kernel of Kant's understanding and advocates of mathematical truths as synthetic *a priori* judgement. The basic assumption of transcendental idealism is that the general properties of phenomena are not the property of objects, but they are properties of ourselves as they are based on mental construct.

One of the most important contributions of Kant is his doctrine of *space* and *time* which is explained in *The Critique of Pure Reason and Prolegomena*. Kant's doctrine of *space* and *time* has brought a Copernicus revolution in philosophy. His theory does not agree with concept of time and space as propounded by Newton. According to Newton *time* and *space* are absolute, infinite and logically exists without any observer. T.E. Wilkerson observes, "For Leibniz there would still be an independent world of objects spatially and temporally related, while for Newton there would still be absolute space and absolute time, containing inanimate objects. One would insist that space and time are relational, the other that they are absolute individuals, but both would assume that they are in a clear sense independent of perceivers. In complete contrast Kant rejects that assumption and insists that space and time are in no sense independent of perceivers, that they are neither relational properties of object independent of us nor absolute individuals independent of us. They are 'in us', forms of our sensibility, fundamental features of the way we look at the world, forms which we project on the world."[39]

Kant formulated the doctrine of *space* and *time* as *a priori* forms on the basis of metaphysical and epistemological arguments. According to metaphysical arguments "space is not a discursive, or, as is said, general concepts of relation of things in general, but a pure intuition. For, in the first place, we can only imagine [*sich vorstellen]* one single space, and if we speak of 'spaces' we mean only parts of one and the same unique space. And these parts cannot precede the whole as its parts... but can only be thought as *in it*. It [space] is essentially unique; the manifold in it rests solely on limitations." The epistemological arguments have been formulated in the *Prolegomena*. The geometry has been interpreted in two different ways, geometry as a branch of physics. It is an empirical science. He in this *geometrical axioms* are inferred from observations which are analogous to Euclidian geometry. This geometry as a branch of physics has been the basis of Einstein's general theory of relativity.

According to Kant geometry is mathematics of space and arithmetic the mathematics of time. 'Kant maintains the parallel as far as possible, and he devotes one paragraph to geometry in the "Metaphysical Exposition" of space (A_{24}), and one to "axioms of time in general" or arithmetic in the "Metaphysical Exposition" of time (A_{31}/B_{47}). Thus in showing to his own satisfaction that experience must also conform to the mathematics of space and time, to geometry and arithmetic."[40]

Another important contribution of Kant is his concept of "*antinomies*". According to Kant there are four kinds of antinomies consisting of thesis and antithesis.

Kant says, "The world has a beginning in time, and is also limited as regards space" this constitutes thesis, the antithesis of which is "the world has no beginning in time, and limits in space: it is infinite as regards both time and space". This is the first antinomy of Kant. Kant's concept of antinomy has made great impact on Hegel. The important argument that constitutes the *Critique of Pure Reason* is the refutation of all kinds of rational proofs of the existence of God. This is a very important from the philosophical point of view. Kant's contention is that God or the absolute is beyond the reach of reason. There is a great similarity between the teachings of *Upaniṣad*[41] and that of Kant. He has demolished ontological, cosmological and theological proofs of the existence of God. The concept of God, Freedom and immortality which are *ideas of reason* cannot prove their existence and reality. Hence, Kant takes shelter in *The Critique of Practical Reason* for formulating the concept of God. This is based on Kant's concept of categorical imperatives. According to categorical imperatives the immortality of soul and the existence of God is an ethical necessity for the realization of highest good in life. There has been great controversy regarding Kant's doctrine of "things in themselves". Bertrand Russell says, "The thing-in-itself" was an awkward element in Kant's philosophy, and as abandoned by his immediate successors, who accordingly fell into something very like solipsism. Kant's inconsistencies were such as to make it inevitable that philosophers who were influenced by him should develop rapidly either in the empirical or in the absolutist direction; it was, in fact, in the latter direction that German philosophy moved until after death of Hegel."[42]

I do not agree with Russell's criticism that the doctrine of *thing in itself* of Kant is an awkward element in Kant's philosophy. I think Kant was aware like Wittgenstein that the thought and language have limitation, there are certain truth like "things in themselves", which are beyond the reach of mind and senses. I find Kant's doctrine of things in themselves as the kernel of Kant's metaphysics. If we remove the Kant's doctrine of things in themselves then his whole metaphysical system would become irrelevant and irrational. I find great similarity between the Kant's doctrines of *thing in itself* with Buddhist concept of *suchness (tathatā).*

Hegel is one of the most original and difficult philosopher and he is the last who is considered as philosophical system builder. According to him the reality is the Absolute. The Absolute is spiritual. He doesn't agree with Spinoza's doctrine that substance has attribute of extension and thought. Apart from this distinction the metaphysical system of Hegel has great similarity with Spinoza. Hegel draws the doctrine of absolute from the concept of reality which does not admit any self-contradictions. He doesn't accept anything real except the whole. The whole is the absolute of Hegel, but he doesn't accept the views of Parmenides and Spinoza who believed in simple substance. Hegel's whole is like an organism. It is a complex system.

The different aspects of the world are not an illusion, but do possess greater or lesser degree of reality. Different parts and dimensions of the world are an aspect of the whole. This follows logically from the doctrine of Hegelian absolute that time and space does not have complete reality.

Hegel is famous for postulating and using a triadic method which is known as dialectic which has been enumerated in his *logics*. His concept of logic is synonym of metaphysics. He refuted the Parmenides doctrine of one being on the basis of his logic. According to him no predicate can qualify the whole of reality. He refuted the Parmenides view on this argument. Hegel's dialectical methods consisting of thesis, antithesis and synthesis would be demonstrated as follows. Let us assume that "The absolute is Pure Being". From the thesis of pure being it emerges that the concept of pure being without any qualities is nothing. This leads to the antithesis that "the absolute is nothing". From the harmonious blending of thesis and antithesis we come to the synthesis that "the absolute is becoming". Again this synthesis that the absolute is becomes the thesis for the second phase of dialectical movement.

According to Hegel we cannot comprehend the truth without going through the rigorous of the triadic movement of dialectics.

Knowledge is a dialectical process. The starting point of our knowledge is sense perception and through the sceptical criticism of senses, the knowledge acquired from sense perception we lend ourselves in pure subjective. "*The Absolute Idea.* The idea, as unity of the Subjective and Objective Idea, is the notion of the idea—a notion whose object (*Gegenstand*) is the Idea as such, and for which the objective (*Objekt*) is Idea—an Object which embraces all characteristics in its unity." According to Hegel the absolute is timeless and time is an illusion. The illusion of time is created due to our limitation and inability to comprehend the absolute. The absolute of Hegel is pure subject thinking about pure thought. In Hegel's own world "This unity is consequently the absolute and all truth, the Idea which thinks itself". The Hegelian concept of God is different from the Plato and Spinoza. Bertrand Russell writes about Hegel, "His life contained few events of importance. In youth he was much attracted to mysticism, and his later views may be regarded, to some extent, as an intellectualizing of what had first appeared to him as mystic insight."[43]

I am in agreement with Russell's view that Hegel retained a belief in the unreality of separateness and his whole philosophy is based on mysticism.

In the contemporary Western philosophy F.H. Bradley occupies a very important position. He is called a new Hegelian. His book *Principles of Logic* contained metaphysical thought which created stir in philosophical world. However, his other important book is *Appearance and Reality*. Bradley belongs to the Idealistic tradition established by Hegel and his successors Lotze and Sigwarts. Surprisingly Bradley doesn't belong to the English empiricist tradition established by Locke, Berkeley and Hume. Bradley's philosophy could be termed as Monism. As he believed that thought and reality are one. There is diversity, but there is no division. Divisions come only when we employ concepts and words to experience. Concepts and words are not real. They are artificial implements.

"Bradley was surely right in emphasizing, as opposed to the empiricist, the artificial character of language, the way it acts as a grid that we place over Reality. For they in their naiveté had believed that once we analyse our ideas into their constituent elements, the simple ideas into which the others can be resolved correspond directly to the simple elements of which the world is composed."[44]

In 1921, a new movement known as Logical Positivism was started by scientist to prove the meaninglessness of metaphysics. This movement is known as Vienna Circle. According to traditional concept, philosophy is a quest for truth. But according to positivist philosophy is not a quest for truth, but it is quest for meaning and sense. Positivist through the method of theory of verifiability tried to demolish the whole of metaphysical system. A.J. Ayer is one of the torch bearers of this movement. His book *Language, Truth and Logic* became very famous.

He postulates that only through experience the validity of the synthetic proposition can be determined. The propositions which cannot be denied without self-contradiction are analytical. He tried to expose the concept of monism by maintaining that it is a mistake to conceive of the various special sciences as expressing different aspects of reality. His whole postulation is based on empirical hypothesis. It speaks of the scientism and not science as such. He writes, "For our part we are concerned to emphasize not so much the unity of science as the unity of philosophy with science. With regard to the relationship of philosophy and the empirical sciences, we have remarked that philosophy does not in any way compete with the sciences. It does not make any speculative assertions which could conflict with the speculative assertions of science, nor does it profess to venture into fields which lie beyond the scope of scientific investigation. Only the metaphysician does that, and produces nonsense a result."[45]

He says that "science is blind without philosophy and philosophy empty without science. His contention that philosophers must become a scientist if he has to make any contribution towards the growth of human knowledge."[46]

Logical positivism's rejection and hostility to metaphysics is based on the employment of a criterion of meaning which is known as the verification principle, but the verification principle is itself not verifiable. There are other important areas of knowledge such as *a priori* statements of logic and pure mathematics and statements of value which cannot be defined by logical positivist. It would be wrong to accept philosophy as logic of science. Philosophy cannot be merged with science. The philosophy and science have distinct area of operation and within that area of knowledge both philosophy and science attain their importance and usefulness as source of our knowledge and understanding of the reality of the phenomena and noumena. However, the positivism played an important role in questioning some of the basic assumptions of metaphysics. In summarizing the outcome of the movement initiated by the Vienna Circle A.J. Ayer states, "It will be seen that the Vienna Circle did not accomplish all that they once hoped. Many of the philosophical problems which they tried to settle still remain unsolved. Perhaps their greatest achievement was to help to introduce a new spirit into philosophy, to set a standard of logical rigour and intellectual responsibility. The producers of what Professor Broad has called "that grateful and comforting mixture of idealistic metaphysics with edifying social and ethical theory" are not extinct."[47]

The whole assumptions of A.J. Ayer's is not based on science, but based on scientism. The recent development in science especially Quantum Mechanics and Relativity have proved that science cannot explain reality in its original form and truth. I shall discuss this in subsequent chapters.

Ludwig Wittgenstein is considered as most original and one of the greatest thinkers that Europe has produced. He has made a great impact on contemporary of Western philosophical movements. His two books *Tractatus Logico-Philosophicus* and *Philosophical Investigations* exercise great influence on the recent philosophical movements especially of Europe and America. I shall confine myself to the impact of mysticism on Wittgenstein's earlier philosophy as formulated in Tractatus. Wittgenstein by making a difference between sayable and unsayable created a theory of Solipsism. His theory of meaning which is the fundamental of the Tractatus is known as the picture theory. He says that "*A proposition is a picture of reality for if I understand a proposition I know the situation that it represents. And I represent the proposition without having had its sense explained to me.*"[48]

Language is a picture of reality. Reality stands here as a fact. Fact means state of affairs. There is a structural similarity between the world of language and the world of facts. The ultimate unit of language is elementary proposition and the ultimate unit of world is atomic facts. This is known as isomorphic relations. However, Wittgenstein's rejected this whole doctrine advocated in Tractatus and he came out with a new thought and idea in *Philosophical Investigation*.

He considers that limit of thought is the limit of language.

"5.61 ... We cannot think what we cannot think; so, what we cannot think, we cannot say either.

"5.62 This remark provides the key to the problem, how much truth there is in Solipsism. For what the solipsist means is quite correct, only it cannot be said but makes itself manifest. The world is my world: this is manifest in the fact that the limits of language (of that language which alone I understand) mean the limits of my world."[49]

According to Wittgenstein proposition does not actually contain its sense but does contain the possibility of expressing it. Proposition contains its form but not the content of its sense. Wittgenstein accepts like *Upaniṣadic* seer that truth and reality cannot be expressed in words because it is indescribable. In place of *Upaniṣadic* dictum '*indescribable*' and Buddhist'*unspeakable*' (*abāchya*) Wittgenstein uses *unsayable*. He accepts that, "6.522 There are indeed, things that cannot be put into words. They make themselves manifest. They are what is mystical. 6.44 It is not how things are in the world that is mystical, but that it exists."[50]

It is very evident from Tractatus that it does not deny the existence of the mystical reality and accept that it is beyond the reach of our thought and language. Wittgenstein's concludes in formulating the seventh and the last proposition in Tractatus "whereof we cannot sayeth thereof we must consign to silence". In Philosophical Investigation Wittgenstein's says that language depicts the cultural form of life. Meaning of word is determined in a cultural context. This is why it becomes difficult to express Oriental ethos in Western language because Oriental tradition is mystical and spiritual whereas Western tradition is dominated by Ontological materialism and rationalism.

Oriental language faces the same problem in describing the Western scientific and technological terminology. However, with the fusion of two tradition and globalization in recent years easing out this problem to great extent. Moreover, language as a means of communication has its own limitations. This is why Wittgenstein's makes a bold declaration that concept of language cannot be defined. After analysis and close examination of the structure of thought and language both Kant and Wittgenstein's draw a line between sayable and not sayable. Kant talked about two realities—phenomena and noumena, whereas Wittgenstein's made a distinction between the worlds of sayable and mystical. Thus, I come to this conclusion that whole Western philosophy is essentially and basically based on Ontological mysticism.

References

1. *Indian Thought and Its Development*, Albert Schweitzer, pp. 10-11, Hodder & Stronghton Limited, 1936, London.
2. D.F. Pears, *Logical Atomism : Russell and Wittgenstein*. The Revolution in Philosophy: London, MacMillan & Co. Limited, 1960, p. 47.
3. *Confessions*, Chapter XX.
4. *The History of Western Philosophy*, Bertrand Russell, A Touch Stone Book, London, 1972, p. 354.
5. Cornford, *From Religion to Philosophy*, p. 201.
6. *A Critical History of Greek Philosophy*, W.T. Stace, Khosla Publishing House, Daryaganj, New Delhi, 2012, p. 33.
7. *The History of Western Philosophy*, Bertrand Russell. p. 37.
8. *Ibid.*, p. 37.
9. *Ibid.*, p. 47.
10. *Ibid.*, p. 48.
11. *The History of Western Philosophy*, p. 47.
12. *A Philosophical Essay on Probabilities*, Marquis de Laplace. French Mathematician, Dover Publications, Inc., New York, 1951, pp. 1-2.
13. *The History of Western Philosophy*, pp. 70-71.
14. *Symposium*, 220.
15. Nietzsche—*Human, Are Too Human.*
16. *A Critical History of Greek Philosophy*, p. 170.
17. *The History of Western Philosophy*, p. 106.
18. William James, "What Psychological Research has Accomplished", In Gardner Murphy and Robert O. Ballon (edition). *William James on Psychological Research*, London, Chatto and Windus, 1961.
19. *A Critical History of Greek Philosophy*, pp. 190-191.
20. *The History of Western Philosophy*, pp. 142-143.
21. *Ibid.*, p. 126.
22. *A Critical History of Greek Philosophy*, p. 217.
23. *The History of Western Philosophy*, pp. 142-143.
24. *A Critical History of Greek Philosophy*, pp. 284-285.

25. *Aristotle*, Vol. 1, p. 204.
26. *Thus Spoke Zarathustra*, Friedrich Nietzsche, Translated by Walter Kaufmann, The Vikcing Press, New York, 1954, p. 12.
27. *Who Was Friedrich Nietzsche, Thoughts in a Centenary Year,* Joachim Kohler, 2000 Inter Nationes. Bonn, pp. 34-35.
28. *Ibid.*, p. 11.
29. *Thus Spoke Zarathustra, Friedrich Nietzsche.* A Book for Everyone and Nobody, Translated by Graham Parkes, Oxford University Press, 2005, pp. xix-xxx.
30. See the Essay, "Nature and the Human "Redivinized": Mahāyāna Buddhist Themes in, Thus Spoke Zarathustra", in John Lippitt and James Urpeth (eds.), *Nietzsche and the Divine* (Manchester: Clinamen Press, 2000).
31. See Thomas H. Brobjer, *Nietzsche's Knowledge of Philosophy* (Urban, III: University of Illinois Press, 2005), cha. 6. For Nietzsche's Japanophile friend, see my 'Nietzsche and East-Asian Thought'. W II: 26[317]; B3 Jan. 1888; BGE 56.
32. Replies to the penultimate counter-objections. *Meditations and Other Metaphysical Writings* by Rene Descartes, Penguin Books, London, 1998, p. 177.
33. *Meditation and Other Metaphysical Writings*, Rene Descartes, The Complete Essays, Penguin Books, London, 1998, p. 669.
34. *Ibid.*, p. 674.
35. *The History of Western Philosophy*, pp. 571-572.
36. *Ethics by Spinoza*, J.M. Dent & Sons, London, 1989. *Every man's Library*, p. xx.
37. *The History of Western Philosophy*, p. 590.
38. *Ibid.*, p. 663.
39. *Kant's Critique of Pure Reason*, T.E. Wilkerson, Oxford University Press, 1976, London, p. 37.
40. Kant's *Critique of Pure Reason*, p. 35.
41. *Taittirīya Upaniṣad*, Verse II. 4. 1.
42. *The History of Western Philosophy*, p. 718.
43. *Ibid.*, p. 730.
44. *The Revolution in Philosophy*, MacMillan & Co. Ltd., 1960, London, p. 19.
45. *Language, Truth and Logic*, A.J. Ayer, Dover Publications. Inc., New York, 1952, pp. 151-152.
46. *Ibid.*, p. 153.
47. *The Revolution in Philosophy*, pp. 86-87.
48. *Tractatus* 4.021.
49. *Ibid.,* 5.61, 5.62.
50. *Ibid.*, 6.44, 6.552.

3

The Oriental Philosophical Background of Science, Spirituality and Ontological Mysticism

TAOISM

Sixth Century B.C. is known in world history as an era of Renaissance. History has never before and after witnessed the presence of galaxy of Great Thinkers who have changed the course of history by regenerating mankind spiritually, morally and intellectually. The Wheel of Change was set in motion in history by The Buddha, Lord Mahāvīra of India, The Lao Tzu and Confucius of China and Parmenides, Heraclitus and Zeno of Greece. Before the advent of these greatest thinkers and philosophers, India was basking in the glory of Ontological mysticism and Advaitism introduced and formulated by Lord Śiva in the form of *Śiva Sūtra* and Vedic verses of Hindu seers. The whole philosophy of the world is elaboration, evaluation, and examination of the issues and the principles that have been formulated by these thinkers. Ascetism is considered as *sine qua non* for mystical experience and spiritual enlightenment. This has been the hallmark of Indian sages and Yogīs, Greek Pythagoreans and Taoist of China. They all considered continuity of life, immortality of self, cycle of birth and death and Transmigration of soul as the kernel of philosophy of life. I would now start with the philosophical thoughts advocated by these thinkers.

Lao Tzu and Confucius are two greatest personage in Chinese history. Confucius is an ethical teacher. Lao Tzu is a philosopher. There is a great controversy regarding the life and the teachings of Lao Tzu. There are some historians who believe that Lao Tzu was not a historical personage. However, after the examination of different views on the historicity of Lao Tzu, I have come to conclusion that he was a historical figure who was a curator during the Chou dynasty. After witnessing the decadence of Chou dynasty he left for some unknown place towards west. On the way he met the keeper of Han-ku Pass named Yin Hsi (Kuanyin), who requested Lao Tzu to write about his philosophical thoughts and leave it for the benefit of the people. The philosophical thoughts that have been handed over by Lao Tzu is known as Tao Te Ching. This is the canonical literature of Taoism. This work has been interpreted by different thinkers and historians in a different way. This book has been written in twilight language, like the canonical literatures of Hindu and Buddhist *Tantra* and works of Zen Buddhism. This probably was the practice to communicate the incommunicable ideas and thoughts through parables, myths and allegories. This is why Tao Te Ching has been explained in various recensions.

Another great work of Taoism is known as Chuang Tzu written or compiled by Chuang Chou. With the passage of time the Taoism has undergone great change. Taoism is spirituality and not a religion. The whole philosophy of Taoism is based on mysticism. There is another important event in the life of Lao Tzu. His meeting with Confucius to me is an historical event which speaks of the Lao Tzu's sublimity and profundity of his mystical thoughts. This meeting has been recorded by the first historian named Ssu-ma Ch'ien of China round about 100 B.C. The work of Ssu-ma Ch'ien is called *The Shih Chi* (Historical Memoirs). In this memoir the meeting of Lao Tzu and Confucius has been recorded in following words: "When Confucius went to Chou, he asked Lao Tzu to instruct him in the rites." Lao Tzu replied, "Even the bones of those you mention have fallen into dust; their only remains are their words. Furthermore, when a gentleman lives in favourable times, he hastens to court in a carriage; but when he lives in unfavourable times, he drifts with the wind. I have heard it said that a good merchant hides his wealth and gives the appearance of want; if endowed with a rich supply of inward virtue, the superior man has the outward appearance of a fool. Get rid of that arrogance of yours, all those desires, that self-sufficient air, that overweening zeal; all that is of no use to your true person. That is all I can say to you."

Confucius withdrew and told his disciplines, "I know a bird can fly; I know a fish can swim; I know animals can run, Creatures that run can be caught in nets; those that swim can be caught in wicker traps; those that can fly can be hit by arrows. But the dragon is beyond my knowledge; it ascends into heaven on the clouds and the wind. Today I have seen Lao Tzu, and he is like the dragon!"

Lao Tzu has been declared as a mystic saint.

The term Tao has been interpreted by different thinkers at different period of history in a different way. Tao is sometimes translated *as path* or *way*. It is sometimes translated as absolute reality. It is considered as totality of all things and beings. Tao is sometimes equated with Order or the Principle of Order and Harmony and Unity. In the Tao Te Ching this word Tao has been used seventy six times with different meanings and connotations. Sometimes it is used as a doctrine as the natural law. However, Tao is not used in the sense of name. Name is the personal and it connotes individual. Tao has been used in the sense of mother also without any kind of Anthromorphic relations. In Tao Te Ching Tao has been used as a mysterious female or mother.[1]

6. The Valley Spirit

The valley spirit not dying
Is called the mysterious female.
The opening of the mysterious female
Is called the root of heaven and earth.
Continuous, on the brink of existence,
To put into practice, don't try to force it.

Tao doesn't undergo any change and metamorphosis. The Tao has no progenitor. It has no life which has been created as the created beings are subject to change and decay.

Lao Tzu's concept of mother and mystical womb is expressed in sense of emptiness. This emptiness is the quintessential principle of Taoism. In verse five and elven of the Tao Te Ching has been expressed in the following words:

5. Heaven and Earth

Heaven and Earth are not humane;
They regard all beings as straw dogs.
Sages are not humane;
They see all people as straw dogs.
The space between heaven and earth
is like bellows and pipes,
empty yet inexhaustible,
producing more with movement.
The talkative reach their wits end
Again and again;
that is not as good as keeping centred.[2]

11. Thirty Spokes

Thirty spokes join at the hub:
their use for the cart
is where they are not.
When the potter's wheel makes a pot,
the use of the pot
is precisely where there is nothing.
When you open doors and windows for a room,
it is where there is nothing
that they are useful to the room.
Therefore being is for benefit,
Nonbeing is for usefulness.[3]

All things and beings have come from Tao and they must return to its source. In Hindu *Tantra* also *Śakti* (mother) is called the womb and seed. In *Yoginī Hṛdya Tantra* mother (*Śakti*) is described as *Yoginī* because she is a relational principle between cause and effect. She is causal matrixes. I find there exists a great similarity between the concepts of mother as enumerated in Taoism with *Śakti* of Hindu and Buddhist *Tantra*. Sometimes in Hindu *Tantra Śakti* has been termed as primordial force which is the progenitor of the universe. In Vedic teachings also we find similar doctrines of evolution of the universe. It has been stated in Vedic verse that everything has come out of the *Brahman* and it is sustained in it and returned back to *Brahman*. "*Guhyasamāja Tantra*, which is considered as the Bible of the Buddhist *Tantra* introduced the concept of the *Śakti* for the attainment of the *Nirvāṇa*. *Guhyasamāja* is considered as the proper and the correct path for obtaining liberation through the esoteric process, while formulating the principles and the philosophy for the attainment of liberation, it has also dealt with the concepts of the *Siddhis*, by virtue of which one can attain lot of occult powers. In the eighteenth chapter *Guhyasamāja Tantra* tries to elucidate and analyse the concepts of the *Siddhis*." Same principle has been enumerated in Tao Te Ching in the following verse (verse 16):

16. Attain the Climax of Emptiness

Attain the climax of emptiness,
preserve the utmost quiet:
as myriad things act in concert,
I thereby observe the return.
Things flourish,
then each returns to its root.
Returning to the root is called stillness:
stillness is called return to Life,
return to Life is called constant;
knowing the constant is called enlightenment.
Acts at random, in ignorance of the constant, bode ill.
Knowing the constant gives perspective;
this perspective is impartial.
Impartiality is the highest nobility;
the highest nobility is divine,
and the Divine is the way.
This Way is everlasting,
not endangered by physical death.[4]

The emptiness is sometimes expressed as the *wu*. Sometimes *wu* is explained as nothingness and non-activity. It would be wrong to identify the *wu* with the Void. In Taoism the Void is pregnant with all potentialities. There are some thinkers who are of the opinions like Han Fei who identify the *wu* with Permanent Tao. But in chapter one of Tao Te Ching the clear distinction has been made between the two.

1. A Way Can Be a Guide

A Way can be a guide, but not a fixed path;
names can be given , but not permanent labels.
Nonbeing is called the beginning of the heaven and the earth;
being is called the mother of all things.

Always passionless, thereby observe the subtle.
ever intent, thereby observe the apparent.
These two come from the same source but differ in name;
both are considered mysteries.
The mystery of mysteries
is the gateway of marvels.[5]

In an inscription of 165 A.D. Lao Tzu has been described as a mystic who had thorough knowledge of meditation. In the hagiographical anthology coming from the same period also confirms that Lao Tzu and the Keeper of the Pass, Yin Si were adept in meditation and other esoteric practices. This is evident from the life and teachings of Lao Tzu. In Indian tradition the holy man is called seers and saints and it is stated that in the state of oneness with *Brahman* seers experience the light which is thousand times brilliant than the sun, but it has a very soothing experience. According to Taoism also life is an inner journey. By identifying oneself with Tao with the practice of meditation and through the self-realization, the man experiences the same light (Ming). This state of spiritual sublimity is unity, transcendentality and emptiness. This is by returning to the Tao and becoming one with the absolute. The word *Te* has also been interpreted in a different way. Sometimes *Te* is used in sense of Virtue, sometimes in the sense of Order. In the Taoist context virtue has no ethical relation; it has been in sense of attainment of perfect harmony and uprightness. We don't find the concept of sin and profane in oriental culture. Taoism also doesn't believe in the doctrine of sin. Ignorance is the root cause of moral degeneration. It is a result of the lack of proper understanding and knowledge of one's own true nature. Man is essentially the Tao like Vedāntic teachings of *I am Brahman* or *I am Ātman*. The kernel of Taoism is to attain and know one's own self. Ascetism is precondition for mysticism. The Tao cannot be explained or communicated in any language, verbal or silence. Tao is beyond the reach of the mind and senses. Here we find a verse in which it has been explained that neither speech nor silence can express the inexplicable Tao. I find there is some great similarity between the teachings of Taoism and Ludwig Wittgenstein. Wittgenstein has concluded in *Tractatus* that there is something which is unsayable and we must maintain silence. Taoism is not content with silence also. It explains that the absolute is beyond the reach of speech and silence.

Chuang Chou has dealt with this problem in the book which is called *The Historical Memoirs*. It has been stated in the book that we cannot enter into the world of mystery of universe with the help of reason. Reason cannot enter into the transcendental world of mysticism. The concept of God is absent in whole Taoism. We can enter into the world of esotericism only with the help of meditation and emptying our mind from all sorts of relativistic knowledge and ethical norms. The phenomenal world is made of *Yin* and *Yang* and it is governed by the relativistic law, but the Tao is beyond the realm of the relativism. It says, "The Tao cannot be affirmed to exist or not to exist. The name Tao is merely an artifice for practical purposes. Hence, whether there is or not a Prime Mover, the question can have a meaning for the detail of things, but whatever could this mean for the Great whole? If speech were really adequate, it would exhaust the problem of the Tao in a single day; but since, it is not so, it can just about exhaust in a day whatever concerns a creature or a thing. The Tao is something beyond seen creatures; neither speech nor silence can convey it. Let us banish both speech and silence: we have reached the farthest limit of thought." [Chapter 25]

As Taoism does not believe in theistic God as creator and hence the problem of origin of universe and existence of God becomes non-sensical proposition. In the context of Tao as absolute and transcendental reality such problems of origin of Tao becomes irrelevant. Chuang Tzu says in chapter six that the Tao is ultimate reality, but it has neither form nor it acts. It is both a trunk and root. It is eternal and totality of all things and being. It is the giver and progenitor of life. But the man who harbours passion and desire cannot have the oneness with the Tao. The realization comes only with purification and emptying our mind and soul by the ascetic discipline. It is a process of emptying himself of one's bondaged self. The enlightenment and illumination comes only after mendicant succeeds in emptying the minds from the cluster of relativistic knowledge and moral virtues.

Like a Yogī the holy man of Taoism establishes complete symbiosis with universe. He establishes himself a complete harmony and rhythm of nature. The search for immortality and enlightenment is the fundamental with all mystic tradition. According to Taoism also the life of immortality and transcendentality resides in the inner most being and existence.

"The Perfect Man is pure spirit. He feels neither the heat of the blazing brush lands nor the cold of the flooding waters; the lightning that splits the mountains and the tempest that stirs up the ocean cannot frighten him. A man like this rides the clouds as his carriages and the sun and the moon as his steeds. He wanders beyond the Four Seas; the alternations of life and death do not concern him, much less the notions of good and evil." [Chuang Tzu, Chapter 2]

According to Buddhist *Tantra* when a man realizes emptiness by emptying his minds and soul from all cravings the world appears as illusion. Such man goes beyond the dualism of subject and object, sin or virtue. He becomes one with *Parāśakti* which creates, maintains and destroys the world. *Parāśakti* is to whom no part of universe remains unseen, there is no kind who doesn't obey her, there is no scripture made by other which is not known to her. Emptiness both in Buddhism and Taoism is transcendental reality. In Taoism it is called the Tao, in Buddhism it is termed as *Śūnyatā*, but both the Tao and *Śūnyatā* have same metaphysical import and signification. The *summum bonum* of Taoism is self-realization which is called enlightenment. It comes only by self-realization. Tao Te Ching explains it in verse thirty three as follows:

33. Those Who Know Others

Those who know others are wise;
those who know themselves are enlightened.
Those who overcome others are powerful;

those who overcome themselves are strong.
Those who are contented are rich;
those who act strongly have will.
Those who do not lose their place endure;
those who die without perishing live long.[6]

The person who lives in the world of dualism of subject and object, sin and virtue, sacred and profane is beyond the reach of self-realization. One will have to rid oneself from snares of cravings. The domain of cravings creates the world of categories. But in the realm of the Tao there is no desire left. Man becomes free from all sorts of cravings and wanderings by emptying his mind and soul from all kinds of defilements. The Tao is ineffable. Lao Tzu through the Tao Te Ching is trying to communicate which is incommunicable. The language of Tao Te Ching is full of symbolism. It is like giving a dumb some sweets and asking him how it tastes. The dumb man will only try to express it through the postures and gestures. The Tao Te Ching speaks of through the same language of postures and gestures. The language cannot express the nature and the reality of the Tao. It can only express the relative truth. No names, no form could be given to the absolute. The Tao is sometimes mysterious being which is beyond the reach of language and thought.

25. Something Undifferentiated

Something undifferentiated was born before heaven and earth;
still and silent, standing alone and unchanging,
going through cycles unending,
able to be mother to the world.
I do not know its name;
I label it the Way.
Imposing on it a name,
I call it Great.
Greatness means it goes;
going means reaching afar;
reaching afar means return.
Therefore the Way is great,

heaven is great,
earth is great,
and kingship is also great.
Among domains are four greats,
of which kingship is one.
Humanity emulates earth,
earth emulates heaven,
heaven emulates the way,
the Way emulates Nature.[7]

Some of the teaching of Taoism is contrary to Confucianism. According to Confucianism knowledge is the basis of the ethical systems. Lao Tzu considers all learning especially the learning of values as impediment in the path of self-realization. All social values are wrong and injurious to the spiritual health of the person because it is rooted in contradictions which cloud the transcendental and divine nature of the ultimate reality. It is only through transcending and going beyond the world of relativistic thoughts and ideas one can enter into the kingdom of the Tao. Tao Te Ching says:

38. Higher Virtue is Not Ingratiating

Higher Virtue is not ingratiating;
that is why it has virtue.
Lower virtue does not forget about reward,
that is why it is virtueless.
Higher virtue is uncontrived,
and there is no way to contrive it.
Lower virtue is created,
and there is a way to do it.
Higher humanity is created,
but there is no way to contrive it.
Higher duty is done,
and there is way to do it.
Higher courtesy is done,
but no one responds to it;
so there is forceful repetition.
Therefore virtue comes after loss of the Way;
humanity comes after the loss of virtue,

duty comes after loss of humanity,
courtesy comes after loss of duty.
Manners mean loyalty and trust are thin,
and disarray's beginning.
Foresight is a flower of the Way,
and the beginning of ignorance too.
Therefore great people dwell in the thick,
not the thin.
They abide in the substance,
not the flower.
So, they leave the latter and leave the former.[8]

Taoism put emphasis for the practice of ascetism. Life of indulgence leads to degeneration of our life. Passions and the cravings bring degeneration of our vitality and loss of soul. The man who lives a life of indulgence cannot experience spirituality and mystical union with the Tao. Such man loses the faculty of listening to the inner sounds of silence and inner light of spirituality. He no longer enjoys the divine bliss of "savour of the Tao".

Wu-wei is one of the root concepts of Taoism. *Wu-wei* is translated into *'No Activity'*. The doctrine of *No Activity* has again been used in many senses. No activity stands for living a natural life. Living a natural life means living a life according to the *Te*. The *Te* distinguishes between natural and unnatural actions.

To live a natural life is the goal of the Indian Yogīs also. Normally, people do not live according to the law of nature and this creates the ripples in the mind in the form of cravings and desires. The whole purpose of Yoga is to rid one-self from the cravings and mundane desires. This is known in *Patañjala Yoga* as *Citta* (tendency). To overcome and root out all the cravings is the purpose and the goal of *Yoga Sādhanā*. And when a practicener through the practice of Yoga root out all the tendencies and cravings he attains mystic Trans (*Samādhi*). It is called *Sahaja Samādhi* (natural state of mysticism). Tao is considered as maternal principle. The concept of mother, female, mystical womb is equated with the Tao and emptiness. This emptiness is equated with the concept of *wu*. Max Kaltenmark writes, "We have several times already come across the expression *wu-wei*: 'without doing', 'absence of action', Wu is not the same as nothingness, and *wu-wei* is not an ideal of absolute inaction; on the contrary, it is particularly efficacious attitude since it makes all doing possible."[9] Inactivity does not mean laziness. In Taoism, this concept has been used in the context of the mysticism. In the state of enlightenment there is no activity. The state of the Tao or the *Brahman* of Hinduism is a state of spiritual sublimity and in that state of enlightenment and *Nirvāṇa,* there is a complete absence of any activity because individuality is merged in the Tao. When there is no individuality there can be no activity. When a man enters into the mystic union with reality he loses his individuality. Action is related to individuality and in the state of *Nirvāṇa* and enlightenment the world becomes unreal and illusion from the transcendental perspective. So, the Taoism here speaks about the inactivity or no action from the perspective of Ontological mysticism. In the Western culture there is complete absence of the concept of enlightenment and *Nirvāṇa*. This is why the Western mind has difficulty in understanding the mystical and the metaphysical import of the concept of the *wu-wei.*

Wu-wei figures three times in the first seven chapters of the Chuang Chou. *Wu-wei* means "by its side you wander in non-action: under it you may sleep in happiness", "Tao has reality and evidence, but no action and form"; "They stroll beyond the dirty world and wander in the realm of inaction". This speaks of the Taoist non-partition in the mundane activities. It means only by inner renunciation and withdrawal from the worldly activities one can enter into the world of the Tao. Both the Lao Tzu and the Chuang Chou adherence to *wu-wei* means no activity springing from the worldly cravings and desires. This is kernel of both Hinduism and Buddhism. One cannot attain *Nirvāṇa* and enlightenment unless one roots out all his cravings and mundane desires. One cannot attain mystic union with cosmic consciousness which is called the mother in all the oriental canonical literatures. The concept of mother has figuratively used as a progenitor and womb of cosmos.

The holy man of China who have played significant role in creating a vibrant cultural milieu lived a life of wandering mendicants and mystics. They have conquered their worldly desires and they used to live in perfect harmony with nature and the Tao. Their mind has never been captivated by worldly desires and attractions because they have attained the heights of incantatory spirituality grandeur. The holy man or the enlightened one lives within one-self with natural simplicity and transcendentality of the Tao. The holy man through the mystic experiences had the realization that they had become the Tao. The Tao is sometimes equated with *Yang* and *Yin* (male and female). This concept of unity of male and female principle is very much prevalent both in Hindu and Buddhist mystical traditions. In the Hindu *Tantra* Śiva and Śakti, male and female are considered as two aspects of the same ultimate reality.[10] The ultimate reality is unchanging, eternal, infinite, one and uncaused. It is supreme reality. It is beyond the categories of existence and non-existence, being and non-being. It is known as *ardhanārīśvara.* In Buddhist *Tantra* also we find the similar concept of *Prajñā* and *Upāya* as the two eternal co-existence, but they are not two entities. They constitute absolute unity. Lalan Prasad Singh writes, "According to *Vajrayāna Prajñā* and *Upāya* reside within the body of sentient being. *Upāya* resides in the high plexus (*Uṣṇīṣa Kamala*) and the *Prajñā* dwells in the lower plexus (*Mūlādhāra*), the sacrococcygeal plexuses. The central objective of the *Tantra Sādhanā* is to awaken the *Prajñā* (*Herukā*), from the lowest plexuses and making her proceed in the upward movement till she becomes united with *Upāya* in *Uṣṇīṣa Kamala*. In *Vajrayāna* man represents *Upāya* and woman represents *Prajñā*. The esoteric commingling of the two is the giver of supreme bliss (*Mahāsukha*), it leads from spiritual discipline and yogic control, and one lives to the spiritual oneness, which is the state of the *Boddhicitta*. *Vajrayāna* accepts and leads to the equipollence of *Prajñā* and *Upāya*."[11]

Feminine concept has been the inevitable principle of practice for attaining *Nirvāṇa* and enlightenment since the origin of mysticism. The kernel of Hinduism, Buddhism and Taoism is a philosophy of non-duality. The concept of feminine principle or mother doesn't speak of dualism of the male and female principles. The reality is not constituted of two principles. *Yang* and *Yin* or the male and the female principles are constituted of undivided ultimate reality. The relation of *Yang* and *Yin* is that of two faces of the same coin. One cannot be separated from the other. However, the feminine principles have been given importance only because of its creativity and as a concept of compassion. Feminine principles have metaphorical use as emptiness and passivity and non-resistance. The concept of *wu-wei* is merely an application to understand the metaphysical and spiritual importance and significance of feminine principles and non-activity. Lao Tze says,

28. Know the Male

> Know the male, keep the female;
> be humble towards the world.
> Be humble to the world,
> and eternal power never leaves,
> returning again to innocence.
> Knowing the white, keep the black;
> be an exemplar for the world.
> Be an exemplar for the world,
> and eternal power never goes awry,
> returning again to infinity.
> Knowing the glorious, keeping the ignominious;
> reopen to the world.
> Be open to the world,
> and eternal power suffices,
> returning again to simplicity.
> Simplicity is lost to make instruments,
> which sages employ as functionaries.
> Therefore the great fashioner does no splitting.[12]

The *Yin* and *Yang* does not confirm with anthromorphism or their Orphism. *Yin* and *Yang* is a metaphysical concept. This is essentially the creative functions which are symbolized by the feminine and the masculine principles like Hindu *Tantra*. In Hindu *Tantra*, Śiva is symbolized as cosmic consciousness devoid of any activity. It is a corpse and Śakti a creative matrix or cosmic principles. Śiva and Śakti form the reality which is absolute and indivisible. Chuang Chou says, "The perfect negative principle is majestically passive. The perfect positive is powerfully active… the interaction of the two results in that harmony by which all things are produced." These two principles are working in complete harmony and unity which is responsible for the very existence of all being. J.C. Cooper writes, "This dual role is also found in the Nature herself, who can be ruthlessly destructive or benevolent in giving unstintingly of life, like the Great Mother, of whom Kwanyin is the

Chinese manifestation in her two aspects of creator and destroyer, life and death, holding within herself the tension of opposites which is the process of transformation through Wisdom (*yin*) and Method (*yang*) into the ultimate unity, the Tao. She is both the Queen of Heaven and the Great Earth Mother, Tellus Mater, from whom all things are born and to whom all return. If she can be cruel and ruthless and fearful she is yet "kind and gentle and indulgent, ever a handmaid in the service of mortals, producing under our compulsion, or lavishing of her own accord. What scents and savours, what surfaces for touch, what colours!... What produce she fosters for our benefit!"[13]

In the second chapter of the Chuang Chou all things and creators are basically identical from the transcendental perspective. The Tao is considered as the basic doctrine of life and unity which is superior to all mundane existence and being. We do not have the experience of the transcendental nature of reality because our mind is clouded by passion, prejudices and cravings. In Taoist tradition heaven has been used in the sense of the supreme principles which guides, controls and illuminates the whole cosmos. To experience the transcendental nature of the Tao one will have to become aware of the relativity of the mundane existence. The notion of good and bad, true and false, sacred and profane are rooted in the very structure of relativistic world. Tao has been compared as "the axis of the cosmos and the hub of the wheel of creation. The mystic who realizes the transcendental nature of the Tao enters into the realm of infinity and eternity. The sages, the holy man and the mystic do not harbour any distinction. They only see and experience unity in multiplicity, spirituality in the mundane world of relativity. In the state of mystic experience the distinction between the subjective and the objective self disappears."

Life and death are not two separate entities. Life and death are the two facets of the same coin. This has been the quint essential teachings of Lao Tzu. Chuang Chou also agrees with the basic and the fundamental principle of unity of life and death. Max Kaltenmark writes, "Life and death are nothing more than natural metamorphoses, mere transmutations of forms, such as the transformation of silkworms into bombyx moths but ancient peasant's beliefs lingering on in the world of learning, held the phenomenon to be much more general. The earliest almanacs taught that sparrows changed into oysters in the fall and oysters into sparrows in the spring. The assumption underlying the *I Ching* is that all phenomena and events interchange premutationally, and can be foretold from the symbolic mutations which are a specialist in the diagrams can decipher."[14]

In the world of the mundane existence there is a perpetual process of change and movement. In the midst of this change and eternal flux there is the absolute Tao which does not undergo change, transformation and metamorphosis. The Tao is supreme unity and oneness in the midst of the world of relativity. The thesis and antithesis, positive and the negative, affirmation and negation are contingent. To experience the underlying unity and the wholeness is the goal and the supreme end of life. Chuang Tzu says, "It is glory of man to know that all things are One and the life and death are the phases of the same existence. Life follows death; death is the beginning of life". Only the enlightened one, know and understand the unity and the wholeness of all things and, therefore, the enlightened one, the dualism of the subjective self and the objective selves is mingled and transformed into the wholeness and unity of the existence and being. The poet Po Chu-I writes:

"Those who speak know nothing,
Those who know keep silence."
These words, as I am told,
Were spoken by Lao Tzu.
But if we are to believe that Lao Tzu,
Was himself one knew,
How come it that he wrote a book
Of five thousand words?

This has been the problem before all the mystics who have expressed their experiences which are inexpressible. Even a modern philosopher like Ludwig Wittgenstein had to make distinction between 'sayable' and 'unsayable'. There is a reality which cannot be expressed in any language and this is why all the mystics have taken help of expressing those mystic experiences through myths, parables and allegories and Lao Tzu is not an exception to this rule. Taoism is a purely metaphysical and ontological mysticism. It is rooted in mysticism. J. Krishna Murthy says, "Truth is pathless".

This pathless path is mysticism. Okakuro-Kakuzo writes, "The Tao is the passage rather than the path. It is the spirit of cosmic change—the eternal growth which returns upon itself to produce new forms. It recoils upon itself like the dragon, the beloved symbol of the Taoists. It folds and unfolds as to the clouds. The Tao may be spoken as the Great Transition. Subjectively is the Mood of the Universe. It is the principle of all energy, yet energy it is not, but merely one of its manifestations. It is the eternal principle of all life, but no life can express it, and all bodies, all material forms, are, but its changing and momentary raiment. Sometimes it called 'The Mother of all Things' the primordial creative cause, the self-existent source, the unconditioned by which all things are conditioned, for although it does not create, it is the source of all creation. The animating principle of the universe; it is 'the unchanging principle which supports the shifting multiplicity'."[15]

There is a great controversy regarding the difference of view on the Confucian moral code and the rejection of Confucius teachings of morality by Lao Tzu as a non-sensical proposition. In philosophy the term non-sensical proposition has been used in a special technical sense. The proposition which does not convey any meaning and sense, it is called non-sensical. However, there is a general agreement between Taoism and Confucianism on the concept of evil or sin. Both according to Confucius and Lao Tzu, sin or evil do not inherently exist in the nature of man. Throughout the teachings of Lao Tzu the concept of God is totally absent. Taoism is not a theology, it is spirituality and in the context of spirituality the God becomes irrelevant. There has been great misunderstanding about Lao Tzu's repudiation of Confucian doctrine of moral code. Lao Tzu's whole teachings are based on Ontological mysticism and hence, from the ontological mystical perspective the sin and virtue, good and bad are irrelevant. The repudiation of the Confucian moral code could be judged from the mystical standpoint, not from socio-cultural, ethical point of view. The state of Tao is pure consciousness, and in that state of pure consciousness any principles of dualism whether it is a concept of sacred and profane, sin and virtue, good and bad do not have any place. If we accept the sin and virtue then the Tao would lose its transcendentality, unity and absoluteness. This is why Taoism does not propagate any doctrine of moral code. But he is not against the

Confucian doctrine of moral code. As such Confucian moral is relevant in the world of relativity and mundane existence. But it is irrelevant in the context of spirituality and Ontological mysticism.

Ethical life is relevant for the normal social being whose very existence is dependent on of social reality. But the Tao which is the origin progenitor and the controller of the whole cosmos is above ethical norms and values. The root cause of our suffering both according to Taoism, Buddhism and Hinduism is erroneous identification of self with non-self. The bondage and the malaise are due to our ignorance of our own real nature of being and existence. This wrong identification of our self and ignorance is the root cause of all kinds of cravings, desires, sense impressions and the wrong ethical values and norms. Life of spirituality is natural and spontaneous. So, any rigorous and moral values would cloud the very transcendental nature of our own being. And in this context the doctrine of morality becomes irrelevant.

For the sages and the enlightened one moral virtue emanates from his thinking and behaviour. *Mahābhārata* says, "The man who has wisdom does not sin, he ceases to do evil and through his wisdom annuls the evil of his former life".[16] There is no element of anthromorphism and theism in Taoism and Confucianism. The anthromorphism is the integral part of the sematic religion—Judaism, Christianity and Islam. However, some element of Pantheons has crept in Mahāyāna Buddhism. But these Mahāyāna Pantheon's in my view is aberration of Buddhism. It is no way related with the basic teachings and concepts of Buddhism. Religion has two parts, i.e., spirituality and the theology. Taoism and Buddhism do not have any theological system. Both Buddhism and Taoism are spirituality and mysticism. To my mind the Tao is pure and transcendental cosmic consciousness. It is eternal and unchanging. It is the cosmic womb out of which like Vedāntic *Brahman* everything has emerged. Hence, according to Confucianism, Taoism, Buddhism and Hinduism there is no creator.

According to Arnold Toynbee society is not constituted of individuals, but their relationship. If the relationship is not based on political social and ethical principles, no society would be able to face the chiasm and disintegration. Hence, the foundation of all socio-economic and political system must have spiritual basis. Man is essentially a spiritual being. All the chiasm, disintegration, conflict and the violence are the result of lack of knowledge and understanding of the true nature of human being. The refutation of moral doctrine of Confucianism should be judged and analysed from the perspective of Taoist concept of spirituality. Lao Tzu does not condemn the Confucian doctrine of moral code and principles. But he shows the lack of spiritual and, mystical content in Confucianism. Without spiritual content and mysticism no social order can exist. To my mind Lao Tzu is right in his rejection of Confucian doctrine of morality because it lacks the basic and the sound philosophical foundation. Without a sound metaphysical foundation no social order could survive the pillage and the plunder of history. Taoism has provided the Chinese culture and civilization the sound philosophical and spiritual foundation and because of this China has survived the viccitude of history.

Taoism is a pathless path. It has to be lived and experienced. It is not to be simply read and sing the glory of the Tao. Tao is a path and the supreme goal. In the light of Tao one can see the reflection of all beings and the existence. It is like a mirror in which nothing is hidden and clouded. It is only through the sensuous indulgence and cravings that man forgets his own true nature and being and he lives a life of inauthentic existence. In Tao Te Ching says,

42. The Way Produces One

The Way produces one;
one produces two,
two produces three,
three produces all beings:
all beings bear yin and embrace yang,
with a mellowing energy for harmony.
The things people dislike
are only to be alone, lacking, and unworthy;
yet these are what monarchs call themselves
Therefore people may gain from loss,
and may lose from gain.
What others teach,
I also teach.
The stronger cannot master their death:
I take this to be the father of teachings.[17]

Here the Lao Tzu has taken the help of parables, myths and allegories to explain the cosmological order. It would be wrong to understand from this verse that the Tao is a creator. To give birth to one, two, three or ten thousand creatures, speaks of the transcendental and primordial nature of Tao. The numbers does not refer to any serial number of creatures. Rather it speaks of the ineffable and undifferentiated beginning of the universe. It should not be compared with Hawkins cosmology.

Chuang Tzu in chapter 12: "At the beginning of all there was a unity, but it had no form." Chuang Tzu and Lao Tzu are thus imagining something anterior to Chaos (the one): a kind of absolute void that Chuang Tzu calls the *wu* and Lao Tzu the *Tao*. This Tao is thus the *Chang Tao* of chapter 1, and the One is the equivalent of the "*Tao* that can be named". It simply speaks of Tao as the primordial source of all existence and being. The cosmological order is the manifestation of this primordial principle of Tao. Tao from one perspective is cosmos. From another perspective it is absolute.

Some of the esoteric and mystical element has been wrongly used as religious doctrines. Taoism is not religion. Tao like the Hindu *Tantra* has been symbolized as the mother. But neither in Hindu *Tantra* nor in Taoism the concept of mother has got any anthromorphic implications and significations. Tao Te Ching says,

6. The Valley Spirit

The valley spirit not dying
is called the mysterious female.
The opening of the mysterious female
is called the root of heaven and earth.
Continuous, on the brink of existence,
to put it into practice, don't try to force it.[18]

The valley spirit has been used in a mythical sense not in a literal connotation. Sometimes some writers derive the esoteric and mystical use of Taoism as a part of religious system. All the symbolism and the myths that has been used in Tao Te Ching have a deeper spiritual and mystical signification. In all the mystical literatures of the world the apparent meaning of different words symbols and myths are quite different from their real meanings. Only those who dive deep into the mysticism could understand the spiritual signification of the different symbols which are used in mystical literatures. The cosmic womb of the mother symbolizes the emptiness and not anthromorphical implications. There is a great similarity between the Buddhist concept of suchness and Taoist doctrine of emptiness. Max Kaltenmark observes "The Void is thus none other than *wu*, the absence of perceptible qualities that characterizes the Tao. This Void is efficacious because, like the bellows, it is capable of producing breath at will: the idea expressed is like the one associated with the symbol of the valley. The Void is efficacious for another reason also: like a wheel hub, a vessel, or a house, it is receptacle. The image of the thirty spokes converging toward the empty space of the hub is often used to symbolize the virtue of the ruler who attracts all creatures inhabited by Tao or, as Ho Shang Kung puts it, by the vital spirits that animate the body. Ho Shang Kung says, 'In the void between Heaven and Earth, the Harmonious Breath [an equal mixture of *Yin* and *Yang*] circulates freely, and the Ten Thousand Creatures are born of themselves. Thus, when man is able to rid himself of his passions, to give up pleasure, and to purify his viscera, then the *shen ming* [spirits and souls from the Heaven and Earth] can dwell peacefully within him' ".[19]

The Western thinkers have used Void in place of emptiness. I think it is due to the lack of proper understanding of the metaphysical signification of emptiness. Emptiness is not void. Both Buddhism and Taoism are of the same opinion that a man when he gets liberated from the sneers of false subjectivity. The sense of pleasure and passions, he realizes the transcendental nature of his own being and existence. Ho Shang Kung rightly made the observation in his commentary, that when man rids himself from passions and pleasures he dwells in the true self. It has been stated in *Mahābhārata* also that *dharma* resides in the innermost recess of human being.[20]

According to Taoism all the creatures in this world are born from *yu* (known) and the ye born from *wu* (unknown). According to the law of nature everything must return back to the point of its origin. The leaves get separated from the tree and it becomes humus and again it returns to the living creatures and in this way the cycle of birth and death continues.

Taoism got recognition and became the leading religious and mystical doctrine during Tang dynasty. Taoism was recognised as great philosophical and mystical doctrine even the family name of the emperors of Tang dynasty were made as Li. The emperor of the Tang dynasty in 1737 was addressed as Nobel celestial. It is stated that about 200 monasteries propagating the doctrine of Taoism were in existence during this period. It is stated that during this period even the royal princesses have embraced Taoism and some of them even enunciated and dedicated their lives for the propagation of Taoism.

The teaching of Buddhism and Taoism are based on ontological mysticism. Having the same root and foundation of their philosophical speculations and reflections Lao Tzu and Buddha were identified as one person. However, after some time the Taoist criticized and considered the famous apocryphal work; the Lao Tzu Hua-hu Ching entitled book – *The Book of Lao Tzu's Conversions of the Barbarians* as false and fabricated. There has been a great conflict for centuries between the Taoist and Buddhist for their dominance in philosophical thinking. Max Kaltenmark writes, "One of these versions deal with 81 *avatāras* of Lao Tzu's conversions. In one he is the Buddha Śākyamuni; in the last, he is Mani, the founder of the Manichaeanism. The inscriptions of A.D. 165 also allude, rather critically, to meditational and long life practices supposed to have been known and, presumably, taught by Lao Tzu. In a hagiographical anthology dating from virtually the same period, it is again said that Lao Tzu and his discipline, the Master of the Pass, were proficient in this kind of exercise. There are also references to the journey to the West and the conversion of the barbarians."[21]

It is evident from the different sources that Lao Tzu was and enlightened person. It seems that like the Buddha Lao Tzu also attained enlightenment through the practice of meditation. When a man attains salvation and becomes one with the reality (cosmic consciousness). He becomes omniscient. It is stated that Lao Tzu was adept in nourishing his vital energy and almost he was having the secret of long life. According to some biographers of Lao Tzu he lived for more than 80 years. According to others he lived more than 200 years. Whatever the length of his life it is apparently evident; Lao Tzu was accepted and revered as sage like the Buddha. "The keeper of the Pass, *Yin* Hsi... was versed in the esoteric sciences and always fed on the purest essences. He kept his virtue secret and went prudently about his business so that no one in his day ever noticed him. When Lao Tzu departed towards the West, *Yin* Hsi, who had already perceived his emanation, knew that a sage was going to pass through. He observed the colours of the signs that preceded him and waited for him on the way; he actually found Lao Tzu. Lao Tzu knew for his part that *Yin* Hsi was an extraordinary person; he wrote a book for him and gave it to him. Then they departed together beyond the Moving Sands and converted the barbarians. They fed on the sesame seeds. No one knows what finally became of them." [Lieh-hsien Chuan, X]

There is a great similarity between the teachings of Taoism, Buddhism and Hinduism. Taoism, Buddhism and Hinduism are based on scientific principles. The search for the secrets of immortality has kept the mind of the Indian Yogīs and Taoists and Buddhist monks engaged in finding the scientific principles behind long life. The practice of meditation and *Prāṇāyāma* (breathing exercise) has been common in all these three schools of thought. Lao Tzu was considered as adept in the practice of meditation and breathing exercise. It has been proved by scientific investigation that the practice of meditation and breathing exercise provides long life and serenity. Disciplining the sexual life and living a life of moderation has been the corner stone of Taoism, Buddhism and Hinduism. Taoism became very popular because of scientific principles based on mysticism and nurture of the life principles. The search for immortality led to alchemy. There has been a belief that the gross substances like mercury, cinnabar can be transformed into immortality. The immortality doesn't mean in spiritual parlance, the immortality of the physical body, but it means the realization of the ultimate reality which is one, infinite and eternal. Thus, the enlightenment attained through the practice of meditation, breathing exercise and observation of sexual discipline leads to life eternal. Meditation was called "connecting on the One" or "keeping the One". In the days of Emperor Wu of the Han, the magicians instituted a cult of the supreme One (T'ai I), then the three Ones (the One of Heaven, the One of Earth, and the T'ai I). In later

Taoism, each of these divinities was imagined to dwell in one of the three Fields of Cinnabar. In points of fact, this unity reimagined a single whole, although it was mentally "visualized" in three dwelling places. This spirituality is gaining ground, but it doesn't mean that science does not replace spirituality. The role of both science and spirituality is important. The most pragmatic approach would be to study science and spirituality and consider the value which each of them have given for the upliftment of mankind. The belief in God or the cosmic religious feeling have been accepted and practised by scientific community from Newton to Einstein. The recent scientific development instead of rejecting the religious and the spiritual contents of Taoism, Buddhism and Hinduism have become integrated into Western world view. In spite of Nobel Laureate, physicist Steven Weinstein and Geneticists Richard Dockings, science could not replace spirituality. Geoffrey Red Mound writes, "One reason to study the relation of spirituality and science in the traditional cultures of China and India is as a prerequisite to understanding their appeal for own culture. However, we must not imagine that current New Age conceptions of Asian Spirituality are identical to those in Asia, either now or in the past. Hence, another reason to study these phenomena is to be able to appreciate them in their own context."[22]

Tao is the most fundamental concept. It is metaphysical, mystical, spiritual and scientific concept in Chinese tradition. It is the fundamental principle through which the origin and the development of the universe is explained. The knowledge of Tao means understanding the nature and the function of ultimate principle that governs the world. In Taoism the understanding and the knowledge of the sage was attained by an implicit process of self-cultivation. Here self-cultivation means self-realization. There is a concept of QI which is related to vital energy of the breath. It is similar to the Indian concepts of *Prāṇa* and the Greek principle of *pneuma*. QI has occupied a central place in Chinese medicine. During the Hang period, QI was considered as a life principle. Zhang Zai considered QI as the life giving energy which gets manifested in different forms of our organism. Li is another fundamental metaphysical concept in Chinese tradition. Li has been used in sense of reason, method and the principle of maintaining natural order. Geoffrey Red Mound writes, "There is never a conception of matter being acted upon by force, in the sense of modern physics. While it has been argued that Chinese nonseparation of matter and energy are related by Einstein's equation, $E = mc^2$, this is anachronistic and scientifically incorrect. The world's most famous equation does not state that matter and energy are the same, rather that they are interconvertible. Nor does there seems to have been any investigation of what *qi* might be in physical terms, beyond purely mental analysis. With *li* as the principle determining coalescence of *qi* into specific things *qi* takes on a meaning much closer to what we think of as matter, but without losing its energetic aspect. The concepts become murky as Zhuxi tries to explain them."[23]

The philosophical explanation of Taoism gives a better understanding of the nature of energy, matter and consciousness. According to Taoism Tao is both the transcendental and immanent reality. It is both separate from the multiple worlds of things and as it is the ultimate reality which gets expressed in myriad things and beings. Taoism like Buddhism and Hinduism believes that ultimate reality can be discovered and experienced by developing intuition through the practice of meditation. The quint essential teachings of Taoism are explained in the famous line of Tao Te Ching, that "a person could know the entire world without looking out of the window". The highest knowledge is intuitive rather than empirical. There is ultimate reality which gets manifested in multiplicity of things and beings. Our life is limited, but knowledge is unlimited. Thus, we cannot know the eternal and the transcendental reality with our limited understanding. There is enough evidence of Taoism believing in previous birth like Buddhism and Hinduism. Tao Te Ching observes:

16. Attain the Climax of Emptiness

Attain the climax of emptiness,
preserve the utmost quiet:
as myriad things act in concert,
I thereby observe the return.
Things flourish,
then each returns to its root.
Returning to the root is called stillness:
stillness is called return to Life,

return to Life is called the constant;
knowing the constant is called enlightenment.
Acts at random, in ignorance of the constant, bode ill.
Knowing the constant gives perspective;
this perspective is impartial.
Impartiality is the higher nobility;
the highest nobility is divine,
and the divine is the Way.
This Way is everlasting,
not endangered by physical death.[24]

The perfect equipoise and tranquillity comes with the experience of the ultimate reality in its totality. One cannot know the reality with the help of the senses and the minds. The minds and the senses give only the relativistic aspects of reality. Max Kaltenmark writes, "The sense yield only points of view, mere aspects of reality, and what is worse, they give rise to desire and passion. Perfect knowledge is of mystical nature; it affects even the distinction between the subjective self and the objective self."[25] He further says that, "The only valid knowledge is all-embracing and intuitive. "Men who cultivated the Tao in former times fostered their learning with quietude. When knowledge made its appearance, they did not use it in order to act; it can be said that they used it solely in order to foster their quietude." "[26]

Taoism outrightly dismiss the concept of creator like God. The concept of Tao cannot be affirmed or denied. It is just an artifice for practical purpose. Taoism imparts its teachings in silence. It believes that only through intuition one can have the experience of reality. The teacher's role is to rid the mind of disciples from the false subjectivity. It is a spiritual practice to get the mind emptied. Once a man attains *satori,* the mind becomes free from all kinds of cluster of opinions views and false subjectivity and defilements. Huai-nam Tzu, Chapter 1 observes, "Man is naturally quiet; this is the nature he receives from Heaven. Under the influence of things, movement occurs in him; this is a deterioration of his nature. His soul responds to the things that present themselves, and his knowledge is thus set in motion. His knowledge puts him in touch with things, and love and hate are thus born in him—love and hate that give body to things—and this knowledge drawn outward can no longer come back to itself. This is how the Heavenly Order is destroyed in man. Those who are initiated into the Tao do not exchange the Heavenly for the Human". Man is the absolute reality, but when man comes in contact with the nature he becomes bondaged self. In Taoism this is why man has been compared with a naturally quiet. In its original form man is a transcendental being. Lao Tzu has used *Heaven* in sense of divinity and there is a great similarity between the Taoism, Buddhism and Hinduism because all these three philosophical systems are based on ontological mysticism. They are the only philosophical systems who propagate the philosophy of oneness and transcendentality. When man attains enlightenment he lives in perfect harmony and symbiosis with the cosmos. He lives in the harmony with nature. This is the life of immortality, infinity and eternity which is different from the normal biological life of a man with its punctuated existence of birth and death. According to Chuang Tzu "enlightened one doesn't believe in good and bad, vice and virtue from the transcendental point of view. The concept of good and bad, vice and virtue are irrelevant. According to Śaṅkrāchārya the propounder of *Advaita Vedānta* says, "I have neither virtue nor vice nor pleasure nor pain, nor the sacred chants nor the pilgrimage, nor the scriptures nor the sacrificial rituals. I am neither the act of enjoying, nor the enjoyable object nor the enjoyer. I am pure knowledge and Bliss, I am Śiva, the cosmic consciousness itself."[27] In Chapter 2 (Ch'i-wu-lun), ends as follows: "Beyond the limits of the world the Holy Man exists, yet does not theorize; within the limits of the world, the Holy Man theorizes yet does not criticize. In the *Spring and Autumn Annals*, a book intended to school the age and to set forth the ideas of the ancient rulers, the Holy Man criticizes, but does not argue. You want to discriminate? Some things cannot be discriminated among. You want to argue? Some things cannot be argued about. So, what is to be done? The Holy Man embraces everything. People who argue do so for show. That is why I say: When you argue, there are some things you are failing to see. In the greatest Tao, nothing is named in; in the greatest disputation, nothing is said; greatest benevolence is not benevolent; if the Tao turns to brilliance, it is no longer the Tao; the speech turns to disputation, it no longer achieves its aim; if benevolence becomes a habit, it is no longer perfect; if humility turns into affection, it is hypocrisy; if bravery turns to aggression, it ceases to prevail. These five qualities degenerate from universality into pettiness, therefore, the best thing is to stop within the scope of cognition. Who knows how to employ disputation without words, the Tao without name? He who could do so would possess a heavenly treasury. Pour into it and it is never full, dip from it and it never runs dry; yet no one would know where this wealth came from. This is what I call the Restrained Light."

Taoism is based on asceticism and mysticism. All life is illuminated by the light (Ming). The enlightened one is not satisfied with the knowledge that governs all life by intellect only. He believes in the realization of Tao in totality and wholeness. It is like Hinduism and Buddhism identifying with the Tao through the attainment of oneness and realization of eternity, emptiness and transcendentality. The knowledge of Tao is what is known in Hinduism as *Parā Jñāna*. Taoism is aware of the futility of discursive knowledge and understanding of the relativistic knowledge. It is not scepticism. This kind of knowledge and understanding leads to contradictions and confusions. It rejects the pseudo-science which is based on incomplete understanding of truth and reality. Taoism believes in emptying the minds from all kinds of defilements and opinions. There is great similarity between Taoism and Hindu *Tantra*. Taoism says that you are both male and female, *Yang* and *Yin*. In Hindu *Tantra* it is called *Ardhanārīśvara*.

Max Kaltenmark writes, "Insofar as it discards discursive knowledge in favour of intuition, and asserts the possibility of reaching, through quietism, a supreme reality, the thought of the Tao Te Ching is indeed a form of mysticism."[28] Loa Tzu is a mystic and his mysticism is based on the realization of Tao which is the fundamental reality. This is why Lao Tzu never dealt in rational exposition of his philosophy. His teachings are obscure and abstract like all other mystics. His teachings are full of parables. As the ordinary language cannot convey or communicate the mystic experience of saints and seers. So, all the saints and seers have taken the help of parables and allegories and anecdotes to convey and communicate the thought which is indescribable in language. The Chuang Tzu has explained in some passages, aesthetics and folklores which were rare in every era of the history. However, he has given a graphic description of some sages who were found in a state of spiritual sublimation.

While describing Lao Tzu when he was in the state of spiritual sublimity and trance the Chuang Tzu writes, "One day, Confucius went to visit the Taoist Holy Man... He found him completely inert and looking like a lifeless body. Confucius had to wait for some time before he was able to address his host. "Did my eyes deceive me?", he said. "Or was it really so? Just now, Sir, my body was like a piece of dry wood. You seemed to have left the world and men, and to have settled into an inaccessible solitude." "Yes", replied Lao Tzu, "I had gone for a stroll at the origin of all things." " [Chuang Tzu, Chapter 21]

This is evident from this anecdote that Lao Tzu was a mystic and a realised soul. We find that the whole Tao Te Ching is a work of ontological mysticism. Lao Tzu's reply to Confucius that he had gone to the origin of "all things" is a spiritual evidence of his attainment of absolute knowledge and he had become enlightened. Only omniscience being can say that he has gone to the origin of all things. The origin of all things means that the knowledge of the principles that guides, controls the cosmos. It is like the Buddha after enlightenment. It is like Indian seers that have experienced the truth and expressed in the Vedic versus like *Upaniṣads*. The Tao Te Ching is like the *Upaniṣad* and *Śiva Sūtra* of Hinduism and *Dhammapada* of Buddhism. Like *Brahman* of Hinduism, emptiness of Buddhism, the Tao is indescribable and supreme reality. It is a cosmic consciousness. It is nameless and indescribable.

Chinese philosophers like Indians believed in transcendental reality which unifies the world of multiplicity. There has been from the very beginning the two complimentary schools of thought in Chinese philosophical traditions. Chinese being down to Earth and pragmatic they have developed two complimentary philosophical systems. The Confucianism provided a sound, moral and social philosophy whereas Taoism was concerned with the realization of ultimate truth and attainment of enlightenment. Chinese has always believed that the monk who will not work shall not eat. So, the Confucius has provided a sound moral social and Governmental structure whereas Lao Tzu has always repudiated the teachings of Confucius because it doesn't lead to the enlightenment. Taoism doesn't give much importance to rationalism as a part of social etiquette. The Taoist is not concerned with this world at all. They have always been concerned with a strong mystical wisdom.

According to Taoism all changes in nature are manifestation of the ultimate reality. The change and transformation occurs in nature out of the innate force. Fritjof Capra writes, "Acknowledging the limitations and the relativity of the world of rational thinking, Taoism is, basically, a way of liberation from this world and is, in this respect, comparable to the ways of Yoga and Vedānta in Hinduism, or to the Eightfold path of Buddha."[29]

There is some misconception about the introduction of feminity in *Vajrayāna*. It is not the first time that feminity has been introduced in both Hindu and Buddhist *Tantra*. Feminity has been the inevitable principles of mystic practise for obtaining emancipation from the very origin of *Tantra*. The genetic idea of Taoism, Hindu *Tantra* and Buddhist *Tantra* is that the feminity is the cosmological order.

The masculine principle is eternal inconceivable, supreme-absolute, is a passive force whereas feminity, the immanent principle is all activity. Masculine and the feminity principle have been anthropomorphically described as husband and wife. The feminity principle is the creation and the recreation of the cosmos. She is the *magna*, *matter*. Feminity is more important than the masculine principles. This is why feminity has been conceived in Taoism as womb of all beings and existence. However, the existence of feminity cannot be thought of in the absence of masculine principles. There is no feminity without masculine principles and no masculine without feminity. Hinduism, Buddhism and Taoism are wedded to the philosophy of non-duality.

There has been great misunderstanding about the practice of mysticism in Taoism. It has been wrongly understood as a magical practice. Geoffrey Red Mound writes, "As Daoism developed, it spawned elaborate practices concerned with increasing longevity. Magic was a prominent part of religious Daoism, particularly the production of *Fu*, or talismans. *Fu* are modified Chinese characters with, magical potency when shown, or even when burned and eaten as ash. To those with knowledge of normal Chinese characters, *Fu* seem odd, even subtly ominous. The practice of *Fu* assumes that the written word has a mystical power to affect events, particularly in the spirit world."[30] In Chinese, Buddhist and Hindu philosophical system knowledge of ultimate reality and ethical understanding of right and wrong are inseparable part of philosophical traditions. The metaphysical dimension to existence does not conflict with scientific rationalism.

Language occupies unique position in Chinese culture and civilization. The Chinese language is logographic. The language represents words in a non-phonetic way. It means the Chinese language represents sounds and not words. There is a very close relation with ancient Sanskrit language. In Sanskrit language also connotes sounds. The whole grammar of Pāṇinī is based on the concept of sounds. Both the Sanskrit and the Chinese language are based on ontological mysticism.

During Tang dynasty Lao Tzu received great honour and recognition in Chinese history. There has been some degeneration also in Taoist movement. Some follower of Taoism were much interested in physical immortality and not the wholly spiritually mortality. This has been a human search from the very beginning of the civilization to find the secrets of immortality and long life. Geoffrey Red Mound writes, "His Wang Mu is an important figure in Taoist mythology and folklore. She seems to have started out in life as a mountain spirit whose appearance, if we are to believe the *Shan Hai Ching* (Book of Mountain and Seas), was none too prepossessing: she had human form, but the tail of the leopard and the teeth of the tiger. Later, however, she became a divinity with rather more charm, and the Taoist took her for the Fairy Queen of the Immortals. A Taoist romance tells His Wang Mu came to visit Emperor Wu of the Han; she offered him some marvellous peaches, and revealed certain things that he was never capable of turning his profit."[31] In search of the secrets of immortality China does discover some scientific principles which could cure the physical and the mental elements. Thus, it could be stated that along with the spiritual tradition initiated by Taoism it also paved the path for scientific discoveries. Taoist are said to be preoccupied with physicians and psychological healers. They considered that cinnabar resides the innermost part of human being.

Of course, some of them indulged in magical practice. According to the mythology there are three Worms or the three Cadaveric demons responsible for the loss of vitality in man. These demons attack different parts of body like eyes, head, belly and kidney and create loss of blood and vitality. To avoid the evil effects they encouraged practising some magical feats and thereby they started using herbs and mineral substances for getting cured from the evil effects of the demons.

All these methods were employed to prolong life and attaining physical immortality. There have been three kinds of drugs; one which were capable of providing immortality, second prolonging life and third curing sickness. The cinnabar, gold, silvers, and pearls and other herbs and minerals were used to prolong life and getting rid from sickness.

There has been an esoteric dance like the Tāntric dances in Indian culture associated with the Taoist practice for attaining supernatural powers. These dances were associated with esoteric practice like Tāntric practices in India. The alchemy was used for prolongation of life with the use of cinnabar and Gold powder. This has been a part of the Āyurveda indigenous Indian medical science. The first actual reference to the alchemy is found in second century B.C. in China.

Wei Poyang is considered the first medical doctor who had written a treatise on alchemy known as *Chou-I T'san T'ung Ch'I*. This work on alchemy deals with the use of cinnabar powder for prolongation of life.

In the beginning of every civilization science was considered as a magic and scientist as a magician. So in all civilization Chinese, Indian and others Europeans civilizations in the beginning, the medical doctors have been considered as magicians. As science has always been associated with mysticism hence in the preparation of drugs or the cinnabar or gold powder for curing of different physical elements and the prolongation of life have been associated with esoteric terminology which was difficult for the non-scientists and the layman to understand the real meaning and the formula of alchemy, that is the case of China also. There is another great scientist who has popularised alchemy and giving it a scientific foundation was Ko Hung. He is the writer of a new treatise on alchemy known as *Pao P'u Tzu*. It has been admitted by the Taoist in early China that apart from the alchemy the secrets of long life, good health and spiritual sublimation lies in the practice of *Prāṇāyāma* (breathing control) and meditation. This is the clear example that the Yoga as propounded by Patañjali was known to the Chinese Taoist. It seems that there has been some communication between the Indian Yogīs and Chinese Taoists. Ko Hung has given a detailed formula and method for the preparation of cinnabar and gold for the use of these precious substances for the prolongation of life and thereby it could be used by the sound body and mind for the spiritual sublimation and tranquillity. The use of *Heaven* in Chinese writings, I consider that this word or metaphor has been employed to express the inexpressible reality that is Tao or divinity.

The immortality does not mean in spiritual parlance the physical immortality. It stands for the ultimate reality which is eternal, immutable and transcendental. In all the earliest writings of every civilization, the saints, seers, sages and *yogīs* have used metaphor, allegories to explain the unexplainable ultimate reality which is mystical in nature. However, the use of the cinnabar, the gold powder and other precious substances has been in practice in China and India for maintaining good health, long life which are essential for practising intuitional science for the attainment of enlightenment and immortality.

A new concept *nei tan* (internal cinnabar), lays light on the secrets of elixir of immortality and enlightenment. The practice of *nei tan* is a pure meditation. Lalan Prasad Singh writes, "Mind cannot maintain its existence without objectivity. Mind is a state in the process of evolution. It is stage in the process of motion. Every motion is an alternated phase of pause and speed. Every movement is pulsative. In the stage of pause it gains momentum which it has to express. Mind resorts to certain inter- and intra-ectoplasmic occupations to express itself. These occupations and conations of mind are known as tendencies or *vṛttis*. These tendencies or *vṛttis* are the ways of expression of mind. In psychology, they are called *expressed sentiments* and *emotions*. Sentiments affecting the subsidiary glands are called instincts. Pineal and pituitary glands are the two important and most vital glands, the rest are called subsidiary glands. *Vṛttis* are the psychic objectivities of the mind. They are the colours and contours of the mental process."[32] Both according to Taoism and Hindu *Tantra* have ultimate reality is neutral by nature. It has two aspects, *Prakāśa* and *Vimarśa*, *Nivṛtti* and *Pravṛtti*, *Yin* and *Yang*. It is rendered as transcendental and immainent, static and dynamic, positive and negative, masculine and feminine principles. Śiva and Śakti, *Yin* and *Yang* are two aspects of absolute reality. Śiva or *Yang* is pure consciousness as such a static principle Śakti or *Yin* is cosmic energy, the world force. She is the dynamic aspects of reality. Neither Śiva nor Śakti, neither *Yin* nor *Yang* is the ultimate reality, they are inseparable.

The mystic unification of Śiva and Śakti or *Yang* and *Yin* under one condition produces the highest state of spiritual bliss and beatitude and under another the manifest world or the phenomenal process as a whole which is called in Hinduism as *Brahmāṇḍa* (cosmos) and in Taoism it is called Heaven and Earth. In both Taoism and Hinduism meditation is the only method to attain enlightenment. "Meditation was called 'concentrating on the one' or 'keeping the one.' In the days of the Emperor Wu of the Han, the magicians instituted a cult of the Supreme One (T'ai I), then the Three Ones (the One of Heaven, the One of Earth, and the T'ai I). In later Taoism, each of these divinities was imagined to dwell in one of the three Fields of Cinnabar. In point of fact, this unity remained a single whole, although it was mentally 'visualized' in three dwelling places."[33]

The mind is always in state of flux. This is the essential nature (*dharma*) of mind. Meditation is a process to concentrate the mind on one point so that mind becomes objectless. The moment the mind becomes objectless it seizes to be a mind and merges into primordial being that is cosmic consciousness (ultimate reality). With the practice of concentrating on the One or keeping the One, the mind is dissolves in pure consciousness. The individual I-ness, is transformed into cosmic being. This is a state of transcendental tranquillity, where life breath is arrested. The mind of the *Yogī* or the Taoist is absorbed in the supreme reality. After the attainment of deep meditation devoid of any form and content is called enlightenment, self-shines by its cosmic light and not by mental thinking and speculation. The man remains in the state of divine transcendence. He goes beyond the world of subject and object. It is eternal life of divinity which is known in Taoism as the Tao and Hinduism as *Brahman* and in Buddhism as *Śūnyatā*.

In Taoist tradition the concentration on One is found *T'ai P'ing Ching* under the title *Shou I Ming Fa*.

The mystic experience of light during the meditation and its resultant state of enlightenment is the quintessential teachings of both Taoism and Hinduism. It is stated that Lao Tzu has experienced such divine light in the state of oneness with the Tao. Chuang Tzu considers the heart of the sages as an empty which is full of light. Chuang Tzu considers it as the experience of Tao in form of light. The Tao which is the ultimate reality and absolute of the Taoism is conceived and experienced as divine effulgence and cosmic consciousness. One experiences this state of divine effulgence only when one becomes one with the Tao or the ultimate reality. In Vedānta also ultimate reality has been conceived as light which illuminates and shines through the different lights in the manifested universe. In the *Muṇḍaka Upaniṣad* it is stated that, "There the sun does not shine, nor the moon or the stars, nor do these flashes of lightening shine there. How can this fire do so? Everything shines as He does so; by His light all this shines diversely."[34]

According to Vedānta *Brahman* or the self is the ultimate source of all light and life in the universe. The whole universe is illuminated by the light and life of the *Brahman*, neither sun nor moon, nor any star or fire do have their own light. They are all illuminated because the *Brahman* is the source of the illumination and life. It has been demonstrated that the lights of life is alone true. Everything is the modification of that ultimate light which is a *Brahman*. According to Vedānta *Brahman* is alone possessed of natural and inherent luminous city and because of the ultimate substratum of all existence and being, the luminous things like the sun, moon, stars and others are illuminated.

There is another treatise which deals with the mystic practices of Taoism entitled as *San Huang Ching*. It is stated that this book was revealed to a Taoist who was meditating on the wall of a cave. It could be compared with *Bodhi Dharma* who visited China from India in 520 A.D. and he for nine years was just gazing towards the wall. This is a form of meditation and through this practice he attained *satori* and after the attainment of enlightenment he started preaching like the Buddha in China and he is now considered as the founder of *Chan Buddhism*. But some of the writers have wrongly considered that the contemplating the wall of the cave as series of talisman's (*Fu*) which is associated with the magical practices to fight the demons. As I have already stated that this is not a magical practice it is a pure intuitional science based on Ontological mysticism.

There have been different treatises associated with the teachings of Taoism. Because of the lack of understanding and the knowledge of the real signification of the different symbols, metaphors and the allegories used by the Taoist these works have been misunderstood as a treatise on black magic and talisman. In course of time there has been happy and harmonious blending of Taoism and Buddhism in China which has been responsible for creating a sound spiritual tradition. The Chinese civilization like Indian is based on sound philosophical and mystical foundation which kept them alive and vibrant till to this date. All the civilizations which didn't have the sound spiritual and Ontological mysticism as their foundations have disappeared from the map of the world and have become now the part of history.

Joseph Needham was a professor at Cambridge University. He spent a considerable time of his life in the study of the origin and the growth of science in China. Science and civilization in China in seven volumes written by Needham is the monumental work. According to Needham the philosophy of Taoism paved the path for the development of scientific realism in China. The philosophy of Taoism is based on ontological mysticism and intuitional science. Ontological mysticism or intuitional science is based on inner spiritual experiences. The spirituality and science are not hostile to each other rather they are complementary to each other and because of the scientific temper and rationalism which was provided by Taoism China and India became a fertile ground for the development of both science and spirituality. Geoffrey Re Mound says, "Chinese spirituality, however, tended to assume that the necessary truths had been determined and that study of authentic texts or with a truly enlightened teacher would reveal them. It was taken for granted that nature was adequately comprehended within Chinese cosmology; investigation of the external world had value, but was tended to be taken as a part of the traditional metaphysics rather than modifying it. Fundamental truths were to be discovered by looking inward, not by empirical observation. Thus, that famous line of the *Dao De Jing* that a person could know the entire world without looking out the window."[35]

It is evident that traditional Chinese medicine and Indian Āyurveda have been the source of great inspiration for the development of medical science in India and China. The discoveries of Chinese and the Indian medical doctors have been the source of inspiration for the development of the science especially in the field of medicine in the West. But the West confined their research and discovery only to the physical aspects of reality because the Western civilization and culture ignored the development of spirituality side by side with science. The West is becoming Faustian. There is no denying the facts that India and China have neglected the study and the development of science and because of this they have lagged behind in scientific development. For the healthy vibrant and the robust civilization development of both science and spirituality is *sine qua non*. China and India have made great discoveries in science in the beginning of civilization like gun powder, the compass, and in astronomy and medicine. But they couldn't keep pace with the scientific rationalism which created lots of problems.

Sometimes the metaphors and symbols used by Tao Te Ching looks like a paradox for the layman. As I have already stated that these metaphors and symbols are pregnant with profound philosophical import, but due to the lack of understanding of the inner and the real meaning of these metaphors and symbols people sometimes consider them as nonsensical propositions and paradoxes. The first chapter of the Tao Te Ching says:

1. A Way Can Be a Guide

> A Way can be a guide, but not a fixed path;
> names can be given, but not permanent labels.
> Nonbeing is called the beginning of heaven and earth;
> being is called the mother of all things.
> Always passionless, thereby observe the subtle;
> ever intent, thereby observe the apparent.
> These two come from the same source but differ in name;
> both are considered mysteries.
> The mystery of mysteries
> is the gateway of marvels.[36]

The real meaning of the teachings of Lao Tzu and Chuang Tzu has been debated for over 2,000 years. It would be preposterous to state that the teachings of Lao Tzu or Chuang Tzu are irrational. There is a limitation of language which has been stated by Ludwig Wittgenstein time without number. The objective aspects of reality are quite different from the subjective experience. As natural science cannot cross or transcends the limitations of the laws governed by time, space and causation it cannot experience the transcendental nature of reality. Geoffrey Red Mound rightly observes, "It has become a cliché that the West developed the objective aspects of thought while Asia developed subjectivity. This is a distortion since all the cultures must develop both the modes of thought. A more accurate to put this is that China saw the universe in human terms, indeed, this is embodied in the tripartite formulation of heaven and earth with mankind in the centre. Chinese philosophy always returns to the human meaning of the phenomena it treats. *Yin* and *Yang* are as much aspects of immediate experiences as they are abstract principles. In this sense, Chinese philosophy always stays close to what we could consider spiritual concerns. Indian philosophy also, despite its vast durations and nearly limitless space, also is ultimately concerned with the human enlightenments, because it always assumes that correct understanding has redemptive value."[37]

Taoism is a philosophical treatise based on Ontological mysticism. Lao Tzu and Chuang Tzu and their followers have taken metaphors and symbols to express the inexpressible. According to Taoism the Tao is unsubjectivated, transcendentality just as light and heat coexist in fire in the same way Tao and Te coexist in the absolute. The absolute of the Tao is beyond the limitation of time, space and causality. It is unchanging, eternal, infinite, one and uncaused. It is the supreme reality. It is beyond the categories of existence and non-existence. It is of the nature of light, bliss, beatitude and consciousness. For the layman who is not conversant with the inner meaning of the metaphors and the symbols used by Taoism for them they are non-sensical and full of contradictions.

Geoffrey Red Mound writes, "It must be said at once that these contradictions are often only apparent: Taoist minds and Western minds (perhaps we should say modern minds) categorize their thoughts quite differently. Yet synthetic, 'organicist' thinking of the ancient Chinese is providing worthier of interest as our knowledge of it increases. Thus, it is true for the history of science as for the history of ideas: the very mysticism of the fathers of Taoism contained some elements that could have favoured the rise of a scientific movement."[38]

Present civilization is foreboding waves of materialism and consumerism. The spirituality and Ontological mysticism of Taoism is hope and promise for better world. It could be the salvation of the crisis ridden present global society.

The crisis in the present world has become a cliché. T.S. Eliott has rightly summarized the crisis of the present civilization as how we have lost the path in the search of the truth and the meaning of existence.

The great civilization like Greek, Roman, Mesopotamia and Egyptians were destroyed due to inner contradictions and fissures created in the absence of proper spiritual anchorage and vision and lack of commitment to higher values whereas Chinese civilization and culture survived the pillage of times and the viscitude of history because of its sound spiritual and ethical foundation provided by Taoism and Confucianism.

Taoism and its teachings published in Tao Te Ching has been translated in almost all languages of the world because of its virtue of absolute tranquillity and sublimity; the most extraordinary appealing of the teachings of Taoism because of its spiritual and mystical content.

References

1. *The Essential Tao*, Translated and Presented by Thomas Cleary, Harpor San Francisco, 1993, Tao Te Ching, p. 11.
2. *Ibid.*, p. 11.
3. *Ibid.*, p.14.
4. *Ibid.*, p. 18.
5. *Ibid.*. p. 9.
6. *Ibid.*, p. 29.
7. *Ibid.*, p. 24.
8. *Ibid.*, p. 32.
9. *Lao Tzu and Taoism*, Max Kaltenmark. Translated by the French; by Roger Greaves. Stanford University Press, Stanford, California, 1969, p. 52.
10. *Yoginī Hṛdaya Tantra*, p. 105. Sarasvati Bhavan Granthamala, vol. 7, Varanasi, 1963.
11. *Buddhist Tantra*: A Philosophical Reflection and Religious Investigation. Lalan Prasad Singh. Concept Publishing Company Pvt. Ltd., 2010, p. 37.
12. *The Essential Tao*, Tao Te Ching, p. 26.

13. *Taoism: The Way of The Mystic*, J.C. Cooper, The Aquarian Press, Wellingborough, Northamptonshire, 1976, pp. 37-38.
14. *Lao Tzu and Taoism*, Max Kaltenmark, Translated from the French by Roger Greaves, Stanford University Press, Stanford, California, 1969, pp. 81-82.
15. Okakuro-Kakuzo, *The Book of Tea* (published by Fox Duffield, New York).
16. *Mahābhārata*, XII.
17. *The Tao Te Ching*, p. 35.
18. *Ibid.*, p. 11.
19. *Lao Tzu and Taoism*, Max Kaltenmark. Translated from the French by Roger Greaves, Stanford University Press, Stanford, California, 1969, pp. 40-41.
20. धर्मस्य तत्त्वं निहितं गुह्याम् ।
21. *Lao Tzu and Taoism*, Max Kaltenmark, Translated from the French by Roger Greaves, p. 110.
22. *Science and Spiritual Traditions*, by Geoffrey Red Mound, Green Wood Press, Westport Connecticut, London, 2008, p. 30.
23. *Ibid.*, p. 67.
24. *Tao Te Ching*, p. 18.
25. *Lao Tzu and Taoism*, Max Kaltenmark, Translated from the French by Roger Greaves, p. 79.
26. *Ibid.*, pp. 78-79.
27. *Nirvāṇa Śatakam*, Verse 4.
28. *Ibid.*, p. 64.
29. *The Tao of Physics*, Fritjof Capra, Bantam Books, New York, 1984, p. 101.
30. *Science and Spiritual Traditions*, by Geoffrey Red Mound, Green Wood Press, Westport Connecticut, London, 2008, p. 60.
31. *Ibid.*, p. 119.
32. *Tantra its Mystic and Scientific Basis*, p. 152.
33. *Lao Tzu and Taoism*, p. 137.
34. *Muṇḍaka Upaniṣad*, Verse Canto II.
35. *Science and Spiritual Traditions*, p. 75.
36. *Tao Te Ching*, p. 9.
37. *Science and Spiritual Traditions*, p. 78
38. *Ibid.*, p. 144.

4

Buddhism

Metaphysics

The Buddha is the greatest philosopher that the world has produced till this date. Historically speaking, he is the only person in the annals of human history, who has founded a school of philosophy and a world religious order. The Buddha after the attainment of enlightenment (*Nirvāṇa*) under *Bodhi* tree at Bodh Gayā reflected on the nature and significance of *Nirvāṇa* which resulted into the birth of new school of philosophy and a new religious order, known as Buddhism. Buddhism is a sublime and profound form of spirituality. It is monotheistic and it represents the highest form of monism. According to Buddhism *Advaya* represents the eternal co-existence of *Prajñā* and *Upāya* which constitute the infinite unity and transcendent reality (*Bodhi Citta*). The most profound ontological doctrine is considered to be the *Mādhyamikā* which claims *Śūnyatā* to be intrinsic in nature, to be the ultimate mode of existence. *Vijñānavāda* (*Yogācāra*) and *Śūnyavāda* (*Mādhyamikā*) deals with soteriological and speculative metaphysics. Buddhism believes in two truths or reality—a conventional or nominal and an ultimate truth. The *Mūlamādhyamākārikā* (literally Fundamental Verses on The Middle Way) of Nāgārjuna the founder of the *Mādhyamikā*—the middle path school of Mahāyāna Buddhism deals with the metaphysical and epistemological problems. This treatise is the foundation of *Mādhyamikā* School in which dialectical analytic arguments have been employed to establish the basic principles of metaphysical and epistemological issues; the central concept of this text is *Śūnyatā* (emptiness). The emptiness is the essence of all things and at the same time emptiness itself is empty. All other Buddhist soteriological concepts and the principles are based on this root concept of emptiness. Jay L. Garfield writes,

"Most bizarre of all, however, at first glance is the doctrine that all phenomena, including self and its objects, are empty. For indeed Nāgārjuna and his followers do argue that the entire everyday world is, from the ultimate standpoint, non-existent. And that does appear to stand just a bit deeper into philosophical left field than even Berkeley dares to play. But if the interpretation I will urge is adopted, the real central thrust of *Mādhyamikā* is the demystification of this apparently mystical conclusion."[1] Buddhism denies the permanent reality as advocated by other schools of Indian philosophical systems except Cārvāka. According to Vedānta self is identical with *Brahman*. Buddha refutes the very existence of permanent self on the argument that if we accept the permanent soul, the *karma* loses its signification and importance. Acceptance of permanent self would destroy the very spiritual life of a man because the belief in self is the source of our all desires. And these desires are the root cause of our sufferings.

> "If prior to desire
> And without desire there were a desirous one,
> Desire would depend upon him.
> Desire would exist when there is a desirous one."[2]

There is some controversy regarding Buddha's denial of self. There are even some believe that Buddhism being a profound philosophical system and world religion could not be dominated by the negative concepts of non-self, suffering and impermanence. Mrs. Rhys David's who has been a great exponent of Buddhism believes that these concepts of *Anitaya* (impermanence), *Anātma* (non-self), *Duḥkha* (suffering) have been interpolated by the latter *pseudo* Buddhist thinkers and followers. According to Mrs. Rhys David's Buddha didn't deny the soul. S. Radhakrishnan writes, "The fundamental difference between the Buddhism and *Upaniṣads* seems to be about the metaphysical reality of an immutable substance, which is the true self of a man as well. We have to decide whether it is the idea of the Buddha to look upon the universal order as coming out of nothing and going back to nothing. It is true that Buddha finds no centre of reality or principle of permanence in the flux of life and the whirl of the world, but it does not follow that there is nothing real in the world at all except the agitation of forces."[3]

The concept of non-self is the root concept of Buddhism. It is not "only restatement of the thought of *Upaniṣad* with a new emphasis, it is the very basis of Buddhist metaphysics." I do not agree with the observation of Prof. S. Radhakrishnan and Mrs. Rhys David's that Buddha believed in the permanent self. This would amount to the rejection of the soteriological and metaphysical foundation of Buddhism. There is another misunderstanding about the teachings of the Buddha. In the *Cūla Maluṅkya Sutta*, Buddha compared the metaphysician with a man wounded by an arrow, would discuss the metal and structure of the arrow instead of treating the wounded man with removal of the arrow. People have concluded from this philosophical enquiry that Buddha was not aware of the metaphysics or he considered philosophy as unnecessary pursuits of knowledge. Buddha was aware of the antinomical character of the reason and this is why he kept mum on some metaphysical enquiries and issues, but this doesn't mean that Buddha was not aware of profound philosophical truth and its knowledge. The fourteen *Avyākṛta* have been interpreted by different scholars differently. In fact Buddha was the discoverer of dialectic and he considered the criticism as a profound philosophy. This has been clear from the opening statement of the Buddha in the *Dīgha Nikāya* (*Brahma Jāla Sūtra*). Buddha didn't define the nature of the absolute. According to Nāgārjuna the absolute is beyond the four categories of *Bhāva* (existence), *Abhāva* (non-existence), *Ubhaya* (nor both existence and non-existence) neither *Bhāva* nor *Abhāva* (neither existence nor non-existence). All the views have been rejected because of the inherent defects. The Buddha's dialectics is used as *reduction ad absurdum*. Dialectic used by Buddha stands for the inability of reason to comprehend the absolute. The absolute is transcendent. It is *Śūnya*, free from any kind of differentiations, change and metamorphosis. There is a great similarity between the philosophy of *Mādhyamikā* and the Kant. Kant also considered criticism is itself a philosophy. *Mādhyamikā* is a profound philosophical system. The whole Buddhist philosophy is based on Ontological mysticism. *Prajñāpāramitā* (perfection) is mystic experience of the truth and reality. It is *Nirvāṇa*. T.R.V. Murti writes, "Metaphysics or true philosophy (*Prajñā*) is non-dual knowledge-Intuition of the real. The possibility of intellectual intuition is not only accepted but is taken to be the very heart of reality. It is the Truth. In intuition, Knowledge and the Real coincide; essence and existence are identical."[4]

Nāgārjuna exposition of emptiness is based on analysis of emptiness. The phenomenal world is empty it means that it is empty of the essence. All phenomena originate in dependence upon conditions. And they are independent. Nāgārjuna metaphysics is based on the concept of essence as eternal and independent. The origination of all other reality and entities are dependent only essence is independent. Nāgārjuna says:

"Essence arising from
Causes and conditions make no sense.
If essence came from causes and conditions,
Then it would be fabricated."[5]

There is some similarity between the Nāgārjuna's concept of emptiness and Spinoza's concept of Substance. Spinoza writes:

I. God is by cause of itself.
II. That thing is said to be Finite in its kind which can be limited by anything of the same kind.
III. By Substance—I understand that which is in self and conceived through itself.
IV. By God (Deus)—I understand a being absolutely infinite, that is, a substance consisting of infinite attributes, each of which expresses eternal and infinite essence.
V. By Attribute—I understand that which the intellect perceives of substance as constituting its essence.
VI. By Mode—I understand the modification of a substance; or that which is in something else through which it is also conceived.[6]

Spinoza's substance is a cause of itself, its existence is self-explanatory. He argues that such a cause must exist and it must be absolutely infinite being. Substance of Spinoza is the basis and explanation of all existence. The concept of substance or the God of Spinoza is esthetical to Christianity and Judaism. According to

Judaism or Christianity and all other theistic Semitic religions God is considered as a person to whom human beings can establish a work in relations. Spinoza's is pantheistic. "Whatever is; is in God. Nothing can exist or be conceived without God."[7]

Concept of creation as conceived and formulated by theistic religion is incoherent with the Spinoza's concept of substance or God. Like the emptiness of *Mādhyamikā*, Spinoza's substance is the ultimate foundation of all beings and existence. Spinoza says, that substance or which is considered to be ultimate reality like the emptiness of Buddhism explains through the nature of all human minds. I would believe that the scientific and the mystical understanding of the reality depend on the last analysis of the nature of reality which provides the ultimate explanation and the basis of all things and beings. And in this sense I would say that both Spinoza and Nāgārjuna are in agreement that there is no conflict between spirituality and science. Both according to me the misunderstanding of the ultimate reality has been the major impediments in understanding the truths and the reality of both science and spirituality. Reality when conceived as many is the basis of all illusions and misunderstanding. Whether it is Spinoza's Substance or Taoist's The Tao or Vedānta's *Brahman* and Buddhist's *Tathatā* (suchness) could be experienced only when mind is rid from the false subjectivity. Buddhism believes that enlightenment could be attained through spiritual regeneration. The supremacy of the mystical experience and its resultant enlightenment is the only way to eradicate desires and passions. It is not the intellect, but the mystical experience which is the supreme means to experience Truth. Reality is the absolute and the highest spiritual value. Kant also considered good as higher value than the reason. And this is why there is a conflict and contradictions in the exposition of *Critique of Pure Reason* and the *Critique of Practical Reason* of Kant. The spirituality is based on consciousness of being which is both transcendent and immanent. The conception of *Prajñāpāramitā* is one of the greatest contributions of Buddhism. *Prajñā* (wisdom) is non-conceptual and mystical experience. *Prajñā* is not a rational intuition. It is free from all kinds of mental reification. *Prajñā* is salvation. Buddhist ethical and mystical practice is always constituted of virtue (*Śīla*), *Samādhi* (contemplation), and *Prajñā* (salvation). The *Śīla* and *Samādhi* pave the path for the attainment of *Prajñā* (salvation). *Prajñāpāramitā* (spiritual enlightenment) is the realization of the transcendental nature of *Tathatā* in its totality. Buddhist concept of *Nirvāṇa* is emptiness. Emptiness is a state which is neither existence nor non-existence nor a combination of two either, nor negation of the two. The Vijñānavāda School enriched the concept of emptiness by affirming the positive aspects of *Vijñāna* (consciousness) which is in the state of flux. The *Vijñāna* of the previous moments gives rise to the *Vijñāna* of the next moment and this process goes on until *Vijñāna* attains *Nirvāṇa* after having eliminated all impurities but the sublimity and the profundity of *Vijñānavāda* lies in the concept that the person will not strive further for *Nirvāṇa* but will continue itself in the spiritual upliftment of all beings. The *Vijñānavādī* would attain liberation only when the whole human beings would be free from the snares of false subjectivity.

On the analysis and elucidation of the concept of *Nirvāṇa* I feel there are two distinct elements that is *Vijñāna* and the *Śūnya*. The Buddhist *Tantra* introduced a new element of *Mahā Sukha* (eternal bliss). There is a clear distinction between empirical and the absolute, *saṁvṛtti* and *paramārtha* in the original doctrine of the Buddhism. Hence, Buddhism retained in some form in the *Abhidharma*. The transient and gross objects of common sense could not be identified from other objects. Such a distinction is the result of the *Abhidharma* metaphysical. According to G.C. Pande, it does form part of the original Buddhism.[8] There has been shifts in the metaphysical stand in *Yogācāra* School where spiritual reality is conceived as infinite beyond empirical flux attainable only to transcendental wisdom. Professor G.C. Pande rightly observes, "Hīnayānī philosophy aims at providing the self-absorbed and ascetical monk with an analytical too which would enable him to objectify his mental states and detach himself from them, and is thus an essentially unworldly and cloistered philosophy which would be charged with encouraging soteriological egoism and an exaggerated attention to the myriad forms of suffering to be abandoned rather than to what is most real and worthwhile. For it every man is totally alone, drowning in a flood of tears, and it proposes to save him by telling him that there is no real person who could be called the drowning man but only an inexorable flood with the taste of tears. Perhaps the Hīnayānīst could retort by saying that the Mahāyānīst proposes to save the man by telling him that he has been either the drowning man or the flood. In a way the retort may be well taken for Mahāyāna does declare all empirical objects or *Dharmas* to be unreal and unborn like the objects of a dream but it concedes them a phenomenal and pragmatic reality. The way it suggests is not simply that of analytic withdrawal (*nivṛtti*), but of positive perfection (*Pāramitā*) culminating in transfiguration or *Paravṛtti*."[9] The mystic and esoteric culture of Mahāyāna which resulted in Buddhist *Tantra* is more spiritual and catholic than Theravāda Buddhism which is reflected in its meditational practice, ethical idealism and religious devotionalism.

The concepts of *Anityā* (impermanence), *Anātma* (non-self) and *Duḥkha* (suffering) are the basic concepts of Buddhism. All the different schools of Buddhism are based on these three basic concepts of Buddhism. The concept of impermanence is based on the proposition, "whatever is existent is momentary". This theory of impermanence is based on the Buddhist doctrine of causation known as *Pratitya Samudapāda* (dependent origination). The logical objection has been raised against the Buddhist theory of causation. If effect is originated from a cause that has ceased to exist, the effect will be destitute of cause because the non-existent cannot be the cause of any existent entity. However, if it accepted that effect has been originated by the existing cause, it entails the cause must be accepted to exist for more than one moment. This brings the Buddhist doctrines of causation between the two horns of dilemma. Neither alternative is in position to give a satisfactory explanation of causation. If we accept the first alternative it is not sufficient basis to explain the causation. If accept the second alternative it *ipso facto* nullifies the doctrine of impermanence. In reply of these charges Buddhist have succeeded in destroying the concept of universal which is the basis of the existent of a permanent reality. According to Buddhism universals are mental constructions. To counter the existence of any ontological universal and permanent entity Diṅnāga and Dharmakīrti advocated a new doctrine of signification and creativity known as doctrine of *apoha*.

H.S. Gill writes, "In the sixth and the seventh centuries CE, the Buddhist logician Diṅnāga and Dharmakīrti, proposed a theory of Signification and Creativity, called *apoha*, which dealt with the complexities of linguistic and ontological universe in terms of dialectical relation between Being and the Other, between the Subject and the Object, and more generally, between all related, but distinct entities of human discourses. Unfortunately, *apoha* has often been presented as a theory of negation, at times, a single, simple negation, at others, a double negation. In fact, *apoha* has nothing to do with any negative or positive proposition. What *apoha* really asserts is the fact that nothing is understood by itself in isolation. All comprehension is dialectical and is highly complex."[10] There is a great similarity between Buddhist doctrine of *apoha* with the theory of signification and creativity propounded by the twelfth century French philosopher Pierre Abelard who explained the phenomenon in terms of *sensus imaginatio intellectus*. Buddhist thinker like Nāgārjuna have always believed in the conventional nature of language and reality as opposed to realist belief of language as a natural phenomenon. Abelard also considers language as a mental construct and the word of language are imposed on the object as they are perceived. Both Nāgārjuna and Abelard reject the basic assumptions of the realist that words contain an objective reference in all its aspects. Buddhist believed that word does not refer to reality. Word only deals with the concepts and the concepts are purely mental constructs. H.S. Gill further writes, "A discursive understanding of the Buddhist theory of *apoha* and *Abelardian conceptualism*, lead us to realize that all creative discourses are specific articulations of specific perceptions of specific existential experiences. There is always a point of departure in the sensuous contact with the empirical reality of existential human condition which stimulates a specific perception and a specific constitution of a conceptual construct that a creative, human discourse is supposed to be. To be is to think and the being of the creative writer or the artist is realized in the conceptual unity of his creation."[11] If we accept language as mental constructs and believe that word is not referred to any objective reality and if word is a conceptual construct in mind and it is hypostatic as an external object, it creates some problem in communication. If we accept that the meaning is the sole possession of subject, how could it be communicated to other? The subjective concept is not the concept of another which ones like to communicate, so what would be the basis of the communication between two persons when the ideas are not communicable and amenable to perceptions by different persons.

Even we accept that the two persons are having the possession of same concept, it doesn't provide the basis of communications, as there is no ground of knowing the mental concept of one is possessed by another.

Satkari Mookherjee writes, "Śāntārākṣita replies that the difficulty would have been actually insurmountable if the conceptual image was confined within its limits and had not extra subjective reference. Though in reality the speaker and the hearer are conversant with what is their private possession, both of them think they understand the objective reality, and the cause of illusion being similar in both, there is no difficulty in intercommunication, just as two persons suffering from ophthalmia, see two moons and when one communicates his experience to the other, his word is believed to refer to an actual fact. Language is, therefore, a convenient instrument for communication of concepts which, however, are fictitious representatives of reality."[12]

The metaphysics is based on the Nāgārjuna's doctrine of *emptiness*. According to this doctrine the essential nature of all existence and being is *emptiness*. It is the *elanvita* and the quint essential nature and source of all reality and it is the essence of all forms and beings. According to D.T. Suzuki *Avataṁsaka* is the quint essence of Buddhism. He writes, "As to the *Avataṁsaka*, it is really the consummation of the Buddhist thought, Buddhist sentiment, and Buddhist experience. To my mind, no religious literature in the world can ever approach the grandeur of conception, the depth of feeling, and the gigantic scale of composition as attained in this *sūtra*. It is the eternal foundation of life from which no religious mind will turn back athirst or only partially satisfied."[13] D.T. Suzuki considers *Prajñā* (transcendental wisdom) and *Karuṇā* (compassion) as the two pillars of Buddhism. *Prajñā* the enlightened wisdom and *Karuṇā* are the two inalienable part of the Buddhist reality. The sublimity and the profundity of concepts of *Prajñā* (wisdom) and *Karuṇā* (compassion) originated in the ideal of *Bodhisattva* which has become the iconic symbol of Mahāyāna Buddhism. According to this tradition *Bodhisattva* is a person who have qualified for attainment of enlightenment and become the Buddha he refuses to attain *Nirvāṇa* for himself unless everybody else would before attains *Nirvāṇa*. Buddhism is a spiritual humanism based on Ontological mysticism. Fritjof Capra writes, "The central theme of the *Avataṁsaka* is the unity and the interrelation of all things and events; a conception which is not only the very essence of the Eastern world-view, but also one of the basic elements of the world-view emerging from modern physics. It will, therefore, be seen that the *Avataṁsaka Sūtra*, this ancient religious text, offers the most striking parallels to the models and theories of modern physics."[14]

Nāgārjuna is credited with bringing the Copernicus revolution in Indian philosophy. A new phase of philosophical thinking and speculation started with *Mādhyamikā*. Dialectic became a spiritual movement. Dialectic is a process to overcome the universal conflict afflicted by the antinomical character of reason. Nāgārjuna succeeded in overcoming the inherent conflict in reason by refuting both the opposites. According to Nāgārjuna real is spiritual and transcendental. According to Nāgārjuna dialectic is mystical experience which takes man beyond the possibility of pain and pleasure. It is the highest end of our spiritual pursuits. It is salvation (*Nirvāṇa*). T.R. Murti writes, "The dialectic as *Prajñāpāramitā* is identified with the *tathāgata* (*dharmakāya*)—the *Ens perfectissimum*, which all beings are in essence and which they attain by spiritual discipline. Religion is the mystic pull of the Transcendent (the Ideal) on the actual. The dialectic consummates the union of all beings with the perfect Being (*Buddhakāya*). In Kant, the critique silences theoretic (Pure) Reason; its function is thus merely negative. It is the Practical Reason that alone guarantees to Kant his ideals, God, freedom and immortality. There is thus the severance of the intellectual from the ethical and the religious. The *Mādhyamikā* Dialectic as negation of thought is intuition of the Absolute as the rooting out of passions it is Freedom (*Nirvāṇa*); and it is perfection as union with the Perfect Being."[15] The Buddhist dialectic culminates in mystical ontology. The terms *Śūnya* and *Śūnyatā* connotes both the relativity and the absolute. The absolute (*emptiness*) is *Śūnya* as it is beyond the conceptual distinctions of existence and non-existence. It is a state of absolute freedom from all kinds of false subjectivity. Philosophy becomes a pursuit of not knowledge, but quest for *Prajñāpāramitā* (perfection).

The Dialogue between Milinda Pañha and Nāgasena occupies a central position in Buddhist philosophical traditions. Nāgasena rejection of permanent self becomes the very basis of Buddhist metaphysics, epistemology and logic. I would like to quote the Dialogue between the Milinda and Nāgasena for the proper understanding of the Buddhist philosophy:

"And Milinda began by asking, "How is your Reverence known, and sir, is your name?"

"'I am Nāgasena. O King, and it is by that name that are brethren in the faith address me, yet this is only a generally understood term, a designation in common use. For there is no permanent individuality (no soul) involved in the matter."

"Then Milinda called upon the Yonakas and the brethren to witness: "This Nāgasena says there is no permanent individuality (no soul) implied in his name. Is it now even possible to approve him in that?" And turning to Nāgasena, he said: "If there be no permanent individuality (no soul) involved in the matter, who it is, pray that gives to you members of the Order your robes and food and lodging and necessaries for the sick? Who is it that enjoys such things when given? Who is it that lives a life of righteousness? Who is it who devotes himself to meditation? Who is it who attains to the goal of the excellent way, to the *Nirvāṇa* of Arhatship? And who is it who destroys living creatures? Who is it who takes what is not his own? Who is it who lives an evil life or worldly lusts, who speaks lies, who drinks strong drink, who (in a word) commits anyone of the five sins which works out their bitter fruit even in this life? If that be so, there is neither merit nor demerit; there is neither doer nor causer of good or evil deeds; there is neither fruit nor result of good or evil *karma*. If, most reverend Nāgasena, we are to think that we were a man to kill you there would be no murder, then it follows that there are no real masters or teachers in your Order, and that your ordinations are void....

You tell me that your brethren in the Order are in the habit of addressing you as Nāgasena. Now, what is that Nāgasena? Do you, mean to say that the hair is Nāgasena?"

"'I don't say that, great king.'

"'Or the hairs on the body, perhaps?'

"'Certainly not.'

"'Or is it the nails, the teeth, the skin, the flesh, the nerves, or the brain, or any or all of these that is Nāgasena?'

"And to each of these he answered no.

"'Is it the outward form then (*rūpa*) that is Nāgasena, or the sensations (*vedanā*), or the ideas (*saṁjñā*). Or the syntheses, the constituent elements of character (*saṁskāra*), or the consciousness (*vijñāna*) that is Nāgasena?"

"And to each of these he answered no.

"'Then is it all these *skandhas* combined that are Nāgasena?"

"'O, great king.'

"'But is there anything outside the five *skandhas* that is Nāgasena?"

"And still he answered no.

"'Then thus, asks as I may, I can discover no Nāgasena. Nāgasena is a mere empty sound. Who then is the Nāgasena that we see before us?"

"And the venerable Nāgasena asked Milinda the king: "did your Majesty come here on foot or in a chariot."

"'I did not come on foot; I came in a chariot".

"'then if you came, sire, in a chariot, explain to me what that is. Is it the pole that is the chariot?"

"'I did not say that.'

"'Is it the axle that is the chariot?'

"'Certainly not.'

"'Is it the wheels, or the framework, or the ropes, or the yoke, or the spokes of the wheels, or the goad that are the chariot?"

"And to all these; he still answered no."

"'Then is it all these parts of it that are the chariot?"

"'No, Sir.'

"'But is there anything outside them that is the chariot?"

"And still he answered no.

"'Then thus, ask as I may, I can discover no chariot. Chariot is a mere empty sound. What then is the chariot you say you came in?" And he called upon the Yonakas and the brethren to witness, saying: "Milinda the king here has said that he came in a chariot. But when asked in that case to explain what the chariot was, he is unable to establish what he averred. Is it, forsooth, possible to approve him in that?"

"And Milinda said: "I have spoken no untruth, reverend sir. It is on account of its having all these things—the pole and the axle, the wheels and the framework, the ropes and the yoke, the spokes and the goad—that it comes under the generally understood term, the designation in common use, of "chariot.""

"'Very good, your majesty has rightly grasped the meaning of "chariot." And just so it is on account of all those things you questioned me about, the thirty-two kinds of organic matter in a human body, and the five constituent elements of being that I come under the generally understood them, the designation in common use, of "Nāgasena." For it was said, sire, by our Sister Vagira in the presence of the Blessed One: "Just as it is by the condition precedent of the co-existence of its various parts of the word 'chariot' is used just so is it that when the *skandhas* are there we talk of a being."

According to Buddhism self is a stream of consciousness. There is a great similarity between the arguments advanced by Nāgasena against the existence of self with David Hume. According to Nāgasena self is not a permanent entity like body. Self is a stream of consciousness and because of the events happening in succession it gives illusion of a permanent entity. Hume also advances the same kind of argument in the rejection of self as a permanent substance. According to him one experiences sensation and perception of heat or cold, light or shade, love or hatred, pain and pleasure, but one does not catch his own self at any time without perception. One can only experience perception but one doesn't observe or experience anything except sensation or perception. In rejecting the self as a permanent substance he says that some thinkers may have a wrong perception of a permanent self. Hume says, "But setting aside some metaphysicians of this kind, I may venture to affirm of the rest of mankind, that they are nothing but a bundle or collection of different perceptions, which succeed each other with inconceivable rapidity, and are perpetual flux and movement". Nāgasena argues that one experiences only suffering, but it doesn't entail that there is an entity that suffers. Self is nothing, but an isolated stream of perceptions. William James also considers consciousness as a stream which are known together in a particular moments of stream of existence. William James says, "the mind is not an enduring being; each subject lasts, but for a moment. Its place is immediately taken by another which exercises its functions, that is, to act as the medium of unity. The subject for the time being knows and adopts its predecessor, and by so doing appropriates what its predecessor adopted."[16]

But if we analyse the teachings of Buddhism then we find that there is a unity behind the eternal flux. The Buddhist philosophy is based on Ontological mysticism, which is based on the concept of absolute which is the source of all existence and being. This is called *Śūnyatā* in Buddhism. This emptiness is beyond the reach of mind and senses. D.T. Suzuki writes, "The fundamental idea of Buddhism is to pass beyond the world of opposites, a world built-up by intellectual distinctions and emotional defilements, and to realize the spiritual world of nondistinction, which involves achieving an absolute point of view."[17]

Buddhism is a philosophy of mind (*Citta Darśana*). Theravāda Buddhism reduces the mind into a set of thoughts and feelings and seeks enlightenment from nescience through detachment. *Mahāyāna* Buddhism considers mind as the seed of enlightenment (*Bodhicitta*). According to *Mahāyāna* meditation is to transform mind into eternal emptiness. This eternal emptiness is called *Bodhicitta*. *Bodhicitta* is bereft of all existence. The *Bodhicitta* remains unpolluted and pure in spite of defilements and cravings. This *Bodhicitta* is pure consciousness and infinite bliss (*Mahā Sukha*). Lalan Prasad Singh writes, "According to Buddhism, reality is in eternal flux. Our experience is only the point instant. Reality is in the state of flux. Existence is contingent. There is no logical foundation for the theoretical basis of natural science. The natural world is known in relation to our modes of experience. The mind is the only instrument through which we know mind and consciousness. Consciousness is a continuum flow. The duality of the physical and the mental does not exist in the state of the pure continuum. This continuum is known as emptiness."[18] Reification in science and philosophy is greatest impediment in understanding the nature of being and reality in totality. The reality exists in relation to our theoretical framework of language and consciousness. The basic question whether world exists the way it appears or whether its mode of existence is different from its mode of appearance. The physical reality does not define in terms of scientific realism. There is truth in Schrodinger's observation that world is nothing but conglomeration of a "construct of our sensations, perceptions and memories".[19]

To me Nāgārjuna's greatest philosophical contribution lies on the formulation of complex doctrine of two truths as a tool for understanding Buddhist metaphysics and epistemology. The Buddha was conscious about antinomical character of reason, and he resolves it by rising to the higher stand point of criticism. Buddha's silence should not be misunderstood as agnosticism, nor it should be understood as his ignorance of metaphysics. He didn't approve speculative metaphysics because of his preference to criticism and ontological mysticism. T.R.V. Murti rightly observes: "The rejection of theories (*diṭṭhi*) is itself the means by which Buddha is led to the non-conceptual knowledge of the absolute, and not *vice versa*. It is no accident then that Buddha concerns himself with an analysis of the various theories or reality and rejects them all. Buddha ascends from the conflict of Reason and the attempt to resolve it by rising to plane higher than Reason is dialectic. And the dialectical method is the *Mādhyamikā* way."[20]

The doctrine of two truths that is a noumena and phenomena is implicit in all philosophical traditions. The propagation of the two truths that is *Paramārtha Satya* (emptiness) and *Saṁvṛti Satya* (conventional reality), indicates the Buddhist stand point. According to *Mādhyamikā kārikā*, "Those that are unaware of the distinction between these two truths are incapable of grasping the deep significance of the teachings of Buddha."[21] The purpose of philosophical deliberation is spiritual. It is to free mind from all kinds of reification. According to Buddhism *Prajñā* is *Nirvāṇa*, it is a state of freedom and bliss. *Prajñā* is a consummation of moral and religious ideas. According to Buddhism state of *Nirvāṇa* cannot be put into any linguistic form, but it is real. The function of *Prajñā* is not to transform the real, but only to create change in our perspective, change in epistemic and not ontological. According to *Mādhyamikā kārikā* "This leads to the other contention of the *Mādhyamikā* that there is no difference whatever between *Nirvāṇa* and *saṁsāra*; Noumena and phenomena are not two separate sets of entities, nor they are two states of the same thing. The absolute is only real; it is the reality of *saṁsāra*, which is sustained by false construction (*Kalpanā*). The absolute looked at through the thought-forms of constructive imagination is the empirical world and conversely, the absolute is the word viewed sub-specie acternatis, without these distorting, media of thought."[22]

Prajñā is a mystical experience of continuum emptiness. It is an analytical knowledge of the empirical world as transient, contingent and suffering. This knowledge leads to the eradication of the belief in intrinsic self and destroys the very foundation of egoism, passion, suffering and defilements. Kant in his *critique* has shown that presentation of speculative philosophy is to provide pure knowledge. Nāgārjuna also holds the same view, but there is an important distinction between Nāgārjuna's dialectic and Kantian critique. For Nāgārjuna dialectic is itself a philosophy, it liberates man from ignorance which is the root cause of sufferings. According to Kant the critique paves the path for the practical reason which provides noumenal values. It is a practical reason which provides freedom and immortality. The analysis and examination of both Kant's critique and Nāgārjuna's dialectic prove that one cannot achieve freedom and enlightenment with the help of philosophical reasoning and disputation. The concept of emptiness and *Prajñāpāramitā* provide the sound philosophical basis of Buddhism. Diṅnāga beautifully summarizes the concept of *Prajñāpāramitā*: "*Prajñāpāramitā* (highest wisdom) is non-dual knowledge, and that is the *Tathāgata*. The Treatise and the spiritual discipline as leading to this end, receive the same application."[23]

Buddhism is a philosophy of non-dual experience of reality. This mystical experience and knowledge of reality cannot be attained as by Hegel through the process of synthesis, but by negation. Negation is a consciousness of its falsity. The awareness and the knowledge of falsity means the awareness of what appears as real is nothing, but a bundle of contradictions. Buddhism is aware of futility of speculative philosophy and hence, it believes in ontological mysticism. The speculative philosophy does not provide sound mystical basis for the realization of the truth and reality rather it results into mental reification. According to Buddhism in the process of reification of our own identity we reify others which results in objectification of our inanimate world. According to Buddhism self does not exist as the body, the mind or the combination of both. The simple negation of self is known as emptiness. The emptiness is the ultimate mode of existence of the self. The experience of emptiness liberates one from the reification of self as an intrinsic reality. It speaks of the ancient wisdom that truth makes a man free from all kinds of reifications and delusions. The realization of emptiness is attainment of *Nirvāṇa*.

According to Buddhism metaphysical, epistemological and soteriological aim is to rid the mind from all kinds of reification to pave the path for the experience of emptiness and supreme bliss. The concept of emptiness and the relation between *Nirvāṇa* and *Saṁsāra* provides the ontological mystical basis of Buddhism. The central teachings of Buddhism are to penetrate into this mystical intuition of the Buddha that doctrine of eternal self is a doctrine of fools. By negating the existence of eternal self the Buddha destroys the very foundation of desires and defilements where they can rest. However, the consciousness is a continuum flow. This continuum flow can never be destroyed or be separated. In this state of pure continuum of consciousness the duality of physical and mental doesn't exist. This continuum is known as emptiness and *Nirvāṇa*.

Buddhist *Tantra*

Tantra forms the esoteric basis of all religion. The central objective of *Tantra* is to awaken the dormant divinity. It is esoteric practice to invoke the spirituality of men and women. All ontological reality is characterized by vibrations. Vibration is serial name or *mantra*, *Śabda* (word) connotes three meanings. (i) Word (*Śabda*) is a symbol or sign, (ii) Word (*śabda*) is a concept, (iii) According to *Tantra* word or *śabda* is an expression of vibrational creative energy. It does not agree with the modern philosophical or linguistic concept of *śabda* (words). Words are esoteric names. *Mantras* (*śabda*) are divine commands. Even Berkeley says that things are nothing, but meanings in the cosmic mind. *Tantra* is esoteric practice to realize the ultimate truth and the real meaning of existence and being. The ultimate reality is called in Hindu *Tantra* as *Ātman* or *Brahman*, in Buddhist *Tantra* it is known as *Bodhicitta*. *Bodhicitta* is bereft of all existence. It is beyond all thought, categories as subject and object. It is of the nature of *Śūnya*. *Guhyasamāja Tantra* defines *Bodhicitta* as "Neither the perception of the absence of existence in non-existence can be called perception, nor the perception of non-existence in existence can be discovered."[24]

There is a controversy regarding the origin of Buddhist *Tantra*. According to one School Asaṅga the founder of *Yogācāra* is an exponent of Buddhist *Tantra*. According to other Nāgārjuna the founder of *Mādhyamikā* school is considered as the founder of Buddhist esotericism. It is believed that Nāgārjuna was initiated into the Tāntric esoteric practice by Buddha Bairochan at the iron tower in South India. However, Tibetan tradition believes that he was initiated in *Tantra Sādhanā* by *Siddhācāra Sarahapada*. And after practising *Sādhanā* he attained *Bajrakāya Siddhi.*[25] But to my mind Buddha himself is founder of *Tantra*. It is the common practice that *Tantra sādhanā* is performed in a cremation ground or a lonely place. When it is practised under the *Kula* tree progress is accelerated. According to *Tantra* belief the banyan tree is considered as the *Kula* tree. It is, therefore, not without any justification or objective that *Siddhārtha* practised his *Sādhanā* under the famous banyan tree at Bodha Gayā and attained enlightenment (*Nirvāṇa*). There is a clear account that Buddha himself practised *asphanāga-yoga*[26] (Yoga of psychic expansion), when he was in search of eternal truth. *Vinaya Piṭaka*[27] says that Buddha's own disciple Bharadvāja rose into the air and brought down the begging bowl which was held high above *Setthi*. Dr. B. Bhattacharya, writes "Buddha recognised *ṛddhis* or supernatural powers and mentioned four *ṛddhipadas*[28] continuously to the attainment of supernatural powers.[29] The element of Tāntricism is further confirmed by the mystic circle (*Maṇḍala*) around the famous *Bodhi* tree under which the Buddha practised meditation and attained *Nirvāṇa*. The *Maṇḍala* of Buddhist *Tantra* is known as *Yantra* in Hindu *Tantra*. Even the formulas of refuse and other ritual practice which were current of all times in all countries of Theravāda Buddhism speaks of *Mantric* character. *Mantra*, *Mudrā* and *Maṇḍala* are the foundation of Buddhist *Tantra* from its very inception. The Buddha revived, regenerated and resuscitated the lost intuitional science of *Tantra*.

There are two traditions of Buddhism (i) *Sūtra* and (ii) *Tantra*. *Sūtra* tradition is known as Theravāda Buddhism. On the other hand the Buddhist Tāntric tradition has been greatly misunderstood. This is due to the fact that *Mahāyāna Sūtras* and their commentaries were little known in the academic world before the end of nineteenth century. Moreover, the whole canonical Tāntric literature is written in *Sandhyā Bhāṣā* (twilight language), The real meaning of which is known only to those who get initiated into esotericism. Hindu and the Buddhist *Tantra* represent special aspects of religious and cultural life of India. *Tantra* and *Veda* are two different, but complementary currents of Indian cultural traditions.

Sādhanāmālā is the canonical literature of Buddhist *Tantra*. According to *Sādhanā Mālā, Tantra* was developed from *Yogācāra* School. *Yogācāra* School was developed out of the *Śūnyavāda* (*Mādhyamikā* school). *Sādhanāmālā* forms the canonical literature of *Vajrayāna* school of *Tantra*. The word *Mahāyāna* has been referred twice in *Sādhanāmālā*. The *Mahāyāna* is according to Buddhist *Tantra* is co-extensive and synonym of *Dharma*. The word *Śūnya* occurs on almost of every page of *Sādhanāmālā*. However, there is a great philosophical, metaphysical and mystical difference between the concept of *Śūnya* as propounded by *Mādhyamikā* and the *Vajrayānist* concept of *Śūnya*. According to *Mādhyamikā* concept and the object are *Śūnya*, there is no reality, either of mind or the phenomenal world. This metaphysical position of *Mādhyamikā* is not acceptable to the *Vajrayāna* School. For Buddhist Tantra, *Vijñāna* is absolutely necessary. There is a little controversy whether *Tantra* is based on *Yogācāra* or *Śūnyavāda* metaphysical treatise. According to philosophical treatise of *Yogācāra* it has explained in detail in many places which leads to infer that the *Vajrayāna* is direct development of *Yogācāra*. The *Vajra* stands for adamantine path or *Śūnya* vehicle. *Śūnya* is referred in an esoteric import to represent the *Vajra*. *Śūnya* is described as *Vajra* because it cannot be changed, it cannot be burnt and it cannot be destroyed. The *summum bonum* of *Tantra* is the transformation of mental energy into the transcendental experience of enlightenment. The mystic transformation and sublimation awakened the human being from his hibernation and this realization is spiritual process of change and metamorphosis from that of *Jīva* (individual) through cosmic being. Man has the inherent energy and spiritual power to enjoy limitless blissful happiness while living and remaining free from the delusion that normally contaminate our mind. With proper transformation all our actions can lead to the path of spirituality and enlightenment. *Tantra* is full of metaphor and symbolism. The concept of *Dhyānī Buddha* is of great mystic significance. *Guhya Samāja* has introduced the concept of *Śakti*. However, *Śakti* has been the inevitable principle of esoteric practice for the attainment of enlightenment, since, the very origin of *Tantra*. *Guhya Samāja* has only introduced the new concepts of five *Dhyāni*

Buddha presiding over the five *skandha* or factors of which the whole universe is composed along with the five *Śakti*. These five *skandhas* are: *Rūpa* (form), *Vadenā* (feeling), *Saṁjñā* (name), *Saṁskāra* (impression) and *Vijñāna* (consciousness). *Guhya Samājā Sādhanāmālā* describes the names, colours and symbols of the different *Dhyānī, Buddhas*. The names are: *Vairocana, Ratna Sambhāva, Amitābha, Amoghasiddhi* and *Akṣobhaya*. Their colours are: white, yellow, red, green and blue and they are depicted in different *mudrās*, namely, *Bodhyāṅgī* (teachings), *Varada* (grace), *Dhyāna* (meditation), *Abhaya* (protective) and *Bhūmisparśa* (earth-touching). The female (*Śakti*) counterparts of the five *Dhyānī Buddhas* are: *Locana, Vairadhatviśvarī, Pandara, Māmaki* and *Tārā*. These five consorts of *Dhyānī Buddhas* belong to the five families of *dveṣa, moha, rāga, cintāmaṇi* and *samaya*. The names of the five *Bodhisattva* of the *Dhyānī Buddhas* are: *Vajrapāṇī, Sāmantabhadra, Padmapāṇī, Ratnapāṇī* and *Viśvapāṇī*.[30]

In *Siddha Sāhitya* (literature) known as *Cārayapada*, the divine love of *Yogīn* and *Yogīnī* has been depicted in a metaphor or courtship between lover and beloved. Individual self is symbolised as male or Lord and *Śūnyatā* as female. The great *Siddha Siddhācārya Kakkurlopa* says in his mystic intoxication "desireless am I and void mind is my husband". Another *Siddhācāra Toilopada* says, "The mind is Lord Vacuity (*Śūnyatā*) is the lady". This male and female principle is always kept ignited in the *Sahaja*. Rāmakrishna also speaks in the same metaphor when he says, "the individual self is merged in his wife Vacuity (*Śūnyatā*) he becomes one with her like the idol of salt when enters into the ocean of existence to fathom the depth and the sublimity dissolves into salt water.

Buddhist *Tantra* is a metaphysical school of non-duality. The five *Dhyānī Buddha* in want of proper understanding and esoteric significance have been wrongly conceived as five primordial gods which smack of polytheism. The concept of *Ādi Buddha* the supreme deity like *Ādinatha* and *Parama Śiva* of Hindu *Tantra* represents the monotheistic spirit and tradition of Tāntricism. According to Dr. B. Bhattacharya this theory of *Ādi Buddha* or *Vajradhara* (the primordial monotheistic Buddha) was originated in the Nālandā monastery in about the tenth century.[31] According to Alexander Csoma de Koros, also the theory of *Ādi Buddha* was introduced at Nālandā in the beginning of the tenth century.[32] There are some misunderstanding and controversy regarding the concept of *Ādi Buddha* that sometimes *Ādi Buddha* is identified with *Vajradhara*. According to some scholars *Bodhisattva* such as *Sāmanta Bhadra* and *Vajrapāṇī* have been identified as *Ādi Buddha*. This misunderstanding is because of the lack of mystic and non-dualistic significance of metaphors used in Tāntric esotericism as *Ādi Buddha* and *Dhyānī Buddha* which are one in essence and reality. Buddhist *Tantra* is not interested in creating any metaphysical system. It is mainly concerned with the enlightenment through the practice of esoteric technique or methods. S.B. Dasgupta writes, "We have said that Tāntric Buddhism was a growth within the province of *Mahāyāna* (the great vehicle), and as such, in aim and ambition Tāntric Buddhism imbibed the spirit of *Mahāyāna* in a marked way. As for the final goal the Mahāyānist believed that every man—nay, every being of the world is a potential Buddha; he has within him all the possibilities of becoming a *Samyaksambuddha*, i.e., the perfectly enlightened one. Consequently, the idea of Arhathood of the Hīnayānīst was replaced by the idea of *Boddhisattvahood* of the Mahāyānīst."[33]

Buddhist *Tantra* considers *Nirvāṇa* as the realization of *Śūnyatā*. *Śūnyatā* is not in any way absolute rejection of reality. It is the negation of subjectivity and objectivity. Buddhist *Tantra* believes that cosmic consciousness is (*Vijñapti-mātratā*) is the ultimate reality. In the state of *Nirvāṇa*, *grāhaka* and *grāhya* are eliminated but the power of consciousness is retained. *Nirvāṇa* is conceived as infinite bliss which has been introduced by *Vajrayāna* and *Sahajayāna*. *Nirvāṇa* is identified with *Mahāsukha*. It is a state of bliss and beatitude, which is beyond the enjoyment and liberation.

Vajrayāna, *Sahajayāna* and *Kāla Cakrayāna* are three main metaphysical and esoteric schools of Buddhist *Tantra*. These three schools of Buddhist *Tantra* represent the three stages of spiritual development of the *Sādhanā. Mañjūśrī-Mūlakalpa, Sādhanāmālā* and *Guhyasamāja Tantra* are the earliest canonical literature on *Vajrayāna*.

Vajrayāna believes that enlightenment cannot be achieved by subjecting the mind and body to sufferings. The Buddha was against the practice of penance and physical suffering. *Mantra*, *Mudrā*,

Maṇḍala and the invocation of deities are the esoteric basis of *Tantra Sādhanā*. The principle of *Śakti* is of great importance. Anaṅgavajra says, "Without *Prajñāpāramitā* emancipation is not possible. T.R.V. Murti while analysing the concept of *Prajñāpāramitā* writes, "Metaphysis or true philosophy (*prajñā*) is non-dual knowledge—Intuition of the real...It is the Truth. In intuition knowledge and reality coincide; essence and existence are identical.... Non-duality, the *Mādhyamikā* is not attained, as in Hegel, by synthesis of particular points of view, but by their negation."[33] But there is great confusion over the word *Paravṛtti*. According to some scholars, "in the *Pravṛtti* of sexual union supreme greatness is obtained". Sylvian Lévi suggests that, '*Pravṛtti* of sexual act' means "the mystic coupling of Buddha's and *Bodhisattvas*' which have much importance in Tantrism. P.C. Bagchi is of the opinion that the Tāntric sexo-yogic practice means the enjoyment of bliss similar to that arising from the sexual act—which is evident in *Sūtra-Laṅkāra* itself."[35]

Vajrayāna is Psycho-spiritual method and spiritual technique to bring about change and metamorphosis of a sentient being into cosmic being. It is intuitional science. It is a mystic technique of inner progression. It makes man richer and fuller and gives him vision and strength. The practice of *Mahāmudrā* (the great woman) is based on mystic ideation and motivation. It all depends on the motivation. A wife is kissed with one motivation and the daughter is kissed with another feelings.

However, it doesn't mean that *Vajrayāna* encourages unethical satisfaction of kernel desires. However, the desires are an enemy, but it can be made an alloy. The physical body of sentient being is a manifestation of *Bodhicitta*. The phenomenal world is manifestation of *Mahāsukha*. In the copulation of man and woman the same happiness and satisfaction is experienced in lesser degree. If it is done with esoteric motivation under strict spiritual discipline the physical enjoyment is ennobled and sublimated. *Vajrayāna* has become very popular because it has embraced all that is the best philosophical and spiritual doctrines. It is an intuitional science and a philosophy of great spiritual significance which leads one to the state of perfection and salvation.

Sahajayāna is a devotional school of Buddhist *Tantra*. Lakṣmikara devi sister of Indrabhūti the king of *Uḍḍīyāna* is one of the greatest exponent of *Sahajayāna*. She introduced the concept of devotion. She created a school of devotional esotericism in Buddhism." She says, "there are no need of undergoing suffering, no fasting, and no rites, or bathing or purification and other rules of society. Nor do you need to bow down before the images of the gods which are prepared of wood, stone or mud. But with concentration offer worship only to your body where all the gods reside."[36]

According to all the spiritual traditions transcendental truth is the ultimate reality. The practice of moral values is stepping stones towards the realization of the *Nirvāṇa* and when man attains enlightenment he transcends the world of good and bad. The state of *Nirvāṇa* is a state of naturalness (*sahaja*). *Sahajayāna* has greatly influenced the Nāthism and Sūfism. M.M. Harparsad Shastri, P.C. Bagchi, Rahul Saṁskritayan have made great contribution by publishing *Siddha* literatures. Suniti Kumar Chatterjee, Sahiudala, Sukumar Sen have also done some valuable works. The word *Siddha* connotes the acquisition of mystic power through the practice of *mantra*. The man who acquires this kind of occult power with the help of incantation of *mantra* is known as *Siddha*. The whole literature of *Siddhācārya* is esoteric (*Guhya*). The real meaning and signification is known only to the initiates. The metaphors and the symbols used in this literature are sexual and have amatory connation, but their real meaning and signification is related to ontological mysticism. The most of the symbols and metaphors refer to the name of the low caste females. In *Hevajra Tantra*, *Prajñā* is addressed as a *yuvatī* (young woman), *jananī* (mother), *bhaginī* (sister), *rajakī* (washer woman), *nartakī* (dancing girl), *dombī* (dome girl). *Prajñā* is called *janani* because she is the cause of creation. She is called *nartakī* because the whole world is nothing, but manifestation of cosmic dance of *Prajñā* and every object is in a state of dancing posture. She is called *dombī* because she is beyond the touch of human mind and senses.

According to Buddhist *Tantra* when *Prajñā* or *Śūnyatā* co-mingles with universal compassion *Karuṇā* it is called *Bodhicitta*. It is believed that *Vajrasattva* eternally co-exist with his consort called as *Vajra Barāhi* and *Prajñāpāramitā*. According to *Tantra* pure and perfect wisdom is the product of unification of *Prajñā* and *Upāya* as fire which is pure and which illuminates everything is a product of two logs of rubbed together. *Dharma Dhātu* extinguishes the fire of pleasure and pain can be attained only by proper churning of the milk of *Prajñā* and *Upāya*. Suzuki traces the concept of *Prajñā* and *Upāya* of the time of Aśvaghoṣa. He says that enlightenment has two attributes: (i) Pure wisdom (*Prajñā*), and (ii) Incomprehensible Activity (*Upāya* or *Karuṇā*). Nāgārjuna has also used the word *Upāya* for *Karuṇā*.[37]

M.M. Gopinath Kaviraj says that there is great similarity between Buddhist and Hindu Tāntric practices. According to him '*Karuṇā* has the same importance in Buddhist Tāntric literature which *Bhakti* occupies in the *Bhāgavata*. The unification of *Prajñā* and *Upāya* transcends and overcomes the ill-effects of defilements. *Karuṇā* alone cannot obtain *Nirvāṇa*.

First there is a practice of *Pāramitā-naya* followed by *Mantra-naya*, both these *naya* (path) have been expounded by Buddha himself. The purposes of both are the same.[38]

There is a lot of similarity between *Vajrayāna* and *Vāmācārya* of Hindu *Tantra*. Both are spiritual and mystical discipline to overcome the instincts and tendencies of sex (*kāma*), anger (*krodha*), temptation (*lobha*), attachment (*moha*), egoism (*mada*), jealousy (*mātsarya*), hatred (*ghṛṇā*), shame (*lājja*), fear (*bhaya*) which are the cause of bondage by veiling the real transcendental nature of sentient beings. *Sādhanā* is performed in cremation ground in dead of night because by seeing the end of mortal frame in form of ashes and skeletons a sense of renunciation and detachments overcome to the practicener which leads to getting rid from the mundane existence and bondage. *Tantra* doesn't believe in suppression and repression of human instincts and feelings. Practice of Tāntric mystic techniques sublimates the baser instincts of human beings. The incantation of *mantra* establishes an esoteric communion which is real individual nature. It is a mystic process of unification of *Śakti* or *Herukā* with Śiva or *Upāya*. The *Vajrayāna* and *Vāmācārya Sādhanā* is recommended by the preceptor for only those who have followed the ethical and spiritual discipline rigorously.

According to *Sahajayāna nirvāṇa* can be attained without undergoing any kind of physical or mental suffering. M.M. Gopinath says that *Sahajayāna* is based on philosophy and practices of *Āgama*. The symbols such *Hakāra* and *Thakāra* represent moon and sun and the unification of these both bring about the unification of moon and sun. According to the philosophy of *Tantra* when the equanimity is disturbed, multiplicity is created. This is the root of creation. The state of dualism is the state of phenomenal world. The state of equanimity is known as *Advaita*. *Sarahapād* who is considered as a great exponent of *Sahajayāna* is also a first exponent of Hindi literature. There is, however, some controversy amongst the scholars and historians about the place of *Sarahapād* in ancient literature. According to some he was a poet of Bengali literature. Other considered him as Oriyā poet, but Rahul Samskritayan says, "that *Sarahapād* is the first poet of Hindi literature because the elements of *apabhraṁśa* elements is found in *Sarahapād* poems. However, it goes without saying that *Sahajayāna* exercised great influence on Bengali, Oriyā, Asamiā, Maithilī, and Hindi literature because of its mystical profundity and its arousal of higher sensibility. The whole *Sahajayāna* literature is full of divine grace and spirituality. Simplicity, grace, mysticism are the hallmark of *Sahajayāna*. The practice of *yoga* and *Tantra* with spiritual commitments and devotion without getting involved in any kind of physical and emotional suffering in the process of awakening of the *kuṇḍalinī* has been the quint essential feature of *Sahajayāna*.

Sahajayāna by introducing and identifying the concept of *Mahāsukha* with *Nirvāṇa* created a great spiritual revolution and transformation in the concept of transcendental reality. *Sahajayāna* has been recognised as the dawn of a new era of *Mahāsukha*. S.B. Dasgupta writes, "The *Mahāyāna* conception of the production of *Boddhicitta* (*Bodhi-cittotpāda*) is transformed in *Sahajayāna* into the production of a state of intense bliss through the sexo-yogic practice; and as after the production, the *Boddhicitta* rises upwards through ten stages (technically known as the *Boddhisattva-bhūmis*) so also *Sahajayāna* practice involves the yogic process of breath-control and other psycho-physical practices through which the disturbed semen should be checked in the *Maṇipūra* (situated near the navel) known generally as the *Nirmāṇa-cakra*, and then it must march upwards through the *Dharma-cakra* situated in the heart and the *Sambhoga-cakra* situated in the throat and then reach the *Uṣṇīṣakamalā* (i.e., the lotus in the head) where it will produce the *Mahāsukha* of the nature of *Nirvāṇa*. The word *Boddhicitta* sometimes in *Vajrayāna* and almost always in *Sahajayāna* is synonymous with the word semen."[39]

There is a great similarity between *Sahajayāna* and Vaiṣṇava *Tantra*. The *Pañcarātra* is the foundation of Tāntric Vaiṣṇavism. *Pañcarātra āgama* is the basis of Tāntric Vaiṣṇava system. It is called *Pañcarātra* because it expounds five kinds of knowledge; both *Sahajayāna* and Vaiṣṇava *Tantra* accept *Śakti* as immanent principle. She is a creative matrix. Like *Prajñā* and *Upāya*, Śiva and *Śakti* are inseparable. Both *Sahajayāna* and Tāntric Vaiṣṇavism adhere to the worship of *Śakti* because it is considered that with the help of *Śakti*, the sentient being will attain liberation from the sneers of false subjectivity. *Śrī Vidyā Kalpa* belongs to the Vaiṣṇava *Tantra*. *Śrī* is consort of Viṣṇu. *Śrī Cakra* is the abode of Viṣṇu. *Śrī* is the womb of universe. *Śrī Vidyā* which is a divine cult and *bhakti mārga* path of devotion constitutes Tāntric Vaiṣṇavism. In both Tāntric Vaiṣṇavism and *Sahajayāna* there is great importance and predominance of devotion. Both *Sādhanā* leads to the state of spiritual enlightenment and enjoyment. In the state of *Sahajayāna* and Tāntric Vaiṣṇavism man becomes God intoxicated. With the awakening of the dormant divinity there is an emergence of great spiritual vibrations in the practicener. This is an inner spiritual journey culminating in the inner happiness and enjoyment of infinite bliss and beatitude. The shedding tears, limping of the body continuous laughing and dancing are some of the outward manifestation of enjoyment of inner bliss and beatitude. In Tāntric terminology it is known as *Aṣṭavabhāva*. The ordinary people who are not aware of the mystic tradition of Tāntricism have greatly misunderstood the Tāntric practices and its achievements.

According to *Rudrayāmala* and *Brahmayāmala Vaśiṣṭa* approached the Buddha in attaining perfection (*Siddhi*). The *Rudrayāmala* states that when *Vaśiṣṭa* went to the Buddha he was shocked to see that Buddha was surrounded by large number of women drinking wine and obscene rites. *Vaśiṣṭa* pleaded to the Buddha to clear his doubts and misunderstandings. According to *Yāmala Tantra* Buddha initiated *Vaśiṣṭa* in *Tantra* and *Vaśiṣṭa* with the practice of incantation of *mantra* and the practice of five *makāras* he attained *Nirvāṇa*. The practice of *Pañcamakāra* and lack of its proper understanding and esoteric significance, both Hindu and Buddhist *Tantra*, have been greatly scandalised.

Sahajayāna and Tāntric Vaiṣṇavism are the finest and profound form of mysticism. The mystic forms of *Sādhanā* lead to the transformation of individual being into cosmic existence. Man enlightened one starts experiencing him in everything. He feels one in all and all in one. Sahajīya cult of Bengal and its literatures have made a great impact on both philosophical and literary thinkings and speculations. This form of Sahajīya cult originated and developed in Bengal and it was enriched by Chaitanya Mahāprabhu and Chaṇḍīdāsa who lived in fourteenth century. The mystic song of bawl have also origin in Tāntric Vaiṣṇavism. The elements of mysticism, Vaiṣṇavism are the kernels of Bawls song. The esotericism of bawl sect speaks of its Tāntric character and traditions. *Sahajayāna* made the Bengali culture and traditions fuller and richer. It is the most sublime form of spiritual culture and tradition and it infused a new life and *elan vita* to the cultural life of Bengal. However, the *siddha* has many connotations. *Siddha* tradition is prevalent in all over India. *Siddha*'s are known as saints and poets. It has enriched all the literary traditions of India. In Tamil Nadu the *Siddha* tradition originates with Thirumool of fifth century. He is considered as great saints and mystics. His work Thiruvanmandirum is considered as the basis of *Śaiva Siddhānta*. *Encyclopaedia of Indian Literature* writes, "We come across names like Bogar, who was a Chinese Taoist (a contemporary of Thirumoolar, so, it is traditionally reported), Macha Muni (Macchendranātha) and Gorakhar (Gorakhanātha), the two names figuring as among the nine originals *Nava Nātha Siddhas*; Kāka Bhusuṇḍar (there is a Kāka Bhusuṇḍa of north-east India, the author of *Bhusuṇḍī Rāmāyaṇa*), Thirumaligai Devar (Malikā Deva), Vālmīki Nandī Eswwarar, etc. There are also *Siddhas* who are reported to have come from Egypt and China and composed poems in a colloquial Tamil tongue which are sung in folk tunes, and then, of course, the places are listed, according to tradition, where they are reported to have attained *Samādhi*."[40]

Siddhas have come from different parts of India. They have lived a life of simplicity and saintliness. *Siddhācārya* have been accepted as mystic poets, saints and philosophers. They have been recognised as man of great wisdom and sanity. They rejected the institutionalized religions and lifeless practice of dogmas and beliefs. Religion is not denominational. It is an art of living with creativity, spirituality, morality and grace. *Sahajayāna* is a spirituality based on ontological mysticism. The state of transcendentality remains ever unpolluted by the humming of longings and desire is known as *Sahaja*. It is a state of desirelessness and choiceless awareness.

This state of *Sahaja* is attained when a man merges his individual consciousness into cosmic consciousness. This state of merger with individual ego with cosmic consciousness is a state of *Mahāsukha* and *Nirvāṇa*. In this state of *Nirvāṇa* the multiplicity of phenomenal world are merged and mingled into eternal and infinite unity. This state of the identification of ego consciousness with cosmic consciousness is known as Buddhahood. This is known as *Sahajayāna*.

Kālacakra Tantra

Kālacakra is the development of *Vajrayāna*. This School of Tāntric Buddhism have been greatly misunderstood. The Tāntric texts and its mystic practices have never been the subject of academic discourse and discussions. However, some commentaries like Vimala Prabhā and Sekoddesatika are available, but it is difficult to dive deep into the real meaning and significance of different metaphors and symbols used in this text. I am trying to present before the academic community the quint essential features of *Kālacakra* both from academic and esoteric perspective. *Kāla* (time) has been interpreted in a different cultural and philosophical tradition differently. It is conceived as supreme force by some cultural and philosophical traditions. Gopinath Kaviraj considers *Kāla* as supreme form of all elements. He says, "*Kāla* is in the form of supreme Godhood". When the *Śakti* manifested in the form of phenomenal world *Śakti* remains immanent as *Idamaḥ Jñāna* (knowledge) and the *Kriyā* (activity) being one of the casual form of activity and the world as manifestation of its knowledge from, it remains one with the *Ātman*. This form of supreme reality as God or *Kālaśakti* is known as *Kālatattva*."[41]

Kālacakra Tantra brings about harmonious and happy blending of dualism and monism. It is esoteric system of meditational practice. The meditational practice enshrined by *Kālacakra Tantra* is to obtain mystic unification of *Śūnyatā* and *Karuṇā*. It is considered that *Kālacakra Tantra* was introduced by *Mañjūśrī* and its commentary Vimala Prabhā was written by Puṇḍarīka.[42]

Dr. B. Bhattacharya says that *Kālacakrayāna* have embodied in its teachings and practices of all the best of *Vajrayāna*, Nāthism and *Sahajayāna*.[43] M.M. Gopinath Kaviraj says that *Kālacakra* aims at a mystical unification of *Prajñā* and *Upāya* technically as *Vajrayoga*. It represents in fact the state of supreme oneness.[44]

Alexander Bergin thinks that *Kālacakra* stands for attaining freedom from the external and internal cycle of time and existence. He writes, "The structure of the external and the internal cycles are analogous, similar to the parallel between macrocosm and microcosm discussed in Western philosophy. This means that the same laws that govern a universe also pertain to atoms, the body and our experience of life. The practices of the alternative cycles also follow this structure so as to allow us to engage with and surmount these forces in an efficient manner. Such mimicking is, in fact, one of the distinguishing features of the *Anuttarāyoga Tantra* technique."[45]

According to the theory of *Karma* life is unfolded according to *kārmic* potential from our past life. Our cycle of birth and death is governed by the metempsychosis (or *kārmic* potentiality). In *Kālacakra* system the cycles of birth and death is known as winds of *karma*. *Kārmic* potentiality manifests into spectrum of impulses, motivations, feelings and desires which control our life. Time has neither beginning nor, however, the spectrum of change would always be associated with the passage of time. The alternate cycles of time when one gets initiated into mystic practice of *Tantra* brings about spiritual change and transformation in one's life.

There has been a happy and harmonious blending of Hindu and the Buddhist systems of spiritual practices and thoughts. It is the result of that blending that lots of Hindu Deities have been incorporated in the *maṇḍala*s of *Śrī Kālacakra*. However, the *Kālacakra Tantra* is the culmination of *Vajrayāna*. It is why the *Śrī Kālacakra*, the supreme Godhood is philosophically and esoterically is of the same nature as the *Vajrasattva* which is found in different *Vajrayāna* texts. *Kālacakra* is the mystic unification of *Prajñā* and *Upāya*. The *Bodhicitta* is the ultimate reality, the supreme bliss, *Mahāsukha* which is without origination and destruction and is embodiment of supreme enlightenment. *Śrī*

Kālacakra is considered as supreme lord and creator of all the Buddhas and *Ādi Buddhas*. Hindu and Buddhist *Tantra* have given a great esoteric importance and significance to *bīja mantra*. The Vimala Prabhā has dealt with esoteric significance of this *mantra* while elucidating the concept of *Kālacakra*. According to Vimala Prabhā *ka* (stands for causality), *la* (stands for absorptions and dissolution), *ca* (signifies unstable mind) and *kra* (means cycle of changes and transformation).[46] According to all the non-dual philosophical system of *Tantra* and mysticism every man and woman is hibernated cosmic beings. The *summum bonum* of life to awaken the dormant divinity and realize the true and transcendental nature of one's real existence and being. *Tantra* considers body as the epitome of the macrocosm. The belief in the identity of microcosm and macrocosm is the basis of *Tantra Sādhanā*. The objective of the *Kālacakra* is to transcend the cycle of birth and death and attain Buddhahood. To transcend the cycle of birth and death one will have to go beyond the reach and the influence of time. It is in flow of *Prāṇavāyu*. Time reveals itself and if *Sādhanā* gets control over *prāṇavāyu* through the esoteric practice of meditation and *vipāsanā* he can have control over time (*kāla*) and he can attain the state of infinite bliss (*Mahāsukha*). *Tantra* considers the whole creation as the organic function of body. Body is the only medium through which one can attain *Nirvāṇa*. Some of the tāntric texts like *Śrī Kālacakratantra-rāja* identify the universe with the body and it locates seas, rivers, mountains and the planets in the different parts of the body. *Tantra* believes that there is an isomorphic relation between human body and the universe, between microcosm and macrocosm. The different letters and syllables of *kālacakra* signify definite mystic meanings; *ca* is the *bīja mantra* of effect (*Kārya Brahman*). *Kālachakra* stands for merger of the individual consciousness into the original cause-potency, which is *Śūnyatā,* i.e., the pure consciousness, the supreme subjectivity. Philosophically speaking, the first state in the process of esoteric practice is to identify the innately misconceived, *the I* as inherently existent. According to Śaṅkara's *Vedānta* bondage is erroneous identification of *I* (self) with non-self. Buddhism believes that there is no inherent existence except *Boddhicitta*. The *Brahma Jāla Sūtra* of *Dīgha Nikāya* considers all the speculations as dogmatism (*diṭṭhivāda*). The Buddha did examine and evaluate different doctrines of reality of his times and rejected all of them. The Buddha transcends the consciousness of the conflict in reason and resolves by rising above the domain of reason. This is dialectic. Buddha says, "To hold that the world is eternal or to hold that is not, or to agree to any other of the propositions you adduce, *Vācchā*, is the jungle of theorizing, the wilderness of theorising, the tangle of theorising, the bondage and the shackles of theorising, attended by ill, distress, perturbation and fever; it conduces not to detachment, passionless, tranquillity, peace, knowledge and wisdom of *Nirvāṇa*. This is the danger I perceive in these views which makes me discard them all."[47] The objective of *Kālacakra tantra* is to get mind free from all kinds of reifications. One who views reified status of the *I* inherent which is rooted in the erroneous belief of I as the real self. Chandrakṛtti rightly says that there is no self-other than the aggregate. Dalia Lama writes, "With such conviction, the decision reached is that the I cannot be found under such analysis; this shows, not that the I does not exist, but that it does not inherently exist as it was identified as seeming to it in the first essential. This infindability is emptiness itself, and realization of its realization of emptiness, selflessness."[48]

The mystic and the philosophical concept of *Kālacakra* have been enumerated by Abhinava Gupta in his monumental work *Tantrāloka*. There is great agreement and similarity between the teachings of *Tantrāloka* and *Śrī Kālacakra* on the point of spiritual significance of *Kālacakra*. Abhinava Gupta in his *Tantrāloka* has explained the doctrine of *kāla* (time) and the spiritual process of keeping one-self above the influence of cycle of time. Abhinava Gupta while enumerating the concept of time in all its dimension has dealt with the importance of *Prāṇa* and *Apāna* which are organically related with our nervous system. *Śrī Kālacakra Tantra* also expounds the same theory and doctrine for going beyond the realm of time for the attainment of enlightenment. *Tantrāloka* also deals with the yogic practice of controlling *prāṇa* and *apāna* for attaining control over *kāla* (time). The Vimala Prabhā a commentary on *Kālacakra* has also discussed in detail the esoteric and the philosophical importance of *Kālacakra Tantra*. According to this treatise Vimala Prabhā, *Śrī Kālacakra* is accepted as unity of *Śūnyatā* and *Karuṇā*. He is symbolised as *Prajñā* and *Upāya*. He is the ultimate and the primordial Buddha.

Vajrayāna, *Sahajayāna* and *Kālacakrayāna* are metaphysical and mystical schools of Buddhist *Tantra*. The different forms of Buddhist *Tantra* do not make any difference to man so long he is truly dedicated to the realization of the sublime and the incomprehensible *Kālacakra*. The mysticism of *Kālacakra* combines science and spirituality, knowledge and wisdom. The different schools of Buddhist *Tantra* are based on the esoteric and philosophical basis which represents the different phases of spiritual development and enlightenment.

Buddhism considers all sentient beings possessing potentiality and spiritual power to attain Buddhahood. The basic philosophical position of *Kālacakra Tantra* is based on *Mādhyamikā* doctrine of fundamental unity of *Nirvāṇa* and *saṁsāra*. Essential nature is inherent *Bodhicitta*. The *Nirvāṇa* is no different from *saṁsāra*. *Saṁsāra* consists in form, in feeling and other faculty of sense. But all these elements are really *Nirvāṇa* and *Bodhicitta*. Only because of illusion they appear as *saṁsāra*. From metaphysical and mystical point of view *saṁsāra* is really *Nirvāṇa*, and then all men are enlightened being. If all sentient beings are enlightened beings then why ever sentient beings have not experienced enlightenment. Metaphysically and mystically it is because of sentient beings are obscure by adventitious defilements and that is why they do not have the realization, that they are the Buddha. The chief objective of the Buddhist *Tantra* is to remove the veil of accidental defilements and with the removal adventitious impurity sentient beings experiences Buddhahood spontaneously. The objective of tāntric practice is to free sentient being from adventitious defilements which comes from wrong view of existence. D.L. Snellgrove writes, "The whole training consists in learning to conceive of existence in knowledge of its non-existence, and one will then automatically realize its true nature which is innate (*sahaja*) and a matter for self-experience (*svasaṁvedya*). But this can only be done by using existence itself as the means (*Upāya*) for there is no other possiblity. One creates mentally (*bhāvayati*) an idealized representation of the process of emanation of existence (*utpattikrama*), which is *saṁsāra*, and by realizing the dream like nature of its apparent diversity, one realizes its unity and this process of realization (*Saṁ panna akrama*) which is *Nirvāṇa*."[49]

Kālacakra is aimed at the attainment of spiritual illumination and enlightenment. It is a state of mystic and metaphysical monism. Both *Viśvamātā* and *Śakti* are inseparable from *Kālacakra* and Śiva. The apparent differences in esoteric techniques and practices are in keeping with the basic mystic necessity for working out the total realization of truth and reality. According to both systems *Sādhaka* enters into esoteric diagram which is known in Hindu *Tantra* as *Yantra* and Buddhist *Tantra* as *maṇḍala*. After taking purificatory bath *Sādhaka* worship deity. The *Sādhaka* considers himself as inalienable part of deity. The *Sādhaka* divinizes himself with incantation of *mantra*. He identifies with *mantra* assigning each part of the body to the corresponding letters of the alphabets according to esoteric arrangements of different *mantras*.

Kālacakra and Hindu, *Tantra* practice of *divyācāra* have great similarity. Both are profound and highest form of esotericism. *Divyācāra* aims at mystic unification of Śiva and Śakti which is considered as true *yoga*.[50] This is an esoteric meaning of coition (*maithuna*) in *Tantra*. Both according to *Kālacakra* and *divyācāra* body is considered as divine abode of deity. The incantation of different *mantra* is associated with techniques of invoking different deities. When the *mantras* are incanted according to the strict esoteric discipline, it gives the desire results as insect becomes a bee by the force of meditation so man becomes God by the attainment of spiritual trance or *Samādhi*.[51] Whole system of Hindu and Buddhist *Tantra* is based on this principle.

Tantra is a very difficult esoteric technique to attain Buddhahood. It is very risky form of mystic discipline. Everybody is not entitled to practice this highest form of *Tantra sādhanā*. A long list of qualification has been laid down by *Kālacakra Tantra* for getting initiation into this form of mystic practice. A person who is a prudent, pure, non-dualist abstaining from violence to all beings with senses control and who takes refuge in *Dharma*, *Buddha* and *Saṅgha* is competent for *Kālacakra Sādhanā*. The *Kulārṇava Tantra* of Hinduism also enumerates long list of qualification necessary for *Tantra Sādhanā*.[52] According to *Kulārṇava Tantra* the person who is heretic, boastful, impotent, wicked, dry, untrue, cruel, foolish, unreliable, plagiarist, passionate, garrulous, lividnous, egoist, coward, crooked, dull, weak, afflicted, ugly, inactive, thief is not entitled to practice *Tantra Sādhanā*.[53]

According to Buddhist *Tantra* the great degree of moral and spiritual discipline is necessary to follow the path of Buddhahood. The door of *Kālacakra Tantra* was never opened for all. *Tantra* was allowed to practice only for a few persons who were equipped with high degree of refinements and power. S.B. Dasgupta writes, "If *Yoga* and *Tantra* are made the common property of all, as it was made by the Buddhist of old, the whole routine of life is upset, and abuses of all tenets follow a matter of course. It is not necessary to state that this psychic culture appealed to men with striking force, particularly when the masters of *Tantra* could perform prodigious feats and miracles, and as such, in time of the *Siddhācāryas* the *Tantras* attracted almost every men without exception, and most of them must of necessity have had to be content with the shadow rather than the substance of *Tantra*. And, as a, matter a fact, owing to the great influence of *Tantras* in earlier days, even at the present time there are very few Hindus in India who are not following the Tāntric practices in some form or other."[54]

The Buddha himself is an exponent of *Tantra* as he was aware that dormant spiritual energy can be awakened only with the ideation and incantation of *mantra*. The incantation of *mantra* reveals the mystery of *Bhūmi* (consciousness) and awakens the dormant divinity which is known in Buddhist *Tantra* as *Herukā*, *Vajratārā*, *Vajrayoginī* and *Vajrachaṇḍikā*.

Pañcamakāra Sādhanā is practiced both in Hindu and Buddhist *Tantra*. It is an esoteric technique for the transformation and sublimation of baser instincts and tendencies to the higher experiences of *Bodhicitta*. The principle behind the *pañcamakāra Sādhanā* is that man must rise with the help of that *Śakti*, which, if misused will cause his fall. The scientific proposition is that the poison which kills can be transformed into elixir of life if it is properly treated by wise physicians. Man has to work out his own salvation, not by negating his desires and suppressing his baser instincts but by sublimating them into the higher form of spiritual life. In *Tantra Sādhanā* man and woman sublimate their corporeal existence and realize that they are the two manifestations of *Upāya* and *Prajñā*.

Buddhism is a philosophy of mind (*Citta Darśana*). *Theravāda* reduces the mind into the set of thoughts and feelings and seeks deliverance from nascence through detachment. On the other hand

Mahāyāna especially Buddhist *Tantra* considers mind as the seed of enlightenment and through esoteric practice one attains enlightenment. The goal of *Theravāda* is to attain eternal quiescence whereas the aim of *Mahāyāna* and *Tantra* is to transform mind into eternal emptiness. This eternal emptiness is called *Bodhicitta*. According to *Tantra Bodhicitta* can be experienced only through the practice of *mantra*, *maṇḍala* and *Herukā* (*kuṇḍalinī*). The practice of Buddhist esoterism leads to the highest form of spiritual perfection and experience and the infinite and eternal unity of *Prajñā* and *Upāya*. Science without spirituality has danger of making man a monster and spirituality without scientific temper makes a man inert and inactive. We are living in the best of times and at the same time we are living in the worst of times. If we fail to resolve the present crisis of civilizations created by misuse of scientific knowledge and power and lack of spiritual vision and commitment there will be inglorious end of a glorious civilization. The need of ours is to bring about the harmonious blending of science and spirituality, *yoga* and *tantra* between man and divinity.

Zen

Zen Buddhism is an ontological mysticism and intuitional science. It is based on the canonical literatures entitled *Laṅkāvatāra Sūtra*, *Prajñāpāramitā Sūtra, Bajra Chedikam Sūtra* and *Avatanaska Sūtra.* This is a branch of *Mahāyāna* Buddhism. According to Zen Buddhism all beings possess the Buddha nature (*Bodhicitta*). Buddha nature is called *Śūnya* or *Tathatā.* The realization of which is the central objective of Zen Buddhism. The *Śūnya* or *Bodhicitta* is known in Chinese as *Chih-mo* or *Shik-mo*. In Japanese the *Bodhi Citta* is known as *kno-mama* or *sono-mama*. The realization of this reality *Bodhicitta* is called *satori*. This state of enlightenment is a mystic experience of state of suchness which transcends all kinds of intellectual and moral considerations. This state of *satori* cannot be explained in terms of logic and language.

There are two views regarding the founder of Zen Buddhism. According to one school Śākyamuni is the founding father of Zen Buddhism. He transmitted this mystic experience and teachings to *Mahākaśyapa*. According to this school the Buddha himself has declared that he has transmitted his mystic power and knowledge of inner spirituality and esoteric mysticism to *Mahākaśyapa*. According to this tradition there are twenty eight patriarchs from Lord Buddha to *Bodhi Dharma* who are considered as the founding father of Zen Buddhism. The names of the patriarch are as follows:

1. Śākyamuni, 2. *Mahākaśśapa*, 3. Ānanda, 4. Savaṁsa, 5. Upāgupta, 6. Dhṛtaka, 7. Miśchaka, 8. Buddhanandī, 9. Bodhamitra, 10. Bhikkhu Pārśva, 11. Puṇyayasgas, 12. Aśvaghoṣa, 13. Bhikkhu Kapimale, 14. Nāgārjuna, 15. Kanadeva, 16. Ārya Rāhulata, 17. Saṅghanandī, 18. Saṅghayaśas, 19. Kumārata, 20. Jayata, 21. Vasubandhu, 22. Manura, 23. Haklenayasas, 24. Bhikkhu Simba, 25. Vaśaśta, 26. Puṇyamitra, 27. *Prajñātārā*, and 28. *Bodhidharma*.

Another school believes that the exponent of Zen Buddhism is *Bodhidharma*. *Bodhidharma* visited China in 520 A.D. and he for nine years meditated looking towards a wall at Shao-Lin-Su temple and after the attainment of *Satori* he transmitted this knowledge to his first Chinese student Hui-ko 468-593 A.D. who is acknowledged as the second patriarch of Zen Buddhism. The *Bodhidharma* practiced for uninterrupted nine years with crossed leg posture (*padmāsana*) and didn't waste any time in going through scriptural reading or practicing any kind of lifeless rituals. According to this school there are six patriarchs: 1. *Bodhidharma*, 2. *Hui-ko*, 3. *Seng-Ts'an*, 4. *Shing-Hsimming*, 5. *Houng-Zen*, and 6. *Hui-Neng*. *Hui-Neng* is called the second *Bodhidharma*. He is considered as the greatest Zen masters who provided the philosophical and spiritual background for this new school of Zen Buddhism during the T'ang dynasty of China. *Hui-Neng* died at the age of seventy-six in 712 A.D. and he was honoured with the robe of *Bodhidharma* by his teachers *Houng-Zen*. There is another controversy regarding the sixth patriarchs. According to this school there were only five patriarchs and after the demise of fifth patriarch the Zen Buddhism was splitted into two sect known as northern school founded by *Shen-Shui* and southern school founded by *Hui-Neng*.[55] Later on Zen Buddhism was divided and splitted into several sects which still exist in China and Japan.

However, the Soto school and Rinzai School became very famous. They are known as northern and southern schools. The basic difference between these schools is related with the nature of enlightenments and its methods.

The Zen derives its mystic and spiritual significance from the Sanskrit word *dhyāna* (meditation). The word *dhyāna* is known in Chinese Ch'an and in Japanese as Zen.

According to Soto school enlightenment is attained gradually. And the southern school believes that enlightenment is undifferentiated and attained spontaneously. This school does not give importance to the practice of rituals and scriptural knowledge. According to this school adopts iconoclastic veneration to the Buddha. The southern school employed mystic techniques as Koan to rid the mind from the familiar track of logical reasoning and creating an inner strength for meditative insight. However, Zen Buddhism is a harmonious and a happy blending of the moral teachings of Confucianism, the meditational practice of Taoism and the religious teachings and the rituals of Shintoism.This happy and harmonious blending of these new schools of Zen Buddhism with Confucianism, Taoism and Shintoism resulted into a vigorous and living religion which redefined the meaning of existence and life and it is a resurrection of man and births of a new socio-religious system within the framework of universal transcendental, philosophical and mystical thoughts. This new school is considered as a harbinger of cultural renaissance and reconstructions which captivated the imaginative and the progressive mind of China and Japan.

David L. Sells says, that "the most remarkable synthesis of Chinese and Indians values was achieved in the meditation school of Ch'an (Zen). While it was based on the auto soteriological principles of Yogīc action, its leadership developed a unique meditative technique, which stressed practical, non-discursive and naturalistic media for attaining enlightenment."[56]

Zen Buddhism provided a new vigour and revitalized the mutilated truth propagated by the religious dogmas and lifeless rituals and dry and orthodox philosophy divorced from social reality and relevant dynamic moral values. The function of philosophy and religion is to promote the art of life and to create a proper psychological, spiritual and moral ambience and background for creating a just society, peace and prosperity for mankind. The truth of philosophical and religious proposition is to be adjudged by their socio-cultural content and their pragmatic values.

Meditation has occupied a prominent and important place in all the schools of *Mahāyāna* Buddhism. The importance and over emphasis on meditation as special technique and doctrines with Taoist influence has emerged as Zen sect, generally considered specifically Chinese product.[57]

However, *Bodhidharma* introduced a new concept of two entrances and four deeds in the technique of *Dhyāna* which enriched the *Mahāyāna* mind, tranquillization. The *Encyclopaedia of Buddhism* says, "the first of the entrances, entrance by reason means (1) to receive the law from a Master and believe that all living things have the same true (Buddha), Nature (2) to meditate on this idea and by having and unshakable faith in it, became one with it, so that, the distinction between oneself and others as well as between the unenlightened man and the Buddha are eliminated, and (3) not to rely completely on the printed word, but to come naturally to truth and dwell peacefully and contently in it".[58]

The concept of meditation has been examined and interpreted in the different schools of Buddhism differently, but it has been accepted and adhered by all that it is an esoteric technique to get the mind free from all kinds of reification. However, the central objective of all schools of meditation to integrate the part with whole and in this process of esoteric unification *satori* is experienced. This mystic experience has been considered as an act of walking with no path, no walker and no goal. These apparent nonsensical statements contain great spiritual significations.

This mystic technique of meditation is a process of emptying oneself from all kinds of mental dispositions and defilements.

Koan

Koan is a mystical language formulated as a riddle pointing to the spiritual experience of awakening. Language is a symbol to express different levels of our experience. The introduction of *koan* is a mystic technique to throw the mind out of its familiar path of logical ratiocination to start the process of emptying it from all kinds of metempsychosis. Mystic experience cannot be explained in ordinary language and logic. For example there is a popular Zen metaphor to show that when someone points out with his finger towards the moon her child sometimes identifies the finger with the moon and he does not comprehend the moon. We also commit the same kind of metaphysical misunderstanding by identifying wrongly ourselves with non-self-known as *pañcakkhaṇḍa* (five aggregrates), i.e., a *rūpa* (corporality), *Vedanā (*feelings*), Saṁjñā* (perception), *Saṁskāra* (mental formation) and *Vijñāna* (consciousness) and fail to know *I* as a part of suchness. Everything is reality; there is not a speck of dust outside the realm of *Bodhicitta*. No scission exists between the phenomenal world and pure essence. There is no difference between *nirvāṇa* and *saṁsāra*. *nirvāṇa* is *saṁsāra* and *saṁsāra* is *nirvāṇa*. Difference lies in our perspective. The use of *koan* is to overcome the riddle of I and world, *nirvāṇa* and *saṁsāra*. It is a mystic technique of unification of *nirvāṇa* and *saṁsāra* which is beyond the reach of any language and thought. So long we live in the world of dualism or subject and object we get used to play the language game. But when one enters into the world of essence after getting free from delusion one becomes aware of the vibrant mystic awareness of living truth. The use of *koan* has been a common tradition of question and answer session between the teacher and disciple. This question and session is called *mondo* in Japanese. To rid the bondaged being from delusion and ignorance to the state of mystic experience is the whole purpose behind the puzzlement and perplexity created by *koan*. D.T. Suzuki says: "on examination we at once notice that there is no room in the *koan* to insert and intellectual interpretation. The knife is not sharp enough to cut the *koan* open and see what are its contents. For a *koan* is not a logical proposition, but the expression of a certain mental state resulting from the Zen discipline."[59]

Koan is a mystical device to unfold the meaninglessness of philosophical polemic and to show that the ultimate reality and the truth of life transcend the domain of mind and senses.

Zen Buddhism is not a philosophical theory or a school. It is an esoteric experience which unfolds the real meaning and truth. It is not based on dialectical method of attaining knowledge. Koan is a mystic experience of uncouth and transcendental reality. This is a path of divinization of man. It is the path of becoming. Koan is not a meditation of any kind of intellectualism but it is uncouth experience of Buddha nature that is the whole truth and whole cosmos. It is an esoteric transformation of mind which culminates in the birth of new consciousness and a new experience of *Bodhi* mind. The purpose of *koan* is to liberate the mind from the sneers of false subjectivity. The apparent enigmatic nature and the subject matter of *koan* have been structured to rid the practicener from naissance so that he can realize the reality. From the positivistic point of view the *koan* is nonsensical utterances. But from the mystical point of view the *koan* is full of esoteric meaning because the mystic experiences are not noetic. The mystic experience requires its expression in form of *koan* because it comes from the innermost depth of being and existence. This is why in all mystical traditions and philosophy the highest truth has been explained with the help of metaphors, symbols and allegories. The practice of *koan* is to prepare the practicener for the experience of oneness with the Buddha nature. Buddha nature is the quint essence of one's own being and existence. It is because of the delusion and false identification with the non-self, one does not get the real experience of being which is a state of *satori*.

The birth of *koan* practice speaks of the spiritual growth of Zen Buddhism into a living religion. The state of Buddha nature is a state of thoughtlessness and nothingness (*wu-yu*). The practice of *koan* has a close relation with the practice of *Nembutsu*. *Nembutsu* is an esoteric technique of incantation of Amita Buddha. This incantation is like the incantation of *bīja mantra* in tāntric tradition. The *Nembutsu* has been related with the founding of the lotus society. D.T. Suzuki says, that "the Chinese Buddhism has been developed along the two traditions of Zen and *Nembutsu*."

Koan and the Mondo are core concept of Zen Buddhism. Mondo is popularly known as question and answer session between the Zen masters and their disciples. This dialogue between the masters and the student disciples is to awaken the dormant divinity and intuitive mind. The subject matter of Mondo are related with the day to day experiences of life. For ordinary people these Mondo's are nonsensical and, but for those who have been initiated in the mystic practice of Zen these *Mondos* are pregnant with profound philosophical and sublime esoteric signification.

According to Zen Buddhism this is the most effective technique to awaken *Prajñā* (wisdom). However, there is a great difference between the Mondo and the Socratic dialogue. The dialogue is based on the dialectical method which leads to scepticism in the undeniable. In the first the purpose of dialogue is to root out the very foundation of monolithic character of rational truth and in the process of dialectic reasoning the seed of new truth is sown. Its movement is in the form of thesis, anti-thesis and synthesis. In the process of second phase the dialectical reasoning the synthesis becomes the thesis which gives rise to a new anti-thesis and new synthesis. This is an endless process which depicts that the ultimate truth is beyond the dialectical reasoning. The dialectical reasoning unfolds and reveals the antinomical character of the reason. Whereas the Mondo is a mystic method to empty the mind from all kinds of defilements and delusions. Master is conversant with the disciple's progress of his spiritualization which comes out of the mental puzzlement and crisis. This is the purpose of *koan* practice. Christians Humphreys writes, "But the *koan* system has its dangers. In the absence of a highly qualified and trained Roshi to assist the pupil there is no one to say when he is on or off the beam in his endeavours, and none to say when he has genuinely 'solved' his *koan*. More important, there is no one to protect him from raising head of steam as one student calls it that without very experienced guidance the whole mind may crack, meaning temporary or permanent insanity."[60]

The Koan and Mondo has been employed to break the barriers of thoughts and reason, so that, one can awaken one's own *Prajñā* (intuition). This was the practice for meditation for days and months sitting in cross leg postures which are called Zazen.

The Zen master is called Roshi. One of the Roshi was very closely watching his disciple who was doing meditation but Roshi saw that disciple was practicing meditation without understanding the proper process of meditative insight and it was a waste of time for the disciple. He inquired from his disciple, "What are you seeking in this way?" The disciple answered, "To become Buddha". Roshi started polishing a stone with the piece of a brick. The disciple was astonished and asked from his teacher "What are you doing sir?" The Roshi replied "Making a mirror." Disciple stated that "You could not make a mirror by polishing a brick." Roshi answered that "no amount of sitting cross leg would make you Buddha." This speaks of the esoteric aspects of meditation unless a disciple practice meditation under the strict guidance of a proper teacher; he or she would not attain the desirable result of awakening *Prajñā*. This process of awakening dormant divinity is known in

Tantra as awakening of serpentine power (*Kuṇḍalinī Śakti*). D.T. Suzuki says, "The problem of *Prajñā*, which constitutes the essence of Buddhist philosophy is really inexhaustible, and no amount of talk seems to suffice. I will give some more *mondo* here and indicate the trend of thought underlying them. Until the relation between *Vijñāna* and *Prajñā*, or that between *Prajñā*-intuition and *Vajñāna* reasoning, is thoroughly understood, such ideas as *Śūnyatā* (emptiness), *tathatā* (suchness), *mokṣa* (emancipation), *Nirvāṇa* and others will not be fully observed as living ideas."[61]

The transmission of spiritual knowledge from Zen master to disciple is called *Śaktipata* in Indian tradition. This transmission of light is esoteric technique to impart spiritual power for the awakening of inner spirituality. This imparts in the spiritual instructions through the metaphors and symbols are known as *Sandhyā Bhāṣā* (twilight language) in India and Koan in China and Japan. The practice of meditation and *koan* forms the foundation for the transmission of mystic knowledge and power from teacher to disciple. This transmission of knowledge is living tradition in Japanese school of Zen Buddhism even today. The person who has spiritual power and knowledge are declared as Roshi. The Roshi is only master entitled to guide the disciple in experiencing the awakening of inner being and dormant divinity through the technique of *koan*. The Zen disciple in the period of *Tang* and early Sung dynasty recorded some of the profound religious teachings of Zen masters which are in the form of *koan*. On the basis of the collection of these *koans* some of the *Mahāyāna sūtras* have been enumerated in the form of the biographies of Zen masters. Rout Fuller says that "these *koan* and stories contain seed-words or the phrases, the master had uttered". These seed words is known as *bīja mantra* in tāntric tradition.

The Zen master accepts disciples only after proper screening and ascertaining the merits and the eligibility of disciples deserving to be imparted the lessons on *koan*.

Satori

Spiritual enlightenment or *Nirvāṇa* is known as *satori* in Zen Buddhism. It is a state of experience of the whole truth and consciousness. It is a spiritual realization of one's own being and existence in totality. D.T. Suzuki says, "The knowledge contains in *Satori* is concerned with something universal and at the same time with the individual aspect of existence."[62]

According to *Mahāyāna satori* is a complete emptiness and total elimination of the feeling of selfness. The Buddha defines this state of enlightenment as immortal (*Amala Dhātu*) because it is the only reality that does not undergo any change and metamorphosis. It transcends the cycle of birth and death. It is immortal because it is free from all cravings (*lobha*), aversion (*doṣa*) and attachment (*moha*). In this state there is no trace of cravings as it is free from the feelings of I-ness which results into clinging to selfhood.

However, there are two kinds of *satori* according to Buddhism: (1) *So-padisess-Nibbāna-Dhātu*, (2) *Anupediśeṣa-Nibbāna-Dhātu*. *So-padisess-Nibbāna-Dhātu* stands for a person who has attained enlightenment, but he is not free from complete annihilation of his metempsychosis (*saṁskāra*). His residual *kamma* still exists as an individualized person which subjects him to undergo suffering. *Anupediśeṣa-Nibbāna-Dhātu* stands for the total and final liberation from the cycle of birth and death. A man doesn't have any chance of going through the wheel of re-birth because he has consumed all the aggregates (*saṁskāra*). This state of liberation abolishes the false distinctions between *saṁsāra* and *Nirvāṇa*. According to Zen Buddhism reality is non-dual. This state of bliss and beatitude is incommunicable and indescribable. In the philosophical terminology *satori* is indeterminate and hence, it cannot be equated with any state of consciousness. It is a transcendental life of inner accesses. It is neither ens (*bhāva*) or non-ens (*abhāva*) nor both nor neither. *Satori* does not have any cosmological activities and function. The concept of transcendental nature of *satori* emanates from the concept of *Prajñāpāramitā*. The theocratic philosophical teachings of Zen Buddhism are evident in seed form in the teachings of the Buddha. However, the Buddhism had undergone great change and metamorphosis required by the socio-cultural determinants of people when it took root in the religious milieu of different people. The every school of Buddhism developed during the different periods of time in history claimed themselves as the real teachings of the Buddha. *Nirvāṇa* is the root concept of Buddhism. The different schools have interpreted this state of *Nirvāṇa* in a different way. The mystic experience of Buddha nature is *satori* which is the result of a long and rigorous practice of *koan* and meditation.

This state of oneness and non-dual is beyond the categories of existence, non-existence, both or neither. The Wu-men-*koan* authored by Hui-kai 1183-1260, is one of the authentic and important treatises of Zen Buddhism. Forty eight events have been enumerated in this book. This book became very famous in the latter part of Shung dynasty in China. It is said that "Hui-kai attained *satori* by practicing *WU*." The first story narrated by Hui-kai of a monk who approached Chao-Chou for Zen practice. The monk inquired "Is the dog endowed with the Buddha nature?" Chao-Chou replied "'WU', it is a pathless path, gateless gate that takes one to attainment of *Nirvāṇa*." According to this method of meditation when one practices *WU*, he attains state of oneness. When one attains this state of oneness he does not need to be told because it is a mystic experience which could not be expressed. The central objective of the teachings of the Buddha is to root out all your cravings. It has been metamorphically stated that when you are trying to cross the sea of existence, i.e., the cycle of birth and death, let not the water percolate in your life boat. If there is any water which has percolated; you must drain out.[63]

It is the cravings which bind you with the cycle of birth and death and you are lost in the sea of sufferings. The practice of WU liberates one from all kinds of cravings and results into the state of no mind. This state of no mind is the state of oneness and *satori*. It is a state of mental equipoise and absolute calmness. D.T. Suzuki compares this oneness or the practice of WU with a dream of dumb. A dumb person is conscious and knows about the content of his dreams, but he is not been able to communicate it to others.[64]

The Zen Buddhism is rooted in the world of facts and reality. It doesn't encourage anyone to renounce the phenomenal world. Even a blade of grass symbolizes Buddha nature. It considers the whole world as it is in its palm. However, some thinkers have equated Zen as a religious form of pantheism. But if we dive deep into the mystical teachings of Zen it is not pantheistic as the Christianity and other form of sematic religion claims to be. I would like to illustrate the dialogue between *Ummon* (Yun-men) and his disciple. It is as follows:

Monk : "What is the Pure Body of the *Dharma*?"

Master : "The hedgerow"
Monk : "What is the behaviour of the one who thus understand?"
Master : "He is a golden-haired lion".

Here the metaphor of the Pure body of the *Dharma* with Hedgerow conveys a sense of pantheism but any explanation of golden-haired lion would explain the mystical symbol used in this metaphor. I would like to quote another Zen *mondo* for throwing some light on the enigmatic nature of the practice of *koan* and *mondo*. It is as follows:

Monk : "I understand that, when a lion seizes upon in opponents whether it is a hare or an elephant, he makes tremendous use of his power—pray tell me what this power is."
Master : "The spirit of sincerity (literally) the power of not deceiving him."[65]

As per the Rinzai school, the golden-haired lion stands for a person who lives the life of sincerity, virility and divinity through the practice of *koan* and *mondo*. To talk in the language of existentialism man who lives the authentic existence because he becomes reality itself. This process of understanding nature and reality demonstrates the Zen love of nature. The Zen does not pronounce polytheism. However, Zen believes each and every individual is an epitome of reality. Each individual is *Bodhicitta*. Everybody is organically related to the other individual. This infinite organic and inter-relationship is the basis of the concept of *Śūnyatā*.

This root concept of reality speaks of the love of nature. The love of nature in Zen is to live and experience the pulsating vibration of the principle of existence and being, i.e., *Bodhicitta*. The Zen concept of aesthetic and love of nature is based on Zen spirituality.

Zen Buddhism was rooted in the cultural life of China because of its down to earth philosophy. In the beginning Buddhism didn't get rooted in the Chinese minds because Chinese had natural dislike for the monks who didn't work for their livelihood and they didn't go for marriage. However, the sublime teachings of Buddhist scriptures especially *Prajñāpāramitā Sūtra*, *Laṅkā Avatāra Sūtra*, *Mādhyamikākārikā* of Nāgārjuna, *Avidhammakośa* of Vasuvandhu and *Avanasaka Sūtra* were made great impact on the creative mind of Chinese. In sixteenth century there were many schools of Buddhism in China which became the cause of great conflict and opposition by the students of Lao Tzu and Confucius. It was *Bodhi dharma* who created a revolution by his spiritual wisdom and mystical power. The then emperor of China in sixth century A.D. was greatly impressed by *Bodhidharma*'s personality and his mystic teachings. He was instrumental in exposing the uselessness of lifeless rituals of religions. *Bodhidharma* stated to the emperor that emptiness is the essence of everything and he decimated the spiritual knowledge to his students saying that each one of us are possessed with Buddhahood and the essence of Buddha mind. The quint essential teachings of Zen Buddhism could be stated as such.

"A Special transmission outside the scriptures,
Not depending upon the letters,
But pointing directly to the mind,
And leading us to see into the Nature itself,
Thereby making us attain Buddhahood".

Zen Buddhism is not a religio-philosophical system; it is a mystic and tāntric tradition. It does not give any importance to philosophical abstractions and conceptualization. It is abhorrent to rational indulgence of religious scriptures. Its approach is direct, integral and total experience of *Bodhicitta*. Its central objective is to rid the mind from the quagmires of moralism because the philosophical and the moral inquiries do not lead to enlightenment. The great patriarch of Southern School of Zen says "Do not think of Good. Do not think of Evil; but look at this very moment upon your original physiognomy, the one which you had even before you were born".

The Buddha before starting his historic meditation under the *Bodhi* tree took a vow for attaining enlightenment or getting himself destroyed. He had received many intellectual discourse and dialogue with the so called teachers and scholars but he couldn't realize the truth. After examining and evaluating the different scriptural teachings he felt that suffering, the impermanence of all things and beings and the continual change and flux of his thought were the only reality on which he established his philosophical system. His inner awareness of the pulsating thought and the process of life revealed the illusion of *I-ness*. After the attainment of enlightenment, Buddha declared that *Nirvāṇa* is the cessation of all suffering. Suffering is rooted in ignorance. To get rid from the wheel of birth and death one must pay full attention to the day to day fact of life. The total attention to day to day facts of life is a state of non-mental observation. Thus, Zen Buddhism is a harmonious blending of science and spirituality. It is a unique spiritual and esoteric system to harmonize the world of inner being with the world of nature. Robert Linssen rightly observes that, "Buddhism is a dialectical pragmatism of psychological and non-mental nature".[66]

Zen Buddhism is philosophy of homogeneity of reality and disappearance of all forms of dualism of subject and object, I and the world, *Saṁsāra* and the *Nirvāṇa*. Zen Buddhism believes that reality is a living truth and is a state of pulsation with wisdom and bliss. It is sudden and spontaneous realization of the Buddha nature. One cannot realize the Buddha nature or the cosmic consciousness in its totality and infinity with the measurement of time and space which are the appearance of reality.

One can realize reality only after transcending the boundaries of time, space and causation. One cannot see light by means of darkness. *Satori* is a state which is free from all kinds of false value and conditionality which are the breeding ground of the notion of darkness. Zen Buddhism is esoteric technique of meditation to destroy all kinds of conditionality and I-ness so that we can attain *satori*. D.T. Suzuki writes, "The Buddha was not the mere discoverer of the Twelvefold Chain of causation, he took the chain in his hands and broke it into pieces, so that, it would never again bind him to slavery".[67]

Zen Buddhism has incorporated the elements of naturalistic mysticism of Taoism and down to earth philosophy of Confucianism. The Buddha nature and the Tao stand for same truth and reality but speak in different language. Zen Buddhism was also very much embraced the Taoist concept of nature. However, it is development of the root concepts of Buddhism propounded by its founder the Buddha. Fritjof Capra observes, "Zen Buddhism is thus a unique blend of the philosophies and idiosyncrasies of three different cultures. It is a way of life which is typically Japanese, and yet it reflects the mysticism of India, the Taoist' love of naturalness and spontaneity and the thorough pragmatism of the Confucian mind."[68]

In Japan, Zen Buddhism transformed the life and culture of people. Japanese Shintoism has incorporated the teachings of Confucianism, Taoism and Buddhism. Confucianism was first to take root in Japan in fifth century A.D. and by seventh century it became part of cultural milieu. Under the influence of Confucianism centralization of political power became as a national cult. The different clans and classes were combined and organized into Japanese mythology in form of an emperor. The *kami* imperial house and tutelary of clans symbolize the *kami* of Japanese nation.

The spiritual humanism profound philosophy and naturalistic ethics of Buddhism were incorporated in Japanese culture. It became part and parcel of their cultural life. Buddhism became almost a state religion of Japan. Buddhism reached Japan in 538 A.D. and eighth century A.D. Buddhism and Shintoism became one and inseparable part of Japanese religious life and culture.

According to the *Encyclopaedia of Britannica*: "After 1192 during the *Kamakura*, theories of Shinto Buddhist amalgamation were established. Two representative examples of such amalgamation were Shintogon Shinto and Tendai-shinto. According to Shin-gon-shinto also known as Ryobu ("Two aspects") Shinto the principle source of whole universe was considered to be the cosmic Buddha. *Mahā-vairocana* also called *Iehi-Jitsu* ("One Reality). Shinto only the Buddha-nature was the source of all things. These two sects also brought various Buddhist rituals of all esoteric nature into Shinto. Buddhistic Shinto was popular for several centuries and influences the majority of Shinto shrines until its extinction at the Meiji Restoration".[69]

According to Shintoism man is a child of *kami*. Being the child of *kami* the life of a man is sacred. It further stands for the respect that enjoys every human being regardless of race, colour and nationality. Man is possessed with divine nature. There is no concept of original sin of sematic religions. However, Shintoism does not have the mystic technique to remove the impurities of soul for the attainment of enlightenment. The Shintoism was greatly influenced by the anthromorphic concept of God. The concept of *Karuṇā* captivated the minds of Japanese. Amitābha Buddha became the religious cult and culture of Japan. There is no concept of future life in Shintoism. The future life and the symbol of Amitābha Buddha as *Karuṇā* captivated the creativity and the imagination of Japanese people and eleventh and the twelfth century Buddhism was firmly rooted in Japanese culture. However, this is era, it is considered by some historians as an age of decadence for Buddhism in Japan because of the different and divergent philosophical schools and sects. The Zen Buddhism revitalized the spiritual and the religious life of Japan with the introduction of new mystic technique of meditation. The emphasis of Zen Buddhism on meditation and rejection is of scriptural teachings and renunciation from the religious and spiritual life.

The only methods for enlightenment were discovered as essential Buddha nature with which every man is endowed. Zen Buddhism became the social reality and mystic experience because it went into the deeper source of life divine. The concept of Buddha mind is in consonance with the concrete living realities of the world and is not a philosophical abstractions and conceptualization of speculative minds. Thus, Zen Buddhism is rooted into the facts and experience.

The Zen love for nature is an article of faith. It introduced a new concept of natural farming which is based on the concept that form is emptiness and emptiness is form. This is a non-discriminating knowledge. The non-discriminating knowledge became the basis of do-nothing farming.

Fukuoka has formulated four principles of his do-nothing farming, which is based on his empirical study and experience. He summarizes his philosophy in the following way:

1. No cultivation or turning of the soil.
2. Do not use fertiliser or prepared compost.
3. Do not weed out either by tillage or herbicides.
4. Do not depend on chemical for pest control.

Natural farming is closely related with natural life.

The concept of *Bodhicitta* for emptiness (*Śūnyatā*) is not concept; it is a mystic experience which binds man with the nature.

This living experience becomes the philosophical basis of love of nature.

The Zen method of love of nature is to eliminate all the barriers between man and nature. The transparency means to clean the mirrors of mind, so that, one can experience the beauty reflected in one's own consciousness. There is an innate aesthetic sensibility or beauty and grace according to Zen Buddhism. The Zen Buddhism provides the philosophical and the spiritual basis for the innate experience of nature. The teaching of Zen is instrumental in the refinement of aesthetic sensibility. This refinement of sensibility exalted and sublimated the sensibility into moral discipline and mystic experience. To make it evident and clear I would like to quote a few lines from Ryokwan a Zen monk. He was living in a solitary retreat on a mountain away from the modern life of crowd. He was a great mystic poet. His solitude was broken by a burglar. However, when the burglar entered into his house he was greatly disappointed because there was nothing worth to be stolen. The Ryokwan was moved by the burglar's disappointment. Burglar left the Ryokwan's room and he was amazed to see the bright light which was coming from the moon into Ryokwan's room. This soothing light of moon awakened the inherent sensibility of the burglar and he wrote:

"A Burglar failing to carry off the moon,
It shines in from the window
Where, I wonder, is he passing the night?
This cold freezing night,
When it is even beginning to storm—
a lonely wayfarer in a world of darkness?"

The modern minds confronts with difficulty in accepting the ontological mysticism because it is based on the experience which can be revealed, felt and lived but cannot be put into words. Only the knowledge and thoughts which are experienced in our day to day life can be expressed in logic and language. However, on the basis of limitation of thoughts and language we cannot doubt the existence of transcendental spiritual reality. The structure of language reveals that there is truth which is sayable and unsayable.

In the words of Wittgenstein what is unsayable we must consign to silence.

The practice of *koan* as a meditational technique to throw the mind of its familiar track of logical reasoning was employed to empty the mind from all kinds of disposition and metempsychosis. The mystical technique of *koan* was devised to transmit the real truth and wisdom through the riddles. The intellectual puzzlement and perplexity created by the practice of *koan* was spiritual necessity to pave the path for enlightenment. It is a normal practice in Zen tradition to create crisis and restlessness in the minds of the disciples to awaken the inner being and divinity which alone can lead one to the realization of *satori*.

Like Indian spiritual tradition Zen master also imparted mystical instructions through transmission of light which is called *Śaktipata* in Indian tradition. The place of teachers is of paramount importance in the mystic traditions of the world. The Zen Buddhism has been accepted both by east and west because scientism and empty natural rhythms are destroying the very inner harmony of our being and existence and nature. Modern man is losing his essential nature and reality slowly and gradually in the process of higher form of civilized life. It is destroying the very natural richness and inner harmony inherent in every living being. Zen Buddhism is based on the philosophy of conformity of life with the rhythm and pulsating living vibrations of nature. The practice of meditation not only leads to spiritual enlightenment, but it also has a soothing effect to our nervous system. It is a psychological and scientific aid to our moral health.

Zen Buddhism is both a sublime form of philosophy, spirituality and scientific way of life to transformation and transfiguration. It is not an institutionalized religion; it is an art of living. It is a way of life. It is a technique to integrate the fragmented and the alienated life of man. It is spiritual process of integrating the part with the whole and man with cosmos. This concept of mystic oneness is the quint essence of teachings of the Buddha. Zen takes life as a whole. It takes the truth in its totality. It takes reality into absolutism. This process of spiritualization through the Zen is a spiritual and scientific transfiguration which makes one to realize that every single moment of life is full of grace, lyricism, spontaneity and significance.

Zen Buddhism became a living philosophical tradition because of its profound metaphysical, moral and mystical foundation. The Buddhist concept of purgatory created a great impact on Chinese creative and religious minds. The three schools of religions were ultimately culminated into one thought and practiced as Zen Buddhism. Zen Buddhism was accepted by the Chinese masses and elites because it has been free from the aliened characters of foreign religion. The Confucianism paved the moral path by widening the mental horizon of Chinese minds because of the philosophical sublimity and spiritual profundity of Buddhism. The Confucianism became a catalytic agent for the acceptance and assimilation of Buddhism into Chinese culture and civilization. Zen Buddhism provided the creative mind of China, a mystic technique to divinize life and attain *satori*. The concept of *Partita Samudapād* and *Nirvāṇa* stirred the Chinese creativity and they have been left with no other choice than to accept Zen Buddhism as a way of life, a way of deliverance and as a way of *satori* to make life richer and fuller. The Zen Buddhist mystical practice of meditation provided spiritual anchor for every man.

The mystical experience of Zen Buddhism is the experience of *satori*. This experience takes man beyond the dualism of subject and object. It doesn't believe in any religious scriptures or philosophical doctrines. It is a freedom from all kinds of denominational teachings and institutionalized religions. However, Zen is based on the original teachings of the Buddha; according to him, *summum bonum* of life is the attainment of *Nirvāṇa*. This is considered as the *summum bonum* of all philosophical schools of oriental traditions because all the oriental traditions are based on spirituality, science and ontological mysticism.

References

1. *The Fundamental Wisdom of the Middle Way*. Nāgārjuna's *Mūlamādhyamikākārikā*, Translation and Commentary by Jay L. Garfield, New York, Oxford University Press, 1995, p. 94.
2. *Ibid.*, p. 16.
3. *Indian Philosophy*, S. Radhakrishnan, Volume 1, Oxford University Press, 1999, p. 375.

4. *The Central Philosophy of Buddhism,* T.R.V. Murti, George Allen & Unwin Ltd., 1960, Ruskin House, Museum Street, London, p. 214.
5. *The Fundamental Wisdom of the Middle Way,* Nāgārjuna's *Mūlamādhyamikākārikā,* Translation and Commentary by Jay L. Garfield. New York, Oxford University Press, 1995, p. 220.
6. *Ethics by Spinoza.* J.M. Dent & Sons Ltd., London, 1989, Everyman's Library, p. 3.
7. *Ibid.,* part 1, Prop. 15.
8. Prof. G.C. Pande. *Studies in Mahāyāna,* Central Institute of Higher Tibetan Studies, Saranath, Varanasi, 1993, p. 45.
9. *Ibid.,* p. 39.
10. *Signification in Language and Culture,* H.S. Gill, 2005, p. 5.
11. *Ibid.,* p. 6.
12. *The Buddhist Philosophy of Universal Flux,* Satkari Mookherjee, Motilal Banarsidass Publishers, Delhi, 2006, p. 139.
13. *On Indian Mahāyāna Buddhism,* D.T. Suzuki, p. 122.
14. *The Tao of Physics,* Fritjof Capra, p. 89.
15. *The Central Philosophy of Buddhism,* T.R. Murti, pp. 142-143.
16. *Principles of Philosophy.*
17. *The Essence of Buddhism,* D.T. Suzuki, p. 18.
18. *Buddhist Tantra: A Philosophical Reflection and Religious Investigation,* Lalan Prasad Singh, p. 140.
19. *Mind and Matter,* Erwin Schrodinger, Cambridge: Cambridge University Press, 1958, p. 1.
20. T.R.V. Murti, *The Central Philosophy of Buddhism,* George Allen & Unwin Ltd., 1960, p. 49.
21. *Ye nayar na vijayanti vibhāgain satyayor dvayoḥ; tetatvaiṁ na vijayanti gambhiraṁ Buddha-śāsane, MK.* XXIV. 9.
22. *Mādhyamikākārikās of Nāgārjuna.* Ed. by L. de La V. Roussin (Bub. Budd. IV), XXV.9.
23. *Prajñāpāramitā Piṇḍārtha tacchabdyyam Nirdesa* of *Diṅnāga,* quoted in Haribhadra's *Abhisamayalaṅkāraloka* twice, pp. 28, 153.
24. *Guhya Samāja Tantra,* p. 11. Oriental Institute, Baroda, 1931,

अभावे भावना भावो भावना नैव।

इति भावो न भावाः स्यात् भावनानोपलभ्यते।।

25. 'A Tibetan Account of Nāgārjuna' an article by S.C. Sarkar in the *Sino-Indian Journal,* December, 1948.
26. *Lalitavistara,* edited by Rajender Lal Mitra, p. 315.
27. *Book of East,* Volume XX, p. 9.
28. *Their Chandu* (will), *Viriyam* (effort), *Cittam* (thought), *Bimalsa* (investigation), *CRC Childers Dictionary of Pāli Language,* p. 157.
29. *The Cultural Heritage of India,* Volume 4th, Ramkrishna Mission Institute of Culture, p. 260.
30. *Tantra: Its Mystic and Scientific Basis,* Lalan Prasad Singh, Concept Publishing Company, New Delhi, 1987, p. 37.

31. *Cultural History of India*, Volume 1, p. 530.
32. *Journal of Asiatic Society of Bengal* (1883), 11, pp. 57 ff.
33. *An Introduction to Tantric Buddhism*, S.B. Dasgupta, University of Calcutta, 1958. p. 58.
34. Lama Angarika Govind in an article on *Mantra in the Stepping Stones*, Vol. II, No. I, published from Kalimpong. p. 21, Sl. 40. *The Central Philosophy of Buddhism*. p. 64, T.R.V. Murty.
35. *Studies in Tantra*, Dr. P.C. Bagchi.
36. न कष्ट कल्पनां कुर्यात्नोपवासी न च क्रियाम् ।

    त्रानं शैचं न चैवात्रग्रामधर्मविवर्जनम् ।।

    न चापि वन्दयेछेवान काष्ठपाषाणमृण्मयाम् ।

    पूजामस्यैव कायस्य कुर्यान्नित्यं समाहितः।।
37. *Mādhyamikāvṛtti* (La Vallu Poussin'a edition), p. 2.
38. *Bhāratīya Saṁskṛti aur Sādhanā*, p. 426.
39. *An Introduction to Buddhist Tantra*, S.B. Dasgupta, p. 173.
40. *Encyclopaedia of Indian Literature*, Vol. V. Sahitya Akademi, New Delhi, p. 4093.
41. *Sanātana Sādhanā Kī Gupta Dhārā*, Vishvavidyalaya Prakashan, Varanasi, II edition, 2002. p. 61.
42. *The Cultural of Heritage of India*, Vol. IV, p. 271.
43. *Ibid.*, p. 271.
44. *Philosophy of Gorakh Nath*, Prepatory note, p. XXVI.
45. *Taking the Kālacakra Initiation*, Alexander Berzin, Snow Lion Publication, Ithaca, New York, 1997, p. 27.
46. *Śrī Kālacakratantra-Raja*. Biswanath Banerjee, Published 1985, rept. 1993, New Asia Printers, Calcutta, p. XIII.

    काकरात् कारणे शान्ते लकाराच्चलयोऽत्रवै।

    चकाराच्चलचित्रस्य क्रकारात क्रमबधनात्।।

    कालोऽसरसुखं ज्ञानमुपायः करुणात्मकः।

    ज्ञेयाकारं त्रगच्चक्रं श्री प्रज्ञाशून्यतात्मिकता।

    करुणाशून्यतामूर्तिः कालशूंवृत्तिरूपिनी।

    शून्यताचक्रमिव्युक्तं कालचक्रोऽदयोमतः।।
47. *Majjhima Nikāya*, Translated by Chalmon, pp. 495-496.
48. *Kālacakra Tantra*, Rite of Imitation, p. 57.
49. *The Hevajra Tantra: A Critical Study*, by D.L. Snellgrove, Part I, Introduction and translation, London Oriental Series, Oxford University Press, London, 1959, p. 22.
50. *Śakti* and *Śākta*, p. 607.
51. *Ibid.*, p. 238.
52. *Tantra Sādhanā*, Chapter XIII.

53. *Ibid.*, pp. 293-294.
54. *An Introduction to Buddhist Esoterism*, p. 168.
55. *Encyclopaedia Britannica*, p. 386.
56. *International Encyclopaedia of Social Sciences*, Vol. I, p. 178.
57. *The New Encyclopaedia Britannica*, Vol. 3, by Encyclopaedia Britannica Inc. 1976, U.S.A., p. 386.
58. *Encyclopaedia of Buddhism*, Vol. III, by G.P. Malalasekera, 1972 Published by the Government of Sri Lanka, Government Press, Cylon, p. 194.
59. *Essays in Zen Buddhism* (Second Series), D.T. Suzuki, Buddhist Society, London, Rider & Company, 1950, p. 87.
60. *Zen: A Way of Life*, p. 112.
61. *Studies in Zen*, D.T. Suzuki, Buddhist Society, Rider-London, Second Impression, 1957, p. 107.
62. *Essays in Zen Buddhism*, Vol. II, p. 39.
63. *Dhammapada, Yamakavagga*, 12, verse.
64. *Essays in Zen Buddhism*, p. 250.
65. *Dentoroku* (Transmission of the Lamp), p. 27.
66. *Living Zen*, p. 46.
67. *Essays in Zen Buddhism*, p. 111.
68. *The Tao of Physics*. Fritjof Capra, p. 108.
69. *Encyclopaedia of Britannica*, Vol. 16, p. 672.

5

Hinduism

Hinduism is most profound school of philosophy. Hinduism is a protean. Hinduism is monastic. Hinduism is non-dual (*Advaita*) and accepts all forms of philosophical concepts as an aspects of one truth and reality.

Indian culture and civilization have had an extremely long and complex development. It is the longest history of continuous growth than any other living cultural tradition of the world. The historical perspective of cultural tradition and philosophical analysis are very useful in understanding the basic and the fundamental cultural spiritual spirit of Hinduism. It is a very difficult and complex task to present a chronological sequence of the philosophical evolution of Hinduism. In the broad outline the philosophical history of Hinduism can be studied in five subtitles: (1) Kashmir Śaivism, (2) *Vedānta*, (3) *Tantra,* (4) *Yoga* and (5) *Yoga Vāśiṣṭha.* I have selected these five topics of Hinduism because they are all based on ontological mysticism. Hinduism is basically and essentially spirituality. Spirituality and science are rooted in ontological mysticism. Ontological mysticism is the common ground of both spirituality and science.

On the analysis and evaluation of these different philosophical religious and the mystical concept of Hinduism, I come to the conclusion that it is rooted in Indus Valley Civilization. The excavation at Mohenjo-Daro and Harappa revolutionized the concept of Indian history and civilization.

The Indus valley civilization goes back to the Neolithic period (7000-6000 B.C.). This was very organised and developed urban culture. Mohenjo-Daro and Harappa were separated by some forty miles, were two of the world civilization's most important cities where the inhabitants enjoyed high standards of living. The city had a developed culture and technology and most of the houses had a drainage system, etc. The antecedents of this culture can be traced to the site of the Mehrgarh (150 miles north of Mohenjo-Daro in Baluchistan) cultural community that existed before 6000 B.C. and has established an unbroken cultural continuity from that early date to the period of the Indus Valley Civilization.

Śaivism and Śaktism represent the beginning of Indian culture and philosophical traditions. Śaivism and Śaktism were the two official religion of the non-Āryan of the Indus Valley Civilization.

Among the aniconic objects of worships are the *liṅgas* and *yonis* together with their dactylic forms (Pl. III. 31-33). The *liṅga* (phallus) worship was prevalent amongst the backward classes of the non-Āryans. E.H. Hartland in a detailed and informative article[1] on phallism deals with the subject from a broader view. His central theme is to trace sex-worship as a part of the history of religion which has been prevalent in the different strata of culture. Sex-worship was a customary practice and was considered to be a part of the religious sacrament by the ancient people belonging to different faiths. With the advancement of the civilization it was transformed into a higher religious symbolism. This practice was so universal that it became an integral part of the evolution of the human mind, and it seems indigenous with the race.[2] Wall observes: "All religions are based on sex, some like the ancient Egyptian, Greek and Roman or the modern *Brāhmanic* worship of Śiva more coarsely so, according to modern civilized thought; others like the Christian religion more obscurely so."[3] Originally, sex-worship was not developed for the achievement of any morbid exaltation and ecstasy. The primitive people were mostly engaged in war, and preservation of progeny was their greatest problem. Sex-worship, therefore, reasonably really stands for procreation and not for any sexual indulgence.

The excavation of Harappa and the Mohenjo-Daro has established beyond any doubt that the Indus Valley Civilization is the oldest living civilization of the world. The indigenous habitants of India were enjoying the sublime form of cultural life. The Indus Valley Civilization didn't have any affinity with the Middle East. A.L. Basham says: "This great civilization owed little to the Middle East, and there is no reason to believe that it was formed by recent immigrants; the cities were built by people who had probably been in the Indus Valley for various or several centuries. The Harappa people were already Indians when they planned their cities, and they altered hardly at all for thousands of years."[4]

The excavation of the Indus Valley has firmly established that it is one of the oldest living civilizations of the world. It is beyond any doubt that the indigenous inhabitants of India were highly developed both spiritually and intellectually. It was the inner conservatism, vitality and the mysticism of Harappan that kept India philosophically and spiritually alive and vibrant. It is quest for one's own identity and destiny that gives birth to philosophy and spirituality. The original inhabitants of the Indus Valley Civilization in quest of identity and destiny discovered the spiritual essence of being and existence which is known as enlightenment. This ontological mysticism gave birth to Kashmir Śaivism, *Vedānta*, *Tantra* and *Yoga*. Man is both rationalist and divine and empiricist and transcendentalist. He has the unique power of living simultaneously in the present and the future. The basic oneness of the universe is the root concept of Hinduism. In our ordinary life, man is not aware of this basic unity. To believe in the world of separate objects and events that are mental constructs of our discriminating and categorizing intellect is called ignorance (*Avidyā*).

The *summum bonum* of Hinduism is to maintain a dynamic balance and mental equilibrium with the practice of *Tantra* and *Yoga*. The mystic method of *tantra* and *yoga* lead one to become the conscious of unity and oneness of the universe. Even the modern science, especially quantum mechanics and theory of relativity, speaks in different language about the basic unity and oneness of the universe. The so called the separate objects and events and the different constituents of matter are all interconnected, interrelated and interdependent. The experience of the separate things and beings as realities is called ignorance in Hinduism (*Avidyā* or *Māyā*). This estrangement of man is known as bondage. This state of oneness is called *Nirvāṇa*. This is a state of spiritual sublimity and self-consciousness where the distinction between 'me' and 'the world' breaks down. It is a state of mystic realization in which the plurality is fused into unified undifferentiable whole, i.e., reality. Fritjof Capra observes, "The picture of an inter-connected cosmic whole emerged from modern atomic physics has been used extensively in the East to convey the mystical experience of nature.

For Hindus, the *Brahman* is the unifying thread in the cosmic wall, the ultimate ground of all beings".[5]

Kashmir Śaivism

The canonical literature of Kashmir Śaivism is constituted of *Āgama* treatise, *Aspanda* treatise and *Prativijñā* treatise. Mālinī Vijaya *Svacchanda*, *Vijñāna Bhairava*, *Śiva Sūtra*, *Rudrāyamala* form the part of *Āgama Śāstra*. *Aspanda* explains the basic intuitional science of *Śiva Sūtra*. *Prativijñā Darśana* expounds the philosophical basis of intuitional science which is called *Tantra*. *Śiva Dṛṣṭi* is the philosophical treatise authored by Somānanda. Somānanda was the disciple of Vasugupta. As per mythology Śiva revealed *Śiva Sūtra* to Vasugupta. According to one tradition Vasugupta was living on Mahādeva mountain near the Shalimar garden of Srinagar where he was revealed *Śiva Sūtra* by Śiva himself. On the waking Vasugupta visited the place whereby touch the stone on which the whole *Śiva Sūtra* was supposed to be incarved as directed by Śiva. According to other tradition the *Śiva Sūtra* was taught to Vasugupta by *Siddha*. Whatever may be the fact the *Śiva Sūtra* is a part of revealed text and this forms the basis of Kashmir Śaivism. *Śiva Sūtra* is a treatise on *Tantra* and it does provide the sound philosophical foundation in the form of a philosophical system which is known as Kashmir Śaivism. Apart from all the above canonical literature of Kashmir Śaivism, Abhinava Gupta wrote *Tantrāloka* which deals with both philosophical and practical aspects of Kashmir Śaivism. This is a monumental work on Kashmir Śaivism in twelve volumes. The teachings of *Tantrāloka* has been summarized in one volume known as *Tantra Sāra*.

Kashmir Śaivism, has acquired its distinctive name of *Trika-Śāsana*, *Trikā-Śāstra* or simply *Trikā* because it deals with the triple principles known as *Śiva-Śakti-Aṇu*, or *Pati-Pāśa-Paśu*, or *Bindū-Nāda-Kalā*. The phrase *naraśaktiśivātmakam trikām* occurs in *Paratriṁsikavimarśinī*. The *Trikā* is known as the mystical school (*rahasyasampradāya*) which is quite different from other forms of Śaivism. It is an idealistic monism (*Advaita*), but differs in fundamental principles from Śaṅkara's *Advaita Vedānta*. According to Kashmir Śaivism, *Advaita* means the eternal co-existence of Śiva and Śakti. *Paramaśiva* is the fundamental reality. He is indeterminable and transcendental existence, beyond all divisibility and separability. He is the all-comprehensive. The authorship of the entire manifest and unmanifest world lies with *Paramaśiva*. He is the only nucleus of this cosmic cycle, the supreme Controller of the world process. Kurti F. Leidecker says: "The difference of the *Īśvarādvaya* system from the Brahmavādins consists herein that the *Cit*-like Exalted One always retains the authorship of the fivefold world process."

Kashmir Śaivism accepts *Māyā* as *Brahmamayī*, *Nityā* (eternal) and *Satyarūpā* (truth). In this school of *Advaita* philosophy, *Brahman* and *Māyā* become one and co-existent. By accepting the principle of *Māyā as a reality, Kashmir Śaivism agrees on the Absolute as all-embracing unlike Śaṅkara's Brahman* which is based on the principle of renunciation and elimination.

Paramaśiva of the *Āgamaśāstra* is the perfect and profound principle of oneness. The plurality and diversity of the cosmos represent the essential spiritual ones of *Paramaśiva*. He is the only Absolute of Kashmir Śaivism, unsubjectivated Transcendentality. He is *Pūrṇahantā*, self-luminous and pure consciousness. Just as light and heat co-exist in fire, in the same way, the universal I-ness (*ahantā*) and Śakti co-exist in pure consciousness. To make distinction between Śiva and Śakti will be a logical abstraction. *Paramaśiva* is unaffected by the limitation of time, space and causality, and unrestricted by his *Vimarśa Kriyā* who is identical with himself. By virtue of his power he is described as the Free Agent. Freedom is the essence of consciousness.

Kashmir Śaivism is the most profound and sublime form of non-dualistic philosophical school. It is also called *Śivādvaita* system. Behind the Tāntric and Yogīc mystical culture and practice there is an evolved philosophical system of thought which provides the intellectual support for the theocratic culture. Kashmir Śaivism believes that reality is of the nature of pure consciousness, self-luminous and all pervading. The reality is called *Parama Śiva*[6]. It is the indeterminable and transcendental existence. It is beyond all divisibility and separability. It is *Advaitam* (supreme unity). *Advaita* stands here as the eternal co-existence of Śiva and Śakti to make any real distinction between them with logical abstractions. All things and beings of the universe are made of the same consciousness Śiva. The transcendental aspects of reality are the fundamental stuff of the cosmos. The creative matrix (*Śakti*) is the cause of multiplicity. *Parama Śiva* in his transcendence is beyond time, space and form and in his immanence is manifested in the universe in the limitation of the sixty four *Tattva*. In his immanence Śiva is transformed into manifest world and in his transcendental aspects he is beyond it. Śiva is consciousness and *stasis* (*Citta*), *Śakti* is consciousness as dynamics (*Chidrūpiṇī*). The absolute reality is *Prakāśa-vimarśa-Samarasyarūpinī.*[7]

Prakāśa is the cosmic effulgence without which nothing can appear. It is Śiva. *Vimarśa* is *Śakti*. It is the mirror in which Śiva realizes his own grace, power and beauty. *Vimarśa* is the creative matrix. The reality is not only cosmic consciousness, but it is creative matrix also. It is transcendental and immanent. The theory of evolution is known as *Ābhāsavāda*. According to Kashmir Śaivism the world is real, in the sense that it is an aspect of supreme reality. M.M. Gopinath Kaviraj says: "The peculiar metaphysical position of the *Tantra* consists in the theory of *Ābhāsa*; which is consistent with this position. It rejects the *Vivartavāda* of neo-*Vedānta*, because the world is not originally a false appearance due to Error. It is real in the same way as an image is real, but it has no existence apart from the medium in which it is manifested.... To the Vedāntist the world appears as such, to the ignorant owing to his ignorance and in the last analysis it is resolved into *Māyā* which is not identical with the *Brahman* and is materialistic; but to a Tantrist the world is real and is the expression of the *Cit-Śakti* or Free Will of the Lord and is really spiritual in essence like the Lord himself."[8]

According to *Pratyabhijñāhṛdayam* the cosmic consciousness (Śiva) by his own Free Will manifests in himself the cosmos where all beings live and exist. Consciousness is the substratum on which the cosmos is supported. In spite of this apparent dualism the cosmos and the cosmic consciousness are essentially one and indivisible. There is no material cause. Cosmic consciousness (Śiva) becomes the cosmos within itself. The cosmic consciousness makes the cosmos from the ultimate substance of his own being. By the power of her own will alone she unfolds the universe upon her own screen.[9]

The jar of clay is still clay. The different ornament of gold is gold. In the same sense the cosmic consciousness that appears as cosmos is essentially still the cosmic consciousness. The goal of Kashmir's Śaivism is to realize this metaphysical truth and become enlightened. The appearance of limitation is the manifestation of non-self. The supreme reality is split spontaneously into subject and object. However, the supreme reality (cosmic consciousness) suffers no change. The cosmic consciousness remains pure, undivided and absolute. The universe of appearances is unmanifest nature of the absolute from which the process of involution emanates which is perceived by subject as different from it. The central objective of Śaivism is the attainment of supreme unification of Śiva with *Parama Śiva*. This state of self-realization is both an enjoyment and liberation. Śaivism does discard the philosophy of nihilism and pessimism.

According to Śaivism world is neither an illusion nor reality. With the practice of meditation one experiences his own true nature as consciousness both in animate and inanimate objects. The realization of all pervading divinity cut ascender the trammels of *Māyā* and puts an end to all kinds of physical mundane and supra-mundane sufferings. Śaivism believes the mystic realization without ignoring the material aspects of life. Śiva and Śakti are two aspects of the absolute[10]. The ultimate reality is eternal, unchanging, infinite one and uncaused. It is beyond the categories of existence and non-existence, being and non-being. *Parama Śiva* is the supreme reality, pure intelligence as well as on including supreme experience. J.C. Chatterjee writes "He is logical in first principle, but not in time".[11] *Parama Śiva* is the supreme cognitive principle. He is a supreme subjectivity (अहंता). He undergoes no change and metamorphosis. There is nothing outside and beyond him. He is the noumenonal cause of this phenomenal world. He is the ultimate cause of manifest universe. *Parama Śiva* is the basic substance out of which the whole of the manifest and un-manifest universe has been created. He creates the whole cosmos out of his power of consciousness (*Cit-Śakti*). *Mahānirvāṇa Tantra* says: "I bow to Thee, the pure consciousness who art in the form of universe."[12]

The absolute is called *Mahā-bindū.* It is without colour and formless point and has position, but no magnitude, it means reality exists, but It cannot be conceived. It is logically indemonstrable. It is beyond the reach of philosophical reflection and ratiocination. The absolute is composite form of consciousness (Śiva) and creative matrix (*Śakti*). Cosmic consciousness (Śiva) and cosmic principle (*Śakti*) are inalienable concomitance.[13] The Kashmir Śaivism is dualistic in theory but monastic in spirit. Śiva and Śakti are inseparable. It is impossible to separate them as the moving wind cannot be separated from the steady fast ether in which it blows. Metaphorically, it has been symbolized as *Ardhanārīśvara*. The absolute is again metaphorically expressed as *Yāmalarūpā*. The Kashmir Śaivism concept of reality resolves the philosophical dilemma of monism and dualism. It also resolves scientist's enigma of mind and matter and *Vedāntins* problem of *Brahman* and *Māyā*.

The inalienable concomitance of Śiva and Śakti is known as *Abhinābhāvi*. This metaphor of *Abhinābhāvi* means inseparable. It means existence of one cannot prove in the absence of other. According to Kashmir Śaivism there is no Śiva without Śakti, no Śakti without Śiva.[14] *Śiva Sūtra* says consciousness is the self.[15]

Nothing exists without consciousness (Śiva). Consciousness is one and the only reality. Self is consciousness in the sense that it is absolutely free in all knowledge and activity. The essence of Śiva has been pronounced as consciousness. Metaphysically speaking consciousness is absolute and it rejects the pluralism which propagates the doctrine of different self and realities. The metaphorically the first *Sūtra* stands for self and its nature of reality. Reality is nothing and separate from consciousness. *Qua* consciousness means the quint essential reality of the cosmos. Consciousness is the sole reality. All existents derive their existence from consciousness.

Parama Śiva is the author of the whole manifest and unmanifest world. He is the nucleus of this cosmic cycle. He is alone the sovereign entity. "*Mahānirvāṇa Tantra* says that, "Through the fear of him; the wind blows, the sun gives heat, the clouds shower rain and the trees in the forests blossom".[16]

The material cause of entire cosmic cycle is consciousness. The cosmic consciousness is the supreme controller of the evolutionary process. Kurt F. Leidecker says: "The difference of the *Īśvarādvaya* system from the Brahmavādins consists here in that the *Cit*-like Exalted One always retains the authorship of the fivefold world process."[17]

According to Kashmir Śaivism the whole cosmos is created out of and the same reality known as cosmic consciousness (Śiva). The material cause and the efficient cause are cardinal principles of creative ideation. Every object has these two causes; over and above there is a conjunctive principle which acts as a catalytic agent between the material and efficient cause. Śiva is a material cause. *Śakti* is a linking force. As efficient cause Śiva is the primary and *Śakti* the secondary factor. Śiva is a consciousness force and all-pervading reality. *Śakti* is always merged in Śiva. She activates the process of creation only when Śiva offers an opportunity and grants divine permission, hence doer-ship lies with Śiva. As an efficient cause Śiva is the primary principle and *Śakti* the secondary.

He is the cosmic consciousness. Śiva is described as one because the reality can be realized by making mind one-pointed with the practice of meditation on *Mahā-bindū* the mind is apexed. An apexed mind realizes reality (*Parama Śiva*) in the state of deep meditation and mystic trance. Mind is dissolved into cosmic consciousness. Mind seizes to be mind. It becomes consciousness. It is called the mystic oneness of Śiva and Śakti, *Kuṇḍalinī* and *Parā-bindū*.

Śiva is cosmic consciousness and *Śakti* is cosmic principle. Śiva is witnessing entity, but without the activation of *Śakti* he remains unmanifested. Śiva is *Jñāna Tattva* and *Śakti* is *Kriyā Śakti*. However, *Śakti* is neither absolute nor independent and separate entity. She is eminent aspects of Śiva. Without *Śakti* Śiva is inactive. Śiva being a supreme subjectivity remains as witnessing force. *Śakti* is a primordial force. The absolute of Kashmir Śaivism is one and eternal, but due to the activation of *Śakti* the absolute appears to have taken different forms and colours. It means that when *Śakti* gets the divine permission and scope of manifestation, Śiva (comic consciousness) undergoes metamorphosis. The singular self is transformed into innumerable finite entity, but consciousness remains the essence the fundamental substance of all physical and metaphysical realities. Śiva does not lose his transcendentality. However, *Śakti* remains and exists in all levels of manifestation and unmanifestation. The transcendentality remains uncontaminated.

"John Woodroffe[18] and J.C. Chatterjee[19] have wrongly conceived *Śakti* as negation, which is a logical principle, whereas *Śakti Tattva* of *Tantra* is a spiritual principle. The principle of Negation as explained by Spinoza and Hegel is a logical dichotomy where 'being' and 'non-being' live together in an unholy alliance.

'Being' and 'Non-Being' are psychic's concepts, and have nothing to do with the mystic and metaphysical principle. A logical principle is conceptual and of dependent origination, whereas a spiritual principle is real and self-existent. As *Vimarśa-Śakti*, she does not negate Śiva (Cosmic Consciousness) in the Western sense; rather she fulfils the desire of Śiva by creating the world. She is said to be *Niṣedha vyāpāra-rūpā Śaktiḥ*. Here *Niṣedha* means the veiling and projecting (*vikṣepa*) *kriyā* of *Śakti* which is quite different from the Principle of Negation."[20]

Parama Śiva which is absolute of Kashmir Śaivism is beyond the question of 'is' and 'is not' and existence (*Cit*) and non-existence (*acit*). The concept of existence and non-existence are rooted in psychic concepts whereas the absolute is unconceivable to human. Rationality is an analytic process. It is rooted in the dualism of subject and object. The absolute (being) is beyond any kind of dualism and ratiocination. Reality is unitary in principle. 'One' and 'Two' are positive mental constructs. According to Kashmir Śaivism, *bindū, nāda* and *kalā* are the three stages of evolution. Involution is the process of crudification of cosmic consciousness which undergoes change and metamorphosis and transforms into phenomenal world. According to variation in the degree of causal matrix consciousness takes different names and forms, but the basic substance is same. When consciousness is metamorphosed he is called qualified *Brahman*. The creation is nothing, but the thought projection of qualified *Brahman*. *Śakti* the *magna matter* is called *Mahā Devī* who conceives bears and nourishes the entire world. Śiva is cosmic consciousness and *Śakti* is the creative matrix. This world is nothing, but the creative ideation of the causal matrix. *Yogīnī Hṛdaya Tantra* says that the world is designed by her own will.[21]

Śakti is absolutely free. *Śakti* exists holding within her that the power that creates, sustains and destroys. Though *Śakti* is creative matrix she is also the means to highest bliss. The cosmic consciousness gets manifested in the cosmos. However, the absolute nature of reality remains indivisible. *Pratyabhijñāhṛdayam* says "*Cit* creates the universe of her own free will."[22]

According to *Pratyabhijñāhṛdayam* Śiva (consciousness) animated by the desire of having manifest universe which is one with himself shines forth as the one *Citta* which is the very void detached from *Māyā*. The creation is nothing, but the metamorphosis of consciousness in form of the totality of different entities. The great commentator of *Śāradā Tilaka,* Raghav Bhatt says that "like the Sāṅkhya concept of appearance of reality from *Sadutapattivāda*, *Śakti* which remains in the dormant state in *Parā-Saṁbit* becomes manifest (*Ucchunāvāsthā*).[23] *Śakti* is uncaused. She doesn't have any beginning. The *Caitanyadhyasena* means the eternal co-existence of Śiva and *Śakti*. The process of evolution animated by *Śakti* is the movement without any feelings. The *Nirguṇa Śiva* does not mean Śiva without *Guṇa* (*Śakti*), but it means *Gunātīta* state of Śiva. The *Śakti Tattva* issues from *Śiva Tattva*. It is further stated that from *Śakti* evolves *nāda* and from *nāda* issues *Bindū* and from the causal *Bindū* proceeds the effect (*kārya*) *Bindū*, *nāda* and *Bīja*.[24] This whole world is nothing, but collection of waves and vibrations. The evolution is the result of self-movement (*Aspanda*) on the part of Śiva-Śakti. The world of waves and vibrations, things and beings is the self-manifestation of non-dual cosmic consciousness. Though the *Śakti* creates infinite forms, but never swerves from essence. According to *Śiva Sūtra* the self is the dancer.[25] This is why every entity from molecules to cosmos is in a state of dancing postures. Nothing in the world is in a state of tranquillity and static. Everything is dynamic. This concept of Kashmir Śaivism that creation is *Aspanda* on the part of the ultimate reality is closer to the modern physics especially the theory of relativity and quantum mechanics. I shall deal with this problem in the subsequent chapters. Gopinath Kaviraj says, "When the universe comes into being it does so as only an image within the unique self. The universe as such varied, but underlying it is the pure and simple unity of *Caitanya* revealing itself to the eye of diligent search (*Anusandhāna*). The manifestation of the universe due to the Free Will (*Svātantrata*) of the Absolute, is thus a process of *Ābhāsa* and for the initiation of this process nothing beyond the play of the will is needed..."[26]

Metaphysically speaking, the *Parama Śiva* creates the cosmos from the substance of his own being. The cosmos is not cosmos, but the consciousness itself. The different things and beings which look different from its essential nature of consciousness is that it remains consciousness itself. The reality which is cosmic consciousness does not lose its perfection, divinity and effulgence. The cosmos of variegated forms and names is the manifestation of consciousness itself which has been created by Śiva's boundless power. *Pratyabhijñāhṛdayam* says, "By the power of Her own Will alone, she unfolds universe upon her own screen."[27]

Consciousness (Śiva) is without any quality and condition. Śiva is impersonal and supreme Lord of the cosmos. Though Śiva (consciousness) is the whole of the world; he does not enter in this world of change and metamorphosis. However, all the shuttle and the crude manifestation is in essence consciousness (Śiva). Śiva (consciousness) alone remains unchangeable, transcendental reality. He is said to be qualified only when one considers him as being the possessor of *Śakti*. The cosmos is a personification of consciousness. The cosmos is both an ideal and real whereas in *Vedānta* reality is *Brahman* everything else is, but an imposition on the reality of *Brahman*. They are ultimately unreal and their unreality is exposed when the person becomes enlightened. In this state of enlightenment cosmos completely seize to exist before the enlightened person. The cosmos in various forms of animate and inanimate is considered as diverse and different forms of consciousness. The cosmos is the thought projection of Śiva and it has been created for the benefit of the *Jīva*. Thus, the Kashmir Śaivism is a happy and harmonious blending of materialism and spirituality, realism and idealism as it is based on Ontological mysticism.

Ultimate reality is called *Parāsaṁvita*. It is cosmic consciousness. It is eternal and unchangeable principle behind all changes. It is beyond the dualism of subject and object. It is supreme subjectivity. *Pratibhijñā Darśana* calls it that reality is constituted of consciousness (*Prakāśa*), *stasis* and *Vimarśa* (consciousness dynamic). In the state of cosmic consciousness subject and object are undivided and indivisible unity. The supreme subjectivity is the *Prakāśa* aspects of the ultimate reality. Object or its consciousness of itself is the *Vimarśa* aspect. The supreme subjectivity that is, the 'I' is the witnessing counterpart of the reality. Mercia Eliade writes, "Western philosopher may perhaps find the jargon of Indian philosophy outmoded, lacking in precision, unserviceable. But all these risks to which the dialogue is subject are of minor importance. The great discoveries of Indian thought will in the end be recognised, under and despite the philosophic jargon. It is impossible, for example, to disregard one of India's greatest discoveries: that of consciousness as witness, of consciousness freed from its psychophysiological structures and their temporal conditioning, the consciousness of the "liberated" man, of him, that is, who has succeeded in emancipating himself from temporality and thereafter knows the true inexpressible freedom. The conquest of this absolute freedom, of perfect spontaneity, is the goal of all Indian philosophies and mystical techniques."[28]

The cosmic consciousness is transcendental self which is divine effulgence and supreme bliss. However, it is hidden from our knowledge and experience on account of our state of dualism of subject and object. The dualism of subject and object is the creation of our thought construct. This is why in *Śiva Sūtra* it has been stated that knowledge is bondage.[29] The whole cosmos is constituted of countless worlds of subject and object. The individuality created out of the thought constructs keeps oneself unaware of the transcendental nature of self. To reveal the real nature of the self which is pure and transcendental, but obscure by the thought constructs of *Jīva*. *Śiva Sūtra* second *Sūtra* has been formulated to understand the metaphysical and epistemological import of the *Sūtra*. If the nature of the entire universe consisting of empirical selves and inert matter is only consciousness or in other words *Parama Śiva* (Highest Śiva), then how is this (apparent) bondage to be explained? In order to remove this doubt, the second *Sūtra* has been formulated. Kṣemarāja cautions – that this *sūtra* is to be read in two ways (1) according to the rules of *Sandhi* (euphonic coalescence of the final and initial letters) with the coalescence of the final and the initial letters in which case this *sūtra* combined with the previous now would stand thus: (*Caitanyamatmajñānaṁ bandhaḥ*), i.e., the form of the *sūtra* would be *Caitanyamatma ajñānaṁ bandhaḥ*, (2) without the coalescence of the final letter of the previous *sūtra* and the initial letter of the second *sūtra* in which case the second *sūtra* would stand separately simply as *jñānaṁ bandhaḥ*.

Ultimate reality is truth, consciousness and bliss.[30] It is truth because it is unchanging, unsubjectivated and transcendental reality. It is the supreme unity without a second. It is luminous and divine effulgence. It is one without second. The *Śakti* is the cause of transformation of cosmic consciousness from reality to relativity. However, the change is not physical but spiritual.

The absolute of Kashmir Śaivism is self-existence and ever the same and serene. It beholds and is the witness of all that is, omnipresent, the self of everything that is. It is eternal omniscience, is hidden and pervades all things. Though the devoid of senses he is the illuminator of all the senses and their powers.[31] The absolute of Kashmir Śaivism is a witnessing entity. Mind is an ever changing function or an organism. It has two chambers—subjective and objective. For the common it is the eye which perceives. But the student of medical science and physics will say that it is the retina which receives the colour vibrations from objects and transmits to the brain. The metaphysician will say that the brain transmits these vibrations to the objective mind which takes the form of vibrations and the subjective mind does the act of perception. Further introspection proves that the subjective mind perceives only because of supreme subjectivity. Cosmic consciousness is the subjective counterpart of the mind. Mind perceives only because cosmic consciousness is the witnessing force behind our all mental activities. The *Parama Śiva* is cosmic consciousness. He alone is the ultimate and the sovereign entity. The *Parama Śiva* is the author and the supreme controller of whole cosmos, manifest and unmanifest. He is the nucleus of this cosmic cycle. The material cause of the entire cosmic cycle is Śiva. He is the supreme controller of the world process. Kurt F. Leidecker says: "The difference of the *Īśvarādvaya* system from the Brahmavādins consists here in that the *Cit*-like Exalted One always retain the authorship of the fivefold world process."[32]

Cosmic consciousness (*Parā Śiva*) is the basic and fundamental reality. It is indeterminable and transcendental existence. It is beyond all divisibility and separability. It is all comprehensive. It is called *Advaitam* (supreme unity). In Kashmir Śaivism *Advaita* (supreme unity) means the eternal co-existence of Śiva and Śakti.[33] Any attempt to make any real distinction will be logical abstraction. Arthur Avalon says: "All that is manifest is Power (*Śakti*) as Mind, Life and Matter. Power implies a Power-Holder (*Śaktiman*). There is no power-holder without Power or Power without Power-Holder. The Power Holder is Śiva. The Power is *Śakti*, the Great Mother of the Universe. There is no Śiva without *Śakti* or no *Śakti* without Śiva. The two as they are in themselves are one".[34]

All the things of Universe are made of the cosmic consciousness. The transcendental aspect of *Param* Śiva is the fundamental substance of the cosmos. *Śakti* the creative matrix is the cause of multiplicity. The material cause and the efficient cause are the cardinal principles of creative ideation. Every object has these causes. Over and above these, there is a connective principle which acts as a catalytic agent between the material and the efficient cause. Consciousness is the material cause. Creative matrix (*Śakti*) is the linking force. As an efficient cause consciousness is primary and creative matrix the secondary factor. Śiva is the consciousness force and all-pervading entity. None else than Śiva can be the material cause of the universe. *Śakti* is always merged in Śiva. The cosmic consciousness of Kashmir Śaivism is the fundamental substance. It is the nucleus of all the nuclei. It is the soul of all soul and the life of all life. It is the ultimate eternal and infinite reality. Consciousness is the fundamental cosmic substance. Werner Heisenberg has come to the similar conclusion after analysing and examining the theory of relativity. The theory of relativity formulations of equivalence of mass and energy brought a revolution in physics. The enormous releases of energy in an atomic explosion are another and still a more spectacular proof of Einstein's equation. The equivalence of mass and energy has—besides its great importance in physics—also raised very old problems concerning very old philosophical questions. It has been the thesis of the several philosophical systems of the past that substance and matter cannot be destroyed. In modern physics, however, many experiments have shown that elementary particles that is positrons and electrons, can be annihilated and transmitted into radiations. Werner Heisenberg writes, "Does this mean that older philosophical systems have been disproved by modern experience and that the arguments brought forward by the earlier systems have been misleading? This would certainly be a rash and unjustified conclusion, since the terms "substance" and "matter" in ancient or medieval philosophy cannot simply be identified with the term "mass" in modern physics. If one wished to express our modern experience in the language of older philosophies, one could consider mass and energy as two different forms of the same "substance" thereby keeping the idea of substance as indestructible."[35]

Kashmir Śaivism accepts *māyā* as *Brahmamayī*, *nitayā* (eternal) and *Satyarūpā* (truth). In Kashmir Śaivism *Brahman* and *māyā* become one and co-existent. Kashmir Śaivism accepts the principle of *māyā* as reality.

The absolute of Kashmir Śaivism becomes all embracing. Unlike Śaṅkaras, *Brahman*, which is based on the principles of renunciation and elimination the absolute of Kashmir Śaivism is the perfect and the profound principle. The plurality and diversity represents the spiritual; and essential oneness of the absolute.

The ultimate reality is beyond the question of *is* and *is not*. Existence (*Cit*) and non-existence (*Acit*) the ideas of existence and non-existence are positive and negative psychic concepts whereas the absolute is inconceivable to human mind and reason. Reason is an analytic process. It involves dualism of subject and object. The cosmic consciousness being the supreme cognitive principle it is beyond the reach of mind and senses. Ultimate reality is singular and unitary in character. One and two are positive mental conceptions. To say that absolute is one doesn't mean that it is within the reach of reason. It is described as one because one can experience by making mind one pointed. With the constant ideation and meditation on *Parābindū* mind is apexed. An apexed mind realizes the cosmic consciousness (*absolute*) in the state of deep meditation. Mind is dissolved into consciousness. Mind seizes to be mind. It becomes consciousness. It is called the mystic oneness of Śiva and Śakti, *kuṇḍalinī* and *paramabindū*. The awakening of the *kuṇḍalinī* opens the gateway to realization. Which is the *summum bonum* of Kashmir Śaivism.

According to Abhinava Gupta liberation is nothing else, but the awareness of one's true nature.[36] The enlightenment means the recognition and recollections (*Pratibhijñā*) of one's true nature. The normal psychological experience is relational. The self-consciousness is in contrast with non-self. The supreme objective of one's spiritual endeavour is to go beyond the dualism of subject and object unless one rids oneself from all kinds of ratiocinations. One cannot attain liberation. When one gets liberated from the thought constructs of the mind one gets experience of the real transcendental nature of self. It is an experience where all kinds of distinctions of knower (*jñātā*), knowledge and object of knowledge are completely annulled. J.

Krishna Murti calls it choiceless awareness and Taoism terms it *wu-wei* (non-interference).

Ābhāsa Vāda (Evolution)

The evolution of Kashmir Śaivism is called *Ābhāsa Vāda*. It is different from the *Śaṅkaras Vivartavāda*. *Bindū*, *nāda* and *kalā* are the three stages of evolution. Involution is the process of crudification of cosmic consciousness which undergoes metamorphosis. Consciousness is transformed and appears in the form of matter. According to the variation in the degree of bondage of creative matrix the cosmic consciousness has taken different forms, but the fundamental substance is one and the same. According to Kashmir Śaivism the cosmos is in the form of potency in the seed form which gets manifested when the creative matrix activates the cosmic consciousness. The cosmic consciousness is the fundamental stuff of the cosmos. Creativity is the very essence of divinity. Abhinava Gupta says, "the cosmic consciousness does not manifest in different forms, but remains co-opt within it. As the great banyan tree remains in the form of seed like that the whole cosmos with all its mundane and supra-mundane manifestation lies in the form of potentia in cosmic consciousness."[37]

The belligerent forces of *Sattva*, *Rajas* and *Tamas*; when they could not maintain the state of equilibrium it bursts and the creation starts. In the modern scientific terminology the universe is explained through the general theory of Relativity and Quantum Mechanics. Stephen Hawking writes, "Today scientists describe the universe in terms of the two basic partial theories—the general theory of Relativity and the Quantum Mechanics. They are the great intellectual achievements of the first half of the twentieth century. The general theory of relativity describes the force of gravity and the large scale structure of the universe; that is, the structure of scales only from a few miles to as large as a million million million million (one with twenty-four zeros after it) miles, the size of the observable universe. Quantum mechanics on the other hand, deals with the phenomena on extremely small scales, such as a millionth of a millionth of an inch. Unfortunately, however, these two theories are known to be inconsistent with each other—they cannot both be correct. One of the major endeavours in physics today, and the major theme of this book, is the research for a new theory that will incorporate them both a Quantum theory of gravity. We do not yet have such a theory, and we may still be a long way from having one, but we do already know how many of the properties that it must have. And we shall see in later chapters that we already know a fair amount about the predictions from a Quantum theory of gravity must make."[38]

The modern cosmologist like Stephen Hawking explained the creation of universe from the concept known as the Big Bang Theory. According to the Big Bang doctrines in the beginning the universe was infinitesimally small and infinitely dense and it burst and with the bursting the creation has started. But the Hawking and the others have not given any logical and scientific explanation of cause of the bursting; if there has not been any pressure within the infinitesimally small and infinitely dense seed of the universe, the seed of the universe would have remained in suspended animation for infinity. And hence I feel that Kashmir Śaivism and other doctrines of Hinduism have given a logical explanation that the nature in the form of belligerent forces which was the cause of bursting and the creation started. And this process is continuous in the cosmic drama. The point from which the triangle of forces burst out is the seed (*Bīja*). It is called *Kāma Bīja*. It is the seed of creation. When this seed of creation is manifested in a metaphysical straight line it is called *nāda*. It is dominated by sentient principles, but due to the activation or domination of static principles the manifestation or creation takes the form of a curvature which is called *kalā*. With the creation of the curvature of *kalā* the phenomenal world comes into being. In the modern scientific terminology cosmos is nothing, but a collection of different waves and curvatures.

Woodroffe writes: "Thus, the *Tantra*s speak of the development of the straight line (*Ṛju-rekhā*) from the point which, when it has gone its length as a point, is turned (*Vākra-rekhā aṁkusakāra*) by the force of the spiralling sack of *Māyā* in which it works so as to form a figure of two dimensions, which again is turned upon itself, ascending as a straight line into the plane of the third dimension, thus forming the triangular or pyramidal figure called *Śṛgataka*."[39]

Mādhavācārya, while enumerating the philosophy of Pāṇinī, says: "the eternal word is called *sphoṭa*..."[40]

The *Sphoṭa* is bursting of the seed of universe (*Kāma Bīja*).

According to Kashmir Śaivism creation starts when the cosmic consciousness (Śiva) and the cosmic principles (*Śakti*) are differentiated due to the bursting of *Kāma Bīja* and the *Parābindū* is transformed into three forms of creation that is *Bindū*, *Nāda* and *Kalā*. *Bindū* is Śiva, *Nāda* is Śakti and *Kalā* is Śiva-Śakti from the point of cause. *Śāradā Tilaka* says: "that which is supreme *Śakti* again divides itself into three, *Bindū*, *Nāda* and *Bīja*"[41], *nāda* or *Śabda* (word) is the first expression of creation. *Śabda Brahman* is the cause of the manifest and differentiated word or meaning or the subtle and crude object without understanding the meaning and significance of *sphoṭa* or the eternal sound one cannot understand the process of creation. *Bindū* is both *Śūnyatā* (void) and *Guṇa*. In the void aspect of it *Bindū* is the supreme *Brahman* and in its *Guṇa* aspects it is *Śakti*.

The phenomenal world is the manifestation of cosmic consciousness. The whole manifest world is being the manifestation of the cosmic consciousness, its existence is life, the reflection of anything in the mirror and hence the manifest world is appearance but it is appearance of the reality and hence Kashmir Śaivism makes a distinction between the reality and the relativity. The question whether the manifest world is real or illusion has been solved by Kashmir Śaivism by declaring the manifestation of the world as an appearance of the cosmic consciousness and hence, it is not illusion. It is a relative truth. According to Kashmir Śaivism the absolute is not only cosmic consciousness, but also a supreme spiritual power. It is both transcendental and immanent. The very nature of the absolute is to manifest. Creativity is the quint essential nature of cosmic consciousness.

The Śakti which is a cosmic principle is called *Chidrūpiṇī*. This is the *Vimarśa* aspects of the absolute reality. *Vimarśa* has been known as *Parāśakti*, *Svātantra*, *Aiśvarya*, *Hṛdaya*, *Sāra*, and *Aspanda*. According to *Aspanda Śāstra* cosmic consciousness is not inert, inactive, but it is full of life and creativity and because the cosmic consciousness is creative the whole world is the manifestation of the absolute and the creation is because of the creativity and the vibrational nature of the absolute so, the whole manifest world and all the objects of phenomenal world are in a state of vibration. That is all the objects of the phenomenal world are in a dancing posture. According to *Śiva Sūtra* the Self is the dancer.[42]

The Kashmir Śaivism has propounded the doctrine of thirty six *tattvas*. *Tattva* means the created being. It belongs to the theory of *Ābhāsa Vāda* (Evolution). These thirty six *tattvas* are as follows: (1) Śiva, (2) Śakti, (3) Sadā Śiva, (4) *Īśvara,* (5) Ṣaḍa Vidyā, (6) *Māyā,* (7) Kalā, (8) Vidyā, (9) Rāga, (10) *Kāla,* (11) *Niyati,* (12) *Puruṣa,* (13) *Prakṛti,* (14) *Buddhi*, (15) Ahaṅkāra, (16) Mana, (17-21) Five sensory organs, (22-26) Five motor organs, (27-31) five *Tanamātrā*, (32-36) five *Mahā Bhūta*. The last twenty five (12-36) *tattvas* have been expounded by Sāṁkhya philosophy also. The sixth *Tattva*, i.e., *Māyā* is part of the *Vedānta* system also. Apart from these thirty six *tattvas Parama Śiva* (the absolute) of Kashmir Śaivism have been endowed with five creativity, i.e., *Citta*, *Ānanda*, *Icchā*, *Jñāna*, and *Kriyā*.

The whole sixty four *tattvas* have again been divided into two kinds that are *Śuddha Tattva* and *Aśuddha Tattva*. This division is based on the elements of *Māyā* present in the *tattvas* (created being). The first five *tattvas* are known as *Śuddha Tattvas*. To my mind the *tattvas* of Kashmir Śaivism is constituted of the manifest world and the division between the *Śuddha* and *Aśuddha* is based on the density of the materiality. However, from philosophical point of view the whole manifest world being the expression of cosmic consciousness the differentiation of the different objects depends upon the density of the crudeness and inertness of the objects. In scientific language it may be explained in terms of the presence of atoms and molecules in different objects. However, essentially the whole world is the part and parcel of the cosmic consciousness.

According to *Tṛikā*, the entire creation is *Ābhāsa*. The phenomenal world is real in the sense that it is a manifestation of *Paramaśiva*. Creation is the result of spontaneous movement (*Spanda*) on the part of Śiva. *The world of waves and vibrations, things and beings, is the manifestation of the non-dual cosmic consciousness with which Māyā* is an essential identical. Gopinath Kaviraj says: "When the universe comes into being, it does so as only an image within the unique self. The universe as such is varied but underlying it is pure and simply unity of *Caitanya*... the manifestation of the universe, due to the free will (*svātantrya*) of the Absolute, is then a process of *Ābhāsa* and for the initiation of this process nothing beyond the play of the will is needed".[43] The world of appearance is real in the same way as an image is real, but it has no existence apart from the consciousness in which it is manifested. Its existence is only the existence of the Absolute.

According to the *Śivādvaita* school of Kashmir Śaivism, Supreme Reality is of the nature of pure consciousness, self-luminous and all-pervading. Its mystic experience is characterized by vividness, directness and bliss. Śiva is *Sat* (Being), *Śakti* is *Satī* (Being as a power). Śiva is *Cit* (consciousness), *Śakti* is *Citi* (consciousness as force). Śiva is *Brahman, Śakti* is *Brahmamayī*. Some say that truth is *Advaita* (non-dual), some others speak of it as *Dvaita* (dual), but it is, in the *Śivādvaita* view, *Dvaitādvaitavivarjitā*: neither the one nor the other. It is beyond dualism and non-dualism.

Vedānta

Vedānta philosophy is the culmination of teachings of the *Vedas*. The philosophy which has been propounded by the seers in *Upaniṣad* is commonly known as *Vedānta*. The canonical literature of *Vedānta* is known as *Prasthāna Trayī*. The *Upaniṣad*, the *Brahma Sūtra* and the *Gītā* form the part of *Prasthāna Trayī*. The *Upaniṣad* belongs to the *Śruti* (oral tradition). There is no authorship of the *Upaniṣadic* teachings. *Upaniṣads* are the work of the seers (*Ṛṣi*) that have experienced the divine truth in their spiritual sublimity. The *Upaniṣads* constitute the revealed texts and it is called *Śruti-Prasthāna*. And this is why they are called *Drāsta Ṛṣi*. *Brahma Sūtra* is attributed to Bādarāyaṇa. The Bādarāyaṇa has condensed the teachings of the whole *Upaniṣads* in *Sūtra* form. The *Brahma Sūtra* is considered as *Nyāya-Prasthāna* because it presents the teachings of *Vedānta* in a logical form. However, *Gītā* belongs to *Smṛti* because it forms a part of *Mahābhārata,* which is a *Smṛti*, hence *Gītā* is called *Smṛti-Prasthāna*. Gauḍapāda is the founding father of school of *Vedānta*. He has incorporated some of the best and the basic ideas and concepts of Buddhism in his philosophy of non-dual school of *Vedānta*. *Māṇḍukyakārikā* of Gauḍapāda is the greatest treatise on non-dual school of *Vedānta*. He is the progenitor of Śaṅkara.

According to *Vedānta Sūtra* the *Puruṣa* and *Prakṛti* of Śaṅkara philosophy are not independent reality, but modification of the one ultimate reality which is called *Brahman* or *Ātman*. Different *Ācārya* (thinkers) at different periods of history have interpreted *Prasthāna Trayī* in a different way and out of which grew the different schools of *Vedānta*. However, I shall confine my deliberation only to the non-dual school of *Vedānta*. George Thibaut, the first Westerners who has commented on *Vedānta* who cannot be charged with any partiality for Śaṅkara speaks of his philosophy in these words: "The doctrine advocated by Śaṅkara is, from a purely philosophical point of view and apart from all the theological considerations, the most important and interesting one which has arisen on Indian soil; neither those forms of the Vedānta which diverge from the view represented by Śaṅkara, nor any of the non-*Vedāntic* systems can be compared with the so-called orthodox *Vedānta* in boldness, depth and subtlety of speculation."[44]

The *Aṣṭābakra Saṁhitā*, the *Avadhūta Gītā* and *Nirvāṇa Śataka* constitute and accredited the classic of monastic *Vedānta*. Śaṅkara is considered as the greatest exponent of monastic *Vedānta*. He has summarized the teachings of *Brahma Sūtra*, *Upaniṣads* and the *Bhagavad Gītā* in a rational and consistent way and he has tried to deal with a metaphysical problem of truth and reality in rational way in course of his exposition of monastic *Vedānta*. According to the monastic *Vedānta* subject and object, self and the non-self are radically opposed to each other and hence, it is a metaphysical error to mistake the one for the other. However, we find this error as universal as we identify our self with non-self. This is the bondage. This is creation of *Māyā*. This is due to the fundamental error on which all our conscious activities are based. To know the ultimate reality, one must get rid from this nescience.

According to the *Advaita* or monastic *Vedānta* pure consciousness pervades our whole life. According to Śaṅkara the reality is pure consciousness or the witnessing entity which does not go about any change and metamorphosis or the witness of change cannot change. The *Brahman* is not merely, but the all. According to *Brahma Sūtra* reality must be its absoluteness. It must remain same beyond the relativistic nature of time, space and causality. Surendranath Bhattacharya writes, Śaṅkara shows that the subject (*viṣayin*) can never be the object (*viṣaya*). The 'I' can never be anything other than 'I'. When I say that I have known myself, what I have actually known is not the self, but something other than it. Whatever becomes an object of knowledge becomes, by that very fact, something other than the self. So, the knower is unknowable."[45]

According to Vedānta, *Brahma* alone is real, world is false and there is complete identity between *Ātman* and *Brahman*. This is the fundamental teachings of *Advaita Vedānta*. According to *Upaniṣad* the *Jīva* is regarded as fundamentally identical with the *Brahman* and hence, according to Śaṅkara *Brahman* is essentially *Nirguṇa* (without attribute), *niṣkriya* (without any activity or movement), *niravayava* (without any parts), *nirūpādhika* (unconditional and absolute) and *nirviśeṣa* (having no distinct elements in it). It has been called by *Upaniṣad* as "thou art that" (*tat-tvam-āsi*).

According to Śaṅkara even the words like *Sat* (truth), *Cit* (consciousness) and *Ānanda* (bliss) do not refer to any attributes or differentiation in the being of *Brahman*. They only employ pure being and pure bliss. Now, the question arises; *Jīva* is converse to all this, then how could it be identical with *Brahman*? The world is always in a state of change, then how it explains the transcendentality of *Brahman* as it is cause (*kāraṇa)* of both material (*Upādana*) and efficient (*nimitta*). How could it be explained the phenomenal world which is said to emanate from *Brahman* exists in *Brahman* and finally get merged in the *Brahman*. These are the metaphysical problems to be solved. The Śaṅkara's answer is the ultimate analysis world is not real, nor does it exists, the only reality is *Brahman* and Gauḍapāda the pre-Śaṅkara exponent of monastic *Vedānta* says, there is neither dissolution nor creation, neither a person in bondage nor any spiritual aspirant, neither any seeker after liberation nor one that is liberated. This mystic experience is the highest truth.[46]

There is a great similarity between the Śaṅkara monastic *Vedānta* and Buddhist view of Nāgārjuna which has been developed by Chandrakīrti. Buddhist also considers the illusionary nature of the phenomenal world without having any basis of transcendental reality, whereas *Śaṅkarācārya* provided the *Brahman* the firm basis of truth and reality. Surendranath Das Gupta writes "*Śaṅkarācārya* called the true perspectives *paramārthika* and *vyavāharika*, the Buddhist called them *paramārthika* and *saṁvṛttika*. The view point of *Śaṅkarācārya* is anticipated by *Asaṅga* and *Vasubandhu* (fourth or fifth century), particularly in the latter's work *Vijñaptimātratā-siddhi*. The philosophical difference between the two viewpoints is almost negligible. This explains why many of the opponents of *Śaṅkarācārya* called him a crypto-Buddhist."[47]

While commenting on the *Brahma Sūtra* Śaṅkara refuted the views of the *Sāṁkhya*, *Nyāya* and Buddhist philosophical schools. However, his enunciation of monastic *Vedānta* is vague and not very logically clear. To establish the monastic *Vedānta* in a proper metaphysical order the scholars like Vācaspati Miśra, Sureśvara, Padmapāda, Maṇḍana Miśra, Shri Harsha and others tried to present the monastic *Vedānta* in a proper metaphysical perspective. There has been a pre-Śaṅkara interpretation of *Vedānta* known as *Vedā-Ved-Vāda*, the concurrence of dualism and monism without excluding any of them as illusory. Bhāskara in his commentary on *Brahma Sūtra* had explained this view with the help of the metaphor of sea and the diversity of waves. There are other great Ācārya like Bhāskara *Yādava Prakāśa*, Keshva Neelkantha, Rāmānuja, Ballava Ācārya, Madhu Sūdana Saraswati, Ballava Ācārya and Vijñāna Bhikṣu who have explained the teachings of *Upaniṣads*, *Gītā* and *Brahma Sūtra* in a different way out of which grew the different schools of *Vedānta*.

However, the most profound school of *Vedānta* to my mind is *Advaita* school. According to this school of thought the essence of reality is absoluteness. It doesn't go about any change and metamorphosis. *Brahman* is real, the world is illusion and there is a complete identity between the *Brahman* and the individual self. This is the fundamental doctrine of monastic *Vedānta*. The *Advaita Vedānta* explains the philosophical problems of how could the *Brahman* be equated with relational world? The world which is always in the state of flux. According to *Advaita Vedānta* only reality is *Brahman* and all else is nothingness.

Gauḍavāda explains the doctrine of *Ajātīvāda* (doctrine of no-creation) which obliterates the distinction between the apparent (*Pratibhāsika*) and *Vyavahārika* (conventional) reality.[48]

There is a great similarity between the doctrine of no-creation propounded by Gauḍavāda and the theory of no-origination advocated by Nāgārjuna. The refutation of the phenomenal world of time, space and causation in the being of *Brahman* the ultimate reality reconciles the contradiction between the *Upaniṣadic* teachings and rational thinking. Śaṅkara introduces the concept of *Māyā* or *Adhyāsa* (superimposition) to overcome the apparent contradiction between the *Brahman* and the world. *Māyā* is mysterious principle which tries to overcome the contradictions, however, *Māyā* is neither real nor unreal, but indescribable. Monastic *Vedānta* has tried to explain the concept of illusion as due to the absence of the real knowledge. This absence of knowledge should not be equated with the negation of knowledge. It is not an *Abhāva,* but a *Bhāva rūpa* (positive entity). However, from the transcendental point of view the *Brahman* alone is real hence, the existence of *Māyā* to me is not properly explained by Śaṅkara.

Satkari Mookerjee tries to explain the concept of *Māyā* while writing an introduction for *Aṣṭābakra Saṁhitā*. He says, "*Māyā* is the prius of the phenomenal world—the principle of unreason, the fountainhead of irrationality, the Enchantress of infinite resources. There is no escape from her hypnotic influence save through knowledge. But there is a silver lining to every cloud. *Māyā* is not the Satan of Sematic conception. She is not Absolute Evil, and is possessed of a redeeming feature in her character, for she is also the embodiment of science and reason. This provides an outlet. Science kills nescienic, reason kills unreason, and both being embedded in the selfsame Principle called variously *Māyā*, *Prakṛti*, or not-self, this Principle carries in its own self the secret of her death."[49]

This, however, the concept of *Māyā* has not been fully explained. *Māyā* being neither the aspects of *Brahman* nor a separate entity neither real nor unreal. It does not stand the scrutiny of logic. I think Satkari Mookerjee is trying to explain the concept of *Māyā* in tune with the concept of *Śakti* of Kashmir Śaivism. According to Śaṅkara *Brahman* is recognized as the cause of the world. The world is simply the appearance, a superimposition. However, the metaphor of rope and the snake does not explain fully the doctrine of *Adhyāsa*. Rope does not lose its reality even when it is mistaken for a snake. World cannot be explained in terms of changing itself into the world. It only appears as a world because of *Māyā*. The *Māyā* is not an independent principle; it is entirely dependent on *Brahman*. It can be conceived only in the context of *Brahman* who is a pure being and cosmic consciousness. Hence, nothing can be accepted without being related to *Brahman*.

Surendranath Bhattacharya writes, "*Māyā*, therefore, by itself is not sufficient to account for this phenomenal world. So, the *Vedāntins* do not hold *Māyā* to be the cause of the world. Rather, it is said that *Brahman* is the cause or ultimate ground of the world. But when *Brahman* is said to be the cause of the world, it must necessarily be supposed to be conditioned (*sopādhika*); absolute (*nirūpādhika*) *Brahman* can have nothing to do with the world. And the *upādhi* (condition) that conditions *Brahman* as the cause is *Māyā*."[50]

The modern commentator of *Vedānta* have been trying to explain the concept of *Māyā* from relativistic point of view. According to this school of thought the world is also real, but it is different from absolute reality and it has been called conventional truth, i.e., reality for reality in the context of relativistic world. Hence, the world is relatively real and it is falsified when one gets the knowledge of the *Brahman* in totality. The world is an illusion but it is not non-existent.

Śaṅkara tries to explain the world from the stand of doctrine of *Vivartavāda*. *Vivartavāda* is different from *Ārambhavāda* of *Nyāya* and *Pariṇāmavāda* of *Sāṅkhya*.

The *Brahman* appears to conventional reality. This may be called that the *Vivarta* is explained as the appearance of absolute reality as conventional reality. In the process of the evolution the consciousness is transformed into relativistic truth. Here *Vivarta* is known as the effect which is neither different nor identical with the cause and hence, it is inexplicable.

"Śaṅkara, however, does not accept or reject either of these views. He says, that all that can be said with any amount of certainty is that the effect has no existence independent of the cause, and that which has no existence by itself cannot be said to have any reality in the true sense of the term. So, the effect neither is not, for if it were absolutely non-existent, no activity would be induced. The world we see before us is neither nor unreal, nor both real and unreal. Hence, it may be logically termed as really indefinable (*anirvacanīya*). This is the fundamental position of the theory of illusory appearance."[51]

Almost all the *Advaita* schools of *Vedānta* accept *Brahman* as the supreme and ultimate reality. The world as false, *Māyā* as neither real nor unreal. The concept of super imposition or the wrong identification of self with the non-self is the bondage. The identity of the self and the non-self has the form of consciousness of self being in the state of bondage. Śaṅkara says, "due to the nescience man erroneously identifies the self with not-self". This is called bondage and it brings about attendant miseries of cycle of birth and death. "Man considers his perishable body as real. He identifies himself with body and he preserves with the help of sense object. This is psychological bondage like the silkworm in its cocoon woven by its own threads."[52]

This individuality arising out of the erroneous identification of the self with the non-self is the cause of illusoriness of the embodied self which is a product of the consciousness of individual self as false in respect of its real individuality and identity. It is the illusion and misunderstanding of individuality which is based on the doctrine of objective illusion called *Anirvacyakhyātivāda*. Śaṅkara introduced the concept of *Māyā* to explain the existence of the unreality of the world. It is the illusion through which self-believes that he is a *Jīva*. *Brahman* is the cosmic consciousness which has neither positive determination nor negative determination; it is characterised as *Sat* (existence), *Cit* (consciousness) and *Ānanda* (bliss). But these are not determination or attributes of the *Brahman*. Individual self has to transcend and rids himself from the false subjectivity for the emancipation. There is a complete identity between the self (*Ātman*) and the *Brahman*. *Ātman* or the ultimate reality is not an entity having freedom, but it is freedom itself. Because of *Adhyāsa Ātman* or *Jīva* thinks he is not free and wants to be free. To know according to *Vedānta* is to be. To know the real identity and destiny of oneself one can be the only way of attaining freedom and discipline that of knowing that is primarily through the *Parājñāna*.

Advaita Vedānta has been discussed and formulated by Maṇḍana Miśra, Vāchasapati Miśra, Sureśvara, Citshup, Madhusūdana, Vijñānabhikṣu and others. Mādhvācārya's *Brahma Vimarśa* occupies an important position in monastic Vedānta.

I would confine my discussion only on Maṇḍana Miśra's *Brahma Siddhi*, Vāchasapati Miśra's, *Bhāvamati* and Mādhvācārya's *Brahma Vimarśa*. There is some controversy regarding the Maṇḍana Miśra's and Sureśvara the disciple of Śaṅkara. According to one school of thought Maṇḍana Miśra was contemporary of Śaṅkara, but he is different from Sureśvara.

According to other school Maṇḍana Miśra and Sureśvara are one and the same person. I believe that Maṇḍana Miśra the author of the "*Brahma Siddhi*" is different from Sureśvara because Maṇḍana Miśra exposition of *Advaita Vedānta* is quite different from the Śaṅkara's *Advaita*. Maṇḍana Miśra is one of the original thinker. According to Maṇḍana Miśra, *Brahman* is identical with the world and he accepted doctrine of *Sphoṭa* enunciated by Bhartṛhari. He tried to bring about the happy and the harmonious blending of the theory of *Śabda Advaita* of Bhartṛhari with *Brahma Advaita* of *Advaita Vedānta*. This is the original thinking of Maṇḍana Miśra. Maṇḍana Miśra gives great importance to meditation to uproot the residual impression or metempsychosis generated by ignorance.

Dinesh Chandra Bhattacharya writes, "The *Jīvas* move in bondage through *Avidyā*, but as reflections of *Brahman* on *Avidyā* they are essentially identical with *Brahman*. Verbal knowledge of the contents of Vedāntic texts, which is mediate (*parokṣa*), cannot produce perception of the reality (*Brahma-sākṣātkāra*) and liberation, unless the proper *vṛtti* (mental image or modification) is formed through constant meditation."[53] Vāchasapati Miśra, the author *Bhāvamati* is considered a most important commentary on the *Śaṅkara Bhāṣya* of the *Brahma Sūtra*. He was one of the most original thinker and expounder of *Advaita Vedānta*. His commentaries of *Sāṅkhyakārikā*, *Yoga Bhāṣya*, *Nyāya Vārttika* and *Vidhiviveka* are a scholarly work on Indian philosophy. His commentary on Maṇḍana Miśra's *Brahma Siddhi* titled *Tattva*, *Samikṣā* in which he tried to adhere to Maṇḍana Miśra's view. Vāchasapati accepted the Maṇḍana Miśra views on *Jīva* as the support of ignorance. However, his most celebrated works on *Advaita Vedānta* is *Bhāvamati*. There has been many commentaries written on this scholarly work by different commentator like Amala Nanda, Apaiya Dikshit, Lakshmi Nirsingha, Swam Prakāśa Anand. Vāchasapati Miśra has advocated a subjective idealism. According to him Vāchasapati holds the view that *Brahman* is both material (*Upādāna*) and efficient cause (*Nimitta*) of the world. Vāchasapati Miśra's exposition of this theory goes against Vedāntic solipsism, according to which individual self with the effects of ignorance is material cause and creator of the world. Vāchasapati Miśra introduced duality of *Avidyā* and plurality of original naissance. One is the psychological naissance in the form of error or illusion, other is the primal or the positive *Avidyā*. One is called *mūlavidyā* or *kāraṇavidyā*.

The *mūlavidyā* can be rooted out only by realization of the true nature of *Brahman*.

Dinesh Chandra Bhattacharya writes, "It is the mind or the intellect (*buddhi*), purified and stimulated by meditation, which produces the final intuition or knowledge of *Brahman*, though the Vedic texts help the mind to a great extent. Immediate cognition, mental or external, requires a sense organ to produce it; and the mind is the sense organ which produces the final perception of *Brahman*. This view also is a heritage from Maṇḍana Miśra and is opposed to the views of the author of *Vivaraṇa* and others who do not hold the mind to be a sense organ or the means (*kāraṇa*) to the final realization. The dictum '*śrotavyaḥ*' does not mean any sort of obligatoriness, as others hold, because it is not at all an injunction (*vidhi*), though it has the semblance of an injunction. It cannot be a *vidhi*, as it is, but a restatement (*anuvāda*) of what we can know by our common sense."[54]

Mādhvācārya expounded the *Brahmavāda* which is in line with other commentators of *Advaita Vedānta* on the *Upaniṣads* and *Brahma Sūtra*. His *Brahma Vimarśa* is one of the great philosophical work on monism expounded by *Upaniṣads*. He considers that the bondage is due to the superimposition of doership on individual. Man thinks that he is a doer only when he becomes the victim of superimposition of naissance and his individuality becomes *Paratantra* (bondage). He refuted the Śaṅkara concept of *Brahman* as *Nirguṇa* (attributeless) and *Māyā* when it is superimposed on *Brahman* it appears as a world. Mādhva considers that Śaṅkara's Vedānta smacks of dualism. On the other hand Rāmānujam expounded the *Viśiṣṭa Advaitavāda* according to which origin of the world is experienced as *Vyakta*. Mādhva refutes both Śaṅkara and Rāmānujam and comes out a new doctrine according to which so long one believes in *Viśiṣṭa* character of *Brahman Advaita* becomes *ipso facto* nullified. Mādhva says *Brahman* is complete supreme and paramount reality. *Brahman* is independent ground of all that is other than *Brahman*. Another salient feature of Mādhva exposition of *Vedānta* is reliance on epistemological considerations. He considers *Vedas* as the only authority and the validity of which depends on being the only source of valid and proper knowledge. Other thinkers have taken ontological refuge a shelter to explain the truth of *Vedas* whereas Mādhva has taken epistemological consideration for expounding the truth of *Vedas*. According to Mādhva *Brahman* is supreme and paramount reality (*sarvottama*). *Brahman* is not among many realities. It is ultimate reality which embraces all and transcends all.

World is the creation and expression of the *Brahman*. *Brahman* provides the reality in all its aspects. Therefore, no reality or truth exists apart from *Brahman*. He takes the help of the *Vedas* where it has been stated that there is non-difference (*Abheda*) in the cosmic consciousness. *Brahman* doesn't undergo any change and transformation while creating the world. Its transcendentality is not lost. The *Śruti* also expounds the theory of difference (*Veda*) between the *Brahman* and the world. However, the difference (*Bheda*) does not speak of the independent existence of reality in form of world. The world is only transcendent nature of *Brahman*. The philosophers and the commentators of the *Śruti* have committed a grave mistake by accepting either *Bheda* or *Abheda* views which is the negation of *Brahman*. According to Mādhva *Vedas* do not put emphasis on *Bheda* (difference) and *Abheda* (non-difference). To Mādhva *Bheda* and *Abheda* are not important philosophical issues. When *Brahman* is the only ultimate reality, he gives a new kind of cosmology. According to him every act affects the whole cosmos and hence every case of any doing is the case of cosmic doing. *Brahman* alone is the supreme doer. He is both the doer and work done. According to him *Brahman* is *Advaita* without a second there is no other than *Brahman* to determine its nature. *Brahma* is *Purṇa* (complete) and paramount reality. *Brahman* is the only doer. The concept of individual doer is based on illusion. According to him *Brahman* is the only substance and substratum of whole existence. And thereby he refuted the Śaṅkara's *Māyāvāda*. He considers that by accepting the Śaṅkara's view of the world as unreal (*Mithyā*) it amounts to Nihilism.

Now, I would like to present the teachings of *Aṣṭābakra Saṁhitā*, *Avadhūta Gītā* and *Nirvāṇa Śataka*. In my opinion these three classical works present the quint essential teachings of *Vedānta*. The greatest problem before the *Advaita Vedānta* is to give a rational and spiritual exposition of the existence of the world. Both science and philosophy have been in search of reality which would satisfy both the philosophy and the scientific quest for unity. The reality has been defined as universal that pervades the parts and provides its meaning. Though *Advaita Vedānta* does not admit any kind of reality apart from *Brahman,* but for the sake of practical convenience it admits three kind of truth, i.e., *Paramarthika, Vyavahārika* and *Pratibhāṣika*. The *Brahman* is considered as *Paramārthikāsatya*, world is considered as *Vyavahārika* truth attributed to the objective world and *pratibhāṣika* truth stands for the naissance of the *Jīva* wrapped in bondage. The illusion of the objective world is a creation of the superimposition of the naissance. *Advaita Vedānta* not only speaks of the illusion of empirical world.

K.A. Krishna Swamy Iyer writes, "Reason which points out the illusion must also be competent to release us from its hold. Śaṅkara is not alone in drawing our attention to the illusory nature of empirical life. Plato, Kant, and Hegel adopt the same view, and in recent times, Bergson, equipped with all the knowledge of modern science, arrives at the same conclusion. The intellect, he says, disguises reality, misrepresents it, and presents to us a static world, while reality is pure movement, change, or a wider consciousness. According to both Śaṅkara and Bergson, the illusion is necessary to practical life, though nonetheless it is an illusion. Śaṅkara does not favour the reality of the idea as against that of the object."[55] The modern science particularly the Quantum Mechanics says that we do not see the nature as it is but as nature is exposed to our method of questioning. Heisenberg writes, "But at this point the situation changed to some extent through Quantum theory and, therefore, we may now come to a comparison of Descartes's philosophical system with our present situation in modern physics. It has been pointed out before that in the Copenhagen interpretation of Quantum theory we can indeed proceed without mentioning ourselves as individuals, but we cannot disregard the fact that natural science is formed by men. Natural science does not simply describe and explain nature; it is a part of interplay between nature and ourselves; it describes nature as exposed to our method of questioning. This was a possibility of which Descartes's could not have thought, but it makes the sharp separation between the world and the impossible."[56]

The ontology of materialism has been questioned by the modern science. Heisenberg further writes, "The ontology of materialism rested upon the illusion that the kind of existence, the direct "actuality" of the world around us, can be extrapolated into the atomic range. This extrapolation is impossible, however."[57]

Vedānta is based on rational metaphysics. However, it goes beyond the reason also. The *Advaita Vedānta* basic concern is to explain the falsity of anything that present as an alternative to cosmic consciousness. The fundamental principles of *Advaita* are the experience and the realization of *Brahman*. According to *Vedānta Brahman* alone is real and the world is appearance and the *Jīva* is conventional reality. Due to the erroneous identification of the self with non-self the bondage is created. Bondage is psychological. It springs from the ignorance of the real nature of the self as *Brahman* is experienced the moment naissance disappears. Freedom entails the freedom from the non-self. The moment a man realizes such the self as *Brahman* and the only ultimate reality, difference and distinction evaporates in the presence of the transcendental knowledge of self. *Aṣṭābakra Saṁhitā* says, "I have neither bondage nor freedom. Having lost its support, the illusion has ceased. Oh, the Universe, though existing in me, does not in reality so exist."[58]

Avadhūta Gītā also speaks the same language. It says, "All is verily the absolute Self. Distinction and non-distinction do not exist. How can I say, "I exists; it does not exist"? I am filled with wonder! The essence and the whole of *Vedānta* is this knowledge, this Supreme Knowledge: that I am by nature the formless, all pervasive Self."[59]

"The cardinal teachings of the *Vedānta* are the knowledge that the self is by nature formless. It is a cosmic consciousness. It is all pervasive."[60]

"The question of the self has been hidden or visible does not arrive when the one self is that self which is a cosmic consciousness."[61]

The bondage is psychological and not metaphysical; it is ideational and not ontological. *Vedānta* as a philosophical pursuit provides rational conviction, but it is not self-realization. The *Advaita Vedānta* has rejected the world of sense and intellect which is embedded in the philosophy of dualism; which doesn't have any logical or ontological justification. All philosophical attempts to give a rational justification of ontological materialism are bound to end in a *cul de sac*. Logic or rationality has limitations and it cannot give any proper presentation of the ultimate reality which is *Brahman* or the self. The *Vedānta* does not ignore the rational philosophical pursuit, but it supplements the results acquired by intuitional science which does not go against the rational presentation of science and philosophy.

The cardinal principle of *Vedānta* is to provide a rational metaphysics and with this rational metaphysics *Vedānta* exposes its limitations and takes man beyond the dualism of subject and object. Because the objective of *Vedānta* is not to provide only a rational ontological metaphysics, but to the realization of the *Brahman* which is the only ultimate substratum and the *summum bonum* of human life.

Śaṅkara writes, "For all the living creatures, a human birth is indeed rare; much more difficult is to attain full manhood; rarer than this is a *Sāttvika* attitude in life. Even after gaining all these rare chances, to have steadfastness on the path of spiritual activity as explained in Vedic Literature is yet rarer; much more so to have a correct knowledge of the deep significances of the scriptures. Discrimination between the Real and the Unreal, a personal experience of spiritual Glory and ultimately to get fully established in the living consciousness that the Self in all; these come only later on, and culminate in one's liberation. This kind of a perfect liberation cannot be had without earned merits of a hundred crores of lives lived intelligently."[62]

According to *Vedānta Brahman* (cosmic consciousness) is the substratum and substance of whole universe. Mundane and supra-mundane consciousness is the substratum of inert object like stone, however, stone is not aware of this truth. The more evolved plant life and animal life do have the consciousness as the only reality behind all the multi-fold expressions in the form of different plants and different species. However, they are not equipped to the spiritual pursuits for the realization of the ultimate truth. The man is the only species who is endowed with the power to realize the truth in its totality and become one with the *Brahman. Aṣṭābakra* answers the query of Janaka as to how the salvation can be attained? *Aṣṭābakra* says, "You are neither earth nor water nor fire nor air nor space. In order to attain freedom know the self as the witness of all these and as cosmic consciousness itself."[63]

The cosmic consciousness or the self is the witnessing counterpart of all our mental activities. The realization of the self as a pure being and consciousness unpolluted and unaffected witness of the phenomenal world would be the dawn of the wisdom and self-realization. So long a man sees another self, this is called naissance. Self-realization lies in seeing nothing, but the cosmic consciousness—the self as the substratum and substance of all beings and existence. The self is the *Brahman* and it is consciousness, existence and bliss. The mind or the *Ahaṅkāra* limits and distorts the pure consciousness as light as seen in the prism. The moment man rids himself from the snares of the false subjectivity, he becomes *Brahman*. *Aṣṭābakra* says, "This is a very significant utterance and one that contains an invaluable lesson for those who wish to attain self-realization. In reality the self is ever free. It never enters into a state of bondage. It is our ignorance that we think ourselves bound; and this thought makes our supposed bondage persist and continue. If, however, we constantly think of ourselves as the eternally free Self, we shall realize that we are ever free."[64]

To talk in the psychological language it is a kind of auto-suggestion. This is the psychological basis of the concentration and meditation. As I have already stated that bondage is psychological and not metaphysical, the only escape from the bondage of the Self from the octopus of sense object is to dive deep into the innermost being which is pure consciousness. In this state of illumination the unity of the cosmic consciousness with all that exists is experienced. In fact the cosmic consciousness is the only truth and reality and nothing else exists apart from the cosmic consciousness. With the experience of this truth the world of objectivity disappears. There is neither plurality of objects nor the plurality of subjects. There is the only one supreme subjectivity or there is no subject.

The *Nirvāṇa Śatakam* of Śaṅkarācārya expounds the quintessence teachings of *Vedānta*. According to *Vedānta* the *Mahāvākya* that *thou art that* is the cardinal teachings of *Upaniṣads*. Though "I am *Brahman*", 'I' becomes the victim of octopus of sense objects and starts thinking in terms of individual doer and enjoyer. Śaṅkara says, "I am not the mind, intellect, ego and memory. I am neither the five sense organs, nor the five physical elements. I am pure knowledge, bliss and I am Śiva – the auspiciousness itself."[65]

Same truth is expounded by *Aṣṭābakra Saṁhitā*. According to *Aṣṭābakra Saṁhitā* "Virtue and via, pleasure and pain, are of the mind, not for you, O all-pervading one. You are neither doer nor enjoyer. Verily you are ever free."[66]

According to *Avadhūta Gītā*[67] "even there is no need of knowledge, reasoning, time, space, instruction from a teacher for attainment of *Samādhi*. I am naturally the perfect consciousness, the real, like the sky spontaneous and steady. Here the sky stands for the *Brahman* itself."

The *Avadhūta* maintains that the practice of *Samādhi* is not required because the self has never been in bondage. The self which is a pure consciousness can never lose consciousness of its true nature. Therefore, to talk of *Samādhi* is frivolous.

Avadhūta Gītā says, "If it is of the nature of the not-Self, how can there be *Samādhi* (super-conscious realization)? If it is of the nature of the Self, how can there be *Samādhi*? If it is both "is" and "is not", how can there be *Samādhi*? If all is one and of the nature of freedom, how can there be *Samādhi*?"[68]

Śaṅkarācārya in summarizing the teachings of *Vedānta* in his last verse of *Nirvāṇa Śatakam* says, "I am devoid of dualities and am formless. I exist everywhere pervading all the sense. Always I am same. (I have) neither freedom nor bondage. I am pure knowledge and Bliss. I am Auspiciousness, I am Śiva." Ervin Schrodinger also agrees with the philosophy of *Vedānta*. The plurality that we perceive is only an appearance and not real. Ervin Schrodinger writes, "Looking and thinking in that manner you may suddenly come to see, in a flash, the profound rightness of the basic conviction in *Vedānta*: it is not possible that this unity of knowledge, feeling and choice which you call *your own* should have sprung into being from nothingness at a given moment not so long ago; rather this knowledge, feeling and choice are eternal and unchangeable and numerically *one* in all men, nay in all sensitive beings. But not in this sense—that you are a part, a piece, of an eternal, infinite being, an aspect or modification of it, as in Spinoza's pantheism. For we should then have the same baffling question: which part, which aspect are *you*? What, objectively, differentiates it from the others? No, but, inconceivable as it seems to ordinary reason, *you*—and all other conscious beings as such—are all in all. Hence, this life of yours which you are living is not merely a piece of the entire existence, but is in a certain sense the *whole*; only this whole is not so constituted that it can be surveyed in only single glance. This, as we know, is what the Brāhmins express in that sacred, mystic formula which is yet really so simple and so clear: *Tat tvam asi*, this is you. Or, again, in such words as 'I am in the east and in the west, I am below and above, I *am this whole world*'."[69]

The examination and elucidations of the concepts of *Vedānta* and modern science leads to the same truth that the reality is beyond the reach of philosophical ratiocination and scientific formulations. It recognises the limitations of reason and it speaks of the transcendental reality which is beyond the reach of philosophy and science. Both science and philosophy are rooted in Ontological mysticism. The natural science which domains are nature leave some basic and the fundamental questions and answers. Eddington says, "We have found that where science has progressed the farthest, the mind has, but regained from nature that which the mind has put into nature. We have found a strange footprint on the shores of the unknown. We have devised profound theories, one after another, to account for its origin. At last, we have succeeded in reconstructing the creature that made the footprint. And Lo! It is our own."[70]

The modern physics is undergoing great change in the light of the development in the field of the Relativity and Quantum mechanics. Search for the nature and the essence of ultimate reality, i.e., of matter of energy and of consciousness, is leading towards the Ontological mysticism. The philosophical insight and the scientific understanding of the concepts need deeper examination and evaluation to understand the mystical nature of the truth. Einstein was the first scientist who visualised a doctrine of unified theory which would explain the mysterious nature of reality and he laid down a new foundation for physics. Whether the assertion of The *Bible* "God is spirit and Vedāntic dictum"—"All is *Brahman*" could be the foundation for the harmonious and happy blending for the science and spirituality. Ken Wilber writes, "If we want to go beyond physics, however, and begin to philosophize, then the world view that can most easily explain modern physics is that not of Democritus, but of Plato. Heisenberg was an excellent philosopher (probably, with Eddington, the most accomplished in this volume), and a metaphysician or mystic of the Pythagorean-Platonic variety. Capable of being rigorously analytical and empirical, he nonetheless despised mere positivism—or the attempt to be only analytical and empirical—and thus in the opening section, Heisenberg, Pauli, and Bohr lament the attempt of philosophy to ape physics."[71]

According to *Vedānta*, the *Brahman* is the ultimate reality which is the inner essence of all things and beings. *Brahman* is beginningless, supreme beyond what is and beyond what is not. *Chāndogya Upaniṣad* says, "that which is the finest essence—this whole world has that as its soul, i.e., reality. That is *Ātman*. Thou art that."[72] The *Upaniṣadic* teachings has to be understood in the context of modern physics. This may lead to the discovery of Einstein's dream of unified theory of reality.

Tantra

In quest of identity and destiny man discovered philosophy and religion. In search of realization of philosophical truth and religious *summum bonum* of life Lord Śiva expounded scientific and mystic tradition known as *Tantra*. *Tantra* forms the esoteric basis of all religion and provides sound philosophical foundation of spirituality. *Tantra* is known as *Āgama Śāstra*. The *Śivādvaita* School of *Tantra* philosophy is unique and sublime contribution of India to speculative metaphysics. In *Tantra*, *Advaita* means the eternal co-existence of Śiva and Śakti which constitute the absolute of *Tantra* philosophy. Śiva is transcendental and *Śakti* is the imanent aspect of the absolute. The *Kuṇḍalinī*, the *Mantra* and the *Yantra* are the three esoteric principles of *Tantra Sādhanā*. Reality is open only to the esoteric experience. The incomprehensible certainty of the absolute cannot be explained by any grammar of metaphysics. The esoteric experience of this intuitional science is vivid, direct and integral. In the intuitive experience the *Yogī* feels the impact of reality and he becomes the absolute, i.e., that which is real identity. The mystery of the ultimate reality cannot be rationally determined. It is beyond the scope of logical concepts. The *Vedas* expound only the negative account of reality as "not this, not this". He is none being. He is nothing, i.e., the *Veda* simply affirm that reality cannot be realized through the various categories of reason whereas *Tantra* is an intuitional science which provides the mystic technique to the realization and experience of the ultimate reality which is variously addressed as *Parama Śiva*, *Brahman* or *Ātman*. The cardinal principles of the intuitional science of *Tantra* are that the ultimate reality is to be realized and experienced with the awakening of the *Kuṇḍalinī*. This awakening of the *Kuṇḍalinī* is a mystic process of divinization and spiritualization. It leads one to the path of inner spiritual transformation. The awakening of the *Kuṇḍalinī* brings about an inner transformation in the physical, vital and psychic forces. The conversion of the mechanical energy into psychic force is called *Upavidyā* and the practice of this force for physical gain is called *Avidyā Sādhanā*. The transformation of psychic energy into spiritual force or bliss is called *Vidyā Tantra*.

From the excavation of Mohenjo-Daro and Harappa we find a historical developed urban life. The proto-Śiva (seal) discovered during the excavation of Mohenjo-Daro is considered 2500 B.C. old. From the skeleton materials unearthed there, whole concept of development of Indian culture and civilization has been revolutionised. The Āryans were not the indigenous population of India, they came here from Central Asia. They contemptuously imposed the name *Anārya* (uncultured) on the natives of this land. It refers to India's heterogeneous community which is of Mongolian, Austric and Austrico-Negroid (Draviḍian origin). From the excavation report of Harappan civilization it is evident that it was a gift of Śaivism or Tantrism. John Marshall says, "The figure represents a prototype of the Historic Śiva."[73]

Sir John Marshall says in the excavation report of Harappa and Mohenjo-Daro that Śiva is the male deity of the non-Āryan pantheon of Pre-Vedic India. The *liṅga* at Gudimallam is ancient (*c.* 200 B.C.) and it has the figure of Śiva with the Mongolian features carved on it. The deity has plaited hair and no holy thread.[74]

M.M. H.P. Shastri says that Śiva is originally the God of the *Vrātyas*, non-Vedic people.[75]

Tantra Sādhanā leads to a higher and spiritual level of perfection, and *Yogī* continues till he achieves the supreme end of life, becomes one with *Parama Śiva*. This is called *Parā Saṁvita*.

Tantra Sādhanā, in fact, is meant for the attainment of the four fold objectives of life, i.e., *Dharma* (virtue), *Artha* (wealth), *Kāma* (enjoyment) and *Mokṣa* (salvation). It is not, as is ordinarily misunderstood, devoted to salvation alone. Human life is multi-dimensional. And any philosophy or religion which does not fulfil these four objectives of life, which follow one another in one's spiritual progress and perfection, remains a futile pursuit.

The material science does not give any holistic view of the Reality. Its method is analytic. It explains the phenomenal world in mathematical forms and physical concepts. These forms and concepts are mere abstractions. The approach to Reality through science remains only partial. Physics, which is employed mechanical models of the universe to explain the fundamental principles of the Cosmos has now changed its course and theme because the models have failed. Of late physicists have taken shelter in concepts and ideas, and agreed with Newton in the view that things 'certainly are not mechanical' entities.

To *Tantra Sādhanā*, both philosophy and science are bound up with mysticism. *Tantra* combines science and spirituality, fact and ideal. Philosophy in India is not mere speculation, but a way of life. Mysticism is a philosophy of oneness. It is based on the rule of identity in life.

The mysticism of *Tantra* denotes a state of consciousness which is characterised by a complete cessation of sensations, ideas, concepts and subject-object relationship. Through *Tantra Sādhanā*, the mind reaches the pure state of Consciousness and Bliss. The *Sādhaka* attains the state of equal-mindedness which finally leads to salvation. *Tantra* leads to an integrated elevation and evolution of human personality. *Tantra* is mysticism as it takes man to the realization of *Parama Śiva* which is beyond the dualism of subject and object. The awakening of the *Kuṇḍalinī*, incantation of *Mantra* and use of *Yantra* (mystic diagram) are mystical in import.

Tantra and the *Veda* are the two streams of Indian culture and civilization. *Tantra* is ancient and indigenous to India. It is a cult whereas the *Veda* is a creed. But all their apparent contradictions and conflicts have long been resolved and both assimilated into the organism of Hindu Culture. *Tantra* is *Āgama* and the *Veda Nigama*. *Tantra* deals with *tattva* and *mantra*, the former a cosmic principle and the latter a mystic sound.

The account of *Tantra* philosophy has mainly been drawn from *Śiva Sūtra*, *Tantrāloka*, *Svachanda Tantra*, *Mālinī Vijjoyottārā Tantra*, *Pratibhijñā-hṛdayam*, *Kāmika Āgama*, *Śiva-Dṛṣṭi* and other works of Kashmir Śaivism. My interpretation of the *Tantra* cult is based on *Śāradā Tilakam*, *ṣaṭcakra Nirūpaṇa* (Serpent Power),

Mahānirvāṇa Tantra, *Kulārṇava Tantra*, *Tripūra Rahasya*, *Saundaryalaharī*, etc. I have also made use of *Hevajra Tantra*, *Sādhanā Mālā* and *Guhya Samāja Tantra* as the base books in dealing with the Buddhist *Tantra*. I have derived considerable help from the works of many authors, especially Sir John Woodroffe, Dr. Gopinath Kaviraj, Dr. P.C. Bagchi, Swami Pratyagatmananda and Dr. Benoytosh Bhattacharya, Lakshman Joo and Jaidev Singh. I am deeply indebted to all of them.

Śaivism and Śaktism the two schools of *Tantra* Metaphysics were the official religions of non-Āryans of the Indus Valley Civilization who practised various aspects of *Tantra Sādhanā*, according to the intellectual abilities and standards. Śiva and Śakti, the dual deities symbolising the two schools, were the principal divine beings and were worshipped. But in essence Śiva was the god of the non-Āryans.

Among the aniconic objects of worship are the *liṅgas* and *yonīs* together their bactylic forms (Pl. II. 31-33). The *liṅga* (phallus) worship was prevalent amongst the backward classes of the non-Āryans. E.H. Hartland in a detailed and informative article[76] on phallism deals with the subject from a broader view. His central theme is to trace sex-worship as part of the history of religion which has prevalent in the different strata of culture. Sex-worship was a customary practice and was considered to be part of religious sacrament by the ancient people belonging to different faiths. With the advancement of civilization it was transformed into a higher religious symbolism. This practice was so universal that it became an integral part of the evolution of human mind, and it seems indigenous with the race.[77] Wall observes: "All religion are based on sex, some like ancient Egyptian, Greek and Roman or the modern *Brahmanic* worship of Śiva more coarsely so, according to modern civilized thought; others like Christian religion more obscurely so."[78]

Originally, sex-worship was not developed for the achievement for any morbid exaltation and ecstasy. The primitive people were mostly engaged in war, and preservation of progeny was their greatest problem. Sex-worship, therefore, reasonably really stands for procreation and not for any sexual indulgence. Further, *Tantra*, a positive science, never encourages sexual indulgence. Rather, it lays down very strict rules and a severe discipline which forbids indulgence, even for a family man though it does not restrain him from leading a normal life. The modern man knows the consequences of mental suppression and repression. But *Tantra* offers an esoteric process, known as *Ṣoḍaśī Sādhanā*, for the sublimation of sex instinct.

Nigama and Āgama

Tantra deals with both the theoretical and practical aspect of spiritual life. The former is known as *Nigama* and the latter is called *Āgama*. Some scholars have tried to prove that *Tantra* is the developed form of the *Sāṅkhya* and *Vedānta* systems that the science of *Sāṅkhya* and *Vedānta* philosophy has been culminated into the Tāntric cult, and, thus, *Tantra* is a part of the *Vedas*. P.C. Bagchi says: "The *Tantra* is regarded as a *Śruti* or *Āgama*, revelation, as opposed to a *Smṛti* or *Nigama*, "tradition". It is thus classed with the *Vedas*. It is usually defined as "*Śrutiśākhāviśeṣaḥ*", a particular branch of the *Vedas*."[79] This contention is untenable.

By no logic or cultural evidence can it be proved that *Tantra* is a branch of the *Veda*. *Tantra* and the *Veda* are the two different currents of India's cultural life. There is no common meeting ground between the two. *Tantra* is a cult and the *Veda* a philosophy. *Tantra* is for the salvation of the soul and the *Veda* for the enrichment of the mind. The difference between the soul and the mind symbolizes the difference between *Tantra* and the *Veda*.

According to Dr. Gopinath Kaviraj, one of the greatest scholars of *Tantra*, the *Veda* is *Nigama* and *Tantra* is *Āgama*.[80] *Tantra* is the superior and sublime form of spiritual life and *Sādhanā*. In the process of Āryanization of Indian culture and life, some scholars have cunningly interpolated some verses in the later Tāntric texts to drive home their points or prejudices.

Rudrayāmala Tantra says that *Āgama* is that class of *Vedas* which has been addressed to *Pārvatī* by Lord Śiva and *Nigama* is referred to as the words of Pārvatī spoken to Śiva.[81] *Rudrayāmala Tantra* is of recent origin. Vedic *paṇḍits* have doubtlessly interpolated this verse to assert the authority of the *Vedas* over *Tantra*. The philosophical and the esoteric exposition of Śiva cannot be classed as the opinion of Vasudeva. Apart from the differences of the cultural contours and climates of these two greatest of spiritual teachers they belonged to two distinct periods of Indian civilization. Their advent in the cultural life of India represents two periods of evolution and elevation of human civilization. Time perspective has always been an important factor in the shaping of a cultural life. In the present case there is a gap of nearly three thousand years between the advent of these two great teachers. How then can the truth propounded by Śiva be equated with the opinion of Vasudeva.

Āgama is the esoteric part of *Tantra* which deals with the problem of awakening the *Kuṇḍalinī* known as *puraścaraṇa kriyā* and meditation. It is the *Sādhanā* part of *Tantra*. According to *Vārāhī Tantra* as quoted in *Śabdakalpadruma*, *Āgama* deals with seven subjects, i.e., cosmology, destruction, worship of God, *Sādhanā*, *puraścaraṇa*, the six black rites and fourfold meditation.[82] *Tantra*, being a science, is amoral. It is a revelation. It unfolds the mystery of mind and soul and takes man to the realization of his own being.

The occult powers which one acquires in the course of *Tantra Sādhanā* can be used for purposes of good and bad. And *Tantra* warns against misuse of the occult science as one would only be exposing oneself to the tortures of animal life. *Āgama* being the cult or *Sādhanā* part of the *Tantra Śāstra*, it is concerned with meditation, *puraścaraṇa kriyā* and *yoga*.

The evolution of psychospiritual philosophy in India is based largely on intuition and mysticism. The search for meaning and authenticity of inner life and the mysteries of the world of the becoming and the world of spirit are the *raison d'ētre* of philosophical speculation and spiritual awakening. The original source of cultural life in India is *Tantra* and *Veda*. The Tāntric tradition has exercised great influence on Āryan civilization. It is generally believed that Indian culture has its roots in *Vedas*; which is not correct. The *Vedas* are later than *Tantra*. It is wrong to think that the primitive non-Āryans were pagan and uncivilized. On the contrary many of the sublime forms of religious worship and the concept of deities are Draviḍian origin. On the basis of available research material it can be safely concluded that Śaṅkarācārya was a great admirer and follower of *Tantra Śāstra*. The mystic power that he had cannot be achieved through the Vedic method. Śaṅkarācārya has displayed occult power to defeat his adversaries on many occasions. This power can be achieved only through *Śakti-Sādhanā*. Śaṅkara was a profound devotee of the *Śrī Vidyā* cult, *Śrī Cakra* is still being worshipped in his *Śṛṅgerī Muṭṭa*. Dr. Gopinath Kaviraj is of the opinion that Śaṅkarācārya will have to be recognised as one of the greatest exponents of the *Tripurāgama* branch of the *Śākta* School.[83]

Kuṇḍalinī

Mind is not the ultimate category of existence and being. There is something which transcends reason for which the term intuition or mysticism is used. Reason cannot comprehend the ultimate reality. *Kuṇḍalinī* occupies an important place in *Tantra Sādhanā*. The *Kuṇḍalinī* is the soul and *Yantra* is the body of *Tantra Śāstra*. *Mantra* and *Yantra* are the warp and woof of the Tāntricism. The *Kuṇḍalinī* is the greatest discovery of Tāntricism. The whole esoteric science of Tāntricism veers around this mystic spiritual force. The awakening of the *Kuṇḍalinī* is the highest objective of *Tantra Sādhanā*. Every man is *Brahman* (God). *Jīva* is Śiva and Śiva is *Jīva*. The only difference is that one is in bondage whereas the other is free.[84]

Kuṇḍalinī is *Parā Śakti*.[85] *Kuṇḍalinī* remains in a sleeping state. With the awakening of the *Kuṇḍalinī* the *Sādhaka* attains the intuitive and mystic power to visualise the absolute. When the *Kuṇḍalinī* is awakened, the trammels of *Māyā* are cut asunder, and the soul becomes free from the bondage of individuation. For the awakening of the *Kuṇḍalinī Mantrā Ghāta*, *Mantra Dīpanī* and *Mantra Chaitana* are required. The incantation of these *mantra* or the *Siddha mantra* is a part of *mantrā ghāta* process, and acoustic vibration is produced in the psychic body which has a whipping effect on the *Kuṇḍalinī*, the slumbering serpent power. *Mantra Dīpanī* stands for inner and the outer purification of the mind. However, the *Kuṇḍalinī* is neither a biological nor a psychic principle; it is spiritual concept. Brown has tried to give an objective view of *Tantra Sādhanā* while editing *Saundaryalaharī*. *Kuṇḍalinī-Yoga* constitutes the main trunk of the *Tantra* cult. The Vedic philosophy takes us to the doors of the Divine, but it cannot let us in; for that intuitional realisation is necessary, which can be attained only by *Kuṇḍalinī yoga*. Surendranath Das Gupta writes,

"So, the all-powerful Śiva though it is the source of all power, behaves as if it were without any power. This power, therefore, remains in the body as the ever-awakening *Kuṇḍalinī* or the serpentine force, and also as manifesting in different ways. The consideration of the body as indestructible is called *kāya-siddhi*."[86] The piercing of different *cakras* by the *Kuṇḍalinī* means the control of mind over the *vṛttis* (tendencies) associated with those *cakras*.

Piercing of the *Sahasrāra cakra* which is called *Uṣṇīṣa kamala* in Buddhist *Tantra* culminates in the attainment of salvation and unification with Śiva. The arousal of the *Kuṇḍalinī* leads to spiritual illumination. It illuminates the different spheres of mind. *Kāmamaya Koṣa* is converted into *Manomaya Koṣa* (subtle mind). *Manomaya* is transformed into *Atimānasa Koṣa* (supramental sphere), and again *Atimānasa Koṣa* is transmuted into *Vijñānamaya Koṣa*. *Vijñānamaya Koṣa* is transformed into *Hiraṇyamaya Koṣa*. This last vestige of mind is ultimately transformed into Self. The *Śruti* says, "Beyond the sphere of *Hiraṇyamaya Koṣa* is transcendental *Brahman*."[87]

Mantra

Mantra is another cardinal principle of Tāntric esotericism. *Mantras* are scientific formulae which are to be practised according to strict spiritual disciplines. Each and every letter from A (अ) to *kṣa* (क्ष) of *Mātṛkā Varṇa* is a living energy. They are the acoustic root of different waves and vibrations of the cosmos. These letters are representative sonoric manifestations of the universe. When these letters are arranged after the Tāntric precepts, a living force is generated which creates parapsychological wonders. The Sanskrit alphabets are of Tāntric origin. They are not called simply alphabets, but *varṇamālā*. Its fifty letters from A (अ) to *kṣa* (क्ष) are the fifty basic vibrations of the cosmos. Each letter is *Bīja Mantra* of fifty human instincts. Here *Bīja Mantra* refers the acoustic root of different psychic expressions. According to *Tantra* the divine nectar that secretes from the pineal gland (*Sahasrāra*) takes different form in six different *cakras* or *Padmas*. These six *cakras* are: *Mūlādhāra, Svādhiṣṭhāna*, *Maṇipūra*, *Anāhata*, *Viśudha* and *Ājñā*. They are called *Padmas* (lotus) because they are in the form of a lotus with a distinct colour and petals. The different petals of respective *cakra* represent the basic human longings and instincts. All the letters are divided into two groups, i.e., vowels and consonants. Vowels are called *Bīja* and consonants are called *Yoni*. Vowels are called *Bīja* because no compound can be made out of them. Consonants are called *Yoni* because they are productive letters. The cosmic creations are a consonantal expression of *Brahman*. Vowels are known as Śiva form and consonants as *Śakti* form. *Mantra* is an esoteric formula to awaken the dormant *Kuṇḍalinī*. It is an Acoustic science which brings the realization of the inner psychic power of a man. The success in *Mantra Sādhanā* depends upon the purity and dedication of *Sādhaka* and the inner potency of the *Siddha mantra* and the grace of Guru. T.M.P. Mahādevan writes, "*Mantra Sādhanā* is an essential part of spiritual discipline. The most potent way of realising a *Devatā* is with the help of these *mantra*."[88] The purpose of *Mantra Sādhanā* is to neutralise the positive effect of *māyā* by arousing the force of fundamental negativity (*Kuṇḍalinī*) and to attain the self-realization. This non-qualified liberation can be attained only by *mantra sādhanā*.

Śiva Sūtra says, "*Mantra* is *Citta*."[89] *Citta* here means cosmic consciousness. *Citta* has not been used here in the sense of objectivated consciousness as described in *Pratyabhijñāhṛdayam*.[90] *Citta* means Śiva. Bhāskara, the great commentator of *Śiva Sūtra* and author of *Śiva Sūtra Vārttika* says, "*Mantra* is that which is of the nature of bringing intuitive realization of Self."[91] The nature of *Mantra* is consciousness.[92] The mantric power is not a mechanical force, but a spiritual principle which awakens the dormant divinity. *Tantra* enjoins upon every man and woman to awaken *mantra*. Mantric Consciousness is the supreme state of evolution. It is a mystic technique for accelerating the process of evolution.

There is a sound wherever there is vibration. Every action is vibrational. The creation or cosmic thought projection in the form of the universe is also an action.

It has vibrations and sounds. We are unable to hear this *supra mundane* sound with our physical ears. But when the mind is tuned with the help of intuitional scientific process we can hear that eternal sound *Oṁkāra*. The *Oṁkāra* is sum total of all cosmic vibrations. All other sounds are different manifestations of this cosmic sound. There is a confusion regarding the concept of

Oṁkāra, in a different Hindu tradition. Even a large section of educated believes in the significance of chanting of *Oṁ*. *Oṁ* is not to be recited, but to be listened in deep meditation. The other great confusion regarding *Oṁ* is about its recitation. A large section of the educated attaches great significance to the chanting of *Oṁ*. *Oṁkāra* is not to be recited, but to be listened to in deep meditation. When the *Kulakuṇḍalinī* awakens in an individual divine self, the later listens to different sounds. When the *Kuṇḍalinī* leave *Mūlādhāra*, one hears the sound of cricket, when she crosses *Svādhiṣṭhāna*, the sound of an anklet is heard, in the *Maṇipūra* one hears the sound of a bell, at the *Anāhata* one hears the musical symphony of flute and finally when the *Kuṇḍalinī* crosses *Viśudha*, the *Sādhaka* hears *Oṁkāra*. Beyond *Ājñā* there is no sound.

The sole objective of *mantra* is to attain liberation from *mundane*, *supramundane* and spiritual bondage. That alone is *mantra* which brings liberation. Incantation of *mantra* brings about the attainment of the four fold objective of life, i.e., *Dharma* (virtue), *Artha* (wealth), *Kāma* (mundane happiness) and *Mokṣa* (liberation).[93]

The existence is mass of waves. Destiny is nailed with multilateral misery. The *summum bonum* of human life is the attainment of *Parama Śiva*—the one singular unrythymic entity. The moment an individual unites his own *Parā Śakti* with *Parama Śiva* his *mantra* begins to vibrate with life and consciousness. *Mantra* becomes *Chaitanya* (consciousness). *Mantra* without conscious force is of no consequence. *Mantra* which are alive with their life force are alone giver of all success and benefits. Bereft of this conscious power *mantras* are combination of mere letters. They do not fructify. "The *mantra* whose potency is asleep does not give any result. In the absence of consciousness force *mantra* becomes mere letters. Even millions of incantations of such lifeless *mantras* do not give any fruit."[94]

The ideation of *mantra* is psychic process of superimposition of cosmic consciousness. It is of two kinds, i.e., auto suggestion and outer suggestion. Both are psychic parts of *mantra sādhanā*. It is of great importance and of scientific nature. With the constant ideation or superimposition of cosmic consciousness, psyche (mind) is transformed into self (*Ātman*). This transformation of psychic into self is the sole objective of *Tantra sādhanā*.

The process of transformation of mind into spirit is scientific and logical. Self or cosmic consciousness is pure and transcendental. In the scientific language we can say that wave of cosmic consciousness travels in a straight line. It means the wavelength of consciousness is infinite or zero. Mind being ever changing relative and functional organism, it is not an absolute reality. Being a relative entity mind is represented by a curvature. With the constant ideation of *Parama Śiva* during *mantra* incantation, the wave length of mind gets gradually straightened and the auspicious moment of spiritual advent the mind attains the wavelength of self which results in the merger of mind into cosmic consciousness. Mind becomes self. The realization of the *Advaita*, i.e., non-dual state of spiritual sublimity is not possible in the state of *Dvaita* dualism. *Jīva* is Śiva and Śiva is *Jīva*. The realization of this identity is the purpose behind *Tantra Sādhanā*. *Mantra* is a liberating force. It wipes away all the blemishes and makes a man pure.

Mantra Sādhanā should be performed under strict esoteric discipline. Adherence to the principles of morality is pre-condition of *mantra sādhanā*. Negligence of esoteric discipline and disobedience to moral principles obnubilate the soul.

There are three kinds of *mantra*-incantation: *Vācanika*, *Upāṁṣu* and *Mānasika*. *Vācanika Japa* is the loud incantation of *mantra*. It is the lowest form of *mantra* incantation.

When *japa* is done in the lowest tone, in other words, when only the movement of lips are observed by others, it is called *Upāṁsu Japa*. The best form of *mantra*-incantation is mental. "The *mantra* which are incanted loudly are no *mantras* at all."[95] *Tantra* rules out loud *mantra*-incantation. This is one of the points of disagreement between *Tantra* and the *Veda*. The Vedic hymns are chanted loudly; they are devoid of consciousness and force. The chanting of the Vedic hymns does not awaken the dormant divinity because it does not create that psychic and esoteric vibration in the psychic body which is the pre-condition for the arousal of the *Kulakuṇḍalinī*. *Japasūtram* discusses in detail the importance of *Japa* in *Tantra Sādhanā*. According to it there should be complete harmony and collaboration between *Vāk*, *Manaḥ* and *Prāṇa* before starting *mantra*-incantation of *Īṣṭa-mantra*.[96] Collaboration between the three factors creates an appropriate field for successful *mantra* incantation. Collaborations of *Śuddhi*, *Ṛddhi* and *Buddhi* create a psychic field for *mantra* evolution. *Vidyā* does not mean theoretical knowledge. It is the right understanding and disposition of things.

Netra Tantram expounds the philosophy and esotericism of *mantra*. It deals with the mystic and the metaphysical nature of *mantra*. According to *Netra Tantram mantra* is composed of three factors and creates the beatitude through the medium of vibration of consciousness. The two *bindūs* (points) white and red represent Śiva and Śakti. They are the cause of word (*Vāk*) and meaning (*Artha*). Śiva is a pure consciousness. Śiva requires the support and active participation of *Śakti* for the creation. Śiva is devoid of force, power and creativity. Metaphysically speaking, *Śakti* is the perfect mirror in which Śiva experiences himself. Out of the mutual enjoyment of Śiva and Śakti, word and meaning have been created. Word (*Vāk*) stands for *Parāpaśyanti, Madhyamā* and *Vaikhari* sounds. *Artha* (meaning) represents thirty six *tattvas* of *Tantra* metaphysics. Śiva and Śakti, the two *bindūs* white and red are inseparable and indistinguishable. *Mantras* are bestowers of desires, are all pervasive and are of all forms. If *mantra* is formless it cannot bestow any power. If it has form it can have only limited power. If *Mantra* is *Śivātmaka*, it is all pervasive and ultimately it becomes void. *Mantra* bereft of material and efficient cause is passive and non-creative. If it is formless it is immutable, static and devoid of creativity. Action warrants individuation. On the other hand if *mantra* is recognised as a principle of individuation then it becomes a subject of bondage. Hence, who is himself under the spell of bondage cannot grant liberation to others. *Mantra* being the liberating principle it cannot be without any force. On the other hand if *Śakti* is recognised as the life force of *mantra* then the question arises that who's *Śakti* it is? The idea of *Śakti* without the one who possess it is not possible. The confusion arises only due to the dualistic or pluralistic approach to the problem. The lack of proper understanding that Śiva and Śakti are not two entities; they are only two facets of the reality. When we experience the monism of Śiva and Śakti, ignorance of duality disappears.

Mantra Sādhanā offers the mystic and scientific process for the realization of non-dual state of Śiva and Śakti. The realization of the unity of the two is experienced in one's state of salvation. Consciousness is the soul repository of *mantra*. Without the force of consciousness *mantra* is dead and useless. The *mantra* consciousness is the *élan-vita* of *mantra Sādhanā*. It is a mystic principle for the unification of internal ectoplasmic vibration with the cosmological vibration and it leads one to the pinnacle of spiritual sublimity. The happy and harmonious blending of the individual ectoplasmic vibration and cosmic vibration is the science and the metaphysics of *mantra-śāstra*.

Yantra or Maṇḍala

Yantra is a mystic diagram. In Buddhist *Tantra*, it is called *maṇḍala*. *Yantra* worship is a marked feature of *Tantra sādhanā*. It symbolizes the higher mystic power. When a *sādhaka* attains a higher degree of spiritual progress, he is initiated into *Yantra* worship. *Yantra* means an apparatus by which anything is accomplished.

Yantra Sādhanā is a higher form of spiritual life. It is an esoteric method to fix the mind on the Supreme Reality. It subdues the *fetters*. *Yantra* is invariably used in higher *Virācāra Sādhanā*.

G. Tucci has done a pioneering work on *Maṇḍala*. His book entitled "*Teoria Praticadel Maṇḍala*" is a landmark in the study and understanding the mystic significance of *Maṇḍala*. According to him *Maṇḍala* is "psychocosmogramme". *Maṇḍala* worship is closely related with empowerment.

The *Abhiṣeka* ritual of *Kālacakra* considers *Maṇḍala* as divine residence as well as mystic diagram of deities. Dalai Lama deals in detail about the concept of *Abhiṣeka* and *Maṇḍala* in his "*Kālacakra Tantra* Rite of Initiation". For the realization of emptiness of inherent existence the deity *Kālacakra* is associated with *Kālacakra Maṇḍala*. *Kālacakra Maṇḍala* emits five colours—blue, red, white, yellow and green. *Kālacakra's* body is blue in colour. He has three necks and black in the centre, red to his right, white to his left. He has four faces. The black face in the centre symbolizes fear. If we walk round the *Maṇḍala* we could see the southern door of the mind *Maṇḍala*. We see that his right face is red and it represents desire. His black face is yellow and it is observed in deep meditation. His left face is white and it symbolizes peace.

The quintessential characteristics of *Maṇḍala* are its geometrical regularity towards the various directions. In the *Yoginī*

Tantra maṇḍala is inhabited with feminine deities. Even the centre is occupied by *Nairātama*, the consort of *Hevajra*. However, *Hevajra* and *Nairātama* are essentially one. The *Nairātama* essentially represents the state of harmony and oneness (*Samarastā*). The purpose of the *mantra* and the *Maṇḍala* worship is to have a mystic experience of essential unity *Nirvāṇa* and *Saṁsāra*. One may select his own divinity (*Īṣṭa Devatā*) and ideate upon it. But the whole purpose of ideation is to comprehend the existence in knowledge of its non-existence and likewise to conceive of *Herukā* on knowledge of his non-existence.

The *mantra Huṁ* is the *Bīja Mantra* to awaken *Herukā* or *Kuṇḍalinī*. Sometimes we complicate the process by envisaging this *Vajra* by transforming itself at the centre of which *Hevajra* is enthroned.[97] The basic function of *Maṇḍala* is to express the truth of emanation. It is considered as the centre of the Universe. Its core is Mt. Meru. It is considered as the Royal *Stūpa* and palace of universal worship and power. It seems that all these ideas and notions have been incorporated in Buddhist *Stūpa*. According to one school of thought *Maṇḍala* is primarily envisaged as *Stūpa*. D.L. Snellgrove writes, "One may envisage the final stage of emanation as the *Maṇḍala* of sixteen divinities, or one may envisage it a countless forms of *Hevajra* filling space in a regularized order in every direction. Then one must realise the identity of oneself with the whole process by associating one's personality with the emanation, which is achieved by a strenuous act of belief: *Oṁ herukā-svābhāvatmako Huṁ* – I am of the essence of *Herukā*."[98]

Yantra and *Mantra* are the body and the soul of the *Tantra Śāstra*. Every deity has its own *mantra*. After the drawing up of the *Yantra* the deity is invoked with his proper *mantra*. The inner life force is aroused to its full potential and is dedicated to the deity through the mystic process of its awakening. John Woodroffe says: "The *Yantra* is an essential part of the *Kaula* worship and without proper *Yantra* the Deity is not pleased to be present. And where worship is offered according to the scripture the Lord himself with the Devī is present."[99]

Mahānirvāṇa Tantra deals in detail with the formation and significance of *Bhairavī Cakra* and *Tattva Cakra*.[100] The formation of *Cakra* is an essential part of *Sādhanā*. *Mantras 'Kling'* and

'Phaṭ' are used by the *Kulacakra* in the formation and the purification of the *Cakra*. *Iṣṭa Devatā* is installed in the *Bhairavī Cakra*. The *Sādhaka* is locked in the mystic unification with the *Kuṇḍalinī Śakti*. "Pārvatī in *Bhairavī Cakra* and *Tattva Cakra* the excellent worshipper should be wedded to his *Śakti* according to the laws prescribed by Śiva."[101]

Yantra worship is a mystic process of awakening the *Kuṇḍalinī Śakti*. The use of *mālā* (rosary) and other articles is made to purify *Yantra* and to awaken the life force of *mantra*. The beads of the rosary represent different letters of *Mātṛkā Varṇa*. 'The *mālā* (rosary) prescribed consists of the letters of the alphabet, strung on the *Kuṇḍalinī* as the thread."[102] The beads of the rosary represent the different expressions of the cosmological order. They also represent the different *vṛttis*. The *Kuṇḍalinī* is the string. It means the different *vṛttis* are associated with the *Kuṇḍalinī Śakti*. With the mystic unification of the *Kuṇḍalinī* with *Parama Śiva*, the *Yogī* becomes free from all *vṛttis*. It is the state of spiritual trance.

Yantra (*Maṇḍala*) is mystic symbol. It stands for transcendental world that exists in the mind of every sentient being. The *Maṇḍala* drawn on the ground or as a painting does not represent true *Maṇḍala*. It is an ideational support for the realization of true *Maṇḍala*. In our mind it is true *Maṇḍala*. It is symbolism which depicts esoteric structure of the universe with the Buddha. It stands for that which exists in our being. This is esoteric process through which a *Sādhaka* must travel in his pilgrimage back to his own centre, the locus of his indwelling *Nirvāṇa*. A. Snodgrass writes, "The formal *Maṇḍala* delineated on the ground can simultaneously depict both worlds, the inner and the outer, because of the strict analogy that exists between them. Each part of the universe is analogous to every other part and to the whole, so that the total cosmos is located at the centre of each mind. When the initiate enters the *Maṇḍala*, he is ritualistically traversing his inner state; in his innermost mind, he is crossing the flood of *saṁsāra*, tracing his way to the centre of the cosmos which is the *bodhi-maṇḍala*, the place where the Buddha's attain Enlightenment."[103]

The symbolism of *Yantra* is pregnant with profound mysticism. *Śrī Cakra* symbolizes the cosmos and its divine cause. There are two sets of triangles, one composed of four males (Śiva) triangles and other five females (*Śakti*). From the macrocosmic point of view, the *Śakti* triangle stands for five vital functions, the census of knowledge, the five census of action and the five subtle and five gross forms of matter and the mind. Śiva triangles represent the four higher *tattvas*, i.e., *Māyā*, *sudhavidyā*, *Maheśvara* and *Sadā Śiva*.

In the centre of *Śrī Cakra*, which is represented by a point (*bindū*), resides Śiva (*Kāmeśvara*) and *Śakti* (*Lalitā*) in an undifferentiated (*abheda*) union, Enclosing the *bindū* is an inverted triangle which symbolizes will (*icchā*), action (*kriyā*) and knowledge (*jñāna*) aspects of *Śakti*. The three *Guṇas* and the deities preside over them. The other *Cakras* are the *Aṣṭakoṇa* (eight triangles), *Daśara-yugma* (two *cakras*, each of ten triangles), *Manvasra* (fourteen triangles), *Aṣṭadala* (eight lotus petals), *Ṣoḍaśadala* (sixteen lotus petals), *Vṛttatraya* (three circle and three squares). These nine *cakras* are ruled over by *Yoginīs* (divinities) presiding over forms of mind, sense and matter. *Yoginīs* are called *Āvaraṇa Devatās* (veiling deities), because they veil the pure consciousness (*cit*) and create the appearance of the world of mind, sense and matter and limited and differentiated (*apūrṇa*). *Śrī Cakra* is the mansion of *Devī*. The realization of *Devī* (*Śakti*) and consequent bliss for the *yogī* comes from her *mantra* which is the *Śrī Vidyā*.[104] The prescription for this *mantra* is given, and it is considered to be the most important esoteric item in Śaktism.

Maṇḍala Sādhanā is not for everybody. It is employed for worldly gains also. After getting initiation into *Sādhanā* the *Sādhaka* draws *Maṇḍala* and meditates upon its esoteric form. The visualization and the empowerment are two potent esoteric techniques with the help of which *Sādhaka* succeeds in liberating himself from the various kinds of mental reifications which leads one to the attainment of Buddhahood.

Maṇḍala undoubtedly gets the primary support from the mind. The crude sand *Maṇḍala* drawn on the ground for painting is not real *Maṇḍala*. It does not give esoteric support for the visualization of the *Maṇḍala* through the process of *mantrika* ideation. It is a thought construct.

It is spiritual structure symbolizing the mystic integration of microcosm and macrocosm. It is the locus of enlightenment, which resides in the recess of one's own being and existence.

Tantra Sādhanā

Mind cannot maintain its existence without objectivity. Mind is a state in the process of evolution. It is a stage in the process of motion. Every motion is an alternated phase of pause and speed. Every movement is pulsative. In the stage of pause it gains momentum which it has to express. Mind resorts to certain inter and intra ectoplasmic occupations to express itself. These occupations and the connation of the mind are known as tendencies or *vṛttis*. These tendencies or *vṛttis* are the way of expression of mind. In psychology, they are called *expressed sentiments* and *emotions*. Sentiments affecting the subsidiary glands are called instincts. Pineal and pituitary glands are two important and the most vital glands, the rest are called subsidiary glands. *Vṛttis* are the psychic objectivities of mind. They are the colours and contours of the mental process.

Vṛttis vary according to the development of the physical body. The developed and higher beings will have an increased number of *vṛttis*. The higher animals will have a greater number of *vṛttis* than the lower ones. There are fifty *vṛttis* in the human structure. They are : *Dharma, Artha, Kāma, Mokṣa, Avajñā, Prasraya, Mūrcchā, Aviśvāsa, Sarvanāśa, Krūratā, Lajjā, Piśunatā, Īrṣyā, Suṣupti, Viṣāda, Kaṣāya, Tṛṣṇā, Moha, Ghṛṇā, Bhaya, Āśā, Cintā, Ceṣṭā, Mamatā, Dambha, Viveka, Vikalatā, Ahaṅkāra, Lolatā, Kapaṭatā, Vitarka, Anutāpa, Ṣaḍaja, Ṛṣabha, Gandhāra, Madhyamā, Pañcama, Dhaivata, Niṣāda, Oṁ, Huṁ, Phaṭ, Voṣaṭ, Vaṣaṭ, Svāhā, Namaḥ, Viṣa, Amṛta, Aparā* and *Parā*.

Vṛttis are represented by different letters of the *Saṁskṛta* alphabet (*Varṇamālā*). The fifty letters of *Saṁskṛta Varṇamālā* are the seed-syllable (*bījākṣara*) of these fifty *vṛttis*. *Tantra Sādhanā* is an esoteric process to control these fifty *vṛttis*. The sublimation of mental activities (*vṛttis*) is the chief purpose of *Sādhanā*. With the sublimation of mind activities, the sense of I-ness disappears. Man becomes free form the fetters of *Māyā*. *Sādhanā* is a mystic process of psychic sublimation. It is an art of restraining the mind stuff (*Citta*) from taking various forms and modifications. Yoga is a mystic process of controlling the mind and restraining it from taking various shapes (*vṛttis*).[105]

The pituitary gland controls two *vṛttis*, i.e. *Parā* and *Aparā*. It is controlling station of the conscious mind. It is *Saṁkalpātmaka* (*parā*) and *Vikalpātmaka* (*Aparā*). *Parā-Vidyā* leads to the knowledge of the Supreme Self (*Parama Śiva*) and *Aparā Vidyā* stands for the knowledge of the manifest universe. The pineal gland is known as the mystery gland in psychology. It is the controller of all the three mental spheres, i.e., Conscious, Subconscious and Unconscious. The pineal controls all the fifty *vṛttis*. These fifty *vṛttis* have one thousand expressions. These fifty *vṛttis* can find expression both internally and externally through the ten agencies of the mind—five sensory organs and five motor organs. The five sensory organs, (*Jñānendriyas*) are: (1) *Cakṣu* (eye), (2) *Karṇa* (ear), (3) *Nāsikā* (nose), (4) *Jihvā* (tongue) and (5) *Tvak* (skin), and their functions respectively are *Darśana* (to see), *Śravaṇa* (to hear), *Agharaṇa* (to smell), *Asvādana* (to taste) and *Sparśana* (to touch). The five motor organs (*karmendriyas*) are: *Vāk* (vocal cord), *Pāṇi* (hand), *Pāda* (legs), *Pāyu* (anus) and *Upastha* (genital organs), and their functions respectively are: *Kathana* (to speak), *Śilpana* (to work), *Cāraṇa* (to move), *Varjana* (to let out the waste) and *Janana* (to give birth). The sensory organs are the receivers of vibrations and the motor organs the creators of vibrations according to the inherent *Saṁskāra*.

Each and every action is the play of *vṛttis*. Every psychic or psychophysical action is the satisfaction of different *vṛttis*. The pineal glands, which is known as *Sahasrāra Cakra*, controls all the fifty *vṛttis* expressed internally and externally by all the ten organs (50 x 2 x 10 = 1000). The awakening of the *Kuṇḍalinī*, the main aim of *Tantra Sādhanā*, alone can bring about a total control over the pineal gland, or *Sahasrāra Cakra*, the abode of Śiva. *Mūlādhāra* is the dwelling place of *Kuṇḍalinī Śakti*. The esoteric coupling (*maithuna*) of Śiva and Śakti brings liberation from the fetters and trammels of *Māyā*.

With the coupling of Śiva and Śakti the secretion of the pineal nectar starts flowing. *Gandharvāmalikā Tantra* says, "Oh beloved one, the Queen of the Devas unites with *Parama Śiva* and in a moment, Oh Devī *Parameśvarī*, nectar is produced. This nectar is issued on the enjoyment of the union of *Kulakuṇḍalinī* and *Parama Śiva*."[106] A man is lost in the world of spiritual beatitude and consciousness. It is the state where he is beyond the approach of all *vṛttis*. Within the scope of *vṛttis* lies the seed of *Saṁskāra* or a sense of I-ness. The attainment of spiritual beautitude means the exhaustion of all the reactive momentum accumulated by *Jīva* in the course of his previous journeys in the cosmic circle (*Brahma-Cakra*). According to *Tantra* the Absolute Reality is neutral by nature. It has two aspects *Prakāśa* and *Vimarśa*; *Nivṛtti* and *Pravṛtti*, which may be rendered as Transcendental and Immanent, Static and Dynamic, or positive and negative. Śiva and Śakti are two aspects of the Absolute Reality. Śiva is pure consciousness and as such a static principle. *Śakti* is the cosmic energy, the world force. She is the dynamic aspect of the Reality. But neither Śiva nor *Śakti* is the Ultimate Reality; they are inseparable. Absolute Reality or *Parama Śiva* (*Brahman*) is the state of neutrality produced through the unification of Śiva and Śakti. The mystic unification of Śiva and Śakti, under one condition, produces the highest state of spiritual bliss and beatitude, and under another, the manifest world or phenomenal process as a whole. When *Śakti* gets the scope of her manifestation, Śiva undergoes transformation and the world of manifestation is produced. Association of Śiva with his consort *Śakti* in the realm of *Pravṛtti* is responsible for the creation of the visible world, but when *Śakti*, in the form of *Kulakuṇḍalinī* rises to Śiva in a process of introversion, their union results in a state of infinite Bliss and Divinity. The metaphysical union or Śiva and Śakti binds and the mystic unification liberate.

Tantra was wrongly downgraded to the class of black magic and condemned as a burial ground of all the dead and the obsolete religious rites. The deeper analysis into its philosophical and mystic imports would throw proper understanding of *Tantra* as a scientific system of spiritual discipline based on human psychology. There cannot be any denying of the fact that the elements of magic and auto-suggestion are contained in the body of *Tantra*. The scientific study of human mind has proved that it has a *Parā*-psychological power. *Pañcamakāra Sādhanā* which is employed in *Tantra* is esoteric process for the transformation of desire. Hunger and sex are in it by logical instincts. They cannot be ignored. The suppression and repression of these desires and instincts lead to abnormal human behaviour. The principle behind the *Pañcamakāra Sādhanā* is that the man must rise with the aid of that *Śakti* which if misused will cause his fall. The poison that kills when cultured by a physician becomes the elixir of life. Man has to work out his own salvation not by incorporating his desires and supressing the biological instincts like sex, but by sublimating and channelizing them into higher forms of spiritual life. The attainment of occult powers and practice of *Pañcamakāra Sādhanā* have created completely wrong understandings about the *Tantra* to the Western minds. A close and scientific analysis of such *parā*-psychological power proves beyond any doubt that they have sound scientific basis. Our knowledge of mind and consciousness is very limited and incomplete. The science of *Tantra* would help one to experience deepest consciousness and become aware of the immense power of mind. The spiritual humanism and intuitional science of *Tantra* would provide sound ethical and spiritual foundation for the harmonious blending of materialism with spirituality, science with religion and philosophy with mysticism. Dr. Benoytosh Bhattacharya rightly observes, "It now remains to be said that the Tāntric culture is the greatest of all cultures, because it aims at the spiritual perfection and psychic development of man, and such no one can deny that the Tāntric culture is the greatest contribution made by India towards the world's civilization.

Whenever in future man awakens to the necessity of psychic, development or spiritual advancement, or stimulating this latent magical faculties, all eyes must turn towards this branch of Sanskrit literature, and to those few *Yogīns* India still possesses, for the most minute, thorough, accurate, easy and practical system of psychic exercise ever conceived by man in any country or in any times in history."[107]

Yoga

Yoga is a spirituality. It is a meditative practice which leads to *Samādhi*. It is not merely philosophical system engaged in systematization of different metaphysical concepts and doctrines. It is an intuitional science. It is science of religion and opposed to and different from the religion of faith and doctrinaire. The mysticism of the meditation of *yoga* combines science and speculation and knowledge and realization. The mystic experience of the cosmic consciousness cannot be achieved through repression and asceticism but through punitive consciousness.

Yoga dives deep into the darkest chamber of mind and the practicener becomes conscious of his own tremendous psychic power. Yoga belongs to the *Madhyamācāra* school of *Tantra*. Psychological schools of *Tantra* consist of *Dakṣiṇācāra*, *Madhyamācāra* and *Vāmācāra*. It is commonly said that *Dakṣiṇācāra* has evolved from the right mouth of Śiva. *Vidyā*, *Mantra*, *Mudrā* and *Maṇḍala* are the four *pīṭhas*, modes of *Sādhanā* of *Dakṣiṇācāra*. Rudra, Skandas, Brahma, Yama, Kubera and Indra *Yāmalas* belong to the *Vidyāpīṭha* of the *Dakṣiṇācāra* School. *Tantras* belonging to this *pīṭha* are *Yoginījāla*, *Yoginīhṛdaya*, *Mantramālinī*, *Aghoreśī*, *Aghoreśvarī*, *Kṛdaghoreśvarī*, *Laṅkinīkalpa*, *Maricī*, *Mahāmaricī* and *Ugravidyāgaṇa*. This school also holds that the *Bhairavas* belong to the *Mantra-pīṭha*. According to it, *Mantra* and *Mudrā* are closely related or connected with each other.

According to this system, *Madhyamācāra* has issued from the upper mouth of Lord Śiva. Vijaya, Nisvasa, Svayambhuva, Vatula, Vīrabhadra, Raurava, Makanta and Vireśa *Tantras* belong to the *Madhyamācāra*. However, no clear mention has been made regarding the *Vāmācāra* School. It belongs to 'the *Tantras* of a higher class'.

Madhyamācāra (middle path) is for all. *Madhyamācāra* in common parlance is known as Yoga. Not much risk is involved in it. However, without proper guru one cannot practise Yoga also. It is a slow and gradual process of self-realization. It is a scientific and universal mystic method to attain salvation. It differs both from *Dakṣiṇācāra* and *Vāmācāra*. Like *Vāmācāra* it is not an aggressive form of spirituality. It is not compromising and pestering process, it is positive and middle path to mitigate the influence of infirmities. It is an esoteric method of constant ideation and incantation. With repeated ideation and incantation a man becomes spiritually evolved and bondage of *māyā* becomes automatically loosen. *Yama*, *Niyama*, *Āsana*, *Prāṇāyāma*, *Pratyāhāra*, *Dhāraṇa*, *Dhyāna*, and *Samādhi* are the constituents of *Madhyamācāra Sādhanā* or Yoga. It is commonly accepted that Patañjali is the founder of *yoga*; but Patañjali is not the exponent of *yoga*. He has compiled and systematised the prevalent practice of *Madhymācāra* school of *Tantra*. In my view it is Lord Śiva who is the founding father of *Tantra* and the exponent of *yoga*.

The Vyāsa is the first commentator on *Patañjali Yoga Sūtra*. Vāchaspati Miśra has commented on the Vyāsa commentary. He was the follower of *Advaita Vedānta* and he tried to interpret the teachings of Patañjali in the perspective of *Vedānta*. The Vāchaspati commentary has become famous as the classical *yoga* school. The *Patañjali Yoga Sūtra*, Vyāsa commentary and Vāchaspati's commentary are considered as the canonical literature on *yoga* philosophical school. Recently Śaṅkara's commentary has been published by Madras Government oriental series in 1952. This work has been published under the scholarly guidance of P.S. Ram Śāstri and S.R. Krishna Murti Śāstri. According to them this is an authentic work of Śaṅkara. King Bhoja is the author of the commentary *Raja Mārttaṇḍa* and Rāmānand Sarswati commentary is known as *Maṇi Prabhā*. The Vijñānabhikṣu has written a scholarly work known as the *Yoga Vārttika*.

Trevor Leggett writes, "A feature of this text is that there is a consistent pull towards the *Vedānta*. For instance, the author will say that as all the *Puruṣas* are consciousness, pure and alone, it is hard to see how they could be distinguished. If indistinguishable, they will be the same. This is against the official view of the Yoga school in the *Yoga-sūtras*. Again, God is presented in this text, at great length, as the creator of the universe by his divine mind. In the *Vedānta* too, God is the all-creating and ruling overlord of the universe, which he projects as a sort of magic show, also entering into it as the Inner Ruler of each thing in it. Release can be affected by worshipping him and reception of his expression word OṀ, leading to experience of the real Self as one with God who transcends the universe and all descriptions. This text continually hints that the universe is unreal, not real as the orthodox view of Yoga would have it. Still, when his duty as a commentator requires it, Śaṅkara presents the formal Yoga view."[108]

Innumerable commentaries have been written on *Yogasūtra*. Man has been conditioned by physiological, social and religious culture and thoughts. The science and philosophy have been trying to understand the structures of consciousness. A man lives in time and history. However, he wants to transcend the boundary of time and history. The *yoga* is considered as a tool and method to take man to trans-historical and a trans-temporal state of spiritual sublimity. According to Indian philosophy man is a hibernated cosmic being. In the essential nature of man's being he is pure being. The real self which is transcendental in nature and cosmic consciousness in reality is a witnessing counterpart of all our mental activities. This has been named as Sākṣīchetā and *Jñātritavanibhandan* (witnessing entity). Mircea Eliade confirms this quintessential teachings of Indian philosophy and writes, "The great discoveries of Indian thought will in the end be recognised, under and despite the philosophic jargon. It is impossible, for example, to disregard one of India's greatest discoveries: that of consciousness as witness, of consciousness freed from its psychophysiological structures and their temporal conditioning, the consciousness of the 'liberated' man, of him, i.e., who has succeeded in emancipating himself from temporality and thereafter knows the true, inexpressible freedom. The conquest of this absolute freedom, of perfect spontaneity, is the goal of all Indian philosophies and mystical techniques; but it is above all through Yoga, through one of many forms of Yoga, that India has held that it can be assured. This is the chief reason we have thought it useful to write a comparatively full expression of the theory and practices of Yoga, to recount the theory of its form, and to define its place in Indian spirituality as a whole."[109]

Patañjali Yoga starts with the *sūtra*: this is the beginning of *yoga*.[110] The second verse contains the quintessential teachings of Yoga. According to this Yoga aims at rooting out all the tendencies.[111] Mind cannot exist without objectivity. Mind is a state in process of psycho-physical evolution. It is a state in the process of psychological evolution of speed and pause. Every movement is alternated by pause and speed. It is pulsating. In the state of pause mind gains momentum which it expresses in the form of tendencies (*vṛttis*). Mind through the help of inter and intra ectoplasmic occupation it expresses itself. These mental occupations and conations are known as tendencies or *vṛttis*. These tendencies and *vṛttis* are known as sentiments and emotions.

The *Ātman* or the cosmic consciousness is neutral by nature. It consists of two aspects *Prakāśa* and *Vimarśa*, *Nivṛtti* and *Pravṛtti* which could be called transcendental and imminent, static and dynamic or positive and negative. The mystic unification of the cosmic consciousness (Śiva) and cosmic principles (*Śakti*) under one condition produces the highest state of spiritual bliss and beautitude, and under another, the manifest world. Yoga is a physio-psycho and spiritual process. It is an inner *yoga* of progression from human into the divine. It is a mystic process of transformation and spiritual sublimation. Mind is always in the state of flux in the form of inter and intra-ectoplasmic occupations. Mind is the greatest impediment in the realization of the true nature of self. Hence for the self-realization one would have to get rid from the very existence of mind. And hence the property of mind is to remain always objectified and hence when mind is made one pointedness it ceases to exist. With the extinction of mind *Jīva* gets himself established in the true nature of its being. When the mind ceases to exist man knows himself as he really is. He has the realization of self. The dualism of his personality or mistaken belief in him as separate from the *Ātman* disappears. This is known as the illumination and salvation or self-realization.

There are four stages of human consciousness, waking (*Jāgarātā*), dream (*Svapna*), *Suṣupti* (Unconscious) and *Tūriya* (*Samādhi*). We are conscious about our waking state, but how would we know that we were in the state of dreamless sleep? *Yoga Sūtra* defines in Chapter I Verse 10 that sleep is a state of consciousness in which man is not conscious about his own I-ness. Suppose a man goes to sleep at 10 p.m. and wakes up 4 a.m., he could infer from the absence of his I-ness between the 10 p.m. to 4 a.m. infers that he was in the state of dreamless sleep.[112]

Radhakrishnan remarks in his Philosophy, Mr. So-and-So, after a good sleep, goes on being Mr. So-and-So, since his experiences unite themselves to the system which existed at the time when he went to sleep, he links to his thoughts and do himself does not fly to any other's. Such continuity makes it necessary for us to admit a permanent Self underlying all contents of consciousness.

The concept of the *Suṣupti* (state of unconscious) is marked by the feeling of weakness and fatigue after one gets awakened from the state of *Mūrcchā* or *Suṣupti*. When a man is put to unconscious state through medication like chloroform when he returns back to the state of consciousness he feels weakness and fatigue. So, this is the finer distinction between the concept of dreamless sleep and the state of unconsciousness. However, the fourth state which is known as *Tūrīya* (*Samādhi*) is the real state of human transcendental nature of his being and existence. In the Western philosophy or psychology this concept of *Tūrīya* doesn't exist because the Western civilization and culture has not attained the pinnacle of human glory in the form of *Tūrīya*, i.e., the state of spiritual bliss and beautitude. When a man goes into the state of *Tūrīya* and when after returning back from *Tūrīya* (*Samādhi*) to the normal state of awakening he feels blissful state, from that he infers that he was in the state of profound and deeper state of bliss and beautitude. So, this is the only proof of the existence of the state of transcendental nature of human being. Man is hibernated cosmic being. Yoga or *Tantra* is a technique to realize the true nature of one's own being. According to *Upaniṣada* man is transcendental being (*Ātman*). According to *Vedānta* to know is to be. When a man knows *Brahman* he becomes *Brahman.*[113]

The Yoga starts with the observation of *Yama* and *Niyama Sādhanā* which constitutes necessary preliminaries for attainment of the self-realization. The *yama* and *niyama* constitutes the moral teachings. The moral teachings are essential and necessary part of Yoga techniques. Without the observation of strict moral codes and values one cannot enter into the higher state of spirituality. *Yama* consists of five principles. They are *Ahiṁsā* (non-violence), *Satya* (truth), *Asteya* (non-stealing), *Aparigraha* (absence of avarice or to live a frugal life) and *Brahmacarya*. *Brahmacarya* has been sometimes wrongly interpreted as the observation of celibacy. *Brahmacarya* means to lead the life with the ideation of the God or the *Brahman*. It results into *Niṣkāma karma*, to work without attachment. The *niyama sādhanā* is also constituted of five principles, *saucha* (cleanliness), *Santoṣa* (contentment), *Svādhyāya* (studious), *Tapa* (austerity) and *Īśvara Prāṇidhāna* (ideation on the divine nature of Self). The *Yama*, *Niyama* propagate and propound the higher principles of morality. But it does not lead to self-realization. It is a stepping stone towards self-realization. Adherence to these moral principles propounded by *Patañjali Yoga Sūtra* paves the path for spiritual ascendance and self-realization. Second and the third factors of *Yoga* are *Āsana* (Yogīc postures) and *Prāṇāyāma* (respiratory discipline). The practice of *Āsana* and *Prāṇāyāma* create a psycho-physical condition for the practice of meditation. All other factors of *Patañjali Yoga Sūtra* have been auxiliary factors and process for creating a psycho-physical condition necessary for the practice of *Yoga Sādhanā*. *Āsana* and *Prāṇāyāma* are important factors in the preparation of *Yoga*

Sādhanā. The purpose of *Āsana* (physical postures) is to put necessary and proper pressure on the different *Padmas* or nerve centres which secretes different types of hormones by different glands. If there is excessive secretion from the particular glands which control particular tendency (*vṛttis*) a man becomes the victim of that *vṛtti* unless the secretion of the hormones are under the normal and required secretion of the hormones it would be difficult for any *yoga* practicener to concentrate his mind and do or practise meditation.

Āsana has been defined by *Patañjali Yoga Sūtra* as physical postures seated in a position which is in the state of relaxation.[114]

The most famous physical posture (*Āsana*) is called *Padmāsana* (lotus posture) in which the *yogī* sits crossed leg. It is a state of stable and enjoyable. *Āsana* is one of the common techniques adopted and practised by Indian ascetics. It has been described in *Upaniṣad* and other Vedic literatures. *Gheraṇḍa Saṁhitā* describes thirty two kinds of *Āsanas*. The *Āsanas* techniques have been practised by almost all spiritual seekers. Patañjali has devoted only three verses on *Āsanas*.

Fourth limb of *Patañjali yoga* is *Prāṇāyāma*. *Prāṇāyāma* is to regulate the movement of inhalation and exhalation of the breathing process. *Patañjali yoga* describes *Prāṇāyāma* as after the mastering of physical posture one should practise *Prāṇāyāma* by controlling and regulating the inhalation and exhalation. Patañjali has devoted only three aphorisms 49, 50 and 51. The forty nine verse speaks of the fourth kind of *Prāṇāyāma* in which the breath is stopped by concentration on external and internal objects. The process of inhalation and exhalation and the suspension of the breathing for certain period as directed by the *guru*. The fourth state of *Prāṇāyāma* is practised by *yogī* who has mastered the other two kinds of *Prāṇāyāma*. *Prāṇāyāma* should be practised with care and devotion. In our common experience we are aware that when our mind is disturbed there is an irregular breathing. This is related with the psychological state of our mind.

However, when we are physically fatigued and we also have the irregular breathing. From this we infer that there is a close and intimate relation with our process of inhalation and exhalation with a state of our mind. So through the practice of *Prāṇāyāma* the *yogī* again creates conducive psycho physical condition for the practice of meditation.

Patañjali has devoted only three verses in dealing with *Prāṇāyāma*. However, Vyāsa, Bhoja and Vāchaspati Miśra have made a detailed analysis and examination of the technique of *Prāṇāyāma* in their commentaries. According to commentary of Bhoja there is intimate connection between respiration and mental states. With the practice of *Prāṇāyāma* respiration of *yogī* becomes rhythmical and it remarkably slows down. This provides a longer and healthy life.

The *prāṇāyāma* is a mystical technique to regulate the pulsation of organic energy discharged by the process of breathing. The higher the *yogī* are allowed to practise the *Pūraka* (inhalation), *Rechaka* (exhalation) and *Kumbhaka* (stoppage of breathing). Only the *yogīs* who have attained mastery over the other kinds of *Prāṇāyāma* and *āsanas* are allowed to practise this kind of *Prāṇāyāma*.

Henri Maspero in his essay "Les Procedes de 'Nourrir le principe vital' dans la religion taoiste ancienne"[115] has considered embryonic respiration. The Taoist objective of the practice of *Prāṇāyāma* has been to attain long life which Taoist termed as "material immortality of the body itself". Dr. Jean Filliozat is of the opinion that this technique of breathing exercise has been borrowed from *Patañjali yoga*. He says, "Taoism could not borrow a notion of the physiological role of the breath in this systematised form from ancient Chinese medicine, for ancient Chinese medicines includes no such notion."[116]

There is enough evidence to conclude that the practice of *Prāṇāyāma* has been adopted and practised by Islāmic mysticism.[117]

Pratyāhāra is a esoteric process to withdraw the mind from the senses. When the mind is withdrawn from sense objects the sense organs also withdraw themselves from the external objects.

And as a result it helps the *yogī* in meditation.[118]

When mind is withdrawn from the senses it helps to have control over the different tendencies (*vṛttis*) and ultimately it helps in rooting out the *vṛttis*. Bhoja in his commentary says that with the practice of *Pratyāhāra* mind instead of directing towards sense objects is rooted in itself. The practice of *Pratyāhāra* helps the *yogī* in having direct knowledge without the help of sensory organs.

Vyāsa says "then the wisdom (*Prajñā*) of the yogin knows all the things as they are."[119]

Dhāraṇā (concentration) is holding the mind onto some particular object.[120] It is a fixing or concentrating a mind on a single point. The objective of *Dhāraṇā* is to control the mental flux and fix it on a single point. The purpose of this is to dissolve the mind into the cosmic consciousness. Vijñānabhikṣu has quoted in his *Yoga Saṅgraha* a passage from *Īśvara Gītā*. According to which *Dhāraṇā* takes the time of twelve *Prāṇāyāmas*. The time necessary for the concentration of mind on an object (*Dhāraṇā*) is equal to the time taken by twelve *Prāṇāyāmas*. All the six-fold paths or limbs of *Patañjali yoga* are termed as *Sādhanāṅga* (the factors of *Sādhanā*). Only meditation is called *Sādhanā*. All other processes and yogic techniques are auxiliary and they help in creating a psycho-physical condition for the practice of meditation. Meditation is the only mystic technique through which one can attain *Samādhi* (self-realization). The attainment of *Samādhi* or *Nirvāṇa* is the *summum bonum* of not only *yoga*, but all other Indian systems except Cāravāka. Meditation is continuous and an unbroken flow of thought towards cosmic consciousness.

There is some controversy regarding the introduction of God by Patañjali. It is considered that under the Vedāntic and the mystical devotional school the concept of God was introduced in *yoga* system. If we go through by the practice of *yoga* in different other systems, the God doesn't become a necessity for the attainment of *Samādhi*. Buddha and his contemporaries and *Tīrthaṅkaras* of Jain systems have attained *Nirvāṇa* or *Kaivalya* without the help of God. Mircea Elliade writes, "Patañjali nevertheless had to introduce *Īśvara* into Yoga, for *Īśvara* was, so to speak, an experiential datum —the *yogins* did in fact appeal to him although they could have obtained liberation by simply following the technique of Yoga."[121]

The cosmos and the self are different modes of reality. Self-realization is by meditation that the cosmic consciousness (reality) is not incompatible with the world and its phenomena. The ignorance of this truth is itself the result of the ultimate reality (cosmic consciousness). In fact there exists nothing, but the reality (consciousness). The phenomenal world is the manifestation in the medium of the cosmic consciousness and hence, it is not unreal. By the constant practice of *Dhyāna* the innermost self is realised.

Tripūra Rahasya says, "That is the oneness of the Self, the same as the identification of the transcendence of the one with that same one in all the diversities of the world apparent to each individual. This destroys the root of ignorance, instantly and completely. *Dhyāna* has been said to develop into *Nirvikalpa Samādhi*. Whereas modifications signify the many sidedness of consciousness, *nirvikalpa* signifies its unitary nature. When the mind does not create pictures due to thoughts, it is in the unmodified state, which is its primal and pure condition. When the pictures on a wall are erased, the original wall remains. No other work is necessary to restore its original condition."[122]

According to *Patañjali Yoga Sūtra* there are two kinds of *Samādhi*, i.e., *Saṁprajñāta Samādhi* (*Savikalpa Samādhi*) and *Asaṁprajñāta Samādhi* (*Nirvikalpa Samādhi*). *Saṁprajñāta Samādhi* consists of several stages. It is not the final and ultimate state of realization of the self. There are five states of *saṁprajñāta Samādhi*, i.e., *Sālokya*, *Sāmīpya*, *Sāujya*, *Sārūpya* and *Sāṣṭi*.

The first state, the *yogin* had the experience that he is on the same level of the ultimate reality, i.e., cosmic consciousness. In the second state he feels he has the closer and the intimate nature with the reality. *Sāujya* means the experience that the self and the *Brahman* are of the same nature. *Viśiṣtha Advaitavāda* of Rāmānujam considers it the ultimate goal of life because it is based on devotion. In the state of devotion there always remains the difference between the devotee and the God. So, this speaks of the nature of dualism. *Sārūpya* is almost the same with *Sāujya*. And in the state of *Sāṣṭi* a *yogī* has the realization that he is God, he is a *Brahman*. Again a distinction of self and the *Brahman* remains in a transcendental form. In the state of *Savikalpa Samādhi* or *Saṁprajñāta Samādhi* the self does not get merged in the cosmic consciousness. In the state of *nirvikalpa Samādhi* there is no trace of individuality. Ramkrishna Paramhansa has beautifully explained this state of *nirvikalpa Samādhi* through a metaphor of a doll of a salt has gone to fathom the depth and the sublimity of the ocean and the moment the doll of the salt enters into the ocean it gets dissolved into the ocean. In the state of *Asaṁprajñāta Samādhi* there is no knower (*Jñātā*), knowledge (*Jñāna*) and the *Jñeya* (the known).

Patañjali also explains the different stages of *Saṁprajñāta Samādhi* in terms of *Vitarka*, *Vicāra*, *Ānanda* and *Asmita*.

According to Vijñānabhikṣu all these four terms are purely technical. These stages are applied conventionally to different forms of realization. These four stages are also called *samapattis* (coalescences).[123]

All these four stages are called *Bīja Samādhi*. According to Vijñānabhikṣu it is called *Bīja Samādhi* because it retains the future manifestations of the metempsychosis. It has not yet exhausted all the metempsychosis and hence, it retains reaction in its potentiality of the *karma* in the seed form. However, in the *Samprajñāta Samādhi yogin* does acquire the faculty of absolute knowledge (*Ṛtaṁbharaprajñā*).[124] According to *Vijñānabhikṣu yogin* by meditation attains and understands that he is self and not body. This state is called the *Dharma Megha Samādhi*.

Asaṁprajñāta Samādhi (*nirvikalpa samādhi*) is the final state of self-realization. It is a state when mind is transformed into *Ātman* (cosmic consciousness). However, there are two stages of *nirvikalpa samādhi* also, *Sabīja nirvikalpa* and *nirbīja nirvikalpa*. When *yogī* attains *nirvikalpa samādhi*, he sometimes takes a vow to retain his physical body to serve the suffering humanity by helping each and every *Jīva* in obtaining the final release from the fetters of ignorance. In Buddhism such *yogins* are called as *Bodhisattvas*. In the state of *nirvikalpa samādhi* the *Sāttvika* metempsychosis still remains with the *yogin*. The living example of this type of great *yogī* who is also called *Paramahaṁsa* we find in the life of Swami Ramkrishna and Ramanamaharṣi. Ramkrishna Paramahansa attained *nirvikalpa samādhi* after getting initiation from his *guru* Totapuri. Totapuri was surprised to see that Ramkrishna attained the *nirvikalpa samādhi* immediately after getting initiation that kind of *Dhyāna yoga* by Totapuri. However, even after the attainment of this state of *nirvikalpa samādhi* Ramkrishna Paramahansa retained his physical body to serve humanity by awakening the dormant spirituality of men and women. Ramkrishna and Ramanamaharṣi remained all the time in the state of *Samādhi*. Such *yogins* are called as *Videhamukta*. Rājarṣi Janaka is also known as *Videhamukta*. When such *yogin* enters into *nirvikalpa samādhi* his existence remains bound by *Sāttvika* vow of such *yogī*. *Ātmā* is called *Sūtra ātmā* because with the threads of the consciousness the *yogī* remains connected or related with the physical body. The *yogī* attains deliverance. He is the *Jīvanmukta*; the liberated in life. He doesn't live in time and history. *Patañjali yoga* defines this state as a *yogin* is established in his own pure nature.[125] Mircea Elliade writes, "Through *Samādhi*, the *yogin* transcends opposite and, in a unique experience, unites emptiness and superabundance, life and death, Being and Non-being. Nor is this all. Like all paradoxical states, *Samādhi* is equivalent to a reintegration of the different modalities of the real in a single modality—the undifferentiated completeness of precreation, the primordial Unity.

The *yogin* who attains to *Asaṁprajñāta Samādhi* also realizes a dream that has obsessed the human spirit from the beginning of its history—to coincide with the All, to recover Unity, re-establish the initial non-duality, to abolish time and creation (i.e., the multiplicity and heterogeneity of the cosmos); in particular, to abolish the twofold division of the real into object-subject."[126]

The *Patañjali yoga* defines this state of seedless *Samādhi* in the last verse of chapter I as, "All the impression of mind is wiped out and no trace of thought and desires remain in the mind then one enters into *samādhi* which is called seedless."[127] In this state of *nirvikalpa samādhi* seeds of all desires and attachments are burnt. There is a continuous continuity of consciousness and it is a state of unqualified, unequivocal unification of *Ātman* and *Brahman*. The *yogī* is free from all cravings. There is no trace of any vestige of duality. This is a state of illumination and eternal bliss. The yogin is fully awake, but he is free from waking life. He is always in the state of full consciousness. Man is free from all sorts of bondage, cravings and longings. All the tendencies (*vṛttis*) have been rooted out. Though *yogin* possess the physical body but he remains united with the *Brahman*. Though he is in a state of finitude but he is united and lives in the world of infinity and transcendence. Even when he returns to a normal consciousness he remains engrossed in godliness. He experiences that *Brahman* is alone real and everything else is a manifestation of that same reality. Knowledge is filled with truth in the state of *Samādhi*.[128]

Chapter III of *Yoga Sūtra* is known as *Vibhūtipāda*. These deal with *siddhis* which are commonly known as occult power.

Yoga is a branch of *Tantra Śāstra*. The central objective of *yoga* is to awaken the dormant divinity which is known as *Kuṇḍalinī*. With the awakening of the *Kuṇḍalinī* and the piercing of the different *chakras* (*Padmas*) *yogī* attains extraordinary psychic power which is known as occultism. Man is a hibernated cosmic being. With the awakening of the *Kuṇḍalinī, yogī* becomes conscious of the cosmic vision and the power. This is the only technique to attain salvation. Swami Vivekananda writes, "But when by the power of long internal meditation, the vast mass of energy stored up travels along the *Suṣumṇā* and strikes the centres, the reaction is tremendous, immensely superior to the reaction of dream or imagination, immensely more intense than the reaction of sense perception. It is supersensuous perception. And when it reaches the metropolis of all sensations, the brain, the whole brain, as it were, reacts, and the result is the full blaze of illumination, the perception of the self. As this *Kuṇḍalinī* force travels from centre to centre, layer after layer of the mind, as it were, opens up, and this universe is perceived by the *Yogī* in its fine, or its casual form."[129]

According to the Yoga system *Dhāraṇā*, *Dhyāna*, and *Samādhi* is known as *saṁyama*. After the practice of *saṁyama* and attainment of awakening the *yogī* acquires a miraculous power, *siddhi*. *Siddhi* is nothing, but the realization of one's own true nature and being. Vivekananda writes, "Wherever there was any manifestation of what is ordinarily called supernatural power or wisdom, there a little current of *Kuṇḍalinī* must have found its way into the *Suṣumṇā*. Only, in the vast majority of such cases, people had ignorantly stumbled on some practice which set free a minute portion of the coiled up *Kuṇḍalinī*. All worship consciously or unconsciously, leads to this end."[130]

The chapter III starts with the aphorism which deals with the concept of *Dhāraṇā*. *Dhāraṇā* is an esoteric process of keeping the mind engaged on a particular object.[131] *Dhyāna* has been defined as continuous and unbroken flow of ideation.[132]

Samādhi has been defined as the result of meditation culminating into mind becoming objectless.[133] The property of mind is to remain always with some object. If at the moment the mind becomes objectless with long practice of meditation, mind loses its properties and with it seises to exist. As a result mind is transformed into consciousness. This transformation of mind into consciousness (*Ātman*) is called salvation. The state of *Dhyāna* is called salvation. Salvation or *Samādhi* is nothing, but getting oneself established in his own true nature. From aphorism Chapter III, Verse 16 to Verse 56 deals with the different kinds of *siddhis*. But these *siddhis* are nothing but the realization of his own being. In verse 51: *Sūtra* deals with that the giving up all the occult powers, a *yogī* becomes free from all kinds of evil and he attains *kaivalya*. This is called the burning of the seeds of all wrong doings. When man rids himself from the feeling and the ideas of omnipotence and omniscience the *yogī* rejects the all kinds of temptations and enjoyments even from the celestial beings. When the Buddha was doing meditation under the *Bodhi* tree the different celestial beings known as *mara* tried to allure the Buddha by offering different kinds of *siddhis*, but the Buddha didn't pay any attention to the allurements and the temptations offered by the *mara's* the celestial beings until he attained supreme knowledge and he became from Siddhārtha to the Buddha. In *Upaniṣad* it has been stated that, "the path to spirituality is like walking on the razor's age".[134] Aphorism 55: "When mind (*sattva*) is like *Puruṣa* in purity, there is Transcendental Aloneness. So, it is."[135] The *yogī* who has attained *Samādhi*, becomes free from all kinds of temptations and allurements because he always lives in a state of divinity and supreme blessedness. Even though *yogī* is conscious of the *siddhis*, but he is not under the control of *siddhis*, but *siddhis* are under the control of such *yogī*. Sometimes such enlightened *yogī* demonstrates those *siddhis* not for the sake of any power, prestige, name or fame, but to prove to the common masses the glory of God. Christ has demonstrated a lot of *siddhis*. The whole New Testament is the story of Christ showing the omnipotent and omniscient power of God. But according to *yoga* this power is not alien to a man. A man himself is a God. And hence according to *yoga* these *siddhis* are the manifestation of man's own cosmic nature. Man is essentially a *Brahman*. Vivekananda writes, "The man who thinks he is receiving response to his prayers does not know that the fulfilment comes from his own nature, that he has succeeded by the mental attitude of prayer in waking up a bit of this infinite power which is coiled up within himself. What, thus, men ignorantly worship under various names, through fear and tribulation, the *yogī* declares to the world to be the real power coiled up in every being, the mother of eternal happiness, if we but know how to approach her. And *Rāja-Yoga* is the science of religion, the rationale of all worship, all prayers, forms, ceremonies and miracles."[136]

Yoga Vāśiṣṭha

The *Yoga Vāśiṣṭha* is one of the monumental works on *Advaita*. There is a great controversy regarding the authorship of this great work. It is considered that Vālmīki is the author of this great work. There is some controversy regarding the date of its composition. According to one school it is pre-Śaṅkara and other believe that the work is post-Śaṅkara and it might have been composed between the eleventh and the thirteenth century. Whatever may be the date of its composition, but it is one of the greatest work of Hinduism. This has been quoted by later *Upaniṣads* such as *Śiva Saṁhitā*, *Pañca Daśī*, *Jīvan Mukti Viveka*, *Bhakti Sāgara*, *Rāma Gītā* and others. The original *Yoga Vāśiṣṭha* contains thirty two thousand verses. This was later condensed to six thousand (6,000) verses. *Chin Māyā* Mission Trust has condensed the whole *Yoga Vāśiṣṭha* into eighty six (86) verses. The *Yoga Vāśiṣṭha* has been composed in a story telling style. There are stories which are full of allegories and metaphors.

This work has been originated from the situation in which Rāma the young prince of Ayodhyā becomes a victim of despair and despondence. On the eve of his departure with Viśvāmitra, the eternal philosophical question disturbed the young mind of prince Rāma. Is there any place where there is no suffering? Can one think of any life which could be free from suffering and grief? Is this world not impermanent? Reflecting on the impermanence nature of the universe Rāma said to Viśvāmitra "Whole phenomenal world are impermanent, of what use are kingdom and happiness to me? Who am I and what is this cosmos? Where this cosmos has come from?"[137] Guru Vaśiṣṭha was requested to dispel the doubts of this eternal philosophical problem which was tormenting the young mind of Rāma. Unless Rāma gets a proper answer to all these eternal philosophical problems he could not be able to travel with Viśvāmitra to protect the religious duties and performances of the sage which was being threatened by the demons. Rāma requested Vaśiṣṭha to solve the riddles and the philosophical enigma which was tormenting his mind. And the doctrine of Vaśiṣṭha which is incorporated in *Yoga Vāśiṣṭha* through philosophical knowledge and wisdom on the riddles and the intellectual doubts of which Rāma had become a victim. Siddhārtha was also tormented by the same problems. Siddhārtha was a protected child and he was not aware of the miseries and other problems of life. When he was passing through the street of Kapilvastu, he was confronted with the old man and he saw the processions which were carrying the dead bodies. This site of old age and death stirred the young mind of Siddhārtha and he reflected on the impermanence nature of the world. In search of truth and salvation he renounced the kingship and became a mendicant. And ultimately he became the Buddha; the enlightened one. Viśvāmitra was delighted to see that the young mind of Rāma is tormented with the eternal philosophical problems and he assured him that Vaśiṣṭha would clarify all his doubts and lead him to enlightenment. Rāma enters into dialogue with *Vāśiṣṭha* on different philosophical problems. This dialogue is known as *Yoga Vāśiṣṭha*. After all the doubts of Rāma was solved and after his enlightenment, *Śri Rāma* leaves with *Viśvāmitra*.

Yoga Vāśiṣṭha is composed of six chapters as follows: (1) *Vairāgya Prakaraṇa*, *Vairāgya* deals with the concept of dispassion or renunciation. (2) *Mumukṣu-Vyavahāra Prakaraṇa*, this deals with the intensity of longings for liberation. (3) *Utpatti Prakaraṇa*, it deals with the origin and development of the cosmos or universe. (4) *Sthiti Prakaraṇa*, it deals with the existence and sustenance of the universe. (5) *Upasama Prakaraṇa*, this deals with the dissolution of the universe. (6) *Nirvāṇa Prakaraṇa*, this deals with the nature of enlightenment.

In course of the narration of the different topics through the metaphors, myths and allegories the central objective of *Yoga Vāśiṣṭha* has been expounded.

The quintessential teaching of *Yoga Vāśiṣṭha* is the self-realization or enlightenment. *Yoga Vāśiṣṭha* is a great treasure of philosophical knowledge. It covers the whole gamut of our life. It speaks of the depth and the profundity of Hinduism. The whole *Yoga Vāśiṣṭha* veers around the problem of the true nature of the existence and being, who am I? The whole Hindu philosophy deals with this central theme.

Human longings are triform, i.e. physical, intellectual and spiritual. Every man runs after enjoyment. The desires never seize and a man's pursuit for happiness goes on. But ultimately after analysis and examination of the nature of his physical desires one comes to the conclusion that the physical objects are not capable of satisfying his eternal longings for eternal happiness. After this realization man abandons his quest for worldly pleasures, this is true dispassion or renunciation. Rāma concludes "If I cannot attain the eternal peace and bliss, I who have renounced all physical longings and do not seek anything except death, I shall remain in eternal silence." It is the feeling of the I-ness that is the cause of the bondage. A man runs after name, fame, power and position. After having the realization of transitory nature of the world, one's mind is free from the ego. He is all the time prepared for embracing death also. And at the same time a man is determined to attain enlightenment.

The quintessential teachings of *Yoga Vāśiṣtha* are both negative and positive. On the negative aspects it is the denial of individuality which is the cause of limitations and imperfections and the positive aspect is affirmation of transcendental nature of self. Without the attainment or realization of *Nirvāṇa* one cannot have the experience of the transcendental nature of the self which is the truth, bliss and state of spiritual sublimity. According to this school of thought *Brahman* is alone real. Everything is *Brahman*. There is nothing other than *Brahman* that is real. *Brahman* is the transcendental nature of our self.

Vaśiṣṭha starts his discourse on the knowledge of self. He propounds the doctrine of liberation. While propounding the doctrine of liberation he stated that liberation is freedom from suffering, fear and tension. Existence of seer and the seen is called bondage. Seer and seen are bound by the influence of seen. When a man is free from the world of the sense perception and gets established in his own true being and existence he becomes enlightened. All relationship is rooted in dualism. When the seed of duality is uprooted man attains the state of spiritual sublimity. In describing the nature of seer or *ātman* the *Yoga Vāśiṣtha* states that it is neither light nor darkness. The profound existence remains nameless and transcendental. But it cannot be said that it is a void. Darkness is the opposite of light and the light is opposite of darkness. The world is always pervaded by the dualistic nature of light and darkness. This is the nature of creation so the true nature of reality is beyond the creation and dissolutions. Vaśiṣṭha says, "The divine Truth (*ṛtam*), the Self, the Supreme, *Brahman*, Truth—such are the names of the great essence that have been invented by the wise for the sake of transaction or communication of knowledge."[138]

According to *Yoga Vāśiṣṭha* the body, mind, ego and intellect are not self. Each of them, i.e., the mind and the body are the object of our consciousness. Self is the ultimate reality in which the universe is rooted. This self-manifests itself in all individual beings. Death brings about a change in the objective world of *Jīva*. It only obstructs the individual from the world in which he is no longer related or doesn't have any rapport after the death. After the death of a person who have rooted out his all longings and desires is emptied of all tendencies, such seeker enters into state of *Nirvāṇa*. *Nirvāṇa* according to *Yoga Vāśiṣṭha* one experiences the total identity with the *Brahman*. According to *Yoga Vāśiṣṭha* it is cosmic mind that has imagined and manifested the idea of the cosmos. This cosmic mind is called *Brahmā* in the *Yoga Vāśiṣṭha*.

The Brahmā creates the world through his thought projection. He is not conditioned by any design. It is cosmic consciousness. He is lord of the whole cosmos. Bhikkan Lal Atreya writes, "The rise of Brahmā in *Brahman*, the Absolute, is the most mysterious occurrence. He is like a sprout come out of the eternal seed of the Absolute when its creative power tends to evolve a cosmos out of itself. The Absolute in its creative aspect or power, in a merely playful overflow, by its own freewill, comes to self-consciousness at one point, which brings about the forgetfulness of the Whole, and on account of intensity of consciousness there, begins to vibrate, pulsate, or agitate in the form of thinking or imagining and assumes a distinct existence for Itself, as if separated from the Whole whose one aspect It is in reality."[139] The creation is the manifestation of the cosmic consciousness with the help of his creative matrix (*Śakti*). This is the inherent power and will to manifest infinite forms. However, the seed of creation is in potential form and resides in the very transcendental nature of reality. It is nothing different from but identical with the reality.

Yoga Vāśiṣṭha propounds the seven stages of spiritual realization. When a man realizes the worthlessness of living without anchoring life with spirituality this is the first stage. In this state one feels that one is totally deluded and wants to get out from this state of delusion and bondage. Such thoughts bring in the company of the man of wisdom. One reflects upon the transitory nature of the world and starts his search for truth. The *Kaṭho Upaniṣad* says that,"Arise, awake and learn by approaching the excellent ones. The wise one describe that path to be as impassable as a razor's edge, which, when sharpened, is difficult to tread on."[140]

A man is sleeping in ignorance and he doesn't have the realization of his true nature. However, the path of spirituality says in the *Kaṭho Upaniṣad* that, it is like walking on the razor's edge. Further *Kaṭho Upaniṣad* describes that the reality is hidden in all beings. And hence it does not appear as the self. But the man who has sharpened his mind and made it one pointed he does realize that it is the self which is verily the ultimate and transcendental reality. The man whose mind has not been purified it is not known to such person. It is only through the one pointed mind and intellect that one gets engaged and in pursuit of ascertaining the nature of ultimate reality which is pure consciousness, truth and bliss.

Vaśiṣṭha while enumerating the different stages of the supreme knowledge, he says, "The seventh state is the highest one." This state of supreme knowledge one delights in self and he is free from all kinds of delusion. In this seventh state the *yogī* becomes completely detached from power, fame and any kind of material possessions. He revels in self alone. This is the state of desirelessness. It is a state of eternal bliss. While concluding the different states of spiritual attainment Vaśiṣṭha describes the realm of liberation in the following verse.

"This fourth state (of consciousness) exists only in those who are liberated while living. Thereafter is the state beyond the fourth which is the realm of liberation without the body. These seven stages are attainable only by the wise."[141]

This fourth state is called *Tūrya*. This has been enumerated for the first time by Gauḍapāda in *Māṇḍūkyakārikā*. The awakening (the *jāgrātā*), dream (*svapna*), senselessness (*suṣupti*) and the *tūrya* (*samādhi*) has been enumerated by Gauḍapāda in *Māṇḍūkyakārikā*.

The Western philosophy and minds are unaware of this fourth state of spiritual enlightenment which has been considered by Hinduism, Buddhism as the *summum bonum* of life. *Muṇḍaka Upaniṣad* describes this state of spiritual sublimity and self-realization and says the knot of the heart is cut ascender all doubts become solved and when the self is realized and all metempsychosis are exhausted.[142]

This is the state of illumination. In this state one becomes free on the eradication of the causes of the bondage. Further *Muṇḍaka Upaniṣad* throws light on the state of self-realization. *Muṇḍaka Upaniṣad* says, "In the supreme, bright sheath is *Brahman*, free from taints and without parts. It is pure, and is the light of lights. It is that which the knower of the self-realises."[143] According to light of the self is the highest light which is not lit by anything else. The *yogīs* who are in pursuit of self-realization alone know this state of illumination. This state has been further enumerated by *Muṇḍaka Upaniṣad*. The *Upaniṣad* says, "There the sun does not shine, nor the moon or the stars; nor do these flashes of lightening shine there. How can this fire do so? Everything shines according as He does so; by his light all this shines diversely."[144] It is the cosmic consciousness (*Brahman*) that illuminates and shines through the different channels of light in the manifested universe. It is, therefore, inferred that the cosmic consciousness (*Brahman*) alone is the source of all energy, life and existence. Anything that is bereft of the consciousness cannot enkindle others. It has been established by the scientific reasoning that cosmic copiousness is alone the light of all lights. It is the source of all energies and life. Everything else is the modification of the cosmic consciousness. This cosmos is nothing, but cosmic consciousness. This world is nothing, but the *Brahman*. This is the quintessential teachings of Hinduism. The various theories are being propounded by the philosophers and the scientists about creation. In the end they are all rooted in Ontological mysticism. There is nothing called ignorance other than the mind. The mind alone is cause of all neissance which is the cause of all bondage. After the realization mind becomes the cosmic being. *Yoga Vāśiṣṭha* says that, "The mind becomes the cosmic being just as a wave rises from the ocean. By that this jugglery of worldly splendour is spread."[145] According to Hinduism, man is God. Only difference is that when man is in a state of bondage he is called *Jīva*. When he is free from bondage he is called God. All existence and reality is cosmic consciousness (*Brahman*). Just like the waves are only ocean in a real form at the same time wave cannot exist apart from the ocean. The wave is ocean, but with the superimposed name and form makes different from the ocean. Similarly, the cosmic consciousness (the *Brahman*) is like the still ocean of consciousness. And from that eternal reality and being emanate the different innumerable names and forms of the world. The world appears, but it is not world in ultimate analysis. It is the *Brahman*. The *Yoga Vāśiṣṭha* describes it as follows, "The names coined for it are ignorance, transmigration, delusion, bondage, *māyā*, impurity and darkness."[146]

Vaśiṣṭha considers the desires (*vāsanā*) are the cause of bondage and they are the greatest impediment in the path of spirituality.

Vaśiṣṭha compares the desires with she elephant which is extremely intoxicated with lust and greed. If it is not rooted out and the seed of desire is not burnt this she elephant will become the cause of endless sufferings and calamities. Further Vaśiṣṭha while enumerating the she elephant of desire he says, "On account of desire, progress in the steps of *yoga* is never accomplished. *Vāsanā*, wish, mind, memory, will, imagination, longing and the like are also names of that she-elephant, i.e., desire. Let one conquer her completely by the great weapon of fortitude."[147]

Yoga Vāśiṣṭha provides a detail account of the chief characteristics of realize souls.

Yoga Vāśiṣṭha says, "He who is awake while in deep sleep, for whom there is no waking, whose knowledge is free form *vāsanā-s* is said to be liberated while living.[148] He who, whether engaged in action or not, has no sense of doership, and whose intellect is not tainted, is said to be liberated while living."[149]

The *Yoga Vāśiṣṭha* believes in scientific temper and rationality. It doesn't accept any authority ancient or modern. According to *Yoga Vāśiṣṭha* the self is to be realized by our own endeavour. Truth is to be revealed through rational interpretations. The Vaśiṣṭha says the philosopher, the sage and the teacher, in the work: "A devotee of reason should value the works even of ordinary persons, provided they are rational and advance knowledge, and should discard those even of the sages, if they are not such. A reasonable statement, even of a child, should be accepted, while the unreasonable ones should be discarded like a piece of straw, even though they are made by the creator himself".[150]

The teachings of Vaśiṣṭha is full of clarity and it is not work of polemical. According to *Yoga Vāśiṣṭha* neither a teacher nor any scripture can ever show God or ultimate reality is to be realized by one's own inner journey through one's own mental purification.

There is only one source of self-realization and supreme knowledge, it is only through one's own endeavour and intuitional experience. This is the basis of all source of valid knowledge. The *Yoga Vāśiṣṭha* is the work of catholicity and generosity. It does propagate that the truth is one and the differences are ephemeral. It teaches and propounds universal and cosmic brotherhood. Vaśiṣṭha says to Rāma, the idea that this one is my brother and that one is not entertained only by petty minded people. How can one said to be a brother and other not, when the same self equally pervades all. All classes of creatures O Rāma are your brothers; there is none here who is not absolutely related to you.

B.L. Atray while summarising the chief characteristics and the universal appeal of the *Yoga Vāśiṣṭha* writes, "Finally, the *Yoga Vāśiṣṭha* is not a work expounding or supporting the teachings of any particular school of thought as distinguished from another. Its teachings are not those of any of the traditional schools of Indian philosophy. It synthesises the best aspects of all systems of thought, particularly those of the Sāṁkhya, the Yoga, the Buddhist, and the Upaniṣadic. It is a thorough going, systematic, and comprehensive idealism, different from the view of all other idealistic schools of Indian thought."[151]

References

1. *Encyclopaedia of Religion and Ethics*, Vol. IX, pp. 815-31.
2. *Sex Worship and Symbolism of Primitive Races*, Percy Brown, pp. 23, 29-30.
3. *Sex and Sex Worship*, Wall, p. 2.
4. *Pre-Historic India*, Harmondsworth, 1950, p. 155.
5. *The Tao of Physics*.
6. *Tantrāloka*, Vol. I, Ch. I, Ver. 108, p. 151. My Book.
   परमः शिवः पुरुषोत्तम विश्वस्य केन्द्रम्। *Ananda Sutram*, p. 4
7. *Yoginī Hṛdaya*, p. 105, शिव:शतयात्मसंघट्टरूपे शिवशक्तंयात्मनो-प्रकाशविमर्शममयोः संघट्टः सामरस्य तद्रूपे...।
8. *Tripura Rahasyam*, pp. 11-12. Sarasvati Bhavan Granthamala, Vol. 15. Varanasi, 1965.
9. *Pratyabhijñāhṛdayam* 2, Nothing exists that is not Śiva, by Swami Muktananda. A Siddha Yoga Meditation Publication. Chitshakti Publications, Chennai, 1999.

10. *Yoginī Hṛdaya*, p. 105, Sarasvati Bhavan Granthamala, Vol. 7, Varanasi, 1963, p. 182.
    शिवशक्ति सामरस्यमयजगदानन्दरूपमित्यर्थ। *Tantrāloka* Āj. XXIX, 84.
11. *Kashmir Śaivism*, J.C. Chatterjee, p. 63, Research & Publication Department, Srinagar, 1962.
12. *Mahānirvāṇa Tantra*, Ch. II, Ver. 59.
13. *Ānanda Sūtram*, p. 1, Ānanda Nagar, Purulia (W. Bengal).
14. *Tantrāloka*, Ahnika 3.
    तयोयद यामलं रूपं स संघट्ट इति स्मृतः।
    आनन्द शर्क्तिः शैवोक्त यतो विश्वं विसृज्यति।।
    न शिवः शर्क्तिहितो न शिववर्जिता।
15. *Caitanyamātma*, *Śiva Sūtras*, Verse I.
16. *Mahānirvāṇa Tantra*, Ch. I, Ver. 34.
17. *Pratyabhijñāhṛdayam*, p. 50.
18. *The Garland of Letters*, p. 97.
19. *Kashmir Śaivism.*
20. *Tantra its Mystic and Scientific Basis*, Lalan Prasad Singh, p. 51.
21. *Svecchā-viśvamayollakha-khachitam, Yoginī-hṛdaya Tantra.*
22. *Pratyabhijñāhṛdayam* 1, Nothing exists that is not Śiva, by Swami Muktānanda, p. 51.
23. *Ya anādirūpa caitanya-dhyasena mahāpralaye sūkṣma sthita. – Śāradā Tilaka.*
24. *Asmacca karanabindoḥ sākṣāta krameṇa kāryabindrotato nadastato bījam iti trayam utpannaṁ tadidan parā sūkṣmasthūlapadam apy ucyate.— Śāradā Tilaka*. Ver. 132.
25. *Śiva Sūtra*. The Yoga of Supreme Identity, p. 152.
26. *Tripūra-Rahasyam*, p. 11.
27. *Svecchayā svabhittau viśvam unimilayati. Pratyabhijñāhṛdayam* 2.
28. *Yoga Immortality and Freedom*, Mercia Eliade, Translated by the French Willard R. Trask, Bollingen Foundation Inc., 1958, p. XX.
29. *Śiva Sūtra* 2.
30. *Yoginī Hṛdaya*, p. 105.
31. *Mahānirvāṇa Tantra*, Chapter 1, Verse 36.
32. *Pratyabhijñāhṛdayam*, p. 50.
33. *Tantrāloka,* Ch. XXIX, 84, *Bharatiya Sanskriti Aur Sādhanā*, Vol. 1, p. 5. M.M. Gopinath Kaviraj, Bihar Rāshtrabhāsā Parishad (Patna).
34. *The Serpent Power*, p. 28.
35. *Physics and Philosophy. The Revolution in Modern Science*, Werner Heisenberg, Harper Collins Publisher, 1962.
36. *Tantrāloka,* Vol. I, p. 192.
37. *Paratriṁsika*, 34,
    शक्तिमदैवयात्म्य लक्षणात् लवणारना लवत्परस्परमेलनात्।

Tantrāloka, 11, 192 Abhinav Gupta, *Tantrāloka*, Kashmir Sanskrit Text and studies, Kashmir Government Publications, Shrinagar.
38. *A Briefer History of Time*, Stephen Hawking with Leonard Mlodinow. Bantom Press, 2005, pp. 15-16.
39. *The Serpent Power*, pp. 35-36.
40. *The Sarva Darśana Saṅgraha*, p. 211.
41. *Śāradā Tilaka*, I.1.9.
42. *Śiva Sūtra* 3.9. *Nartaka Ātmā. Śiva Sūtra, The Yoga of Supreme Identity.* Jai Deva Singh. Motilal Banarsidass Publishers, 2008, p. 152.
43. *Tripūrarahasya*, p. 11.
44. *Introduction to B.S.*, p. xiv. *The System of Śaṅkara*, according to Sir Charles Eliot, "In Consistency, Thoroughness and Profundity, holds the first place in Indian Philosophy" (*Hinduism and Buddhism*, Vol. ii, p. 208).
45. Surendranath Bhattacharya. *The Philosophy of Śaṅkara: The Cultural Heritage of India*, Vol. III, 1969, p. 239.
46. *Māṇḍūkyakārikā* II, 32.
47. *The Philosophy of Śaṅkara. The Cultural Heritage of India*, Vol. III, 1969, p. 7.
48. *Māṇḍūkyakārikā* II, 32.
49. *Aṣṭābakra Saṁhitā*, Swami Nityāsvarūpānanda. Advaita Ashrama (Publication Department), 2010, p. XIX.
50. *The Philosophy of Śaṅkara. The Cultural Heritage of India*, Vol. III. 1969, p. 242.
51. *Ibid.*, p. 243.
52. *Vivekacūḍāmaṇi*. Verse 36.
53. *The Cultural Heritage of India*, Vol. III. *Post-Śaṅkara Advaita*. Dinesh Chandra Bhattacharya, p. 256.
54. *Ibid.*, pp. 267-268.
55. *Philosophy of the Advaita*. K.A. Krishna Swamy Iyer. *Cultural Heritage of India*, Vol. III, p, 221.
56. *Physics and Philosophy: The Revolution in Modern Science*, Werner Heisenberg, p. 55.
57. *Ibid.*, p. 119.
58. *Aṣṭābakra Saṁhitā*, Chapter II.18.
59. *Avadhūta Gītā*, Chapter I, Verse 4.
60. *Ibid.*, Verse 5.
61. *Ibid.*, Verse 10.
62. *Vivekacūḍāmaṇi*. Verse 2.
63. *Aṣṭābakra Saṁhitā*. Chapter I. Verse 3.
64. *Aṣṭābakra Saṁhitā*. Chapter I. Verse 11.
65. *Nirvāṇa Śatakam*. Verse 1.
66. *Aṣṭābakra Saṁhitā*. Chapter I. Verse 6.
67. *Avadhūta Gītā*. Chapter I. Verse 58. p. 31.
68. *Avadhūta Gītā*. Chapter I, Verse 23, p. 12.

69. *My Views of the World*, Ervin Schrodinger, Ox Bow Press, Woodbridge, Connecticut, 1983, pp. 21-22.
70. *If Science is Conscious of its Limits. Quantum Question*, Shambhala Publications, Inc., 1984, p. 74.
71. *Quantum Questions*, Ken Wilber. Shambhala Publications, Inc., 1984, pp. 31-32.
72. *Chāndogya Upaniṣad*. VI.I 9.4.
73. Sir John Marshall, *Mohenjo-Daro and the Indus Civilization*, p. 57. Arthur Probsthain, 41, Great Russell Street, London, 1931.
74. T. Gopinath Rao, *Elements of Hindu Iconography*, Vol. 1, Pt. I, Introduction, p. 6.
75. *Journal of the Asiatic Society of Bengal*, Proceedings 1921, pp. XXI-XXIV.
76. *Encyclopaedia of Religion and Ethics*, Vol. IX, pp. 815-31.
77. Brown, P., *Sex and Sex Worship of Primitive Races*, pp. 23, 29-30.
78. Wall, *Sex and Sex Worship*, p. 2.
79. *The Cultural Heritage of India* (2nd edition), Vol. IV, pp. 211-12. Ramakrishna Mission Institute of Culture, Calcutta, 1956.
80. *Bhāratīya Saṁskṛti Aur Sādhanā*, Bihar Rāshtrabhāsā Parishad, Patna, 1963, p. 1.
81. *Tantras—Studies on their Religion and Literature*, p. 2. Punthi Pustak, Calcutta, 1963.

    आगतं शिववक्त्रेभ्योगतश्च गिरिजानने।
    मतश्च वासुदेवस्य तस्मादागमुच्यते।।
    निर्गतं गिरिजाववक्त्राद गतश्च गिरिशश्रुतौ।
    मतश्च वासुदेवस्य तस्मान्निगमुच्यते।।
82. *Ibid.*
83. *Bhāratīya Saṁskṛti aur Sādhanā*, Vol. 1, pp. 13, 115.
84. *Kulārṇava Tantra*, p. 241, Ganesh & Co., Madras.

    जीवः शिवः शिवो जीवः स जीवः केवलः शिवः।
    पाशबद्धः स्मृतो जीवः पाशमुक्तः सदाशिव।।
85. *Tantrāloka* II, p. 77.

    परैवसूक्ष्मा कुण्डलिनी शक्तिः।
86. *History of Indian Philosophy*, Vol. V, p. 59.
87. *Muṇḍaka Upaniṣad*. II.2.9
88. *The Garland of Letters*, p. VIII.
89. *Śiva Sūtra Vārttika* Ch-1 Kashmir Series of Texts, and Studies, Shrinagar, 1916.

    चितं मन्त्रं।।
90. *Pratyabhijñāhṛdayam*.

    चितरेव चेतनपदादवरूढा चेत्थसङ्कोचिनी चित्तम्।।

Prativijña hṛdayam Leidicker, Kurt F. (Ed.) Adyar Library and Research, Madras, 1996.

91. *Śiva Sūtra Vārttika*, p. 30.
स्वात्मानुभवंर्धर्भित्वात्समन्त्र इति गीयते।
92. *Ibid.*, p. 29.
93. *Kulārṇava Tantra, Ullāsa*, 15. VV. 2-2, p. 320. Ganesh & Co., Madras, 1965.
शृणु देवि प्रवक्ष्यामि यन्मांत्वं परिपृच्छसि।
तस्य श्रवणमात्रेण मंत्रतत्वं प्रकाशते।।
जपज्ञयात परोयज्ञो नापरोऽस्तीह कश्चन।
तस्माज्जपेन धर्मार्थकाममोक्षाश्चं साधयेत्।।
94. *Ibid.*, p. 326. Verse 61.
चैतन्यरहिता मंत्राः प्रोक्ता वर्णास्तुकेवलम्।
फलग् नैव प्रयच्छन्ति लक्षकोटिजवादीप।।
95. *Śiva-Sūtra-Vimarśinī*, p. 48.
उच्चार्यमाणा ये मन्त्रा न मन्त्राश्चापि तदिबदुः।
96. *Japasūtram*, p. 106.
97. See Tucci, *Teoria Pratica del Maṇḍala*, p. 31.
98. *Hevajra Tantra*, Part I, pp. 32-33.
99. *Kulārṇava Tantra*, p. 74.
100. *Mahānirvāṇa Tantra*, p. 233.
101. *Ibid.*, p. 237.
102. *Ibid.*, p. 124.
103. A. Snodgrass, *The Symbolism of the Stūpa*, Ithaca, Cornell University, Southeast Asia Program, 1985, p. 107 and passim.
104. *Saundaryalaharī*, p. 9.
105. *Patañjali Yoga Sūtra*.
योगश्चितवृत्ति निरोधः।
106. *Tāntric Texts*, Vol. IX, Luzac & Co., Great Russell Street, London, 1992, p. 60.
107. Benoytosh Bhattacharya, *An Introduction to Buddhist Esotericism*, p. 174.
108. *Śaṅkara on the Yoga Sūtra*, A Full Translation of the Newly Discovered Text. Trevor Leggett, Motilal Banarsidass Publishers Private Ltd., Delhi, 1990, pp. 7-8.
109. *Yoga Immortality and Freedom*, Mircea Eliade. Bollingen Series Princeton. 1954, p. XX.
110. *Patañjali Yoga Sūtra*, Chapter I, Verse 1.तदा द्रष्टुः स्वरूपेऽवस्थानम्।
111. *Patañjali Yoga Sūtra*, Chapter I, Verse 3.
112. *Patañjali Yoga Sūtra*, Chapter I, Verse 10.
113. ब्रह्म विद ब्रह्मेव भवति।
114. *Patañjali Yoga Sūtra*, Chapter II, Verse 46.
115. *Journal Asiatique*, CCXXVIII (1937), 177-252, 353-430.

116. *Taoisme et Yoga, Dan* Vietnam, III (Aug., 1949), 120.
117. *Cf.* I. Goldziher, *Vorlesungen uber den Islam*, p. 164; M.M. Moreno, "*Mistica musulmana e mistica Indiana*," Annali Lateranensi, X (1946), 102-212, especially pp. 140 ff.; and particularly L. Gardet, "*La Mention du nom divin* (dhikr) *dans la mystique musulmane*," Revue Thomiste, LII (1952), 642-79; LIII (1953), 197-216, a study that we use below, pp. 217 ff.
118. *Patañjali Yoga Sūtra*, Chapter II, Verse 54.
119. *Patañjali Yoga-Bhāṣya*, II, 45.
120. *Patañjali Yoga Sūtra*, Chapter III, Verse 1.
121. *Patañjali Yoga, Immortality and Freedom*, Mircea Elliade, pp. 75-76.
122. *The Mystery Beyond the Trinity: Tripūra Rahasya*. Śrī Ramanasramam, Tiruvannamalai, 2011. Chapter XVII, Verses 70-73.
123. *Patañjali Yoga Sūtra*, Chapter I, Verse 41, with the commentaries of Vyāsa and Vāchaspati Miśra.
124. *Patañjali Yoga Sūtra*, Chapter I, Verse 48.
125. *Patañjali Yoga Sūtra*, Chapter I, Verse 3.
126. *Patañjali Yoga Immortality and Freedom*, Mircea Elliade, pp. 98-99.
127. *Patañjali Yoga Sūtra*, Chapter I, Verse 51.
128. *Patañjali Yoga Sūtra*, Chapter I, Verse 48.
129. Conquering the Internal Nature, *Rāja Yoga*. Swami Vivekananda, Advaita Ashrama Publications, 2012, pp. 59-60.
130. *Ibid.*, pp. 60-61.
131. *Patañjali Yoga Sūtra,* Chapter III, Verse 1.
132. *Ibid.*, Verse 2.
133. *Patañjali Yoga Sūtra,* Chapter III, Verse 3.
134. *Kaṭho Upaniṣads,* I. iii.14.
135. *Patañjali Yoga Sūtra*, Chapter III, Verse 55.
136. *Conquering the Internal Nature, Rāja Yoga*. Swami Vivekananda, Advaita Ashrama Publications, 2012, p. 61.
137. *Yoga Vāśiṣtha Sāra Saṅgraha*, Verse 6, Central Chinmaya Mission Trust, Mumbai, 2012.
    Asthira sarva evaite
    Sacarācara-ceṣṭitaḥ
    Kiṁ me rājyena kiṁ bhojagaiḥ
    Ko'haṁkimidam agatam.
138. *Ibid.*, p. 48. Chapter III.
    Ṛtam-ātma paraṁ brahma
    Satyam-ityadika budhaiḥ
    Kalpita vyavahāratham
    Tasya saṁjñā mahātmanaḥ (6)
139. *Yoga Vāśiṣtha* III. 55.47; III.3.33f; VIb.208.27.29; IV.44.14f; IV.42.4; VIa.114.15-16; VIa.33.21; III.114.10.20; VIa11.37; IV.42.5. *The Cultural Heritage of India*, Volume III, *The Philosophies*, p. 432.
140. *Kaṭho Upaniṣad*, I. iii, Verse 14.

141. *Yoga Vāśiṣtha Sāra Saṅgraha*, Verse 10, Chapter V. Central Chinmaya Mission Trust, Mumbai, 2012.
Jīvanmukteṣu caisa hi
Tūryavastheha vidyate
Videhamukti-viṣayas-
Tūryatitam-ataḥ pąram
Bhūmikā-saptakaṁ caitad
Dhimatameva gocaraḥ (10)
142. *Muṇḍaka Upaniṣad*, Chapter II, Verse II. 8.
143. *Ibid.*, Chapter II, Verse 9.
144. *Ibid.*, Chapter II, Verse 10.
145. *Yoga Vāśiṣtha Sāra Saṅgraha*, Chapter III. Verse 8, Central Chinmaya Mission Trust, Mumbai, 2012.
Manu bhāvati bhūtama
Taraṅga iva varidheḥ
Teneyam-indrajalaśrīḥ
Jagati pravitanyate (8)
146. *Ibid.*, Chapter III. Verse 9.
Avidyā saṁsṛtir-moho
Bandho māyā malaṁ tamaḥ
Iti namāni tasyas-ca
Kalpitāni bhāvanti hi (9)
147. *Ibid.*, Chapter VI. Verses 8-9.
Bhūmikasu ca sāravasu
Sanacaro naiva sādhyate
Vāsaneha manas-cittam
Saṁkalpo bhāvanaṁ spṛha (8)
Ityadini ca nāmāni
Tasya eva bhāvanti hi
Dhairya-nāmna varāstrena
Caitaṁ sarvātmana jāyet (9)
148. *Ibid.*, Chapter IV. Verse 3.
Yo jāgarti suṣuptistho
Yasya jāgran-na vidyate
Yasya nirvasano bodhaḥ
Sa jīvanmukta ucyate (3)
149. *Ibid.*, Chapter IV. Verse 5.
Yasya nahamkṛto bhāvo
Yasya buddhir-na lipyate
Kurvato kurvato vapi
Sa jīvanmukta ucyate (5)
150. *Ibid.*, II.18.2, 3.
151. *The Cultural Heritage of India*, Volume III, *The Philosophies*, p. 426.

PART – II

6

Science and Mysticism

Stephen Hawking in the beginning of his book entitled *The Grand Design* writes, "How does the universe behave? What is the nature of reality? Where did all this come from? Did the universe need a creator? Most of us do not spend most of our time worrying about these questions, but almost all of us worry about them some of the time. Traditionally these are questions for philosophy, but philosophy is dead. Philosophy has not kept up with the modern development in science, particularly physics."[1]

Philosophy is not dead, rather science has become a philosophy. Problem of 'why' has been the fundamental issue of philosophy since its very inception and the problem of 'how' comes within the domain of scientific investigation and discovery. Now, science is trying to understand, reflect and solve the problem of why. It is a welcome step. Scientist propagating their theories on the foundation of ontological materialism coming out of Plato's cave to new awareness of Truth and Reality. Truth and Reality is postulated by Ontological mysticism (ontological spiritualism). There is a convergence of science and philosophy today. Philosophy is not only alive and vibrant, but it has made science a living subject. The problem whether the matter is wave or particle is rooted in misunderstanding and the wrong notion of wave and particle. Matter is neither wave nor particle it is consciousness. Whole cosmos is the modification of cosmic consciousness (*Brahman*, *Ātman*), Emptiness (*Śūnyatā* or Tao). Whole cosmos is the modification of cosmic consciousness. Consciousness is the *Reality* and the sole *Truth.* Science and philosophy are the quest for truth and reality. The classical science was concerned with the objective truth. The theory of Relativity and Quantum Mechanics have transcended the boundary of classical science in search of the understanding and knowledge of true nature of reality and entered into the subjective domain of philosophy. If science would not have entered and made inroad into "*subjectivity*" it would have become dead and would have lost charm, beauty and relevance. Unless we understand the true nature and structure of truth we would become the victim of such dilemma. Einstein has revolutionized the science by his famous formulation of $E = mc^2$. He was the first scientist who came face to face with truth. For him matter is not dead, but it is energy and alive. By this formulation he rejected the age old scientific dogma of dead matter. The universe is vibrating with life. It is a living reality because it is a modification of consciousness. Consciousness is the quintessential nature and structure of the cosmos. Both science and philosophy culminate in spirituality. It is the goal and the end of the quest for science and philosophy. This is Ontological mysticism. According to Spinoza, the human body is a modification of infinite substance (God) in so far as it is expressed in the attribute of extension. According to him the material world is a modification of God. Hence, it follows from Spinoza's philosophy that there is consciousness which corresponds to the vital processes of our body. Ervin Schrodinger, one of the founding father of Quantum Mechanics writes, "And then, on the other hand, we say that consciousness is that by which this world becomes manifest, by which indeed, we can quite calmly say, it first becomes present; that the world consists of the elements of consciousness—this world within which we have just discovered the emergence of the brain as a highly specialized phenomenon, something which has emerged, but which might quite well have remained non-existent and which is, in any case, by no means *sui generis*. And now we are asked to believe that this special modification in the evolution of the higher mammals had to happen in order that the world should dawn on itself in the light of consciousness; whereas, if it had not emerged, this world would have remained nothing, but a drama played to an empty house, not present to anyone and hence not in a real sense present at all! If this is really the ultimate wisdom to which we can attain in this question, then to me it seems to be utter bankruptcy of our picture of the world. And we thought at least to acknowledge it, and not act as though it did not matter to us, or jeer, in our rationalistic wisdom, at those who try to find a way out, however, desperate."[2]

Danish physicist Neil Bohr (1855-1962) came out with a new theory of complementarity to explain the dilemma of wave and particle. A single model may not be adequate to explain all observations made of atomic or subatomic systems in different experiments. For example, "electron diffraction is best explained by assuming that electron is a wave, whereas the photoelectric effect is described by assuming that it is a particle." The idea of two different, but complementary concepts to treat quantum phenomena was first put forward by him.

Wave and particle dilemma is due to incomplete understanding of reality. The reality is beyond wave and particles. The nature is not governed by whims and caprices. There is some system, some rules, some principles, behind the movement of the phenomenal world. The uncertainty principles which explains certain natural functions like Newtonian Classics Physics which also explains gravitational movement some natural bodies, but which does not give scientific explanation of particle and waves but it has some limitations. The principles of uncertainty entail absence of our proper knowledge and understanding of the movement of particles and wave which has given rise to the principles of uncertainty. The movement of particles and waves would be explained by some law. Einstein didn't agree with the Copanhagen interpretation of Quantum mechanics. Einstein's rejections of Bohr's doctrine of complementarity are based on some scientific thinking and reflection.

It is to be ascertained whether Einstein is right in his assertion that God does not play dice with the world. If we accept the theory of complementarity then the logical doctrine of principles of identity and contradiction will have no place in science.

Washington Post writes, "In science, revolutions take time. So, the day after news broke of a possible revolution in physics 'particles moving faster than light'—a scientist leading the European experiment that made a discovery calmly explained it to the few present at CERN the giant particle acceleration straddling the Swiss-French border. The physicist, Danrio Anterio made no sweeping claims."[3]

In the *Washington Post* of 25th September, 2011 highlighted the new discovery by science which has almost falsified the findings of Einstein that nothing travels faster than light. Some particles according to the report travel faster than the speed of light. It is called the "God Particle". However, I believe that the cosmic consciousness has the speed of infinity. It may be called in mathematical terms that the cosmic consciousness travels with absolute speed and at the same time it has a zero speed. The whole cosmos exists in between zero and infinite speed. The cosmic consciousness which is called in Hinduism as a *Brahman* or Śiva, Tao in Lao Tzu metaphysics and *Śūnyatā* (emptiness) in Buddhism is the ultimate reality. It has absolute speed and absolute stillness (pause). From philosophical perspective we can say that consciousness has got infinite speed and from other perspective it may be called that it has a zero speed. Conceptually, there is no dilemma between absolute speed and absolute pause. The root of knowledge is spirituality, the trunk is science and the branches are all other schools of social sciences and humanity. Knowledge bereft of ontological mysticism is Pyrrhonism. In mystical experience, knowledge and wisdom become one. Monism is true philosophy and ultimate basis of science. Oneness with reality is the goal of spirituality and the proper understanding of reality is the end of scientific journey. I feel the convergence of science and spirituality will herald a new era of ontological mysticism. Science and spirituality are the integral form and part of human existence.

A French mathematician Marquis de Laplace (1749-1827), has made a very logical and rational assertion that all our knowledge is problematical. And in that background we have to examine the different scientific doctrines.

I think that the Einstein's assertions about the speed of the travelling light is the fastest, i.e., it is a relative truth. So, there is every possibility of its limitation and falsifications. As I have already asserted that the phenomenal world exists between zero and infinity and hence any scientific formulation which has not reached infinity has every possibility that it would be falsified by other scientific formulation. Scientific formulation being relative in nature, it doesn't entail that the Einstein assertions were totally wrong. As I have already stated, every scientific postulation is relative and subject to being corrected, improved and modified by another scientific postulation. Marquis de Laplace writes, "Strictly speaking it may be even said that nearly all our knowledge is problematical; and in the small number of things which we are able to know with certainty, even in mathematical sciences themselves, the principle means for asserting truth—induction and analogy, are based on probabilities; so that the entire system of human knowledge is connected with the theory set forth in the essay. Doubtless it will be seen here with interest that in considering, even in the eternal principles of reason, justice and humanity; only the favourable chances which are constantly attached to them, there is a great advantage in following these principles and serious inconvenience departing from them; their chances like those favourable to lotteries, always end by prevailing in the midst of the vacillations of hazard."[4]

There has been a constant debate between the domain of philosophy and science. We have been making arbitrary distinction between philosophy and science, between speculative and logical aspects of science. However, it would be wrong to assume that philosophy must develop into logic of science, which has been asserted by A.J. Ayer. He writes in his concluding celebrated book *Language, Truth and Logic* that, a person who is engaged in understanding the logical relationship of the different hypothesis and defining it in form of symbol is a philosopher. According to him, it is one and the same thing to address such people who are engaged in logical relationship of hypothesis as a philosopher or a scientist. He concludes with this sentence that "What we must recognise is that it is necessary for a philosopher to become a scientist, in this sense, if he is to make any substantial contribution towards the growth of human knowledge."[5] A.J. Ayer being a positivist he is biased for science. He could not comprehend the whole gamut of philosophical thinking and speculation. There is no necessity of philosopher becoming a scientist, when scientists are becoming philosophers in pursuit of truth, beauty and reality. Pure physics and pure mathematics are branches of philosophy. The root of knowledge is ontological mysticism, the trunk is philosophy and science and other forms of knowledge are different branches.

Karl Popper is of the opinion that scientific knowledge and all other theories are open to be proven false. However, mediating between two planes of perception and reflection given by science and philosophy would be the greatest intellectual adventure and most rewarding of our times.

I would analyse, examine and evaluate the findings and the postulations of classical physics, theory of Relativity and Quantum Mechanics in the larger background of philosophical reflection and ontological mysticism.

According to classical physics the universe is governed by the laws that are susceptible to rational understanding. And the chief purpose and objective of classical physics has been the application of those laws for extending our knowledge about the phenomenal world. Newton was a deeply religious man. He considered these laws as the manifestation of God's perfection. However, to great extent the classical physics became a tool for understanding the laws that governed the phenomenal world. However, the classical physics failed to explain some problems that govern the events on sub-atomic level. It failed to make enroot into some atomic phenomena with any certainty.

Strictly speaking quantum physics does not believe in the world of waves and particles, of position and velocity. We enter into the world of inconsistency and contradictions when we try to explain the quantum world in the language of classical science.

Actually the measurement of the object measured and the subject doing the measuring are inexplicably involved.

David Lindley in the introductory remark of Werner Heisenberg's celebrated book *Physics and Philosophy* writes, "In stressing the inadequacy of either the wave or the particle picture alone, Heisenberg tells us that "by playing with both pictures by going from one picture to the other and back again, we finally get the right impression of the strange kind of reality behind our atomic experiments." This, I fear, will strike a good many readers as a bit of dodge. That's all very well, Professor Heisenberg, these readers might say, but can you spell out for us just what this "strange kind of reality" consists of? Alas, that is ultimately what we cannot do, at least not in a very satisfactory way."[6] On the basis of the analysis of different concepts of classical physics, relativity and quantum mechanics, we come to the conclusion that the physics of today has not been able to formulate any satisfactory doctrine of reality. Schrodinger and Heisenberg both accept the role of consciousness and subjectivism in formulating the concept of reality. I shall deal with this problem in detail later on. Before that I would like to give the brief historical account of the development of science in the west. It is necessary to understand the development of the doctrine of reality in course of the scientific development which ultimately culminates to my mind in Ontological mysticism.

Modern Western science begins with Thales, who stated that 'everything is made of water'. Thales was born in Miletus, in Asia Minor. However, a number of other writers consider Thales as the founding father of philosophy. I have already dealt with this problem in previous chapters on Western Philosophy. I consider Galileo as the father of modern science. His greatest contribution in the field of in science is his doctrine that the object in absence of resistance falls at the same rate. It is considered that he made this experiment from the leaning tower of Pisa. However, some consider it as a myth. But this lays downs the sound foundation of classical physics. He was a son of music theorist and luteinise. He was the first scientist who used technology to explore and uncover the mystery of nature. He was the first to use telescope to explore the strange world of stars. This application of technology in exploring the mystery of the universe was a great revolution in the field of science. He discovered the stars which have never been thought of before. His observation of the movement of different stars leads him to believe that Copernicus was right and thus he made a historic observation that the earth is not the centre of the universe. Earth moves around the sun. It is the sun which is the centre of the galaxy around which all planets move. For this discovery Galileo was severely punished by the church because Galileo's discovery went against the biblical doctrine. Under the pressure of the church and to escape the capital punishment Galileo declared Copernicus theory was false and erroneous in 1616. In 1632 Galileo opines, "Take note, theologians, that in your desire to make matters of faith out of propositions relating to the fixity of sun and earth you run the risk of eventually having to condemn as heretics those who would declare the earth to stand still and the sun to change position—eventually, I say, at such a time as it might be physically or logically proved that earth moves and the sun stands still."[7] In 1963 Galileo's good friend became the Pope and he tried his level best to get the 1616 decree revoked. His book dialogue concerning the two chief world systems was published in 1632 which had become very famous throughout Europe. In this book Galileo had come out with strong argument in favour of heliocentric world as propagated by

Copernicus. The Pope became very angry though he was his friend and he sentenced Galileo to house arrest for the rest of his life and asked him to make public announcement of the falsification of Copernicanism. Before his death in 1646 Galileo, he succeeded in smuggling his another manuscripts which was published as '*Two New Sciences*' in Holland and this became the foundation of the classical physics.

In 1609, when Galileo Galilei was scanning the night sky with a telescope he observed that planet Jupiter was having several small satellites or moons that revolved around it and it went against Aristotle and Ptolemy who had thought that everything orbit directly around the Earth. It was a polish priest Copernicus, who had propagated this heliocentric doctrine that earth is not the centre rather the sun is the centre around which all other planets revolve. Kepler, a German scientist, made some improvement in the Copernicus theory by introducing a new concept that planets do not orbit in circles but in ellipses. This was the end of the Ptolemy's theory that earth is the centre. The sound foundation of classical physics was laid by Isaac Newton. He published his book entitled, *Philosophaie Naturalis Principia Mathematica.* It is considered as the greatest single publication which revolutionised the scientific world. He presented a scientific explanation for the planets orbiting the sun by introducing a path breaking doctrine of gravitation. In *Principia*, Newton presented a law that all objects are by nature in the state of rest until some external forces work upon to move or change the movement. And Newton gave a scientific explanation that why any object falls to earth instead of remaining at rest, and he called this force, gravity. Newton was of the opinion that this law of gravitation was applicable to all objects of the universe from the falling of an apple to the stars and planets. It was a great change and revolution in the scientific thinking because it was for the first time that the theory of gravitation explained the movement of the planets and other objects and he laid down the foundation for classical modern physics and modern astronomy. According to modern classical physics, matter was considered as the fundamental reality. The phenomenal world of things existed in space and time. The matter would be modified and it could be acted upon by forces. Every event is the result and cause of other events and it is all because of the interaction between the matter and the forces. Galileo observed the interplay of the things and events that provided the basis of scientific materialism.

According to classical physics the universe is governed by a set of laws. These laws could be analysed for better understanding. With the application of these laws that govern the universe we could exert change and influence our environments. Newton was a deeply religious person. He considered these laws as the manifestation of God. The understanding of these laws enhanced the dignity and honour of man which were reduced to the cog of a machine during the middle ages by the birth of Western natural philosophy.

The success and importance of any scientific theory depends upon the strength of predictability of events and provides a rational model of the universe. The Newton's theory became very famous because of his doctrine of gravitation, which would predict the motion of the sun, moon and other planets of our galaxy with higher degree of certainty. According to the theory of Gravitation, each body attracts other with the force proportional to the quantity (mass), universally proportional to the distance between them. This is a very simple scientific model. But all theories howsoever important it may be are based on the degree of probabilities. Marquis de Laplace says, "It is remarkable that science, which commenced with the consideration of games of chance, should be elevated to the rank of the most important subjects of human knowledge."[8]

According to Newton's law of gravitation, it was predicted with great amount on certainty about the movement of earth, moon and other planets. Ever since the birth of civilization the philosopher and the scientist have been grappling with the problem of a single theory that would explain the whole universe, though it is very difficult to formulate a theory that would provide a proper scientific and rational doctrine, which would explain universe in one go. In the process of understanding the mystery of nature we develop and discover a number of different theories to explain and predict certain events. One of my central objectives is to search for a new theory which would explain the universe in terms of science and philosophy. Stephen Hawking writes, "But ever since the dawn of civilization, people have not been content to see events such as unconnected and inexplicable. We have craved an understanding of the underlying order in the world.

Today we still yearn to know why we are here and where we came from. Humanity's deepest desire for knowledge is justification enough for our continuing quest. And our goal is nothing less than a complete description of the universe we live in."[9] But the nature of any scientific theory is always provisional. It doesn't matter that our experiments is in agreement with some theory, but one cannot be certain that next time his experiment may contradict the theory. Even discovering a single observation which goes against the prediction of the theory there is enough basis for the existing theory for its rejection and falsification. But it simply speaks of the limitation of any theory. Newton was a staunch believer in absolute God. He was very much upset when his own doctrine didn't approve of the idea of absolute God. Both Aristotle and Newton were in agreement that, time is absolute. The idea of the absolute time and absolute space was refuted by Einstein's theory of Relativity. Hawking's writes, "Newton was very worried by this lack of absolute position, or absolute space, as it was called, because it did not accord with his idea of an absolute God. In fact, he refused to accept the lack of absolute space, even though his laws implied it. He was severely criticized for this irrational belief by many people, most notably by Bishop Berkley, a philosopher who believed that all material objects and space and time are an illusion."[10]

Modern science today is trying to discover a basic law from which the motion of matter and all elementary particles and their properties could be mathematically understood. Thales was the first who considered that water is the material cause of all things. And with this postulation of Thales science took birth in the West. The German philosopher Nietzsche formulated three basic philosophical principles to understand the mystery of the universe. The first condition was that to find out the material cause of all things. Secondly, the analysis and postulation must be based on logic and rationality. And these fundamental laws should be reduced to one principle. This has been the search from the beginning of human civilization.

Werner Heisenberg one of the greatest physicist of last century observes, "The constant element in physics since Newton is not a configuration or a geometrical form, but a dynamic law. The equation of motion holds at all times, it is in this sense eternal, whereas the geometrical forms, like the orbits, are changing. Therefore, the mathematical forms that represent the elementary particles will be solutions of some eternal law of motion for matter. Actually this is a problem which has not yet been solved. The fundamental law of motion for matter is not yet known and, therefore, it is not yet possible to derive mathematically the properties of the elementary particles from such a law. But theoretical physics in its present state seems to be not very far from this goal and we can at least say what kind of law we have to expect. The final equation of motion for matter will probably be some quantized nonlinear wave equation for a wave field of operators that simply represent matter, not any specified kind of wave or particles."[11]

The basic difference between classical physics and Relativity theory and Quantum Mechanics are that according to classical physics there is an objective world which exists apart from us. We can measure, observe and experiment about the external world without changing it. The external world is completely indifferent to us. Galileo's success is dependent on quantifying the phenomena of the external world. The whole idea of external objective world depends upon the postulation of 'it is out there'. The new physics believes that the reality undergoes change in the process of our observation. Gary Zukav writes, "According to quantum mechanics there is no such thing as objectivity. We cannot eliminate ourselves from the picture. We are a part of nature, and when we study nature there is no way around the fact that nature is studying itself. Physics has become a branch of psychology, or perhaps the other way round.

Carl Jung, the Swiss psychologist, wrote:

The psychological rule says that when an inner situation is not made conscious, it happens outside, as fate. That is not to say, when the individual remains undivided and does not become conscious of his inner contradictions, the world must perforce act out the conflict and be torn into opposite halves. Jung's friend, the Nobel Prize winning physicist, Wolfgang Pauli, put it this way:

From an inner centre the psyche seems to move outward, in the sense of an extraversion, into the physical world..."[12]

The classical physics postulated by Newton has a limitation. It has failed to explain the functions and the structure of electrons in an atom. However, it doesn't mean that the classical physics is based on wrong and misleading scientific postulations. Newton's classical physics does explain the macroscopic matter constituted of innumerable atoms. However, there has been a great change and revolution with the advent of the theory of relativity and quantum physics.

Relativity

Albert Einstein the founding father of Relativity says in 9th June, 1952, as a Note to the fifteenth edition of the publication of his book on *Relativity of The Theory of Special and General Relativity* "I wish to show that space-time is not necessarily something to which one can ascribe a separate existence, independently of the actual objects of physical reality. Physical objects are not in space, but these objects are spatially extended. In this way, the concept 'empty space' loses its meaning."[13]

In the world of modern physics, the theory of relativity has exercised a historical role in changing the concept of time, space and reality. It could be said that Einstein's doctrine of relativity is a philosophical treatise. If we examine the development of modern physics, it is evident that Einstein's was awakened from the dogmatic slumber of classical physics which failed to explain the electrodynamics of moving bodies. Maxwell's discovery of electrodynamics nature of light waves has thrown a new revelation on the subject which could not be explained by classical physics before the advent of relativity belief in the empty space. The scientists used to believe that as the sound waves travels through air, but it creates difficulties in explaining the movement of light waves. The sound could not travel outside when the vessel is emptied whereas light travels easily through the evacuated volume. It was postulated that ether fills the empty space through which the light waves could travel. Einstein writes, "As long as one was convinced that all natural phenomena were capable of representation with the help of classical mechanics, there was no need to doubt the validity of this principle of relativity. But in view of the more recent development of electrodynamics and optics, it became more and more evident that classical mechanics affords an insufficient foundation for the physical description of all natural phenomena. At this juncture the question of the validity of the principle of relativity became ripe for discussion, and it did not appear impossible that the answer to this question might be in the negative."[14]

Einstein's foundation of relativity is based on the fundamental postulation that laws of science must be same for all freely moving observers. The Michelson-Morley experiment postulated the ether in explaining in terms of objects contracting and slowing down when they move through the ether. In his famous paper in 1905, Einstein rejected the concept of ether as unnecessary and along with that he refuted the concept of absolute time. According to Einstein, time is not separate from space but is combined with it to form an object known as space–time. This has changed the very basis of modern physics. The concept of time has been the best and difficult problem for both philosophers and scientists since the very beginning of civilization. St. Augustine's views that Time is an aspect of human cognition has played an important role in the formulation of theory of relativity.

He has discussed this problem in the eleventh book of *Confession.* This is a purely a philosophical treatise and not a religious work. While discussing what is "What then is time" he asked "If no one asked me, I know; if I wish to explain to him who asks, I know not," Various difficulties perplex him. Neither past nor future, he says, but only the present, really is; the present is only a moment, and time can only be measured while it is passing. Nevertheless, there really is time past and future. We seem here to be led into contradictions. The only way Augustine can find to avoid these contradictions is to say that past and future can only be thought of as present: "past" must be identified with memory, and "future" with expectation, memory and expectation being both present facts. There are, he says, three times: "a present of things past, a present of things present, and a present of things future." "The present of things past is memory; the present of things present is sight; and the present of things future is expectation."[15]

However, Augustine's concept of time has not solved all the problems but it has definitely laid a foundation of the future development of physics, especially in the form of relativity and quantum mechanics. It does lay down the foundation of a new dimension of reality in the form of subjectivism which I shall discuss later. But to divide time in the form of past, present and future is to escape from the philosophical contradictions and difficulties. One of the founding fathers of quantum mechanics, Erwin Schrodinger, also says that there is only eternal present. He writes, "For eternally there is only now, one and the same now; the present is the only thing that has no end."[16] Schrodinger's formulation of the concept of time is different from that of St. Augustine's and Kant. His whole concept of time is based on Vedāntic teachings which will be dealt in detail later.

There is another important answer to Einstein's *Relativity of Simultaneity.* When two events occur at the same point in space simultaneously we believe that they coincide. This term is not very clear. If we think of three points in space that exist on a straight line in which the middle point is at the same distance from each other/outer points. Einstein has dealt with this problem by imagining a lighting stroke happening at *A* and *B* simultaneously. We understand that the rays of light emitted at places *A* and *B* where the lightning strokes meet each other at the midpoint *M* between the length of *A* and *B*. Imagine *M* be the midpoint of the distance *A* and *B* on the travelling train. But it doesn't mean that when two events are simultaneous for one observer they may not be simultaneous for another observer if he is moving in a train. Einstein says "Now, in reality (considered with reference to the railway embankment) he is hastening towards the beam of light coming from *B*, whilst he is riding on ahead of the beam of light coming from *A*. Hence, the observer will see the beam of light emitted from *B* earlier than he will see that emitted form *A*. Observers who take the railway train as their reference – body must, therefore, come to the conclusion that the lightning flash *B* took place earlier than the lightning flash *A*." This throws a light on events which are considered simultaneous with reference to the embankment are not simultaneous with respect to the train and *vice versa.* This is known as relativity of simultaneity. Every reference observer depicts its own particular time. Einstein writes, "Now before, the advent of the Theory of Relativity it had always tacitly been assumed in physics that the statement of time had absolute significance, i.e., that it is independent of the state of motion of the body of reference. But we have just seen that this assumption is incompatible with the most natural definition of simultaneity; if we discard this assumption, then the conflict between the laws of the propagation of light *in vacuo* and the principle of relativity disappears."[17] According to relativity there is no real difference between the coordinates of space and time. We believe that there is no real distinction between the space coordinates. However, the most fundamental contribution of Einstein has been his legendary scientific formulation $E=mc^2$ (where, E is energy, m is mass and c is referred to as the speed of light). This is known as the principle of relativity in the form of inertia of energy. The formulation presents the equivalence of mass and energy.

This has enhanced the experiments and formulations of atomic energy. This was possible by this equation that elementary particles can be created from kinetic energy, i.e., the theory that speaks of the particles annihilated to form radiations. Transmutation from energy into mass and mass into energy. The unthinkable release of energy in an atomic explosion stands out as most revolutionary evidence of the correctness of Einstein's formulation. On the basis of this formulation matter was converted into pure electromagnetic radiation. The atom bomb that devastated the city of Hiroshima on the 6th August, 1945 was the result of this transmutation matter in energy in the form of bomb which was less than one ounce. Einstein limits the speed of any object which would never be equal to the speed of light. Einstein believed that the speed of light is the highest. The object cannot reach the speed of light because the mass of it would become infinite. It means the equivalence of mass and energy will have to gather infinite amount energy to reach the speed of light. Einstein believes that the light or other waves that doesn't contain mass can move at the speed of light. The new researches and experiments which are the Large Hydron Collider (LHC) which came in existence on 20th November in 2009 is trying to understand the mystery of dark matter and energy. In recent experiments it has claimed that it has succeeded partially in overcoming the speed of light. I would discuss this matter later.

The equivalence of mass and energy has questioned some of the philosophical concepts of a substance which cannot be destroyed. In modern physics a lot of experiments have been carried out in which the elementary particles like positrons and electrons were annihilated and transmuted in radiations. But I would not consider it the rejection of the philosophical concept of substance. It could be explained in modern scientific formulation that mass and energy are the modes of the ultimate reality, i.e., cosmic consciousness. This has been postulated and discussed in detail in Kashmir Śaivism and Vedānta of Hinduism, *Tathatā* (suchness) and emptiness in Buddhism and Tao and Teh of Taoism. The matter and energy are not ultimate truth and reality, but they are modifications of the ultimate reality which is known in Kashmir Śaivism as Parama Śiva, in Vedānta as a *Brahman*. I shall deal with this problem in a detailed manner in the next chapter in the context of the dark matter and the origin of the universe.

Albert Einstein, a clerk in the department of patent company at Berne, Switzerland presented the general theory of relativity at the age of 26 in 1905. He died in 1955 at Centre of Advance Study, Princeton (USA). He was forced to immigrate to U.S.A in 1932. The theory of relativity was confirmed by Arthur Edington in 1919 when he witnessed the bending of light at the solar eclipse on the island of Principe. He was awarded a Nobel Prize in physics in 1921 on Photo Electric Effect and not for his theory of relativity.

The first force when it was explained which is known as force of gravity, it heralded a new era of awakening in modern physics. The second electromagnetic force advanced the scientific development and paved the path for the theory of relativity and quantum mechanics. The third and the fourth forces were the two nuclear forces the weak and the strong forces. When the atom was split in the 1930's, scientists for the first time started understanding the forces that light up the heavens. This revealed the secrets behind the stars. Not only this unleashed immense power of atomic weapons, but it also created a hope to harness this power for the betterment of the society. Some of the discoveries have been awesome and made us wonderstruck. These discoveries laid down the foundation for a new physics, chemistry and biology.

The unification of electricity and magnetism created by James Clarke Maxwell, (1831-1879) provided a new theory of light. According to electromagnetism, light is an electromagnetic wave. According to Maxwell, the visible light is only a tiny part of the electromagnetic spectrum. Maxwell's theory of electromagnetism was confirmed by the discovery of radio and X-rays.

In 1916 Einstein wrote another historical paper known as the Theory of General Relativity. The basic assumptions of general relativity are the relation between inertia and gravity. Werner Heisenberg while summarising the scientific importance of the theory of general relativity writes, "Though the experimental basis of general relativity is still rather narrow, the theory contains ideas of greatest importance. During the whole period from the mathematicians of ancient Greece to the nineteenth century, Euclidean geometry had been considered as evident; the axioms of Euclid were regarded as the foundation of any mathematical geometry, a foundation that could not be disputed. Then, in the nineteenth century, the mathematicians Bolyai and Lobachevsky, Gauss and Riemann found that other geometries could be invented which could be developed with the same mathematical precision as that of Euclid, therefore, the questions as to which geometry was correct turned out to be an empirical one."[18]

Another important contribution of Einstein theory of relativity, space-time is carved due to mass and energy. General relativity always adheres to the four dimensional space-time. It means that the gravitational field should also bend the light. According to this theory, time is also influenced by the force of gravity. Time doesn't mean same things for different observers at different heights in a gravitational field. And this resulted in the rejection of the concept of absolute time. Space and time are also influenced by the events of the cosmos. It is not a one way traffic that space and time only influence the events of the universe. While enumerating the importance of the theory of general relativity, Stephen Hawking's writes, "Another prediction of general relativity is that time should appear to run slower near a massive body such as the earth. Einstein first realized this in 1907; five years before he realized that gravity also altered the shape of space, and eight years before he completed his theory. He derived the effect using his principle of equivalence, which played the role in general relativity that the fundamental postulate played in the special theory."[19]

There is a startling discovery that the total amount of energy coming from ordinary matter and dark matter is only twenty seven per cent of the total energy. Scientists are struggling to know and discover the source of the seventy three percent which is termed as dark energy. This is the most mysterious part of modern physics. Lisa Randall writes, "The discovery of the dark energy matter was the most profound physics wake-up call of the late twentieth century. Although there is much we don't know yet about the evolution of the universe, we have a spectacularly successful understanding of the universe's evolution based on the so-called Big Bang Theory supplemented by a period of exponential expansion of the universe known as cosmological inflation."[20] This cosmological inflation which is known as cosmological constant is now considered by scientists as the greatest discovery of Einstein. This new energy which is called dark energy is postulated to maintain the balance and the very existence of the universe. Dark energy is not found in particles or other matter. It doesn't disappear in the face of expanding universe but it does maintain a constant and required density. Scientists feel that it is only due to this dark energy which is called the cosmological constant that keeps the universe expanding. Lisa Randall writes, "Einstein had originally proposed that such a form of energy in what he called the universal constant, which later became known to physicists as the cosmological constant. Shortly after, he thought it a mistake and, indeed, that his use of it to try to explain why the universe was static was misguided. The universe does in fact expand, as Edwin Hubble showed soon after Einstein proposed the idea. The expansion is not only real, but it now seems that its current acceleration is due to the funny type of energy that Einstein had introduced and quickly dismissed in the 1930's."[21] Einstein's theory of general relativity entails the expanding universe. It is not only a theory that exercises negative pressure on the environment. This is known in physics in the absence of any other terms as a dark energy. The expansion of universe is possible only with the cosmological constant that has been coined by Einstein. The dark energy is equated with the cosmological constant in absence of any other proper explanation of the source and the cause of expanding universe. Einstein's assumptions that every property of the universe does not change but there is a mystery that the universe which was found by Hubble's as expanding under the force of gravitation but still collision does not take place.

This gravitational attraction is a puzzle. To solve this puzzle and perplexity Einstein coined a new concept of cosmological constant which according to this concept every cubic centimetre of empty space has a fixed amount of energy. Einstein termed this constant energy density of the vacuum as cosmological constant which he denounced as the greatest blunder of his life in 1930's. Alex Vilenkin writes, "Another puzzling feature of the big bang is the precarious balance between the power of the blast that sent all particles rushing away from one another and the force of gravity that slows the expansion down. If the density of matter in the universe were a bit higher, its gravitational pull would be strong enough to halt the expansion and the universe would eventually recollapse. If it were a bit lower, the universe would continue expanding forever. The observed density is within a few percentage points of the critical density, at the borderline between the two regimes. This is very peculiar and calls for an explanation."[22] The balance, equilibrium and the very existence of the universe is a mystery for the scientists. The scientists postulate to explain this mystery with a new concept of vacuum which is the state with ephemeral particles. But instead of explaining the mystery it complicates the problem. It looks like a scientific fiction. Lisa Randall writes, "And these are not the only puzzles evoked by the energy of the universe. The value of the dark energy, in particular, is actually the tail end of a much large mystery: why is the energy that pervades the universe so small? Had the amount of dark energy been greater, it would have dominated matter and radiation much earlier in the evolution of the universe and structure (and life) would not have the time to form. On top of that, no one knows what was responsible earlier on for the large energy density that triggered and fuelled inflation. But the biggest problem with the energy of the universe is the *cosmological constant problem.*"[23]

The concept of matter and its existence including the concept of vacuum are scientific puzzles. The scientists even raise the question: why there is universe at all? Why there is a matter in the universe? If the concept of matter and anti-matter having same value, then why they didn't destroy each other and go out of existence? Why and how the asymmetry between matter and anti-matter was created? These are some of the unanswered questions of modern science.

Penzias and Wilson discovery of cosmic microwaves on which they were awarded the Nobel Prize in 1978 is another mystery. What is the source of the cosmic microwaves, background of radiation; which has not been answered? Sir Arthur Eddington says, "We have found a strange footprint on the shores of the unknown.

We have devised profound theories, one after another to account for its origin. At last, we have succeeded in reconstructing the creature that made the footprint. And Lo! It is our own". According to Einstein, the universe is finite and yet it has no limits. The concept of the finite universe was first conceived and demonstrated by Johannes Kepler in 1610. If the universe would have been infinite, the stars and the galaxies would have distributed energy uniformly throughout the infinite space. If that would have been the case, if we have looked in the sky we could have experienced constant brilliance. If that would have been the case there would have never been dark at night and on the basis of this he for the first time conceived the idea that the universe is finite. There is a possibility that the number of stars within the radius is finite. The concluding lines of Einstein's formulation of relativity are as such "If we are to have in the universe an average density of matter which differs from zero, however, small may be that difference, then the universe cannot be quasi-Euclidean. On the contrary, the results of calculations indicate that if matter be distributed uniformly, the universe would necessarily be spherical (or elliptical). Since, in reality the detailed distribution of matter is not uniform, the real universe will deviate in individual parts from the spherical, i.e., the universe will be quasi-spherical. But it will be necessarily finite. In fact, the theory supplies us with a simple connection between the space-expanse of the universe and the average density of matter in it."[24]

In summarising whole the discussion on relativity I come to the conclusion that the cosmological constant does not denote dark energy but it is a form of a cosmic consciousness. To my mind the cosmic consciousness which is ultimate reality is the source and origin of all the forces that operate in the universe. The laws that govern this ultimate reality are not blind. Moreover, in the enumeration of the physical universe in terms of four dimensional: space-time remains unexplained without introducing the subjectivity. The role subjectivity has been accepted in explaining the quantum mechanics by Heisenberg and Schrodinger. Schrodinger has gone further and he explained the mystery of universe with the help of the Vedāntic concept of *Brahman*. I would deal with this in the next subsequent pages. To my mind the universe is not only five dimensional, subject being fifth dimension, but it is multi-dimensional because the subject or the consciousness doesn't function singularly. This cosmic consciousness is called *Ātman* or *Brahman* in Hinduism which may be called cosmological constant because the cosmic consciousness is in a state of absolute and absolute pause. The concept of empty space in the manifest universe is illogical. *Śūnyatā* (emptiness) of Buddhism and Tao of Taoism and the *Brahman* of Hinduism are the only eternal source of cosmological constant and origin of *Élan-vita.*

Quantum Mechanics

Quantum mechanics as a theory was developed to explain electromagnetic waves and atomic structure. Classical physics failed to explain both the electromagnetic waves and atomic structure. At the beginning of the twentieth century the atomic structure puzzled the physicists in explaining the emission of electrons from the surface of the metal illuminated by light. Einstein was the first scientist to realize that the classical description of light as a wave on an electromagnetic field does not explain the photoelectric effect. The experiments proved that electrons could be emitted only if the incident light was of a sufficient wavelength while the intensity of light appeared to be not relevant. Einstein postulated that photoelectric effect, light behaves as a shower of particles, E with the energy given by Planck's expression, $E=hf$. Here f stands for light frequency and h is the Planck's constant. However, in non-relativistic Quantum theory, particles are assumed to be neither created nor destroyed, to move slowly relative to the speed of light, and to have a mass that doesn't change with velocity. This postulation is applicable to atomic and molecular structure which is considered as an aspect of nuclear physics. The relativistic quantum theory applies to particles that travel to or near the speed of light.

Quantum mechanics is replaced by classical mechanics and Maxwell's electromagnetic theory. It was a new revolution in the world of pure physics.

Max Planck (1858-1947) laid down the foundation of modern quantum physics by postulating the theory that nature is not continuous but it is marked by discrete packets or quanta. He was awarded Nobel Prize in physics in 1918. He published his quantum postulation in December in 1900. The Planck's theory of heat radiation and the postulation that energy is emitted or absorbed only in discrete energy form called quanta was inanalogous with the traditional classical physics of Newton. Light can be interpreted in terms of electronic magnetic waves propounded by Maxwell's theory or it could be interpreted in terms of light quanta, i.e., energy packets passing through space with higher velocity.Werner Heisenberg writes, "This time it was the young Albert Einstein, a revolutionary genius among the physicists, who was not afraid to go further away from the old concepts. These were two problems in which he could make use of the new ideas. One was the so-called photoelectric effect, the emission of electrons from metals under the influence of the light. The experiments, especially those of Lenard, had shown that the energy of the emitted electrons did not depend on the intensity of the light, but only on its colour or, more precisely on its frequency. This could not be understood on the basis of the traditional theory of radiation. Einstein could explain the observations by intercepting Planck's hypothesis as saying that light consists of quanta of energy travelling through space. The energy of one light quantum should, in agreement with the Plank's assumptions, be equal to the frequency of the light multiplied by the Planck's constant."[25]

The theory of uncertainty initiated by Heisenberg in 1927 and Bohr's doctrine of complementarity are the fundamental basis of quantum mechanics. According to Heisenberg electrons do not occupy any fixed location in atoms as has been the basis of classical physics. One can know and ascertain the average position of an electron. But any measurement of the movement of the electron is worked under the principle of uncertainty. According to the new postulation of Quantum Mechanics we can have proper understanding of movement of electrons only at quantized levels. And it was assumed that the laws of classical physics do not apply at the quantized movements of electrons in an atom. This paradigm of quantum mechanics is applicable at the atomic scale. It only throws light on the limitations of classical physics in the interpretations of nature. At the macroscopic level of nature or material world, the laws of classical physics are operated. But at the microscopic scale of atom classical laws breaks down. Newton's work entitled *Philosophiae Naturalis Principia Mathematica* postulates that the all objects at rest remain in that state unless it is moved by some external force. And he explained the movement of the planets around the sun in the elliptical orbits in terms of force of gravity.

Now, the universe is described and explained in terms of two fundamental theories of general theory of Relativity and Quantum mechanics. The general theory of relativity is capable of explaining the macrocosmic level of universe. Quantum mechanics deals with microscopic level of phenomena. However, these two doctrines one which works at the macroscopic level other with microscopic level of nature are analogous to each other. Now, the scientists and the philosophers are in quest of a doctrine which could resolve this ambiguity and provide a doctrine which Einstein dreamed of as 'theory of everything'. However, one should be conscious about the limitation of the rational thinking. It is an impossibility to discover and arrive at some absolute truth with the help of rationality. Heisenberg writes, "The philosophic thesis that all knowledge is ultimately founded in experience has in the end led to a postulate concerning the logical clarification of any statement about nature. Such a postulate may have seemed justified in the period of classical physics, but since quantum theory we have learned that it cannot be fulfilled. The words "position" and "velocity" of an electron, for instance, seemed perfectly well defined as to both their meaning and their possible connections, and in fact they were clearly defined concepts within the mathematical framework of Newtonian mechanics. But actually they were not well defined, as is seen from the relations of uncertainty."[26]

"The essence of substance" is beyond the reach of our mind and senses. James Jeans (1877-1946) has dealt with this problem in his celebrated work the mysterious universe. According to him the objective reality exists because they affect our consciousness. But we believe that that objective reality is either real or ideal. He explains everything in mathematical language. According to him, "God is a mathematician and the universe begins to look more like a great thought than a great machine". There is an echo of Pythagorean mysticism in his thought. However, it rejects the Humean thesis of solipsism, i.e., "All this is creation of my own mind, and exists in no other mind". Rationality has limitation. He says, "A mathematical formula can never tell us what a thing is, but only how it behaves; it can only specify an object through its properties. And these are unlikely to coincide *in toto* with the properties of any single macroscopic object of our everyday life." The modern science is trying to discover some basic law of motion for matter from which all elementary particles and their properties could be deduced mathematically. This elementary particle is being postulated to basic substance which is known as energy or matter. Energy is considered as the basic substance. Elementary particles and all atoms are made from this basic substance. But the greatest problem before the modern scientists is to ascertain the mathematical forms of elementary particles which could be a solution of the eternal laws of motion for matter. Heisenberg says that the fundamental law of motion for matter is not known and, therefore, it is not possible to drive mathematically the properties of elementary particles from such a law. The concept of matter has undergone great change and metamorphosis. According to Aristotle matter is in itself not a reality but only possibility "*a potentia*". Matter exists through the means of form. Matter according to Aristotle is not a specific matter like Thales water or anything else. It is a kind of indefinite material substratum which is the basis of possibility of passing and transforming into actuality with the help of forms. As for example the statue is potentially in the stone before it was transformed into a splendour or beauty in form of statue by the sculpture. According to Heisenberg this concept of *Potentia* could be compared with the modern concept of energy. The division between matter and form doesn't exist in modern physics. Elementary particles not only produce some force, it is activated by some force, it represents a certain field of force. According to Copenhagen interpretation matter and force are the appearance of waves and particles. However, the theory of special relativity and quantum mechanics presents two different concepts and throws light on two different aspects of nature. Theory of special relativity deals with the space time continuum which is quite analogous to classical physics. According to Einstein the maximum velocity of light cannot be surpassed by any other moving objects. The theory of special relativity which postulates the structure of space and time put infinitely the boundary between the regions of simultaneousness.

On the contrary quantum theory of uncertainty put a definite limitation on the position and momenta, i.e., time and energy which could be measured simultaneously. Heisenberg writes, "Therefore, any theory which tries to fulfil the requirements of both special relativity and quantum theory will lead to mathematical inconsistencies, to divergencies in the region of very high energies and momenta. This sequence of conclusions may perhaps not seem strictly binding, since any formalism of the type under consideration is very complicated and could perhaps offer some mathematical possibilities for avoiding the clash between quantum theory and relativity."[27]

According to Einstein's theory of special relativity, time is affected by gravity. According to the special relativity the experience of time for a person in a relative motion is quite different from another stand point of theory of general relativity. According to later the person observing from a different height in a gravitational field will have different notion of time. According to first person observing from the relative motion and another person observing from different height there would be a difference of one second between the signals because time moves more slowly, closer to the surface of earth because of the effects of gravitation. And this rejected the Newton's concept of absolute time. In summarising the Einstein theory of relativity Stephen Hawkins writes, "Space and time are now dynamic quantities: when a body moves or a force acts, it affects the curvature of space and time—and in turn the structure of space-time affects the way in which bodies move and forces act. Space and time not only affect but are also affected by everything that happens in the universe. Just as we cannot talk about events in the universe without the notions of space and time, so in general relativity it became meaningless to talk about space and time outside the limits of the universe. In the decades following 1915, this new understanding of space and time was to revolutionize our view of the universe."[28]

Copenhagen interpretation of quantum theory has thrown a new light on the elements of subjectivism into theory. According to the Copenhagen interpretations of quantum mechanics our knowledge of the position of the particle is complementary to our understanding of velocity. Space-time postulation of atomic events is complementary in providing the proper description of the structure of space-time. This has been formulated from the epistemological and ontological standpoints. Here epistemology and ontology help each other in having a proper understanding of nature. Quantum mechanics represents two analogous pictures of waves and particles. The complementary doctrines of waves and particles has been of great debate between Einstein and Schrodinger criticising the doctrine of complementarity advocated by Copenhagen interpretations of quantum theory and formulated by Neil Bohr and supported by Heisenberg and the others. The misunderstanding of the dualism between the two descriptions of reality in the form of waves and particles posed another serious problem about the actual happenings in atomic events. It is believed that the results and mechanism employed in observation can be formulated in classical concepts. But mathematical formulations of the combined statements about the possibility and our knowledge of facts cannot be described what happens between this observation and the next. Heisenberg writes, "This looks as if we had introduced an element of subjectivism into the theory, as if we meant to say: what happens depends on our way of observing it or on the fact that we observe it. Before discussing this problem of subjectivism it is necessary to explain quite clearly why one would get into hopeless difficulties if one tried to describe what happens between two consecutive observations."[29] In the theoretical explanation of any experiment involves two steps. For example the experiment of source of monochromatic light that radiates towards a black screen with two small holes. The wavelength of the light and the diameter of holes create the problem. Distance behind the screen of a photographic plate which witnesses the events of light can be explained in the experiment in terms of wave picture one may observe that the primary wave penetrates through two holes and there is a possibility of secondary spherical waves that begins from the holes that interfere with one another. This interference would create a pattern of varying intensity on the photographic plate. If the experiment is multiplied the light quantum that has gone through the first hole blackening of the plate due to, would correspond to the probability distribution. Heisenberg writes, "This example shows clearly that the concept of the probability function does not allow a description of what happens between two observations. Any attempt to find such a description would lead to contradictions; this must mean that the term 'happens' is restricted to the observation."[30] If we enumerate this interpretation of an experiment which has been started with two steps, we in the first place deal with the arrangement of the experiment in the light of classical physics which is explained in terms of probability function. This is a very important factor which throws light on the probability function of laws of quantum theory. In the second step it could be measured in the initial condition. Heisenberg writes, "The probability function combines objective and subjective elements. It contains statements about possibilities or better tendencies ("potentia" in Aristotle philosophy). These statements are completely objective, they do not depend on any observer; and it contains statements about our knowledge of the system, which of course are subjective in so far as they may be different for different observers. In ideal cases the subjective element in the probability function may be practically negligible as compared with the objective one. The physicists then speak of a 'pure case' ".[31] The Heisenberg's theory of uncertainty is based on the probability function which is the combination objective element of tendency and the subjective element of incomplete knowledge. This has been the basis of Heisenberg postulations that the result of observation cannot be normally predicted with certainty. We can only predict of the probability of certain results of observation which could be about the repeated confirmation by repeating experiments. According to Quantum mechanics our observation of the knowledge of system undergoes change which doesn't have continuity and with the result the mathematical also undergoes discontinuous change which is termed as *quantum jump*. This speaks of a very significant development in quantum physics of transition of events from the *possible* to the actual which happens during the process of observation. Quantum mechanics throws a new light on the events that takes place in atomic experiments. The events are related to the observation and not to the state of affairs between two observations. The psychological act of observation doesn't apply, while it does apply to the physical events. In other words, while we can summarize that transition from the *possible* to actual happens as soon as the interaction of the object with the measuring device takes place. And thereby it entails that the rest of world also takes place in the drama of this place. Heisenberg comes to the conclusion that in the objective description of the world especially in the reference of the atomic world in classic physics, science starts with belief or may be termed as from illusion, the description of the world or the parts of the world without any reference to the observer. Quantum theory does contain the real subjective element. However, it does divide the world into the object and the rest of the world. The Copenhagen interpretation of quantum theory starts with the paradox. The starting point of formulation of quantum experiment is in terms of classical physics. At the same time from the knowledge that these concepts do not adhere to nature accurately. This is the root of the paradox which speaks of the statistic character of quantum theory. This paradox leads to the uncertainty in relation to the macroscopic behaviour of the world, when it enters into the quantum theoretical system. Heisenberg writes, "Therefore, that apart of matter or radiation which takes part in the phenomenon is the natural "object" in the theoretical treatment and should be separated in this respect from the tools used to study the phenomenon. This again emphasizes a subjective element in the description of atomic events, since the measuring device has been constructed by the observer, and we have to remember that what we observe is not nature in itself but nature exposed to our method of questioning."[32]

While understanding and describing the harmony in the cosmic drama of nature we are both a choreographer and a spectator. In describing and understanding the laws of nature and our scientific relations we become very important when we enter into dialogue with parts of nature with the help of nature by using most effective, scientific tools. The introduction of the "*subject*" in postulating Quantum Physics, Heisenberg writes, "It is understandable that in our scientific relation to nature our own activity becomes very important when we have to deal with parts of nature into which we can penetrate only by using the most elaborate tools."[33]

To my mind Heisenberg's acceptance of active role of subject in understanding nature opens new vistas in modern science and philosophy. I postulate that Einstein's four dimensional world of space-time does not provide the proper scientific and philosophical understanding and knowledge of the world without introducing and accepting the role of the subject. And hence I feel space-time-subject does provide the true and the real picture of nature. As subject being a conscious element it has a singular function. When the four dimensional world is subjectivised in the prism of subjective consciousness of an observer in multidimensional world. Subject is definitely one of the most important relevant fifth dimensions of world and in the spectrum of this space-time-subject world becomes multidimensional.

Werner Heisenberg formulation of uncertainty principle puts limits on our ability to predict the future in terms of scientific laws. It follows from the principle of uncertainty that the concept of determinism does not hold well. According to quantum theory, even one quanta of light could disturb the structure of particles. According to this principle, there is an uncertainty in the position of particle times and uncertainty in velocity times. The concept of uncertainty of position and velocity of particles is the quintessential nature of atomic structure. The theory of uncertainty is fundamental principle on which the whole Quantum mechanics has been founded. Heisenberg, Erwin Schrodinger and Neil Bohr are the founding fathers of this new and revolutionary scientific postulation of quantum physics. The application of uncertainty principle entails the dualism of waves and particles. The nature is explained in terms of either particles or waves from one perspective and from other's perspective it is a particle. This has been enunciated by Neil Bohr which is called concept of complementarity. Though Quantum theory has been very successful especially in the field of life science and creating the technological wonder in the form of electronic device like television, computers, etc. it has failed in the large scale structure of universe. Quantum physics provides a new concept of reality. The classical physics was to great extent successful in providing a concept of reality which has been successful when applied to macroscopic level. In one of the root concept of waves-particles dualism, when applied it does explain the microscopic mystery of atomic structure. According to this new scientific postulation of Quantum mechanics in spite of all our knowledge and understanding the physical events cannot be predicted with certainty because it is not deterministic in nature. The future course of nature according to Quantum mechanics is basically uncertain and unpredictable. Stephen Hawking writes, "Quantum physics might seem to undermine the idea that nature is governed by laws, but that is not the case. Instead it leads us to accept a new form of determinism: given the state of the system at some time, the laws of nature determine the probabilities of various futures and pasts rather than determining the future and past with certainty. Though that is distasteful to some, scientists must accept theories that agree with experiment, not their own preconceived notions."[34]

The refutation of Copenhagen interpretations led by Einstein is based on ontological spiritualism. There has been great debate between Einstein and Bohr, on the validity of Quantum mechanics. Bohr observes, "There is no Quantum World. There is only an abstract mechanical description. It is wrong to think that the task of physics is to find out how nature is. Physics concerns what we can say about."

Einstein differing with Bohr based his assessment of Quantum Mechanics on his belief in the existence of a causal, observer-independent reality. Einstein observes, "What we call science has the sole purpose of determining what is. Einstein believed in the observer independent reality, whereas Bohr believes that Quantum Mechanics considers that there is no possibility of having knowledge of nature without getting it modified and tinged in the process of observation and experimentation. Manjit Kumar writes, "For Bohr the theory came first, then the philosophical position, the interpretation constructed to make sense of what the theory says about reality. Einstein knew that it was dangerous to build a philosophical world-view on the foundations of any scientific theory. If the theory is found wanting in the light of new experimental evidence, then the philosophical position it supports collapses with it."[35] Einstein reiterates, "It is basic for Physics that one assumes a real world existing independently from any act of perception." However, he admits but 'This we do not Know'[36]. Einstein refutation of Copenhagen interpretation of Quantum Mechanics is based on his implicit faith in God that doesn't play dice with the world. However, Einstein does not reject the whole theory, only that it does not provide complete picture of physical reality at the Quantum level. However, Einstein accepts his profound ignorance about the world as it is. Science has its own limitation. It cannot comprehend the transcendental nature of reality. The whole debate between Einstein and Bohr is about the kind of Physics that is acceptable as a theory which speaks of the nature of reality in itself. It doesn't provide a complete picture of reality. Einstein has been working throughout his life to provide a complete picture of world view in the form of unified theory. In the absence of proper understanding and knowledge of "reality as it is" which is beyond the reach of scientific rationalism, it is not possible to enunciate any philosophical or scientific doctrine to explain the reality in its totality and wholeness. In the ultimate analysis of the whole philosophical pursuits and scientific experiments and reflections divorced from Ontological mysticism is incomplete. To my mind the ontological mysticism is the only possibility to fulfil the dream of Einstein's formulation of unified theory.

According to this belief it is postulated that scientists have been dealing with the world which has not been made by them. The world remains essentially unchanged even if the scientists would not be there. Copenhagen interpretation does not provide the proper understanding and knowledge of atomic structure. The arguments of Einstein and other have been rebutted by the adherents of quantum mechanics with the view that the whole doctrine of ontological materialism is based on illusion that existence and the actuality of the world could be extrapolated into atomic structure. Heisenberg says that this extrapolation is '*an impossibility*'. Though modern science comprising of the classical physics, theory of relativity and quantum mechanics does not provide the real understanding of the reality and nature, the modern scientific theories deals with the very limited part of nature and reality and it has left the other part for the future scientific investigation and discovery. This is a welcome step by the scientists who have realized their limitation in their understanding of truth and reality. Heisenberg says, "In this way modern physics has perhaps opened the door to a wider outlook on the relation between the human mind and reality."[37]

Quantum Mechanics postulates that electron does not occupy a fixed position in the atoms. It could be found and located at any particular point in space. But the measurement of the particular position of the electron is bound by the principle of uncertainty. The atomic structure is constituted of nucleus and electrons orbiting around it. The atom is composed of particles like electrons, protons and neutrons. Protons and neutrons are composed of eight smaller particles called quarks. Each of these atomic particles entails the existence of anti-particles. Anti-particles have the same mass but are opposite in their charge and other attributes. In the dance of energy the meeting of anti-particles with particles result into annihilation of each other.

But a new discovery has postulated a theory which is called Sting Theory which claims that sting is the fundamental particles. However, this theory is also being questioned and a new concept known as M-theory which has been formulated by scientists like Stephen Hawking's in his famous book *The Grand Design*. Hawking's claim that this could fulfil the dream of Einstein and it could be considered as the theory of everything. I shall deal with this concept but to me M-theory as postulated by Hawking's seems to be more of a scientific fiction than a scientific doctrine. Hawking does claim that this new theory would explain the problem of quantum gravity. We shall examine, analyse and evaluate the veracity of whether it is a scientific fiction or a scientific doctrine. Heisenberg is honest and forthright in accepting that the experiments are carried out about atomic structures but "the atoms or the elementary particles are not as real; they form a world of potentiality or possibilities rather than one of things or facts".[38] Einstein's dream of having a unified theory of matter has become a deep concern for scientists of all hues. The unification of theory of Relativity and Quantum Mechanics may provide a foundation for future scientific investigation and discovery. Hawking had postulated the theory of Quantum gravity on the basis of the unification of the above two lines of scientific thinking, postulations and formulations. In spite of all the knowledge and development in the realm of mathematical formulations, the scientists do accept that we fail to provide an unambiguous behaviour of an electron in the interior of an atom. Heinrich Hertz (1857-1894) has formulated the limitation of scientific thinking and postulations in his introduction to the principles of mechanics published in 1876, he states that natural science is one whose proposition on limited domains of nature can have only a corresponding limited validity, that science is not a philosophy developing a world view of a nature as a whole or about the essence of things. The proposition of science does not have the task or the capability of unfolding the inherent essence of nature. The conclusion derived from our scientific investigation and observations does have any valid causal relationship on the basis of which we can make a prediction about truth and veracity of scientific proposition. Science must be conscious about its own limitations otherwise it would make nonsensical assertions in the name of scientific truth and revelations. Eddington states that, "We have found that where science has progressed the farthest, the mind has, but regained from nature that which the mind has put into nature. We have found a strange footprint on the shores of the unknown. We have devised profound theories, one after the other, to account for its origin. At last, we have succeeded in reconstructing the creature that made the footprint. And Lo! It is our own". Heisenberg's formulation of scientific proposition speaks of his deep understanding and knowledge of not only physics, but of philosophy too. His whole formulations and postulations of scientific propositions are a philosophical treatise dealing with the most profound philosophical issues and problems. He says, "The philosophical content of science is only preserved in science is conscious of its limits. Great discoveries of the properties of individual phenomena are possible only if nature of the phenomena is not generalized *a priori*. Only by leaving open the question of the ultimate essence of a body, of matter, of energy, etc., can Physics reach an understanding of the individual properties of the phenomena that we designate by these concepts, an understanding which alone may lead us to real philosophical insight."

Quantum mechanics states that however sophisticated tool we may employ for the measurement of any events it has intrinsic uncertainty. Uncertainty does exist in spite of our best efforts of designing our technology for the measurement. The inherent uncertainty cannot be overcome. Theory of Relativity is closely related with cosmological constant, i.e., velocity of light. The relation between space and time is dependent on this cosmological constant. Whereas classical physics considers the velocity of light as infinite. Thus the classical physics breaks down in explaining some of the basic behaviour and natural functions in the field of electromagnetic wave. Quantum Theory on the other hand is related with Planck's Quantum action. Planck considers its constant as infinitely small. And with this help the quantum mechanics have been able to predict to great extent the proper understanding of structure and the function of interior atom.

Heisenberg speaks about a third constant which would be able possibly to determine the masses and other properties of elementary particle. Scientists have been engaged in determining the third hypothetical constant which would give an approximate accuracy about the function and nature of atomic interior structure and function of the atoms. Heisenberg does admit that this is for future research and investigation in the field of atomic physics. He writes, "But all these problems will be a matter of future research of atomic physics. One may hope that the combined effort or experiments in the high energy region and of mathematical analysis will some day lead to a complete understanding of the unity of matter. The term "complete understanding" would mean that the forms of matter in the sense of Aristotelian philosophy would appear as results, as solutions of a closed mathematical scheme representing the natural laws for matter."[39] Before Edwin Hubble an American astronomer discovered with his advanced and sophisticated telescope on Mt. Wilson in California that universe was expanding. There are lots of stars and galaxies and Milky Way in the terrestrial paradise of cosmos. The scientists believed that earth is static. Hubble discovered that the galaxies are moving with faster speed going beyond our solar system. This forced Einstein to reject his own postulation of cosmological constant because he believed in static universe. His postulation was based on the mutual attraction of all the matter which entails according to him the static universe. The concept of cosmological constant on the other hand speaks of a new anti-gravity force which is responsible for maintaining balance in the universe. Stephen Hawking believes that Einstein's concept of cosmological constant is true and a proper theory to explain the expansion of the nature of stars, galaxies and milky ways while maintaining the balance and equilibrium of the cosmos. Hawking writes, "He later disavowed the cosmological constant, calling this fudge factor his "greatest mistake". As we will soon see, today we have reason to believe that he might have been right to introduce if after all. But what must have disappointed Einstein was that he had allowed his belief in a static universe to override what his theory seemed to be predicting: that the universe is expanding. Only one man, it seems was willing to take this prediction of general relativity at face value. While Einstein and other physicist were looking for ways of avoiding general relativity's non-static universe, the Russian physicist and mathematician Alexander Friedmann instead set about explaining it."[40]

Friedmann formulation of universe was based on a very clear postulation that if the universe would have been static it would have looked same and identical from every direction. And he concluded that the universe was not static. This was much before the Edwin Hubble's discovery of the expanding universe. The Friedmann postulation that the universe looks same from different directions, it entails that the universe would look identical in all directions as looked from other galaxies also. However, there is some limiting factor in Friedmann postulations which is the nature of all scientific postulation and theories. The recent observations have proved that the movements of different galaxies and stars are speeding up rather than it is slowing down. Hawking further writes, "no one is sure yet, but it could be an evidence that Einstein was right about the need for the cosmological constant (and in antigravity effects) after all."[41] In fact Einstein's theory of general relativity entails the nature of expanding universe. However, he didn't believe that his theory of general relativity speaks of the expanding universe because nobody before had any inkling about the expanding universe and this is why in 1930 he declared his biggest blunder while postulating the cosmological constant. Lisa Randall writes, "After Hubble's measurements, Einstein dispensed with the fudge he had made, calling it "his biggest blunder." This modification was not entirely erroneous, however. We will soon see that more recent measurements show that the cosmological constant term he added is actually necessary to account for recent observations—although the measured magnitude, which accounts for the recently established acceleration of its expansion, is about an order of magnitude bigger than the one Einstein proposed to merely stall it.

The expansion of the universe was a nice example of a convergence of top-down and bottom-up physics. Einstein's theory of gravity implies that the universe expands, yet only with the discovery of the expansion did physicists feel confident they were on the right track."[42]

Planck laid down the foundation for Quantum Mechanics as stated earlier. If we go through the development of Quantum Mechanics then we find that '*h*' has been used for the first time in 1900 by Max Planck while explaining the black body radiation. However, its physical significance and importance in the scientific world was not very clear. In 1905, it was the genius of Albert Einstein who examined, evaluated and clarified Planck's theory in the background of understanding the nature of light. The nature of light has been explained in terms of both as a wave and a particle. In the scientific formulation a particle known as photon is considered massless, which has the speed of light *c* and it is denoted by energy *E* and it has been formulated that $E=hv$. When the scientists started examining the nature and the structure of a photon, it was considered that a photon has energy, it must be associated with momentum. In 1923 Louis de Broglie came out with a new concept that the electrons which were considered as particles are waves. In Neil Bohr's concept of atomic structure electron orbiting is an integral multiple and the quantity denoted by letter *h* which played a significant role in postulation of modern Quantum Mechanics in which *E*, *h* play a significant role. Heisenberg's doctrine of uncertainty put limitation on the accuracy in explaining the structure of atom. Edward Gerjuoy defines Quantum Mechanics in the following words, "The modern theory of matter, of electromagnetic radiation and of the interaction between matter and radiation, also, the mechanics of phenomena to which the theory may be applied. Quantum Mechanics, also termed as wave mechanics, generalizes and supersedes the older classical mechanics and Maxwell's electromagnetic theory. Atomic and subatomic phenomena provide the most striking evidence for the correctness of Quantum Mechanics and best illustrate the difference between Quantum Mechanics and the older classical physical theories. Quantum Mechanics is needed to explain, many properties of bulk matter, for instance, the temperature dependence of the specific heat of solids."[43]

However, Quantum Mechanics cannot be applied in all domains of scientific enquiry. In explaining the Quantum mechanical relations the role of Planck's constant has been very important even in Schrodinger's equation and Heisenberg's principle of uncertainty. However, Planck's constant doesn't play any important role in classical physics. According to classical physics the structures of nature are measurable with small error. According to classical physics it was believed that the position and velocity of the particles could be ascertained and examined. But the uncertainty principle postulated by Heisenberg in 1927 stated that measurement of quantity leads to uncertainty. There is another enigmatic nature of wave particles, dualism, which has not been as it has been found satisfactory and scientific answer. The propagation of the new theory known as complementarity and postulation of dualism of wave particles enunciated by Neil Bohr in 1928 opposed by Einstein and Schrodinger have kept the best scientific minds engaged in providing a satisfactory answer. The combination of theory of uncertainty and complementarity doctrines put a limit to our experimental ability in explaining and describing the physical system.

There is another enigmatic scientific concept known as *cosmological concept* which is being debated. And it is being discussed by almost all the modern scientific minds dealing with pure physics and cosmology. It is now equated with dark energy which constitutes seventy three per cent of total energy. Quantum Mechanics does accept the existence of cosmological constant with very high energy density. This energy density is so high that it doesn't come within the purview of scientific observation. And hence cosmological constant has become one of the greatest enigmas of physics. To examine and evaluate the scientific significance of cosmological constant is one of the greatest searches for understanding and ascertaining the veracity of this concept. Robert Cald Well writes, "The cosmological constant was introduced by Albert Einstein in 1917 in the first application of general relativity to cosmology.

In order to balance theoretical and practical considerations in constructing a mathematical model of the universe, Einstein found it necessary to invoke a new cosmological term. He regarded this term as a universal constant whose value would be determined empirically. The effect of adding the (inverted *V*) was to cut off the gravitational influence of distant matter and balance the field equations for a static universe. This cosmological model was consistent with contemporary observations of the slow kinetic motions of stars and nebulae. Though the 1929 discovery of the cosmic red-shift distance by Edwin Hubble, soon interpreted as expansion, invalidated Einstein's construction, the cosmological constant survived. Later, when discussing the discovery of the expanding universe with George Gamow, Einstein is reputed to have called the introduction of the cosmological constant "the greatest blunder" of his life."[44] The concept of Cosmological constant was postulated by Albert Einstein in 1917 in explaining cosmology with the application of his another theory known as general relativity. Einstein considered it inevitable to postulate this new concept known as cosmological constant in bringing about harmony and synthesis between the theoretical and practical formulation of the mathematical model of the universe. This new concept was consistent with the contemporary observations of slow kinetic motions of stars and nebulae. The whole theory was based on the concept of static universe. Einstein postulated that the universe was static. Universe is neither expanding nor contracting. It is eternally in the state of static harmony. But with Hubble's discovery of expanding universe and the movement of the stars and galaxies with tremendous speed, Einstein postulation of static universe was falsified and Einstein was forced to denounce his greatest discovery known as cosmological constant as the greatest blunder of his life. However, to the great surprise and satisfaction of the scientific world the cosmological constant is considered as the greatest discovery as it explains the maintaining of the balance and harmony in the expanding universe. Yakov Zeldovich in 1967 considered the cosmological constant as a source of Quantum vacuum. The cosmological constant is now equated and interpreted as cosmological vacuum. It has to be ascertained whether cosmological constant is the result of the geometry of space, time or the gravitational sources. Now, the scientists think that the concept of Einstein, the cosmological constant based on space, time continuum inherently speaks of the expansion of universe. Stephen Hawking writes, "The most impressive fine-tuning coincidence involves the so-called cosmological constant in Einstein's equation of general relativity. As we've said in 1915, when he formulated the theory, Einstein believed that the universe was static that is, neither expanding nor contracting. Since all matter attracts other matter, he introduced into his theory a new antigravity force to combat the tendency of the universe to collapse onto itself. This force, unlike other forces, did not come from any particular source, but was built into the very fabric of space-time. The cosmological constant describes the strength of that force. When it was discovered that the universe was not static, Einstein eliminated the cosmological constant from his theory and called it the greatest blunder of his life. But in 1998 observations of very distant supernovas revealed that the universe is expanding at an accelerating rate, an effect that is not possible without some kind of repulsive force acting throughout space. The cosmological constant was resurrected."[45] The cosmological constant implies the presence of cosmological events horizon, which would be spherical in boundary. It means the light signal emitted from the centre would not reach the spherical boundary because of the expansion of space and time. If we consider the cosmological as dark energy it would become impossible to measure the horizon located at a radius of immeasurable magnitude.

Robert Caldwell writes, "Precision measurements of the cosmic distances and the evolution of the universe will help refine the evidence for the cosmological constant. Current evidence is ambiguous as to whether (inverted *V*) is dark energy. If it is not, it will likely be accepted in practice that (inverted *V*) is zero.

Confirmation of the existence of a non-zero cosmological constant would have a tremendous impact on physics and our view of the universe."[46]

To my mind the cosmological constant that maintains the harmony and balance in the universe is the result of interaction between two aspects of the same Ultimate Reality known as cosmic consciousness (Śiva) and cosmic matrix (*Śakti*). The cosmic consciousness and the cosmic matrix are two facets of the same coin. They coeternally exist and it could not be separated from one another. The cosmic matrix (*Śakti*) may in modern scientific terminology be called as Cosmic Energy. In fact, the whole universe is the reflection of this ultimate reality (cosmic consciousness) which is called *Paramaśiva* in Kashmir Śaivism. *Ābhāsavāda* of Kashmir Śaivism provides both the scientific and philosophical explanation of origin and development of the universe in the form of innumerable galaxies, milky ways, supernovas, stars and other celestial bodies.

The discovery of the expanding universe and cosmic acceleration has confirmed the existence of cosmological constant. Lisa Randall writes, "Most of the universe is made of stuff whose identity remains a mystery. Twenty years from now, people might smile at our ignorance. And these are not the only puzzles evoked by the energy of the universe. The value of the dark energy, in particular, is actually the tail end of much larger mystery: why is the energy that pervades the universe so small? Had the amount of dark energy been greater, it would have dominated matter and radiation much earlier in the evolution of the universe, and structure (and life) would not have had time to form. On top of that, no one knows what was responsible earlier on for the large energy density that triggered and fuelled the inflation. But the highest problem with the energy of the universe is the cosmological constant problem."[47] Quantum Mechanics postulation of dark energy and the vacuum with no permanent particles present are the greatest enigma. It is present in a paradox that in the presence of density of dark matter and dark energy which are the source of origin and development of the universe is rooted in ontological mysticism. In the modern scientific world the concepts of dark matter and dark energy is posing the greatest problem in explaining the mystery of the universe. Scientists do accept that they are unable to provide and resolve this problem in the realm of scientific postulation, discovery and experiments. It has been accepted now that there are innumerable universes with multi-dimensional structure and functions.

Lisa Randall writes, "Why is there matter in the universe at all? Our equations treat matter and antimatter on the same footing. They annihilate when they find each other, and both disappear. Neither matter nor antimatter should remain when the universe has cooled."[48] The existence of the asymmetry of matter and antimatter is another enigma for the scientists and the cosmologists.

According to Kashmir Śaivism, *Vedānta* and Buddhism there is existence of non-zero vacuum. The whole universe is pervaded by cosmic consciousness and its modification due to the activation of cosmic matrix energy. Ultimate reality is known as Parama Śiva for *Brahman* in Hinduism and emptiness (*Śūnyatā*) in Buddhism and the Tao in Taoism. This different terminologies used by Hinduism, Buddhism and Taoism speak of the same reality and truth. There is inherent limitation and difficulties in expressing and communicating the real and ultimate nature or reality. Even the common experiences of colour *red* and *blue* cannot express the true nature of what is in reality colour red or blue as has been postulated by Heisenberg. We shall deal with these problems of ultimate reality and its structure, functions and modifications in the form of the cosmos in subsequent chapters. It is the domain of Ontological Mysticism as has been accepted by even Schrodinger and others. Scientists are facing this problem and showing their inability to resolve this mystery because their whole postulation is based on ontological materialism. Planck accepts that science cannot resolve the ultimate mystery of nature. And that is because, in the last analysis, we ourselves are part of nature and, therefore, part of the mystery that we are trying to solve.

A theory which doesn't have inherent possibility of its falsification is not scientific. Here possibility is used not in the sense of total rejection and falsification but in the sense of its limited validity.

Genesis

Philosophers and the scientists have been trying since time immemorial to understand and explain the origin and the development of the universe. Stephen Hawking's writes 'In the beginning the universe was infinitesimally small and infinitely dense, and it burst'. This is known as the "big bang theory". The scientists before the postulation of Einstein's theory of relativity and Max Planck, Heisenberg's, Schrodinger's and Neil Bohr's postulation of Quantum Mechanics believed that the universe constituted of space-time was smooth and flat. But with the advent of the new discovery and concept of big bang, the doctrines who believed the static and the flat universe is broken down. The question which is unanswered till today is why the infinitesimally small and infinitely dense universe did burst. Scientists don't have answer to this why. If there has been no other force, in that case, the infinitesimally small and infinitely dense would have remained in the state of eternal in animated state. Kashmir Śaivism, *Vedānta*, Buddhism have answered this "why" problem. I believe that Kashmir Śaivism provides a scientific and philosophical explanation of this problem. According to Kashmir Śaivism, Parama Śiva is the fundamental reality. Śiva (cosmic consciousness) and *Śakti* coalesce into one undivided unity of transcendentality. The cosmic consciousness is illuminating (*Prakāśa*) and knowing entity and *Śakti* (cosmic matrix) is veiling (*Vimarśa*) and activating entity. Śiva (cosmic consciousness) is consciousness in *stusis*. The creative matrix is consciousness dynamic. It is in the nature of the ultimate reality to create and manifest in the form of universe. So long, the cosmic principles (*Śakti*) remain merged in cosmic consciousness, it does not get any scope of activation and manifestation. The theoretical dualism of cosmic consciousness (Śiva) and cosmic matrix (*Śakti*) is symbolically represented by a grain of gram having two seeds closely joined and covered with the sheath of *Māyā*. The evolution starts only when they come apart. When the cosmic matrix which is the cosmic energy starts acting and reacting, the differentiation is started. This differentiation between cosmic consciousness and cosmic principles of energy is the cause of creative ideation and the modification of consciousness in the form of universe. This differentiation in the form of modification of cosmic consciousness is meant objectivisation of the ultimate reality. Evolution is known according to Kashmir Śaivism as *Ābhāsa*. According to *Ābhāsavāda*, world is real, in the sense that it is an aspect of supreme reality. Dr. Gopinath Kaviraj says, "The peculiar metaphysical position of the *Tantra* consists in the theory of *Ābhāsa*, which is consistent with this position. It rejects the *Vivartavāda* of neo-*Vedānta*, because the world is not originally a false appearance due to Error. It is real in the same way as an image is real but it has no existence apart from the medium in which it is manifested. To the Vedāntist, the world appears as such, to the ignorant, owing to his ignorance, and in the last analysis, it is resolved into *Māyā* which is not identical with *Brahman* and is materialistic, but to a Tantrist the world is real and is the expression of the C*it-Śakti* or Free Will of the Lord and is really spiritual in essence like the Lord Himself."[49]

Bindū, *Nāda* and *Kalā* are the three stages of evolution. Involution is the process of crudification of cosmic consciousness which undergoes metamorphosis. The cosmic consciousness is transformed and modified into matter. According to the variation in the degree of bondage of creative matrix (*Śakti*) the cosmic consciousness (Śiva) has taken different modifications. But the fundamental reality is one and the same. Creation is nothing, but the thought projection of the *Brahman*. The *creative matrix*, the *magna matter* conceives, bears and nourishes the entire universe. Śiva is pure consciousness and *Śakti* is the activating principle. This universe is nothing, but the creative ideation of the causal matrix. The creative matrix (*Śakti*) is constituted of sentient, mutative and static principles. These three principles after the formations of these three triangular forces which are belligerent in nature burst from the *Bindū* (the point) and in the form of *Nāda* (*Śabda*) and *Kalā* (curvature). The triangle of forces bursts from one of the vertices. The point from which the triangular forces burst out it is called *Kāma Bīja* (the seed of the universe). The seed of creation is expressed in a metaphysical word as *Nāda* (word). It is dominated by sentient principles.

But due to the activation or domination of the static principles the expression takes the form of the curvature. It is known in Kashmir Śaivism as *Kalā*. With the creation of the universe in the form of *kalā* the phenomenal world comes into being. In scientific language the universe is nothing, but a collection of different waves and curvatures. In philosophical terminology it is called the modification of the cosmic consciousness. Spinoza also believes that the world is a modification of God. God is the ultimate substance and reality.

The bursting of the point (*bindū*) is known in Hindu philosophy as a *Sphoṭa*. This *Sphoṭa* concept of Hinduism is called the Big Bang theory in modern scientific terminology. Stephen Hawking while enumerating the postulate of the Big Bang writes, "The first actual scientific evidence that the universe had a beginning came in the 1920's. There was a time when most of the scientists believed in a static universe that had always existed. The evidence to the contrary was indirect, based upon the observations Edwin Hubble made with the 100 inch telescope on Mount Wilson, in the hills above Pasadena, California. By analysing the spectrum of light they emit, Hubble determined that nearly all the galaxies are moving away from us and the farther away they are, the faster they are moving. In 1929 he published a law relating their rate of recession to their distance from us and concluded that the universe is expanding. If that is true then the universe must have been smaller in the past. In fact we extrapolate to the distant past, all the matter and energy in the universe would have been concentrated in a very tiny region of unimaginable density and temperature, and if we go back far enough there would be a time when it all began—the event we now call the big bang."[50]

According to the Catholic priest, Georges Lemaitre was the one who postulated the theory of big bang in 1927. According to other it was British astrophysicist Fred Hoyle who first conceptualized the big bang theory. According to big bang theory in 1949 universe was originated at about 13.75 billion years ago. According to this theory in the beginning the universe was a very hot fire ball. But in the period of 13.75 billion years of its formation it cooled down and it took the form of innumerable galaxies, milky ways, stars and other celestial bodies. Einstein's concept of gravitational field is the cause of distribution of matter. He applied this theory of gravitational field in explaining the structure and the function between the earth and the sun. But the scientists think that it could be very useful tool and theory to explain the structure and the function of the universe.

The universe is a curvature and it has taken different forms and modification of the ultimate fundamental reality, that is cosmic consciousness and it has been originated in the form of different galaxies and other celestial bodies is inherent in the theory of evolution of Kashmir Śaivism known as *Ābhāsavāda*. In spite of all the knowledge and the monumental achievements in the field of scientific discovery, the scientists have not been able to explain the origin of the universe out of the ultimate energy which is considered mysterious. Lisa Randall accepts the inability of modern science in explaining the origin, nature and the function of the energy that resulted in the expansion of the universe. She writes, "The shocking observation was that the measurements of the characteristics of the universe required the presence of this new form of energy that's not carried by matter. This energy is not carried by particles or other stuff, and it doesn't clump like conventional matter. It doesn't dilute as the universe expands, but maintains a constant density. The expansion of the universe is slowly accelerating as a consequence of the mysterious energy, which resides throughout the universe, even if it were empty of matter."[51] Lisa Randall does accept the inability and profound ignorance about the cause of the big bang. Why the universe which was in the beginning infinitesimally small and infinitely dense banged or erupted. The evolution and the beginning of the universe in spite of the big bang theory is a mystery. However, the Big Bang theory does explain to a great extent the expansion and evolution of the universe. It was Einstein who first conceived the idea of the expanding universe and formulated his historic scientific theory of general relativity.

In this new theory of general relativity he postulated a new source of energy and tried to adjust with his concept of static universe. However, with Hubble's discovery of the expanding universe in which he dropped that idea which was in the form of the cosmological constant. Now, scientists are trying to use the concept of cosmological constant in explaining the balance and the harmony of the universe. The big bang theory was further confirmed by NASA's COBE (Cosmic Micro-Wave Background Explorer) satellite launched in 1992 with the presence of micro-waves throughout the space. Micro-wave radiation was discovered accidentally by Penzias and Wilson in 1965 on which they were awarded Nobel Prize. Lisa Randall is of the opinion that in spite of the confirmation of cosmic radiations, it is a scientific means for understanding the cosmology as a scientific discipline. But it doesn't confirm the big bang theory. She writes, "The cosmic radiation has proved to be a tremendous tool—not just for confirming the Big Bang, but for turning cosmology into a detailed science. The cosmic microwave background (CMB) radiation gives us a very different way of observing the past than traditional astronomy measurements."[52]

The COBE satellite mission launched in 1989 has thrown some light on the mysterious nature of the universe's expansion in terms of cosmological inflation, dark matter and dark energy. Unless we have scientific knowledge about the cosmological inflation, dark matter and dark energy we won't be able to have proper understanding of the nature and the structure and the functioning of the universe. In spite of all the discoveries and exploration, the origin of universe is shrouded in mystery for the scientists. The Indian seers have given metaphysical postulation of the universe which is being confirmed by modern science. Einstein (1879-1955), Heisenberg (1901-1976), Schrodinger (1887-1961), Max Planck (1858-1947), James Jens (1877-1946), Louis De Broglie (1892-1987), Wolfgang Pauli (1900-1958), they have thrown great light on unveiling the mystery of the universe with their monumental scientific postulations. I shall deal with it in later chapters. In understanding the mystery of the universe and in exploring the mystery in scientific and philosophical postulation the sematic concept of personal God has been the greatest stumbling block. And this is why since the very advent of modern science from the seventeenth to the modern age the first rank scientists and original thinkers like Galileo and Charles Darwin have been prosecuted and condemned by Christianity and sematic religious tradition and belief. Albert Schweitzer writes, "And distinguishing Indian world view from ours, there is yet another difference, which lies just as deep as that between world and life affirmation and world and life denial. That of India is monastic and mystical, ours is dualistic and doctrinaire. Mysticism is the perfect form of world view."[53] Dualistic world view expounded by the semetic religions does not correspond with reality. According to the semetic religious dualistic doctrines universe cannot be made to square with facts. It is based on faith and belief. Unfortunately, the theistic religions do not have sound metaphysical foundation. Schweitzer further writes, "The theory of the universe which these doctrine world views represent is dualistic. They assume two principles in the history of the events starting from the very origin of the being. One principle is conceived as an ethical personality who guarantees that what happens in the universe has an ethical goal; the other is represented as the natural force dwelling within the universe and operative in a course of events governed by natural laws. This dualistic world view exists in very many variations. In the teachings of Zarathustra the Jewish prophets and Christianity what happens in the universe is interpreted as the battle in which the super-natural ethical power wins its way through in conflict with the natural non-ethical. When more critical forms of thought engage in the problem it strives in so far as it can cover up the dualism. But it is there nevertheless. Even the philosophy of Kant is dualistic. It works with the idea derived from Christianity, of an ethical creator of the universe without making clear to itself how it can succeed in identifying him with the Primal cause of being."[54]

For the proper understanding of the universe we have to understand the reality of which the universe is composed. Einstein dreamed of a unified theory which would explain the mystery of the universe. Stephen Hawking has postulated the Grand Design which he thinks is a theory of everything. He writes, "That more fundamental theory is called M-theory, as we mentioned earlier. No one seems to know what the "M" stands for but it may be "master", "miracle" or "mystery". It seems to be all the three. People are still trying to decipher the nature of the M-theory, but that may not be possible."[55] If nobody knows what the "M" stands for then how can it be called a scientific postulation or a logical proposition? It does not have any truth value. It becomes an enigma. It can be put under the category of tautology or contradictions. The words "master", "miracle" and "mystery" put together do not convey any meaning. The so called term, "master", "miracle" and "mystery" connotes different sense and meanings and denotes different objects and things. Hence I am of the view that "M"-theory is a nebulous concept. Further he says, "It could be that the physicist's traditional expectation of a single theory of nature is untenable and there exists no single formulation. It might be that to describe the universe, we have to employ different theories in different situations. Each theory may have its own version of reality, but according to model-dependent realism, that is acceptable so long as the theories agree in their prediction whenever they overlap, that is whenever they can both be applied."[56]

Hawking's formulation of M-theory is based on ontological materialism. The scientists and philosophers have examined, analysed and evaluated Ontological materialism and they have found that materialism cannot solve the enigma of "Why" of nature. This enigma of nature is related with the problem of ultimate reality. The mystics and seers of different views are unanimous that this problem is rooted in ontological mysticism. World is true till one realizes the truth that is ultimate reality. The seers and mystics have had the direct experience of ultimate reality (cosmic consciousness). It is through meditative insight alone one can have realization through direct experience of the cosmic consciousness or cosmic being. Meditation is unlearning. The meaning of word is determined in a context. The word master, miracle and mystery have been used by Hawking's in the context of matter or ontological materialism. If the same words are used in the context of cosmic consciousness their meaning would be different. I feel the ontological mysticism may be the answer in finding and fulfilling dream of Einstein in providing a *theory of everything*.

According to M-theory, the universe has eleven space time dimensions. Let us analyse, examine and evaluate the M-theory postulated by Hawking. After the analysis and examination of the concept of M-theory we may arrive at the conclusion whether M-theory is a scientific doctrine or a scientific fiction. But in the course of his postulation and arriving at the concept of the theory of everything Hawking has dealt in some detail about the constituents of the universe and he has dealt with the concepts of universal inflation, dark matter and dark energy. His whole thesis is based on

Ontological materialism. In the light of the basic and the fundamental assumption of ontological materialism we will deal with the subjects like cosmological inflation, dark matter and dark energy for the better understanding of structure and functions of the universe.

Now, the scientists who have considered atom as the basic indivisible unit of matter out of which the whole phenomenal world have been created out of the atoms as the building blocks. Now, atom is no more considered as indivisible; with the advancement of the scientific research and experiments it is now considered that atoms is made of smaller particles like electrons, protons and neutrons. Now, it is believed that the proton and the neutron themselves are constituted of smaller particles known as quarks. The protons that contain quarks are bound together through gluons. The mass of proton, however, does not come from the mass of quarks that it contains. The mass of the proton is the result of the energy involved in binding the proton together.

The proton moving with high momentum has lot of energy. Protons are sea of quarks, anti-quarks and gluons in excess of three valence quarks which are essential for the charge of proton. However, proton is heavier than electron. Scientists believe that the mass of proton is approximately two thousand times greater than that of an electron. The discovery of quarks inside the protons and the neutrons is the result of Friedman, Kandl and Taylor's experiments conducted during 1967-1973. And they were awarded a Nobel Prize in 1990 for their discovery. However, it was British physicist Paul Daric who came out with a new discovery known as antimatter in 1927, in the process of understanding the nature and structure of the electron. The discovery of antimatter heralded a new thinking in conceptualizing matter-antimatter symmetry in laws of physics which govern the functioning of the universe. According to the scientists, the phenomenal world is constituted of matter and not antimatter. This is putting a greatest enigma of the existence of asymmetry in matter and antimatter. The scientists are profoundly ignorant about the birth of this antimatter. Though antimatter does play an important role in particle physics, but the source of it is still a mystery. Apart from the subatomic particles, scientists believe in the existence of an anti-particle. Anti-particles are of the same mass as their parental particles but are opposite in nature and other attributes. The anti-particles and electrons are positrons which have positive charge. This is in opposition of the charge of electron. The meeting of anti-particles and particles results into annihilation of each other. There is another particle called photon which is a massless particle. The photons of earth come from the sun which exists closely with the nucleus furnace of the sun. Hawking's writes, "All old physicists have discovered dozens of these particles. Over time, as the universe has undergone a complex evolution, the make-up of this zoo of particles has also evolved. It is this evolution that has made it possible for planets such as earth, and beings such as us, to exist. One second after the big bang, the universe would have expanded enough to bring its temperature down to about ten billion degrees Celsius. This is about a thousand times the temperature at the centre of the sun, but temperature as high as this is reached in H-bomb explosions."[57]

Scientists have succeeded in understanding the makeup of the universe to a great extent. But with every advancement in the knowledge of science it gives to a new problem. Scientists do accept that there is a lot of critical gaps in understanding the makeup of the universe.

Mass is one of the properties of particle along with charge and anti-reactions. It is believed that particles is made up of non-zero energy, but mass is intrinsic properties that which can attain many possible values which also includes zero.

Lisa Randall writes, "One of the Einstein's major insights was to recognize that the value of a particle's mass tells how much energy it has when it is at rest. But particles don't always have a non-vanishing value for their masses. And those that have zero mass, like the photon, are never at rest. However, the non-zero masses of elementary particles, which are an intrinsic property they possess, are an enormous mystery. Not only quarks and leptons, but also weak gauge bosons—the particles that communicate the weak force—have non-zero mass."[58]

All the particles contain masses still there is another bigger problem that scientists are facing to answer the questions "what are these masses as they are?" Another big question which is the best minds of the world fail to understand and explain is called the dark matter and the dark energy. The matter and the dark matter constitute only twenty seven percent of the total energy of the universe. Seventy three percent of the energy is called dark energy about which the scientists and the cosmologists are profoundly ignorant. Another puzzling problem is the cosmological inflation which has been the force behind expansion of the early universe. Lisa Randall writes, "The shocking observation was that measurements of the characteristics of the universe required the presence of this new form of energy that is not carried by matter. This energy is not carried by particles or other stuff, and it doesn't clump like conventional matter. It doesn't dilute as the universe expands but maintains a constant density. The expansion of the universe is slowly accelerating as a consequence of the mysterious energy, which resides throughout the universe, even if it were empty of matter."[59] As I have already discussed and explained that this mysterious energy is nothing but the cosmic matrix (*Śakti*), i.e., co-eternally exists with cosmic consciousness (Śiva).

The cosmos is constituted of many universes and the whole cosmos is a modification of cosmic consciousness with the activation of cosmic matrix. Kashmir Śaivism and *Vedānta* have already dealt with metaphysical problems. According to *Vedānta* the cosmos has been originated from the *Brahman* (cosmic consciousness) and is sustained by cosmic consciousness and again it merges into cosmic consciousness. The process of creation is continuous from the time immemorial. The calculation of the modern cosmologists that the universe was created about fourteen billion years ago may be applicable to the universe in which our present solar system is one of the integral part, but the cosmos is made of many universes. The astronomers with the help of telescopes have discovered the myriad of universe. The collection of innumerable stars, galaxies is called Milky Way galaxy. It has been confirmed that there are many stars constituted of planetary systems encircling them. Some of the stars are much more brighter than our stars, others are fainter also. They are sprinkled in the space and closely clustered in the Milky Way. When we examine the view of universe on a larger scale, it is known as cosmological expansion. The American Astronomer Hubble found that on the cosmological scales the galaxies are moving away from one another with the velocity of recession being linearly proportional to the distance of the object. In cosmological language, it has been termed as Hubble Law. The Hubble law says that roughly 10 billion years ago the mass of the matter in the universe was closely put together in a very dense state. Everything then exploded in a big bang which resulted into the explosion in the form of galaxies of stars, created out of the debris of mass of matter. Hawking had stated that in the beginning the universe was infinitesimally small and infinitely dense and it exploded. However, the scientists and the cosmologists have not given any logical or scientific explanation of why it exploded. I have already explained before that the problem of "why" belongs to the domain of philosophy and this problem is philosophical and is explained by Kashmir Śaivism and *Vedānta*. The scientists do agree that they have not as yet found the proper answer to the origin of the universe. *Encyclopaedia Britannica* writes, "The observed expansion of the universe immediately raises the spectre that the universe is evolving, that it had a beginning and will have an end. The steady state alternative, postulated by a British school of cosmologists in 1948 is no longer considered viable by most of the astronomers. Yet, the notion that the cosmos had a beginning while common in many theologies, raises deep and a puzzling question for science, for it implies a creation event—creation not only of all the mass energy that exists in the universe, but also perhaps of space-time itself."[60] The universe is expanding and it would continue to expand till indefinite future or whether after some time the expansion will be reversed by the effects of gravitational attraction. There is no simple answer to this question. Scientists have now accepted that there are unknown amount of hidden matter which is unknown to us. And which is the key in the understanding that explains the gravitation of the universe. This hidden mass in my opinion is cosmic consciousness which was termed by Einstein as cosmological constant. The birth of the universe with incredible heat and life to the gatherings on earth of atoms became the chemical foundation of life. The Hubble observation heralded a new era of extra galactic astronomy. He discovered that the different galaxies are spirals, elliptical and irregular. *Encyclopaedia Britannica* writes, "Hubble's findings provided the empirical justification for the so called cosmological principle, a term coined by the English Mathematician and astrophysicist Edward A. Milne to describe the assumptions that at any instant in time the universe is, in the large, homogeneous and isotropic—i.e., statistically the same in every place and in every direction. This represented the ultimate triumph for the Copernicus Revolution."[61]

Einstein's formulation of theory of general relativity in 1916 revolutionized the classical Newtonian conception of gravitation. According to the new thinking the gravitation is not only a force but it should be considered as a dynamic of space and time. With the discovery of Hubble's expanding universe and Einstein's propagation of theory of general relativity a new world view has emerged. However, I do not agree with the interpretations given by the present scientists. The *Encyclopaedia* observes, "The discoveries of Hubble and Einstein gave rise to a new world view. The new cosmology gave empirical validation to the notion of a creation of event; it assigned a numerical estimate, for when the arrow of time first took flight, it eventually led to the breath-taking idea that everything in the universe could have arisen form literally nothing."[62] The universe has not been created literally out of nothing. This speaks of the biblical or the sematic religious prejudices which believed that Lord created sun, moon and everything out of nothing. Einstein is of the opinion that the doctrine of personal God should be abandoned. He believes in a religion without any theology. Einstein writes, "A God who rewards and punishes is inconceivable to him for simple reason that man's actions are determined by necessity, external and internal, so that, in God's eyes he cannot be responsible, any more than an inanimate object is responsible for the motion it undergoes. Science has, therefore, been charged with undermining morality but the charge is unjust. A man's ethical behaviour should be based effectually on sympathy, education and social ties and needs; no religious basis is necessary. Man would indeed be in a poor way if he had to be restrained by fear of punishment and hope of reward after death. It is, therefore, easy to see why the churches have always fought science and persecuted its devotees. On the other hand, I maintain that the cosmic religious feeling is the strongest and the noblest motive for scientific research."[63] If we examine the development of science since Galileo to Einstein, Heisenberg and Schrodinger, I find that their findings and discoveries had been a revolt against the biblical conception of genesis. This has been disputed by Charles Darwin, Dawkins and others, the eminent biologists and scientists. I shall take up this matter and discuss in the subsequent chapters. The discovery of astronomers has confirmed that the most of the matter in the universe is concentrated in the galaxy. There is another mysterious nature of universe which has become one of the greatest riddles. They have discovered that the universe does contain a large amount of quantities of mass that does not emit any light. This hidden mass is called dark matter. Berkley has long before asserted that the "*essence of substance*" is unknown and unknowable. Descartes, the founder of the modern philosophy, has asserted that there could be no interaction between mind and matter. The essence of matter is extension in space and the essence of mind is thought. Hence, there is no possibility between the connection of mind and matter. However, the idealist philosophers have taken a clue from Berkley and Descartes and considered this philosophical issue in a different way. The idealist thinkers while agreeing with Berkley and Descartes that matter and mind are basically different in nature and hence there is no possibility of their interaction but they found that both mind and matter do interact and on the basis of this interaction of mind and matter the idealists deduced that the matter must be of the same nature and form as that of the mind which was postulated by Berkley as eternal being. This eternal being or the Spinoza's substance is nothing, but cosmic consciousness.

Prince Louis De Broglie writes, "This goal as we have seen is, without doubt, to succeed in penetrating further into knowledge of natural harmonies, to come to have a glimpse of a reflection of the order which rules in the universe, some portions of the deep and hidden realities which constitute it. Even the scientists or philosophers who, pragmatic in tendency have reduced to a utilitarian role the value of scientific theories such as, for example, the eminent physicists Pierre Duhem, have had to recognise that these theories establish between the phenomena a "natural classification," allowing us to sense the existence of an "Ontological order" which is beyond us."[64]

The principle of uncertainty and complementarity entails the limitations of scientists ability to describe the physical nature and form of the universe and hence scientists possibility to predict the result of measurement on that system. The cosmological constant is a parameter that was introduced in general relativity by Einstein to explain the non-vanishing curvature to space-time even in the absence of matter. This very concept which was the soul of the theory of general relativity was considered as the greatest blunder of his life by Einstein. But the cosmological constant has resurrected in explaining the very harmony and order in universe. As I have already stated that this cosmological constant is not anti-gravity which keeps up the universe in order and harmony but it is cosmic matrix (*Śakti*) that may be considered as cosmic energy which has created the whole cosmos with the so called substance cosmic consciousness. Cosmic consciousness is the only ultimate reality which explains the emergence, sustenance and the disappearance of some galaxies which again give birth to a new galaxy, a new Milky Way and a new universe. To explain the formation of the universe now I shall take up the concept of the dark matter and dark energy.

Ontological Materialism is based on the concept of matter which is considered as the building blocks of universe. In the process of elucidation, examination and analysis of the concept of matter, scientists first discovered an *atom* as the ultimate and indivisible unit of matter. Then with the progress of science, it was found that structure of atom is constituted of nucleus, electron, proton and neutron. Credit goes to Paul Dirac for the discovery of antimatter in 1927 which has played an important role in understanding the structure and the functions of the particle physics. Further advancement in understanding the atomic structure Friedmann Kendall and Taylor discovered quarks inside the proton and neutron. And they were awarded the Nobel Prize in 1990 for their discovery. But the credit goes to Rutherford for providing the basic analysis for the discovery of the nucleus which revolutionised the very concept of particle physics. Rutherford writes, "It was quite the most incredible event that has ever happened to me in my life. It was almost as incredible as if you fired a 15 inch shell at a piece of tissue paper and it came back and hit you. On consideration, I realized that this scattering backward must be the result of the single collision, and when I made calculations I saw that it was impossible to get anything of that order of magnitude unless you took a system in which the greater part of the mass of the atom was concentrated in a minute nucleus. It was then that I had the idea of an atom with a minute massive centre carrying a charge."[65]

Atomic structure is very complex and it is still surrounded by mystery. Matter is the building block of the world and not antimatter. The mass of ordinary matter is normally constituted of protons or neutrons. Protons and neutrons which carry the mass of matter are not constituted by their antiparticles. However, the asymmetry in matter and antimatter is considered as an important factor of the phenomenal world. However, scientists are profoundly ignorant about its present.

The scientists are engaged in unveiling the mystery of atomic structure further and there is every possibility that with the discovery of present concept of matter may be falsified. The acceptance of scientific world view entails the acceptance of the laws of nature which govern the universe. But if we accept the view presented by the scientists of today that world was created out of nothing, science becomes a fiction. How can something comes out of nothing? There is another puzzling problem that governs the quantum world, i.e., the principle of uncertainty and complementarity. The principles of uncertainty invalidate the laws of nature and the theories of complementarity are against the laws of identity and contradiction. However, I don't deny the importance of the principles of uncertainty which has revolutionised Quantum Mechanics. My contention is that it doesn't give the complete picture of the Quantum world in its totality.

There are other concepts which have been postulated by scientists while explaining the structure and function of universe which are puzzling and posing great problem such as the concept of dark matter, black holes and dark energy.

To me the ultimate reality (cosmic consciousness) is unknown, but knowable. Every spiritual tradition have discovered the methods and esoteric techniques to experience the Truth, but the religions which are based on faith and rituals, postulation of reward and punishment are greatest impediment in the path of realization of the ultimate reality (cosmic consciousness). The realization of ultimate reality (cosmic consciousness) is known as *Nirvāṇa* or self-enlightenment. *Nirvāṇa* is not a myth, but a living truth. The mystic and the seer have had the experience of the Truth since the very advent of human civilization. Ontological Mysticism is the foundation of science and spirituality, physics and philosophy. However, before discussing Ontological Mysticism and its philosophical and scientific importance and relevance in presenting a world view consistent with the laws I would like to discuss the concept of the matter, dark matter, dark energy, black holes and the fuller understanding of the ontological materialism and its failure to provide the scientific picture of the world view which has been acclaimed by it.

Matter

As I have stated earlier that matter is a complex substance and surrounded with mystery. The elementary components that combine together to form the substance which is known as matter is quite different from which we experience with our sensory organs. According to the scientists, the components of substance which is called matter functions not according to physical laws. According to the scientists who are engaged in understanding and deciphering the nature and the function of substance known as matter is puzzled by the behaviour of matter when its scales decrease. The matter is administered by properties quite different as if they do not belong to this world. Different theories have been postulated to describe the inner functioning and the form of matter to understand the phenomenal world. The most puzzling feature of the substance atom is that it consists of basically empty space. The nucleus of the centre of the atom is much smaller in radius than their electron orbits. The nucleus is very small in comparison to the radius of an atom. The concept of empty space of which the atom is constituted is of course puzzlement. But the greatest puzzle is the concept of wave nature of matter which is one of the root concepts of quantum mechanics for understanding the atomic electrons. As we have already discussed that the location and the momentum of the particle cannot be understood with certainty which was paramount necessity for understanding the path of an object in time. The uncertainty principle of Werner Heisenberg developed in 1926 postulates that the position with accuracy is known limits the maximum precision which one can measure momentum. The principle of uncertainty is in contradictions with the Newtonian classical physics. Quantum Mechanics postulates that electrons occupy the fifth position in the atoms; which was the basic assumption of classical physics. According to Quantum Mechanics the electrons could be seen in any particular point in space and it is a question of probabilities. Any measurement of the movement of the electrons is governed by uncertainty principle. Neil Bohr came out with a new solution for this contradictory theory of Newtonian physics and the principles of uncertainties propounded by Heisenberg and as a compromise formula, he stated that the Newtonian classical physics does not apply at the Quantum world. He didn't repudiate the classical Newtonian physics whole hog, he simply said that the classical Newtonian physics breaks down at atomic level. So far scientists consider that the electrons and the quarks are the basic substance of which matter is constituted. However, with the advancements of the recent discoveries in physics we are still groping in the dark to understand the make-up of the universe. There is another mystery of the concept of mass of elementary particles. Lisa Randall writes, "Mass is one of the properties—along with charge and interactions —that define a particle. Particles always carry non-zero energy, but mass is an intrinsic property that can take many possible values including zero. One of Einstein's major insights was to recognise that the values of a particle's mass tell how much energy it has when it is at rest. But particles don't always have a non-vanishing value for their masses. And those that have zero mass, like the photon, are never at rest. However, the non-zero masses of elementary particles, which are an intrinsic property they possess, are an enormous mystery."[66]

Dark Matter

Dark matter is a puzzle. Dark matter is essentially matter. It is called dark matter because it is not seen as it absorbs light. There is a great controversy regarding the percentage of dark matter that exists in the universe. According to Hawking, matter in galaxies, clusters and possibly between clusters that have not been observed directly but can be detected by its gravitational effect. As much as 90 per cent of the mass of the universe may be in the form of a dark matter.[67] Large amount of the dark matter contained by galaxies is not known directly but we postulate the existence of dark matter on the basis of its gravitational attraction on the orbits of stars. Whereas Lisa Randall considers that dark matter constitute only twenty three percent of the total energy of the universe.[68] She considers that the dark matter contains the right and the proper amount of energy to exercise proper gravitational effects. Dark energy occupies an important issue both for particle physics and cosmology. The interaction between dark matter with the ordinary matter is being investigated by the pure physicists and the cosmologists. Hawking's thinks that the dark matter contains greater amount in comparison to the ordinary matter in the universe. The existence of elementary particles called the neutrino which was considered as massless hence, it doesn't have any gravitational attraction. But the recent experiments have shown that neutrino does have very small amount of mass. And on the basis of this it is inferred that it might be another form of dark matter.

Dark Energy

This is another mystery that operates in the universe. It is considered that the dark energy is not constituted by particles and it doesn't belong to conventional matter. The dark energy does not evaporate with the expansion of the universe but strangely enough it maintains regular density. This dark energy is considered as a cosmological force behind harmony and order that exists in the universe. Einstein postulated this form of energy and termed it as the universal constant which was later on known as *cosmological constant* in the world of physics though he considered that as his greatest blunder of his life. However, the concept of cosmological constant as resurrected in explaining the mysterious nature of the harmony and orderliness in the multi-universe. Lisa Randall writes, "Ordinarily matter and dark matter still do not provide the sum total of the energy in the universe—together they constitute only about 27 per cent. Even more mysterious than dark matter is the substance that constitutes the remaining 73 per cent and that has become known as dark energy."[69] The microwave radiation discovered by Penzias and Wilson accidentally poses another mystery. In the absence of any certain scientific evidence or the existence of the micro wave radiation in the universe, it is postulated that apart from the amount of matter and dark matter which do not explain the source and the nature of microwave radiations. Physicists and cosmologists have postulated the existence of another mysterious substance called dark matter. The mystery of dark energy holds the key for understanding the nature, function, harmony and orderliness that exists in the universe. Whether it is a cosmological constant postulated by Einstein or it is something unknown to the world of physics and cosmology. However, we have to make a thorough investigation both scientifically and philosophically to have a proper and complete understanding and knowledge of the universe.

To my mind we can have the proper understanding and knowledge of dark matter and dark energy only if we engage ourselves in pursuits of spirituality. The whole universe is the reflection, and manifestation of the cosmic consciousness which is ultimate reality.

CERN and LHC

European Organization for Nuclear Research (CERN) and Large Hadron Collider (LHC) are two greatest centres to study and make experiments to determine the basic constituents that form the universe. The central objectives of these two research institutions are to make experiments to ascertain the nature and the function of matter, dark matter and dark energy. These research institutions have been made and developed to provide proper research facilities for the physicist in different parts of the world to collaborate on their joint experiments at these international research centres. The original objective of CERN was to accelerate protons and antiprotons.

In 1950 a UNESCO conference was held in Florence, Italy to establish a laboratory to make experiments with the nuclear energy where the scientific community in Europe could collaborate and work together. The CERN is the result of that UNESCO conference in Florence. On July 1st, 1953 representatives from twelve European countries met to create the research institution which is now known as the European Organization for Nuclear Research. It is an institution of advance research facilities and programmes to unfold the mystery of nuclear power. It is basically a research centre where the scientists are working on research projects connected with sub-nuclear and particle physics. This highly sophisticated research centre has been build up in the centre of Europe at the Swiss and French border near Geneva. This is one of the most successful international scientific ventures after the Second World War. CERN is the greatest centre of experimental particle physics. Now, the membership of the countries representing has increased from original twelve to twenty member states. It is most surprising that USA is not the official member of CERN. The CERN research centre is funded by the member countries. The major funding has been done by Germany. On 16th December, 1994, the CERN Council put its signature and gave approval for the establishment of another gigantic research centre which is known as LHC (Large Hadron Collider). Japan became the member of the Board of LHC in 1995 and India in 1996 followed by Russia and Canada, United Sates became its official member in 1997. LHC has undertaken a most unimaginative project to understand the structure and the function of the nuclear energy. It is named after the particles known as Hadrons. 10th September, 2008 heralded a new history in Nuclear Physics when the first experiment was made at LHC. It has been constructed between the Gura Mountains and Lake Geneva which touches French-Swiss border. It is a 26 km circular tunnel deep underground. It is designed with scientific purpose to have a proper and comprehensive knowledge of the constituents of the cosmos. The cosmos was created out of the substance that is known as atomic structure and with the gradual evolution the universe was created from infinitesimally small and infinitely dense substance after the Big Bang. It is expected that the experiments that are carried out at LHC bring revolutionary change in our world view and of the fundamental nature and functions of matter and space. It is both a physical science and astronomical investigation. It is expected that LHC would herald a new era for Particle Physics and Cosmology. On November 23 LHC undertook the experiment of its first collision. On 29th October, 2008, the LHC was inaugurated in the presence of 1500 physicists and eminent world leaders outside Geneva. It has undergone great tests and turmoils. At one time it was thought that it would not succeed after the initial failure in its adventure. But on 20th November, 2009 it was a new beginning with tremendous success when LHC made an experiment with proton beams by colliding and successfully creating a spray of particles. On 23rd November LHC undertook its first collision. Millions of protons were collided with the injection of necessary energy. However, with the ambitious and unprecedented research project of creating a black hole became an international debatable point amongst the scientists and political leaders. Stephen Hawking's postulation that quantum mechanics provide a safety valve for the matter imprisoned and engulfed in black holes, which means that quantum mechanics provides black holes to decay and degenerate. There is a dark side of the scientific discoveries and development also. Scientists are responsible for the dangerous applications of its knowledge and successfully creating a nuclear bomb with the help of Einstein's formulation of equivalence of mass and energy. Scientists would have to be very careful in playing with this dangerous experiment in the field of particle physics by transforming the matter into its explosive form. The creation of black hole poses greater danger because if it is not carefully handled the creation of black holes may wipe out the very existence of the planet Earth.

It is making experiments to create a microscopic low energy black hole. Black holes exist throughout the universe. These black holes in fact are present at the very centre of most of the lost galaxies. For the creation of the black holes an enormous amount of energy is required bigger than any laboratory that could create. When this project was undertaken by LHC the scientists of the world were divided on the feasibility and its possible devastating effects. A section of scientists were worried that with the creation of a black hole, it would destroy the very existence of the planet earth. Black hole devours whatever comes within the radius known as *event horizon.* Gravitational pull is so much an enormous power of the black holes that they engulf and devour all that comes within their known radius. They are called black holes, for no amount of energy comes out as everything is sucked by its gravitational pull and power.

Before the establishment of the LHC nobody had ever imagined that a black hole can be created in a laboratory. For creating a black hole in laboratory unimaginable minimum mass is required. The gravity of black hole is so strong that the known gravitational force of any particle is almost negligible. Lisa Randall writes, "Black holes form when enough matter gets concentrated inside a small enough region that the force of gravity becomes indomitable. The size of the region required to make black hole depends on the amount of the mass."[70]

The whole concept of LHC was conceived by CERN Council which was approved in December 1994. As the CERN institute is confined to Europe it was considered by the international community and the scientists that apart from the CERN there should be an international research centre to carry out the specific research and experiments with particle physics with sole objective of finding out the ultimate unit of the substance of which the whole universe has been constituted. Now, CERN and LHC are working with coordinated cooperation. However, there is a difference both qualitatively and quantitatively in the research projects and the objectives with which these both highly sophisticated and advance centres in nuclear particle physics are working.

The *Washington Post* published a new item on 25th September, 2011, with a caption "Faster Than Light : Revolution or Error". In science, revolutions take time. So, the day after news break of possible revolution in physics—particles moving faster than light—Scientists leading the European experiment that made a discovery calmly explained it to a standing room at CERN. The Giant particle acceleration straddling the Swiss-French border. The Physicists, Dario Anterio made no sweeping claims. This news has created a ripple in the scientific world. According to some the ultimate particles of matter is called Boson. Boson has been named after the eminent Indian Scientist Satyan Bose, who worked in collaboration with Albert Einstein. Some others call this as a God Particle. However, this discovery is still surrounded with mystery. Nothing has been said with accuracy and certainty. So, it is still a hypothesis. But there is a possibility according to me that some particles may travel higher than the speed of light. As I stated earlier that universe exists between zero and infinity. So, there is a possibility some particles may travel nearer to infinity. But, there is no possibility of any particle to acquire the infinite speed. The cosmic consciousness alone has infinite speed. There is an absolute speed and absolute pause in the realm of cosmic consciousness which is the ultimate reality and source of the entire cosmos. The whole cosmos is the modification of the cosmic consciousness with the activation of cosmic matrix. The creation of black holes is another problem on which the scientists and the engineers are engaged. As we have already discussed that this adventure is both beneficial and dangerous also.

To talk from the scientific conceptual point of view I think that there is another potentiality which could be created by scientists with the high and more sophisticated instrument which would have the potentiality and power to unleash the untold energy which may destroy our galaxy. If the process of evolution from the infinitesimally small and infinitely dense point from which the big bang occurred, if this process is reversed and the different elements of matter like air (*vāyu*), fire (*agni*), water (*jala*) and earth reverse with the technological marvels of transforming the ether into air, air into fire, fire into infinitesimally small and infinitely dense and if it bursts then it would bring an untold release, untold energy and it would result in the destruction of the existing galaxy. But it would create many galaxies and Milky Ways. This is the process that would continue. Science is neither moral nor immoral. It is revelatory. It reveals the hidden properties of nature. There are many Milky Ways and galaxies, some of the galaxies and stars whose light has not reached this earth even after billions of year. So with this reality and truth it is very difficult for anybody to imagine the vastness of the cosmos. Now LHC is engaged in finding out Higg's Boson. Higg's Boson is still in the state of conjecture whether the LHC would be able with its experiments to establish the existence of Higg's Boson depends upon the strength of its hypothesis. The physicists are working on this project which would throw some light on the nature of matter and space.

Lisa Randall observes, "This is because the Higgs Boson and nothing else leads to another enormous enigma known as the hierarchy problem. The hierarchy problem concerns the questions of why particle masses—and the Higgs mass in particular—take the values that they do. The weak mass scale that determines elementary particle masses in ten thousand trillion times smaller than another mass scale—the Planck mass that determines the strength of gravitational interactions."[71]

The creation of the universe from infinitesimally small infinitely dense beginning is a Quantum act. To understand the significance and the formation of universe we must combine Einstein's General Relativity theory with Quantum Mechanics. According to Hawking, the universe exists with many different sets of laws. Universe is in a state of expansion and inflation. Hawking observes, "But according to even conservative estimates, during this cosmological inflation, the universe expanded by a factor of 1,000,000,000,000,000,000,000,000,000,000 in .00000000000000000000000000000000001 second. It was as if a coin 1 centimetre in diameter suddenly blew up to ten million times the width of the Milky Way. That may seem to violate relativity, which dictates that nothing can move faster than light, but that speed limit does not apply to the expansion of space itself. The idea that such an episode of inflation might have occurred was first proposed in 1980, based on consideration that goes beyond Einstein's theory of general relativity and takes into account aspects of Quantum theory. Since, we don't have a complete Quantum theory of gravity, the details are still being worked out, and physicists aren't sure exactly how inflation happened."[72]

There are other scientists who do not agree with the big bang theory to equate the origin of the cosmos about fourteen billion years ago. Arnold Benz writes, "All the atoms that are heavier than lithium on our earth bear witness to the history of the Milky Way. The carbon and oxygen in our bodies stem from the helium combustion zone of an old star. Two silicon nuclei, merged in the early phase of a supernova explosion, become the iron in our blood haemoglobin. The calcium in our teeth formed during a supernova out of oxygen and silicon. The fluoride which we brush our teeth was produced in a rare neutrino interaction with neon. The iodine in our thyroid glands arose through neutron capture at the onset of a supernova. We are connected directly with the development of stars and are ourselves part of the cosmic history."[73] He further writes that "it would be wrong to equate of the cosmos with the big bang about fourteen years ago, just as it will be wrong to compare cosmic history to the running of a clock."[74]

The physicists from the university of Melbourne and Royal Melbourne Institute of Technology have postulated that after investigating the cracks and crevices common to all crystals including ice, our understanding of the nature of the universe would give another revolutionary theory that the universe is not an outcome of the big bang but a Big Chill.

A new theory which has been developed called Quantum Graphity. According to this space may have been made out of individual building blocks like tiny atoms. These individual blocks may be equated as similar to pixels that make an image on a screen. These building blocks of space are so small that it is impossible to see directly. However, the theory of big bang is nearer to truth. But it would be wrong to assume that the cosmos has been originated about fifteen billion years ago. According to Kashmir Śaivism,

Vedānta and Buddhism the origin of cosmos cannot be fixed in the scale of time. This has happened from the beginning of the existence of the ultimate reality which doesn't have any beginning.

In spite of all the unprecedented and spectacular discoveries and progress in scientific knowledge the problem of the origin of the universe and the real nature of the substance out of which the universe has been created remains a great mystery. The concept of dark energy which is present in enormous amount in the whole universe remains a mystery. According to modern science the biggest problem with the energy of the universe is cosmological constant problem. This has been established beyond doubt that there are many universes which are governed and contained by different value of dark energy.

Lisa Randall writes, "As I said then, I'm not convinced. Nonetheless, neither I nor anyone else has a better answer. The explanation for the value of the dark energy is perhaps the most major mystery particle physicists and the cosmologists face today. In addition to puzzles about energy, we also have a further cosmological mystery about matter: Why is there matter in the universe at all?"[75]

Lisa Randall's treatment of theoretical physics is tinged with profound philosophical import. In philosophy anyone who reveals the new dimensions in existing philosophical problem or who raises a new metaphysical issues and problem is considered as most original thinker. If we judge Lisa Randall's treatment of science with philosophical reflection and speculation I consider her as one of the most original thinker. The problems which she has raised are unanswered till this day because these problems don't belong to the domain of science. She has raised some most original and transcendental metaphysical problems which would be solved and answered in taking recourse to ontological mysticism.

I feel the convergence of science and spirituality has become a historical necessity to resolve the mystery and live in peace and in state of spiritual effulgence. *Nirvāṇa* is the only goal and in itself of all our scientific or philosophical pursuits. I shall discuss this subject in the next and the last chapter.

The modern scientific world is with full of puzzles and enigma. The presence of matter and antimatter is one of the great puzzlement because the presence of one annihilates the other. So, with the process of cooling of the universe, after the Big Bang inflation, there would have been neither matter nor antimatter. The how and the why this matter and antimatter asymmetry came into existence. This is the enigmatic scientific problem before the theoretical particle physics and cosmology and the greatest and unanswered problem is the formation of dark matter and dark energy. These are some of the unanswered questions scientists like Lisa Randall thinks the experiment at LHC throw some light in the process of the solution of these problems.

However, I am not sure rather doubtful whether the scientific experiments and investigation are carried in the right directions. However, I wish that LHC succeeds in solving these riddles which are standing in the path of pure theoretical physics and cosmology as the greatest monster.

I would like to conclude this chapter by quoting a most profound statement made by Erwin Schrodinger. He writes, "I have, therefore, no hesitation in declaring quite bluntly that the acceptance of a really existing material world, as the explanation of the fact that we all find the end that we are empirically in the same environment, is mystical and metaphysical."[76]

Science and spirituality are integral forms and parts of the cosmos and human existence.

References

1. *The Grand Design*, Stephen Hawking & Leonard Mlodinow. Bantam Press, London, 2010.
2. *My View of the World*, Ervin Schrodinger. Ox Bow Press, Woodbridge, Connecticut, 1983, p. 40.
3. *Washington Post*, 25th September, 2011. Faster than Light: Revolution or Error. Particles Burst Einstein's Speed Limit by Brian Vastag.
4. *A Philosophical Essay on Probabilities*, Marquis De Laplace. Dover Publications, Inc., New York, 1951, pp. 1-2.
5. *Language, Truth and Logic*, A.J. Ayer, London, Victor Gallanez Ltd., 1936, p. 248.
6. *Physics and Philosophy, The Revolution in Modern Science*, Werner Heisenberg, Harper Perennial Modern Thought Publishers, New York, 2002, p. XIII.
7. Galileo, 1632. *Science and Religion: Opposing Viewpoints*, ed. Janelle Rohr (Greenhaven Press, 1988), p. 21.

8. *A Philosophical Essay on Probabilities*, Marquis De Laplace, Dover Publications, Inc., New York, 1951, p. 195.
9. *A Briefer History of Time*, Stephen Hawking & Leonard Mlodinow. Bantam Press, London, 2010, p. 18.
10. *Ibid.*, pp. 23-24.
11. *Physics and Philosophy: The Revolution in Modern Science*, Werner Heisenberg, Harper Perennial Modern Thought Publishers, New York, 2002, p. 46.
12. *The Dancing Wu Li Masters: An Overview of the New Physics*, Gary Zukav, Perennial Classics, New York, 1979, p. 33.
13. *Relativity, The Special and the General Theory*, Albert Einstein, Mahaveer Publishers, New Delhi, 2011.
14. *Ibid.*, p. 26.
15. *Confessions*, Chapter XX.
16. *My View on the World*, Erwin Schrodinger, p. 22.
17. *Relativity, The Special and the General Theory*, Albert Einstein, p. 39.
18. *Physics and Philosophy, The Revolution in Modern Science*, Werner Heisenberg, p. 97.
19. *A Briefer History of Time*, Stephen Hawking & Leonard Mlodinow, Bantam Press, London, 2010, p. 44.
20. *Knocking on Heavens Door*, Lisa Randall, Harper Colin Publishers, p. 122.
21. *Ibid.*, p. 123.
22. *Many Worlds in One, The Search For Other Universes*, Alex Vilenkin, Hill and Wang Publications, New York, 2006, p. 47.
23. *Knocking on Heaven's Door*, Lisa Randall, Harper Colin Publishers, p. 374.
24. *Relativity, The Special and the General Theory*, Albert Einstein, p. 126.
25. *Physics and Philosophy, The Revolution in Modern Science*, Werner Heisenberg, p. 6.
26. *Ibid.*, p. 59.
27. *Ibid.*, p. 136.
28. *A Briefer History of Time*, Stephen Hawking & Leonard Mlodinow. Bantam Press, London, 2010, pp. 48-49.
29. *Physics and Philosophy, The Revolution in Modern Science*, Werner Heisenberg, pp. 24-25.
30. *Ibid.*, p. 26.
31. *Ibid.*, p. 27.
32. *Ibid.*, pp. 31-32.
33. *Ibid.*, p. 32.
34. *The Grand Design*, Stephen Hawking & Leonard Mlodinow. Bantam Press, London, 2010, p. 72.
35. *Quantum, Einstein, Bohr and the Great Debate about the Nature of Reality*, Manjit Kumar, Hachette UK Company, 2008, p. 320.
36. *Ibid.*, p. 320.
37. *Physics and Philosophy, The Revolution in Modern Science*, Werner Heisenberg, p. 176.

38. *Ibid.*, p. 160.
39. *Ibid.*, p. 140.
40. *A Briefer History of Time*, Stephen Hawking & Leonard Mlodinow, Bantam Press, London, 2010, pp. 58-59.
41. *Ibid.*, pp. 66-67.
42. *Knocking on Heavens Door*, Lisa Randall. Harper Colin Publishers, p. 355.
43. *Encyclopaedia of Science and Technology*, 10th Edition, McGraw Hill, New York, 2007, p. 691.
44. *Ibid.*, p. 813.
45. *The Grand Design*, Stephen Hawking & Leonard Mlodinow. Bantam Press, London, 2010, pp. 161-162.
46. *Encyclopaedia of Science and Technology*, 10th Edition, McGraw Hill, New York, 2007, p. 814.
47. *Knocking on Heavens Door*, Lisa Randall, Harper Colin Publishers, p. 374.
48. *Ibid.*, pp. 375-376.
49. *Tripūra Rahasyam*, pp. 11-12. Saraswati Bhavan Granthamala, Vol. 15, Varanasi, 1965.
50. *The Grand Design*, Stephen Hawking & Leonard Mlodinow, Bantam Press, London, 2010, p. 124.
51. *Knocking on Heaven's Door*, Lisa Randall, Harper Colin Publishers, p. 123.
52. *Ibid.*, p. 358.
53. *Indian Thought and its Development*, Albert Schweitzer, London, Hodder and Stonghton Ltd., 1936, p. 10.
54. *Ibid.*, pp. 11-12.
55. *The Grand Design*, Stephen Hawking & Leonard Mlodinow. Bantam Press, London, 2010, p. 117.
56. *Ibid.*, p. 117.
57. *Ibid.*, p. 70.
58. *Knocking on Heaven's Door*, Lisa Randall, Harper Colin Publishers, p. 116.
59. *Ibid.*, p. 123.
60. *Encyclopaedia Britannica*, p. 762.
61. *Ibid.*, p. 766.
62. *Ibid.*, p. 766.
63. *Cosmic Religious Feelings. Quantum Questions*, the Mystic Writings of the World's Greatest Physicists, Ken Wilber. Shambhala Publications, Boston, Massachusetts, 1984, p. 105.
64. *The Aspiration towards Spirit, Quantum Questions*, Ken Wilber, p. 120.
65. *The Making of the Atomic Bomb*, Simon and Schuster, 1986, Quoted for Example in *Richard Rhodes.*
66. *Knocking on Heavens Door*, Lisa Randall. Harper Colin Publishers, p. 116.
67. *The Grand Design*, Stephen Hawking & Leonard Mlodinow. Bantam Press, London, 2010, p. 150.
68. *Knocking on Heaven's Door*, Lisa Randall. Harper Colin Publishers, p. 120.

69. *Ibid.*, p. 122.
70. *Ibid.*, p. 169.
71. *Ibid.*, p. 296.
72. *The Grand Design*, Stephen Hawking & Leonard Mlodinow. Bantam Press, London, 2010, p. 129.
73. Future of the Universe, Arnold Benz., Continuum, New York, London, 2000, pp. 32-33.
74. *Ibid.*, p. 33.
75. *Knocking on Heaven's Door*, Lisa Randall, Harper Colin Publishers, p. 375.
76. *My View of the World*, Erwin Schrodinger, Ox Bow Press, Woodbridge, Connecticut 1983, p. 94.

PART – III

7

Ontological Mysticism

The twenty first century will usher a new era of spiritual renaissance. This renaissance would come in which mankind would discover that the ethical and spiritual truths are the highest truths. It would liberate mankind from the miserable obsession of the reality which is based on Ontological Materialism. The integration of multi-dimensional kaleidoscope of science with monastic and spiritualistic kaleidoscope is Ontological Mysticism. East is monastic and the West is theistic. East is mystical and the West is dualistic. East is spirituality and west is science. Ontological mysticism is the happy and harmonious blending of East and West and science and spirituality. Nature has not set any limit to the realization of human hopes and aspirations. Spirituality is a path of truth, virtue and *Nirvāṇa*. Science gives us knowledge, spirituality brings wisdom. In the state of spiritual sublimity we are face to face with truth and reality. Integrating and mediating between these two planes of ratiocination and reflections given by science and spirituality would be the greatest intellectual and moral adventure and the most rewarding achievement of today. The impact of Ontological Materialism which has disastrous impact on our civilization is that it is far more developed materially than spiritually. With the scientific and technological advancement the forces of nature at our command, in such an unprecedented way, have polluted the very civilization which was born out of love and compassion. We value material achievements and we do not keep in our mind the importance of ethical and spiritual values. Albert Schweitzer writes, "The essential nature of civilization does not lie in its material achievements, but in the fact that individuals keep in mind the ideals of the perfecting of man, and the improvement of the social and political conditions of people, and of mankind as a whole. And that their habit of thoughts is determined in living and constant fashion by such ideals."[1]

Modern science has succeeded in revealing some of the mysteries of nature and in the course of their penetration deeper into the knowledge of natural harmony it has become conscious of the fact that it is harmony and order which rules the universe. And this harmony and order is beyond the realm of scientific ratiocination and experiments. This natural harmony and order is the result of the activation of some hidden reality which I consider as cosmic consciousness. However, scientists do accept the existence of an *Ontological order* which is beyond the reach of scientific enquiry. Prince Louis De Broglie considers that the truth is that humanity has been able to adapt itself to live in this world in which there is some isomorphic relation with our mind. If there would not have been so, perhaps humanity would not have been able to survive. He writes, "How remarkable is the harmony between the resources of which our mind disposes and the profound realities which conceal themselves behind natural appearances. To bring this harmony more completely into the light, to glimpse yet more the Ontological order of which Duhem spoke--such appears to be the true mission of pure science. Removed from all utilitarian preoccupation, solely devoted to the search for truth, it appears to us as one of the noblest activities of which we are capable. By the wholly ideal nature of the goal it pursues, by the intensity and the disinterested character of the efforts that it demands, it possesses a moral value which cannot be denied."[2] Henry Bergson, the author of *Creative Evolution*, has warned against the power of destruction that man has acquired for the first time in the history with the technological advancements and the monumental discoveries of modern physics. He thinks that, we are living in an era of inexpiable strife which has surpassed the limit and the magnitude of horrors of all the wars of the past have witnessed the potential of destruction that could destroy the whole humanity from the surface of the earth.

And he thinks "Let us add that this increased body awaits a supplement of the soul and that mechanism demands mysticism."[3] Humanity doesn't know that the future depends on itself. It is for it to see if it wishes to continue to live, says Bergson.

Prince Louis De Broglie writes, "Confronted by the dangers with which the advances of science can, if employed for evil, face him, man has need of a "supplement of soul" and he must force himself to acquire it promptly before it is too late. It is the duty of those who have mission of being the spiritual or intellectual guides of humanity to labour to awaken in it this supplement of the soul."[4]

The theory of relativity and Quantum Mechanics has brought a revolution in human thinking and understanding of both nature and man. However, Einstein dreamt of postulating a unified theory for the understanding of universe and man. It was a revolution in itself. I consider that the Ontological Mysticism may be considered as a unified theory because it does explain the mystery of the universe and the mystery of the soul.

In the last chapter we have discussed in some detail, in the context of Quantum theory, that there exists a deep metaphysical and an epistemological relation between the object and the subject, between the observer and the facts observed. We cannot have any understanding and knowledge of an object divorced from the subjective involvement. Quantum mechanics believes that the subject and object relation which tinged and modified the object in the process of observation by the observer is neither irrelevant nor completely surveyable. After any number of observations the object is left in a state where which some features (the last observed ones) are known, but others those inferred with by the last observations are not known. This speaks of our limitation and this is why any explanation or, faultless description of physical object is not possible. Schrodinger writes, "I say this interpretation suggests itself: that there is a fully determined physical object in existence, but I can never know all about it. However, this would be a complete misunderstanding of what Bohr and Heisenberg and those who follow them actually mean. They mean that the object has no existence independent of the observing subject. They mean that recent discoveries in physics have pushed forward to the mysterious boundary between the subject and the object, which thereby has turned out not to be a sharp boundary at all. We are to understand that we never observe an object without its being modified or tinged by our own activity in observing it. We are to understand that under the impact of our refined methods of observation and of thinking about the results of our experiments that mysterious boundary between the subject and the object has broken down."[5] According to classical mechanics once sufficient data is provided it gives yes or no answer for all the further questions. While Quantum Mechanics simply leaves unanswered some questions in theory to be answered by our experience and further reflections.

According to quantum mechanics, we are not in a position to provide any information about the physical objects or the phenomenal world without having personal experience. This experience or interaction is very important. Even while perceiving an object we modify the object by the light rays with which we hit the object. In the process of perception, the light rays reflect into the retina of the eye and it transmits the inferred object to our mind. So, in the process of obtaining knowledge about an object, we tinged and modified the object. This is an eternal problem of philosophy and Kant has rightly argued that the things in itself is unknown and unknowable. Kant, however, does agree that all knowledge begins with experience but it doesn't mean that it is not always derived from experience. Experience teaches us that certain things have such and such properties but it doesn't provide complete knowledge that it could not be different. Any emphasis on the theory of complete logical clarification would lead to scientific impossibility. Heisenberg says, "It has been pointed out before that in the Copenhagen interpretation of Quantum theory we can indeed proceed without mentioning ourselves as individuals, but we cannot disregard the fact that natural science is formed by men. Natural science does not simply describe and explain nature; it is a part of the interplay between nature and ourselves; it describes nature as exposed to our method of questioning."[6]

Quantum mechanics is a paradox. According to Quantum Mechanics scientists explain its experiments in vocabulary of classical physics. And at the same time, it asserts that those concepts do not agree accurately with nature. The paradoxical nature of Quantum Mechanics combines objective and the subjective elements. It is all about possibilities and not certainty. Heisenberg further says, "This looks as if we have introduced an element of subjectivism into the theory, as if we meant to say: what happens depends on our way of observing it or on the fact that we observe it."[7]

While making experiments to understand the atomic structure one starts with the belief that one is making experiments with physical objects and facts which are considered as real. But in the process of experiments, one realizes that the atoms or elementary particles are not real. They belong to the world of possibility rather than as one of the things or facts. The science then becomes an esoteric because scientists cannot define the meaning of concept with absolute certainty. The Quantum Mechanics postulation that every knowledge depends on both subject and object which are inextricably interwoven is the echo of the Pythagorean and the Democrats formulations who postulated that all our perceptions, experiences and observations have strong personal and subjective tinge.

Rene Descartes, the founder of the modern philosophy postulated that there is no possibility of intimate connection between mind and matter. According to him essence of matter is extension in space and that of mind being thought. And he is considered as the father of the dualism. The world of mind and the world of matter are two completely different worlds independent like two parallel rail lines running together without any meeting point. However, he postulated that these two independent entities do meet at the mysterious pineal glands. Against the background of the rationalist doctrines of Descartes, Berkley and the empiricists and the idealist's thinkers that did agree as mind and matter fundamentally belong to different world and nature, they could have never interacted. Berkley argued that matter and mind do interact contagiously and he argued that matter must be of the same nature and substance as mind. And hence the essence of matter must be thought rather than its extension otherwise there is no possibility of their meeting. On the other hand, Locke postulated the "*real essence of substance*" is unknown and unknowable. The theory of empiricism fathered by Locke culminated in *solipsism* of David Hume. The epistemological and philosophical problems raised by Hume are still unanswered. According to Locke, knowledge is the perception of agreement or disagreement of two ideas. This thesis of Locke had logical corollary in Berkley's formulations "*Essest Percipi*", which means that the existence of things lies in their being perceived. To be perceived is identical with existence. This line of argument culminated in extreme scepticism which is known as solipsism of Hume. According to Hume, we have experience or perception of only ideas. He refuted any induction or causation. If the extreme form of Hume's scepticism and solipsism is accepted it would annihilate the very basis of empirical science. I feel Hume's assertions have certain limitations, but it is not wholly and completely false. Even modern scientists are grappling with the problem of nature and the understanding of complete and irrevocable knowledge. The scientists and mathematicians from the time of Greek and philosophical thinkers of Hinduism and Buddhism have been of the opinion that the knowledge acquired by empirical science is true till we have the total experience of the ultimate reality. The complete knowledge is integral, total and direct which could be obtained only through intuitional science and meditative insight.

Sir James Jeans writes, "Most scientists would agree that they are nothing more than pictures—fictions, if you like, if by fiction you mean that science is not yet in contact with the ultimate reality.

Many would hold that, from the broad philosophical standpoint, the outstanding achievement of the twentieth century physics is not the theory of relativity with its welding together of space and time, or the theory of quanta with its present apparent negation of the laws of causation, or the dissection of the atom with the resultant discovery that things are not what they seem; it is the general recognition that we are not yet in contact with the ultimate reality. To speak in terms of Plato's well-known simile, we are still imprisoned in our cave, with our backs to the light and can only watch the shadows of the wall. At present the only task immediately before science is to study those shadows, to classify them and explain them in the simplest possible way."[8]

We do not have knowledge of the thing in itself. This throws a new light on the relation on the integration and the intimate relation between the subject and the object. The barrier between subject and object would not have been broken down which has been accepted by Heisenberg and Schrodinger if both the subject and the object would not have belonged to same reality or substance. This is the fundamental philosophy of Ontological Mysticism. The Subjectivisation of the so called external object is knowledge and the Subjectivisation of supreme subjectivity (cosmic consciousness) is wisdom or *Nirvāṇa*. This speaks of a hidden reality of which both the subject and object are modification and manifestation. I consider that the cosmic consciousness is the only truth and reality. The dualism of subject and object is real till we have the realization of ultimate truth and reality (cosmic consciousness).

Lisa Randall writes, "Understanding nature, life and the universe poses extraordinarily difficult problems. We all would like to better understand who we are, where we came from and where we are going—and to focus on things larger than ourselves and more permanent than the latest gadget or fashion."[9] This is the basic and fundamental concern for both science and philosophy. Philosophy has been in quest of truth and reality which would bring the realization and experience of cosmic consciousness. "*Know thy self*" has been the central objective of the Eastern philosophical and mystical tradition. Schrodinger also comes to the same conclusion while speaking about the importance of the knowledge and the experience of "*who are we*?" He writes, "I do think I am prejudiced against the importance that science has from the purely human point of view. I had expressed by the original title of these lectures, and I have explained in the introductory passages, that I consider science an integrating part of our endeavour to answer the one great philosophical question which embraces all others, the one that Plotinus expressed by his brief : who are we? And more than that, I consider this not only one of the tasks, but the task of science, the only one that really counts."[10] The Laws of Causation is the fundamental rule of science. But it has its own limitations. The principle of uncertainty has not totally rejected the concept of causation but in explaining the functioning of atomic structure it has failed. I personally believe that the principle of uncertainty is incomplete. There cannot be any irrevocable and universal theory or postulation; it is based on potentiality and possibilities. However, the categorical imperative postulated by Kant as a moral concept has great relevance today. Dictate of beauty and adherence to moral norms and values has important place in our life. Though I am aware that the moral values are not universal and absolute in character, it has certain limitations of time, place and cultural milieu which are considered as the greatest value in one tradition that is considered as the greatest sin in other traditions. For example according to the Hindu tradition one who knows the *Brahman* or God (cosmic consciousness or ultimate reality) one becomes *Brahman* or God. But in Islamic tradition, anybody proclaims himself or herself to be God is considered the greatest sin and blasphemy. However, one will have to give place to moral values and character and scientific knowledge to spiritual awareness and sublimity. Planck in reply to the question when he was asked that the progress of science consists in discovery of new mystery the moment one thinks that something fundamental has been solved. In answer to this question he says, "Science cannot solve the ultimate mystery of nature. And that is because, in the last analysis we, ourselves are the part of nature and, therefore, part of the mystery that we are trying to solve."[11]

Erwin Schrodinger while enumerating the problem of reality or individual he comes to the conclusion that the concept of individual or reality is wrapped up in mystery. Take for example the concept of particles. What are these particles if they are not individuals? When we examine the nature and the form of ultimate particles in our environment which is considered as an attribute of individual sameness becomes enigmatic, as we know that an atom is constituted of a number of particles and a molecule is constituted of several atoms. The molecules are of different size, i.e., small and big but there is no limit, beyond which we call it a big molecule. According to modern science size of the molecule has no upper limit. It may contain hundreds of thousands of atoms. Schrodinger writes, "It may be a virus or gene, visible under the microscope. Finally, we may observe that any pulpable object in our environment is composed of molecules, which are composed of atoms and which are composed of ultimate particles..... and if the latter lack individuality, how does, say my wrist watch come by individuality?"[12] Where is the limit? How does individuality arise at all in objects composed of non-individuals? Schrodinger has raised a very fundamental, scientific and philosophical issue. I personally feel that in absence and without reference to transcendental reality (cosmic consciousness) the objective world loses its identity and meaning. Scientific materialism is not clear and sure about the material reality out of which the phenomenal has been created. Science only deals with the partial aspects of reality which is considered the very nature and form of the objective world. Science does admit that the quasi-metrical aspects of reality don't explain the whole truth. There is hiatus in ratiocination and reasoning but it doesn't mean that we should all together reject the process of ratiocination and reasoning. It does explain that there is something which transcends the world of reason and scientific materialism. As I have already mentioned before that the world is real till we realize and experience the ultimate nature and the form of the absolute (cosmic consciousness).

The Gauḍapāda, the founder of *Advaita Vedānta*, developed the line of argument that the world is real only till we realise and experience the ultimate reality (cosmic consciousness) or *Brahman*. According to him there are four stages of our consciousness, i.e., awake (*jāgrata*), dream (*svapna*), dreamless (*suṣupti*) and enlightenment (*tūrya*). *Tūrya* is known as the transcendental state of pure consciousness. It is a state of truth (*sat*), consciousness (*cit*) and wisdom (*bliss/ānanda*). When one experiences the transcendental reality which is called *Samādhi* also the world disappears. Gauḍapāda argues that the world disappears in the state of *tūrya* or *samādhi* (state of cosmic consciousness) because the world is not real in the sense of absolute reality. And hence only which is unreal can disappear in the state of salvation or *Nirvāṇa*. Śaṅkara's whole philosophical basis is the exposition of Gauḍapāda's doctrine of *Advaita* which is developed in *Māṇḍūkyakārikā*. Śaṅkara's famous aphorism, states that the *Brahman* is real and the world is unreal and there is complete identity between *Jīva* and the *Brahman*. There is a qualitative difference between the dreamless sleep, state of pure consciousness, i.e., *tūrya* and senselessness (*mūrcchā*). When a man goes into deep sleep or that is termed as dreamless sleep, he does not enter into the state of pure consciousness. When he wakes up, he infers that from 10 p.m. to 4 a.m. his I-ness or the sense of individuality was absent and on that basis he infers that this is the only proof that he was in a state of dreamless sleep. The identity of the individual *Jīva* is established on the basis of the absence of his I-consciousness before and after the dreamless sleep. On the basis of this inference that when his I-ness was absent he was in the state of dreamless sleep. But the dreamless sleep is not the state of pure cosmic consciousness.

Some Western writers have wrongly equated this state of dreamless sleep with *Samādhi,* i.e., the state of pure consciousness when one becomes one with the *Brahman* or cosmic consciousness. The state of *Samādhi* is a state of infinite bliss. With the same line of arguments our seer and the mystics infers that he was in a state of *Samādhi* because when he returns to normal consciousness, he experiences the scattering state of blissfulness. And on that basis the mystic and the seer infers that he must have been in a state of greater bliss and that is called the state of divine effulgence and *Samādhi*. There is again qualitative difference between the state of senselessness and *Samādhi*. When any person with the application of chloroform or some such medicine loses his awareness or when gets a great mental or physical shock out of physical injury or intense mental shock, he loses normal consciousness. But when he returns back to a normal consciousness he feels and experiences a great weakness. After returning back from the state of *Samādhi* one experiences a scattering and fleeting bliss. While one returns back from senselessness, one experiences extreme weakness, so, there is a qualitative and quantitative difference between the state of dreamless sleep, *Samādhi* and senselessness.

There is again a qualitative difference between the Hindu concept of self and mind and the Western concept of self and mind. According to most of the Western thinkers there is no much qualitative difference between the mind and the self rather for modern Western psychology and other Western philosophers the mind is the self. But according to Hindu psychology and philosophy there is a vast and fundamental difference between mind and self. According to Hindu psychology and philosophy there are five stages of our psychic or mental consciousness. They are called conscious mind (*Kāmamaya koṣa*), the sub-consciousness mind (*Manomaya koṣa*), supramental consciousness (*Atimānasa koṣa*), causal mind (*Vijñānamaya koṣa*) and supracausal mind (*Hiraṇyamaya koṣa*). The normal conscious mind deals with the physical aspects of our day to day function like sex and hunger. The *Manomaya koṣa* (subconscious mind) deals with our subtle mental activities like discrimination, thinking, etc. Other three supramental, causal and supracausal mind may be termed as unconscious mind according to modern psychological terminology. But the Indian concept of unconscious mind is again is qualitative which is different from Freudian and Jungian concept of unconscious mind. However, Indian concept of unconscious is closer to Jungian concept. But according to Hindu psychology self or *Brahman* is quite different from mind. Only when one transcends these five stages of mind, i.e., also called sheaths one realizes the cosmic consciousness and the *Brahman*. According to *Muṇḍakopaniṣad*,

"The stainless, indivisible *Brahman*, the pure, the light of all lights, is in innermost sheath of the supramental divine hue—the highest. That is what the knowers of the *Ātman* know."[13] This is the state of *Samādhi* which is not a myth, but spiritual reality. This has been proved beyond any doubt with scientific experiments that have been done by one of the greatest *Yogī* named Swami Rāma at the research institute known as Menninger Foundation, Topeka Kansas, USA. "In 1970, he became a consultant at the Menninger Foundation, Topeka, Kansas, and started working with Dr. Elmer Green of the research department. In 1973, *Time-Life Nature/ Science Annual* in which some of his experiments were published, reported: "At the Menninger Foundation, Topeka, Kansas, performing in a laboratory, monitored by a battery of instruments..... Swami [Rāma] demonstrated that he can speed up his heart rate without moving any of his skeletal muscles or changing his breathing. He has also shown that he can produce a 10 degree difference in temperature between different parts of the palm of his hand." In 1973, the *Encyclopaedia Britannica* Yearbook of Science and the Future published, "The Swami could voluntarily maintain his production of *theta* and *delta* brain wave..... During one five minute test, Swami Rāma demonstrated *theta* waves were 75 per cent of the time. The next day he deliberately produced *delta* waves for 25 minutes. He appeared asleep and even snored gently, but afterwards he could repeat almost perfectly thing said in the room at that time." The *New York Times*, magazine, September 12, 1971, also repeated that "For 17 seconds his electrocardiogram showed 300 beats per minute. These rapid contractions, known as atrial fibrillation, mean that the heart can no longer pump the necessary volume of blood—a critical state, which if not reversed, will be fatal.... [In Delta Experiments] Swami Rāma who called this state "yogic sleep" could enter it at will. He did so in the laboratory producing an EEG record much like deepest sleep with 40 per cent *delta* waves."

The veracity of the mystic experience of *Samādhi* and transcendental reality has been proved experimentally by Swami Rāma and others ancient seers and mystics, the world of dualism on which the whole scientific materialism is based, loses its very meaning and truth. Only in the context of consciousness the world becomes meaningful and relatively true. According to modern scientific discovery and experimentation the whole of reality is nothing, but the modification and transformation of cosmic consciousness. Consciousness is the only reality that exists. Without the acceptance of the cosmic consciousness or *Brahman* as substance the scientific thinking breaks down in explaining reality and truth. Schrodinger writes, "I say this danger arises if we forget that the casual nexus that we are talking about is situated in our idea of the external world—if we insist on locating it in a self-supportingly 'existent' external world not dependent on our psychic experience. It seems to me that this brings us to a somewhat paradoxical conclusion: if, without involving ourselves in obvious nonsense, we are going to be able to think in a natural way about what goes on in a living, feeling, thinking being (that is, to see it in the same way as we see what takes place in inanimate bodies)—without any directing demons, without offending against, say, the principle of increase of entropy, without entelechy or *vis-à-vis* or any other such rubbish—then the condition for our doing so is that we think of everything that happens as taking place in our experiences of the world, without ascribing to it any material substratum as the object of which it is an experience; a substratum which, as the rest of this investigation will show, would in fact be wholly and entirely superfluous."[14]

Scientific materialism is based on dualism. Dualistic theory of universe is based on the two theories. One theory postulates that the theistic God of sematic religion that has created the world. Other principles are conceived as natural laws that governs the universe. This dualistic doctrine is the foundation of Christianity, Islam and Judaism. And this view has always stood against the scientific rationalism and opposed the scientific discoveries since Galileo. The concept of God as a creator and ethical principles which govern the world and impart judgement on all kinds of human activities. The theory of reward and punishment is based on personal God as has been conceived in the canonical literatures of sematic religion. Albert Einstein feels very strongly to do away with the concept of personal God. He writes, "But I am persuaded that such behaviour on the part of the representatives of religion would not only be unworthy, but also fatal. For a doctrine which is able to maintain itself not in clear light but only in the dark, will, of necessity, lose its effect on mankind, with incalculable harm to human progress. In their struggle for the ethical good, teachers of religion must have the stature to give up the doctrine of a personal God, that is, give up that source of fear and hope which in the past placed such vast power in the hands of priests."[15]

The concept of personal God was the greatest impediment in the path of development of scientific rationalism in the past. On the other hand, the Berkeliun idealism, Humanian solipsism and Leibnizian monastic idealism is also detrimental to the scientific world view, though it has raised some basic issues in philosophy and science which is being debated even today. Russell and Whitehead have tried to bring about some kind of reconciliation between the mind and body concepts. In philosophy and psychology consciousness is being debated and discussed from the very beginning of its inception, whether the world is a mind like or body like or there is a harmonious blending between the two. The characteristic of mind is assumed as consciousness and the defining characteristics of body are extension in space. Consciousness in Western philosophy and psychology is taken normally as sensation. Bertrand Russell and Whitehead conceived a new reality called *élan-vita.* And they assumed that the sensation or consciousness and extensions are the result of combinations of this neutral reality *élan-vita.*

But the *élan-vita* cannot be accepted as the sole reality out of which everything has emerged because consciousness and the extensions are two contradictory concepts. Hence either *élan-vita* is body like or it is mind like reality. The dualistic element of contradictory natures constituting reality in the form of *élan-vita* is unscientific and unphilosophical.

Saul Paul Sirag has a new theory. According to him unification of all the forces is possible if a new world view is created out of the unification of theory of general relativity (Einstein's theory of gravity) with Quantum Mechanics. But again the possibility of unification of two world views which are incompatible and contradictory in nature poses another philosophical and scientific problem. General relativity is deterministic in nature and on the other hand, Quantum Mechanics is basically non-deterministic. He postulates that "Quantum Mechanics has a deterministic side as well as non-deterministic side. The unification and the reconciliation of these two incompatible views is possible in the theory postulated as Quantum measurement problem."[16]

To strengthen his view he gives an example of a Buddhist monk Fa Tsang (643-712 A.D.) who demonstrated before empress Wu at an Octagonal room which was covered with mirrors all around including floors and the ceilings. In the centre of that, he put an image of Buddha with a burning light. When the Empress entered the room he demonstrated of Totality in *Dharma Dhātu* which was mirror within the room all over the idol of the Buddha. The reflection of image of Buddha was being mirrored within the rooms without any omission or misplacement. On the basis of this Fa Tsang wanted to prove the concept of inter-penetration and contentment. In short, he wanted to prove the principle of one in all and all in one. This is the mystery of reality embracing one and the infintum is revealed. This explains that the concept of simultaneousness arising out of different realms is so clear that no justification is necessary. "These infinite reflections of different realms now simultaneously arise without the slightest effort. They must naturally do so in a perfectly harmonious way. As far as the principle of the non-obstruction of space, it can be demonstrated in this manner. Your Majesty, now, we see all the mirrors and their reflections within this small crystal ball. Hence, we have an example of the small containing the large as well as the large containing the small. This is demonstration of the non-obstruction of the "sizes" of space."[17] Further he demonstrated the non-obstruction of time, i.e., the past entering the future and future entering the past cannot be exemplified by any demonstration because of the static nature of reality which is lacking the dynamic quality of temporal elements. The example and demonstration of non-obstruction of time and space is quite problematic to demonstrate through ordinary means. For, that one will have to reach a different level in which one will have the capabilities of witnessing a demonstration such as that. This has demonstrated the hyper dimensional nature of reality which is being postulated by modern science to bring about unifying physical forces in a unified field theory. Scientists believe that this is one of the possibilities with the help of hyper dimensional nature of reality to postulate the theory of consciousness that could serve the proper rational and scientific world view.

Bertrand Russell in his *Analysis of Mind* holds a different view altogether. According to him all mental states are made from the same kind of elements as body. Simply it has been a different permutation and combination. However, Bertrand Russell had a different view in his book entitled *Human Knowledge* (*Human Knowledge: Its Scope and Limits*, Part VI, Chapter 6, p. 480). He thinks that some thinkers have strong reservation in the existence of the external world. These two statements as recorded in Human Knowledge and its Limits and the Analysis of Mind are mutually contradictory. Erwin Schrodinger has made a detailed analysis of this problem in his book *My View of the World*, Chapter VII, titled Consciousness, Organic, Inorganic, Mneme. He postulates that the world has first manifested from the consciousness.

The world consists of elements of consciousness in which we have witnessed the emergence of a brain which is a highly specialised phenomenon. While discussing the concept of inorganic and organic, he raised the issues whether the organic is a special modification of inorganic or the other way round. While analysing the concept of organic he says that "our world of organism is composed of living tissues which are compounded in a special relatively small number of elements. Then he tries to understand the concept of organic and he debates whether it is simply *protein* or *protoplasm*. In the organic being, the life and its existence is an organic being. It consists of constant change of matter while the form remains the same. The fundamental contrast and contradictions between organic and inorganic is not constituted in the constitution of an object but it is related with the attitude of the observer. Now, the question arises whether we pay attention to unchanging material with changing form or the unchanging form with the changing matter. We cannot reconcile both at the same time. Now, the question arises which material events are directly associated with consciousness because not all brain processes and functions are associated with consciousness. It includes the regulatory reflect process in the ganglia of spinal cord which controls the nervous system but it is associated with a number of reflex actions which involve the brain but they do not enter into consciousness. The organic is accompanied by consciousness. Erwin Schrodinger writes, "It seems to me that the wish to reduce the whole of reality to mental experience has much deeper foundations than a mere obstinate desire to deny an idea (that of the real external world) without which we cannot achieve a single step in practical life. This idea is itself a mental construct and is not being questioned in the least."[18] While analysing the concept of reality Schrodinger thinks that the concept, reality and existence, etc., are all empty words because they do not denote any objects with certainty. And thus, he comes to the conclusion that we cannot understand fully and wholly the true forms and the function of nature. It is beyond our reach to formulate and postulate a complete reconstruct of nature in our mind. He makes a very bold assertion that, "What we are acknowledging and asserting here is something more: it is impossible to have so much as a completely certain, unambiguous mutual understanding between human beings; it is a goal which we are forever approaching, but which we can never reach. On this ground alone exact science is never really possible."[19]

It is considered that the transcendental reality (cosmic consciousness) is beyond the reach of our mind and senses. Pythagoras was one of the great Greek philosopher and mystic. He is acknowledged as the father of the Western scientific tradition. However, according to him philosophy was considered as a means of spiritual purification. He was the first Western thinker who believed in the destiny of soul with the possibility of rising to union with divine. We find a harmonious blending of ecstatic practices of the then Orphic cult of mystery which he tried to reform. I believe that his belief in the concept of the theory of rebirth and transmigration of soul and concept of soul's union with divine is the impact of Indian philosophical and mystic influence on him. Now, the historians have new evidence that there has been a cultural exchange of ideas and thoughts between the Indian thinkers and mystics with the Greek thinkers and it has benefited both in the enrichment of Indian and Greek culture. But this much is certain and evident that Pythagoras emphasis on the reformation on knowledge and science as a path to salvation is the direct impact of Indian Ontological mysticism and philosophy. Jeffrey Mishlone writes, "Scholars suggests that Pythagoras incorporated the ecstatic practices of the Orphic mystery cult, known for its raw emotional manifestations which he attempted to reform with his emphasis on knowledge and science as a path to salvation."[20] Another thinker,

Montaigne, considers that none of our beliefs is beyond doubt. Even the father of modern Western philosophy, Rene Descartes, thinks that we cannot reduce the transcendental reality of God into the limits of human concepts and postulations.

Our understanding of the phenomenal world is also not beyond any doubt. He writes, "But the uncertainty of human knowledge is not limited to the speculation about God. Our senses frequently deceive us. "Anybody can provide as many examples as he pleases of the ways our senses deceive or cheat us, since so many of their faults or deceptions are quite banal."[21] Why should we, therefore, not doubt whether our thinking and acting are but another dream; our waking, some other species of sleep."[22] Our analysis of scientific knowledge and philosophical speculation culminates in pyrrhonism. We cannot have the total understanding of nature and reality with the help of reason and ratiocination. And all our scientific knowledge and philosophical speculations are an attempt to discover the mystery of nature and reality with the tools of scientific realism and philosophical postulations which are inadequate and incapable in providing the knowledge of nature and reality with certainty and totality.

Einstein writes, "The individual feels the futility of human desires and aims and the sublimity and marvellous order which reveal themselves both in nature and in the world of thought. Individual existence impresses him as a sort of prison and he wants to experience the universe as a single significant whole."[23] Einstein here talks like an oriental mystic because he is aware of the limitations of scientific knowledge. And at the same time he is a great critic of Christianity also which is based on the concept of personal God and he has no hesitation in denouncing the doctrine of personal God which is based on the principles of fear and hope. The concept of personal God has been the greatest detriment in the development of liberal social system and postulation of scientific theories. But he is aware that the reason has its own limitations. It is beyond the reach of mind and the senses to comprehend truth and reality. All the rationalistic theories and postulation are expressed in a crass form. The rationalistic cannot provide the knowledge and understanding of the fundamental and ultimate goal. The knowledge acquired by scientific discoveries and experiments is useful to a great extent in the attainment of certain pragmatic ends, but the *summum bonum* of our life does not come from this kind of ratiocination. We have to ultimately depend and explore the ground and possibility of ontological mysticism to make our life richer and fuller. The knowledge which is based on the collection of simple datum does not provide the understanding of truth and reality. The datum acquired by rationalists and scientific materialists are based on the spacial and temporal multiplicity of phenomenal world and individual thinking. This does not give and express the true nature and form of existence and being. Multiplicity is appearance, it is not reality. Schrodinger writes, "The plurality that we perceive is only an appearance; it is not real. Vedāntic philosophy in which this is a fundamental dogma, has sought to clarify it by a number of analogies, one of the most attractive being the many-faceted crystal which while showing hundreds of little pictures of what is in reality simple existence object does not really multiply that object."[24]

Science deals with the shadow of sound and colour. It does not deal with sound or colour as such. The journey of science and philosophy culminated in ontological mysticism. Science based on ontological materialism breaks down at the level of relativity and quantum physics. Schrodinger does recognise the importance of profound knowledge taught by oriental seers and mystics. He talks very high of the Upaniṣadic teachings. He writes, "In Christian terminology to say: "Hence, I am God Almighty" sounds both blasphemous and lunatic. But please disregard these connotations for the moment and consider whether the above inference is not the closest biologists can get to proving God and immortality at one stroke. In insight is not new. The earliest records, to my knowledge, date back some 2500 years or more. From the early great *Upaniṣads* the recognition ĀTMAN = BRAHMAN (the personal self-equals the omnipresent, all-comprehending eternal self) was in Indian thought considered, far from being blasphemous, to represent the quintessence of deepest insight into the happenings of the world. The striving of all the scholars of *Vedānta* was, after having learnt to pronounce with their lips, really to assimilate in their minds this grandest of all thoughts."[25]

The quest for infinite bliss and beatitude has been instrumental in discovering the transcendental nature of man's being and existence. Man is just not another creature; he is a hibernated cosmic being. If man does not have this longing for the transcendental nature of being and existence, he would not have discovered the ultimate reality (*Brahman* or cosmic consciousness) and he would not have established his identity with ultimate reality. This is the most profound and the greatest discovery of Hinduism and Buddhism. I am self (*Ayamātma*), I am *Brahman* (*Ahaṁ Brahma Asmi*), *thou art that, that thou art* (*Tattvamasi*), I am that (*So'ham*) are known as the words of wisdom (*Mahāvākyas*). These words of wisdom are not just philosophical truth experienced by seers and saints, *yogīs* and *munis* in Indian tradition in their state of spiritual sublimity that is known as enlightenment (*Nirvāṇa*), but are a living reality. The state of *Nirvāṇa* is a state of self-consciousness where the distinction between 'me' and 'the world' breaks down completely. It is fused into unified undifferentiated whole that is *Brahman* or *Ātman*. Fritjof Capra observes, "The picture of an inter-connected cosmic whole which emerged from modern atomic physics has been used extensively in the East to convey the mystical experience of nature. For Hindus, the *Brahman* is the unifying thread in the cosmic wall, the ultimate ground of all beings."[26] The basic oneness of universe is the root concept of Ontological mysticism. In our ordinary life we are not aware of this basic unity. We believe in separate objects and events that are mental constructs of our discriminating and categorizing intellect and is called illusion (*Avidyā*). The central objective of Ontological Mysticism is to maintain a dynamic balance and mental equilibrium because in this state of mental equilibrium alone one would become conscious and experience the absolute oneness of the cosmos. Modern science especially Quantum Mechanics and the theory of relativity express in different ways that there is a basic unity in the universe. The separate objects and events, the different constituents of matter and the phenomena are all interconnected, interrelated and interdependent, though we understand as isolated and separate entity. To consider these abstract concepts of separate things and beings as natural realities is what is called in Hinduism '*Māyā*'. This estrangement of man has been viewed by Hinduism and Buddhism in the form of bondage. According to *Sāṁkhya* and *Vedānta* systems, the erroneous identification of man with non-self is nascence or *Avidyā*.

"Man is *Brahman* but due to the *Avidyā* he is estranged with himself. The Upaniṣadic seers have been in the quest of liberation from this estrangement. '*Know thyself*' is the *dharma* of man. It is sacramental and sacerdotal. It is a soteriological commitment to value and the goal. Man is a unit of value and the quest for his own identity and destiny is the *dharma* of man. Man is both rationalist and divine, an empiricist and transcendentalist in the present and the future. This uniqueness makes him the most superior creature in the world and provides him the spiritual power of transcendence. According to Hinduism: "*Dharmasya Tattavaṁ Nihitaṁ Guhyam*".

The *dharma* resides in the innermost recessed of one's being and existence. This is the quintessence of Hinduism. *Dharma* is the root concept of Hinduism. Different concepts and religio-philosophical systems of Hinduism are corollaries of this root concept. The concept of *karma*, rebirth, *ātman* or *Brahman* and *mokṣa* are different dimensions of *dharma*. However, Kashmir Śaivism and *Vedānta* have gone deeper into the philosophical and the mystical enquiry. *Śiva Sūtra* begins with *Chaitanya—ātma*, conscious self, which has absolute freedom of all knowledge and activity is the self or nature of reality. In the meditative insight and philosophical investigation, Ontological mysticism discovered the path of liberation and christened it as *mokṣa*. *Mokṣa* or *Nirvāṇa* is nothing, but the realization of one's own being. In the realization of one's own identity with the *Brahman*, lies the solution of man's estrangement and freedom. Thus Ontological Mysticism is a socio-spiritual discipline that aims at the realization of the supreme goal of life, not by renunciation, but by enriching the social system. According to Ontological Mysticism, human society is one and indivisible because there is only one *dharma* of man. This is the basic thrust of Ontological Mysticism.

Ontological mysticism works against the destruction of spiritual values that bind man with himself and with the society. The scientific and technological advancement is getting out of balance with our moral, spiritual and social performances. Instead of having control over the biosphere we must exercise control over ourselves. Ontological Mysticism speaks of control over ourselves and makes life fuller and richer with the help of meditative insight and esoteric techniques and discipline.

Science and social systems are organic and integral. In the socio-economic system this organic relation manifests in a linear cumulative and quantitative form. In this process of growth and differentialism, man is becoming more and more independent of nature. According to Ontological Mysticism only man possesses the scientific knowledge, power and spiritual vision to create a society of his own imagination and requirements. Yet, man does not enjoy absolute freedom. He is constrained by axial facts that each social system has a different rhythm of change. All social changes are not compatible with one another. Our analysis and examination of social change and transformation from pre-historic to modern times have revealed that our perception of time, space and causation have undergone a great change. The power that we possess today to transform nature and the extent and the range of man's socio-political and cultural life are on a scale that our ancestors would not have been able to comprehend. Our socio-political and economic and moral structures have undergone tremendous change and transformation through scientific and technological advancement. However, under technological society, man is becoming bereft of self-identity. This process of dehumanization is a bad omen. The genetic engineering, eugenics and test tube babies have made a great impact on our social systems and ethical values. The unholy alliance of science and technology is leading man towards a technological society that would unleash courses of history that would be self-destructing.

Albert Schweitzer writes, "Our Civilization is going through a severe crisis. The disastrous feature of our civilization is that it is far more developed materially than spiritually. Through the discoveries which now place the force of nature at our disposal in such an unprecedented way, the relation to other individuals, of social groups and of states have undergone a revolutionary change. We value two highly material achievements and no longer keep in our mind as vividly as desirable the importance of the spiritual. The essential nature of civilization does not lie in its material achievements, but in fact that individuals keep in mind the ideas of the perfecting of man, and the improvement of social and political condition of people and of mankind as a whole and that their habit thoughts is determined in living a constant fashion by such ideas."[27]

Annul the dangerous fissures of the present socio-political system. We have to learn to live together in harmony in spite of differences of civilization, culture, religion, race, languages and nationality. The situation is both delicate and dangerous. Arnold

Toynbee has stated in his monumental work *The Study of History*, "we are now waking up to the truth that we have unintentionally put ourselves in a new position in which mankind may have to choose between two extreme alternatives of committing genocide and learning to line hence forward as a single family..... Historical forces can be more explosive than an atom bomb. The very survival of mankind is in doubt. It is human nature that threatens its total annihilation. The question of survival is related to human nature. The very existence of mankind depends on the cultivation of such motives and thoughts that would annihilate the very geniality in man and lead to the harnessing of real being which is divine. Man is essentially a divine being. The experience of divinity has given birth to religion?" Ontological mysticism with its mystic techniques and spiritual humanism has the vision and the power to lead the bewildered humanity to the Vedāntic truth—"All is *Brahman* were self and the ultimate reality become one and to lead the vision of one world and one humanity (*Vasudhaiva Kuṭumbakam*)".

Arnold Toynbee was of the opinion that the West is well equipped to resist the temptation to despair because of its adherence to Christianity which has given it a unique power and distinction to overcome all kinds of temptations.

However, if we analyse Thales thoughts we would find that he is as dogmatic and pessimistic as Spengler. Spengler considered and viewed Western civilization as Faustian. H. Stuart Hughes, writes, "So much for Toynbee's empirical pretensions. For all of his scholarly scruple, his appeals to common sense, when on scratched the surface, one found him as dogmatic as Spengler—perhaps even more so, since his religious beliefs kept skewing his data. At bottom, what he had composed was a history of salvation. Still more, by the time he completed his work, Christianity itself could no longer contain his all-embracing piety. By then he had enveloped the entire roster of higher religions in a single paean of praise. He had become a living embodiment of "syncretism" in belief he had stressed as characteristic of "late" epochs. Thus, Toynbee's work threatened to collapse under the strain of elaborations and rectifications he had introduced into it. His ambiguous achievement suggested that a historian was possibly not the right sort of scholar to bring good sense to the job of cultural comparisons across time and space."[28]

However while writing an introductory note for India's Contribution to World Thought and Culture, Arnold Toynbee opines, "Today we are still living in this transitional chapter of the world's history, but it is already becoming clear that a chapter which had a Western beginning will have to have an Indian ending if it is not to end in the self-destruction of the human race. In the present age, the world has been united on the material plane by Western Technology. But this Wester skill has not only 'annihilated distance', it has armed the peoples of the world with weapons of devastating power at a time when they have been brought to point-blank range of each other without yet having learnt to know and love each other. At this supremely dangerous moment in the human history, the only way of salvation for mankind is an Indian way.... In the Atomic Age the whole human race has a utilitarian motic for the following this Indian way. No utilitarian motive could be stronger or more responsible in itself. The survival of the human race is at stake. Yet even strongest and most respectable utilitarian motive is only a secondary reason for taking Ramakrishna's and Gandhi and Ashoka's teaching to heart and acting on it. The Primary reason is that this teaching is right—and is right because it flows from a true vision of spiritual reality."[29]

The Western Civilization and science based on ontological materialism provides the concept of universe which is doctrinaire world view based on dualism. This dualistic view which has culminated in the philosophy of Descartes and which became the basis of classical physics assumed two principles in history of civilization. The first principle is conceived as ethical personality that guarantees that whatever happens in the historical process has a moral goal. And other force is the law that governs the nature. This dualistic principle is the basis of semetic religion. Albert Schweitzer writes, "The dualistic world view does not correspond with reality, for it comprises doctrines about the universe which cannot be made to square with the facts. It derives from a habit of thoughts which is under the influence of ethical belief. So, whilst Indian thought rests in the perfected form of world view, in mysticism, our own thought strives after a form of world view which is essentially naïve and not in agreement with the facts. Spinoza, Fichte Selling and Hegel's are concerned with the spiritual union with man with infinite being. Although their philosophy does not repose as mysticism, it is mysticism nevertheless in its essential. It is monastic thought under the influence of modern natural science that undertakes the great forward push against dualism. In actual facts the monastic method of thoughts, the only method with harmony with reality, has already gained the victory over the dualistic."[30]

Spirituality as conceptual knowledge and meditative insight is preparation for the life divine. The great truths of science and philosophy are not proved but experienced. This integral experience is a vivid and vibrant realization of ultimate reality. According to Ontological Mysticism ethics is important and significant as a stepping stone towards life divine. However, ethical values and norms are not the *summum bonum* of human life. The transcends of ethics, should not be misconstrued as nullification of the importance of ethics as it speaks of its intrinsic embodiment in the very existence of the being. According to ontological mysticism, the *summum bonum* of life is to become one with the ultimate reality (cosmic consciousness). The attainment of the enlightenment on *Nirvāṇa* is no longer bound by ethical norms and values. The enlightened being is vitally interested in the welfare of the world like Buddha. The Buddha has burning passion for social righteousness. *Nirvāṇa* cannot be attained by treading ethical path as enlightenment is an altogether different dimension of reality and being. However, the Ontological Mysticism does not deny the significance of ethics. Its basic concern and philosophical postulation is rooted in the concept of salvation. Civilization is an expression of cosmic spirit. All life is sacramental. All truth about God has its source in God. True knowledge is to know one's ignorance. The law of *karma* affirms the implicit presence of the past in the present. Ontological Mysticism is based on the close relationship of metaphysics and ethics. There is an indispensible relationship between the ultimate reality (*Brahman*) and man. Ethical theory must be rooted in transcendentality of metaphysics in philosophical conception of the relation between Human conduct and ultimate reality.

The values of ethical norms would be philosophically indicated if and only if the structure of cosmic process is spiritual. The *summum bonum* of life is to realize the ideal possibility and spiritual endeavour to divinize the life of a man because man is essentially *Brahman*. Spirituality is not hostile to science nor is true science detrimental to spirituality. The happy and harmonious blending of science and spirituality would alone herald a new era of human understanding and renaissance.

Ontological Mysticism alone corresponds with the truth and reality. It does provide the complete and total world view because it provides philosophical solution of fundamental questions of how man is to become spiritually one with reality? To become one with reality is in other words becoming spiritually one with infinite being that is cosmic consciousness, which is nature and destiny of all existence and being. All other world views and philosophical doctrines provide a fragmented picture of the truth and the reality. William James while summarising the importance and the relevance of mysticism observes, "In psychology, physiology and medicine whenever a debate between the mystics and the scientists has been taken once for all decided, it is the mystics who have usually proved to be right about the facts, while the Scientifists had the better of it in respect to theories."[31]

On the question of the cosmic origin or the first principle as why there is something not anything has occupied human enquiry since the dawn of the civilization. Science and philosophy have been trying to understand universal and a historical principle by which to speculate on the matter of ultimate reality. We live in the universe that contains both matter and consciousness. Matter and consciousness are the salient constituents of the universe. Matter and consciousness have been regarded as strange partners. Both are contained in reality which is the inner aspects of the web of the universe. At the present, the understanding of reality is undergoing great change. Scientific world views are making room for mysticism. The foundation of logic is ratiocination that any logical proposition must be either true or false. Logical reasoning does not accept any middle ground for partial truth or falsity. It follows from the above that if any proposition confirms that if a single logical statement and its negation is both simultaneously true and false then nothing can be ascertained. The logical propositions are true in logic but not in the physical world. According to logic, two plus two is four but if we mix two drops of water and two drops of water it will become one big drop. The logical proposition are too illogical but not in the physical world. It follows from the above that the universe in a limited circumstances only adhere to the propositions of logic.

Kant has long before stated that we cannot know things in themselves. He was the first original thinker to challenge the objectivity, the ideal that we know the things as they are because the concept with the help of which we know the things are our concepts due to our own understanding which pass through *a priori* categories of sensibility. Everything we know has a subjective element. Therefore, absolute objectivity is impossible. We know that the dilemma of appearance cannot be resolved by reason. Wittgenstein is nearer to truth when he says, "Whereof we cannot sayeth, thereof we must consign to silence".[32]

Our unity of life is based on esoteric experience. It speaks of the depth and of the dimensions of mystic experience. Thus some kind of esotericism forms the basis of all religion. However, different religious traditions have some salient features but the subterranean spiritual flow is the same. Hinduism and Buddhism emphasize immanence rather than transcendence. Both of them believe in continuous rather than discontinuous, both in theory and in experience, but underlying spirit is marked by spirituality. Though Buddhism denies the existence of transcendental creator 'God' in favour of an indefinable, non-personal absolute sources or dimension that can be experienced as the depth of human subjectivity. However, there is a presence of transcendence. Zen Buddhism and *Advaita* experience of *Satori* and the realization of *Brahman* speak of deeper spirituality. It is true that transcendence cannot be defined. In Karl Jaspers words, "Everything thinkable is rejected as invalid by transcendence. Transcendence can be defined by no predicate, objectified by no representations, and attained by no inference, although all the categories are applicable as means of saying that it is not a quality or a quantity, it is not a relation, it is not one, not many, not being, not nothing etcetera."[33] Karl Jaspers only affirms the traditional wisdom of all the religious scriptures and he speaks in the language of ontological mysticism.

Ontological Mysticism is a spiritual path to take man and woman from the *mundane to supra mundane* existence, from the dualism of subject and object to the higher and sublime state of oneness of infinity and divine being. It provides a moral and spiritual anchorage to mankind. The central object of ontological mysticism is to make man free from false subjectivity.

Philosophers have gone beyond an investigation of things in being to a systematic knowledge of being itself. We have been trying to understand reality, which has been hitherto appeared in different forms of metaphysics—materialism (everything is matter), spiritualism (everything is spirit) and hylozoism (cosmos is a living spiritual substance). In every case being has been defined as something existing in the world from which all these other things originated. But this kind of investigation has been rejected by Karl Jaspers. Karl Jaspers has shown that being *per se* unlike thing is being, is not an object and can never become one.

That is to say those things are those appearances of phenomena with the help of categorization; appear as clear, distinct and thinkable. Man can become an object only in part as physical existence. However, it does awaken in us a faculty of sensing what authentically is in the phenomena. Philosophy's search for reality or being is to secure a sound foundation for rational metaphysics of religion. Philosophy does change our entire consciousness of being and reality. It is at the heart of every philosophy. Religion based on such vision and philosophy succeeds in arresting the decline of moral values and enthroning it once again to the wills and minds of the people. True religion is that which provides sound rational metaphysics to seek to live in organic harmony with reality, the highest religious experience is categorized by mystical oneness. It is a quest to seek such transcendence within human self. Spiritual life is one of harmony with both mental and human orders. It is a mystic act of submersion of individuality in an organic relationship and in a mystic experienced oneness with reality.

Man is a spiritual being. In the words of St. Augustine, man is a spiritual substance. Transcendence is the essence of man. However, man is in the state of hibernation. He has forgotten his true being and transcendentality. In the words of T.S. Eliot "Where's the life we have lost in living". The task of Ontological Mysticism is to awaken the dormant divinity and to take man to the state of spiritual sublimity.

Einstein opins that, "man's ethical behaviour should be based effectually on sympathy, education, and social ties and needs, no religious basis is required." It speaks of Einstein's disenchantment with Christianity which is based on faith and not on Ontological Mysticism. Any religion which doesn't have sound Ontological Mysticism as the basis would become fundamentalist in nature. Einstein has spoken very highly of oriental religious tradition, he writes, "The religions of all civilized people especially the peoples of the Orient are primarily moral religions".[34] I have already provided a synoptic view of Taoism, Buddhism and Hinduism in previous chapters which speak of their spiritual profundity and divine sublimity.

Schrodinger writing "The striving of all the scholars of Vedānta was, after having learnt to pronounce with their lips, really to assimilate in their minds this grandest of all thoughts. Again, the mystics of many centuries, independently, yet in perfect harmony with each other (somewhat like the particles in an ideal gas) have described, each of them, the unique experience of his or her life in terms that can be condensed in the phrase : DEUS FACTUS SUM (I have become GOD)."[35]

The phenomenal world of plurality is only an appearance, it is not real this Vedāntic philosophy demonstrated by a number of analogies and metaphors. One of them is many faceted crystal which while showing innumerable pictures remains one object. This has already been quoted before in the context of the Buddhist monk demonstrating it before the Chinese empress. Schrodinger also talks very high of the *mahāvākya* of *tattvamasi*—Thou art that. This *mahāvākaya* symbolizes the basic truth, "I am this Whole World" or "I am the Cosmic Being (*Brahman*)".[36]

Consciousness is singular and not plural. Plurality is unreal. According to Schrodinger, the idealism of Berkley does not help in the proper understanding of the world. At the same time the plurality based on ontological materialism does not provide the true and the real picture of the world. According to Schrodinger, the only solution to this conflict in so far as any is available to us at all, lies in the ancient wisdom of *Upaniṣad*. We are living in the world which is both mystical and metaphysical. We all represent different aspects and modifications of the ultimate reality which in the Western terminology is called God, while in the *Upaniṣad* its name is *Brahman*. Schrodinger writes, "There is no plurality whatever. This is simply the mystical-metaphysical doctrine of the *Upaniṣads* itself: the plurality of sensitive beings is mere appearance (*māyā*); in reality they are all only aspects of the one being. The eschatology, which is really disturbing, is in the second half: the indispensible condition for liberation, that is the ending of the eternal cycle of birth and death, is that one should genuinely appropriate this doctrine as one's own, understand it, and assent to it not only with one's lips but with one's whole soul."[37] Nothing is inevitable in life except *Nirvāṇa* and oneness with cosmic consciousness. Essence of life is creativity. Authentic existence is a genuine becoming. There is a difference between knowledge and wisdom. Knowledge is bondage and wisdom is salvation. In the Indian tradition, it has been termed as *Aparājñāna* (knowledge) and *Parājñāna* (wisdom). *Aparājñāna* the knowledge is Subjectivisation of external objectivity and *Parājñāna* (wisdom) is subjectivisation of the supreme subjectivity. In *Śiva Sūtra*, in the second *sūtra* (aphorism) it has been said that the knowledge is a bondage.[38] The meaning of the word is determined in a cultural context. Here the word *jñāna* (knowledge) has been used in the relativistic context. Word does not have always a fixed meaning. According to *Amarakośa* the famous Sanskrit treatise, it has been discussed in detail. *Amarakośa* refers the word *hari* which is being used in the sense of deity, serpent and frog. Now, the meaning of Hari would be determined in the semantic context, otherwise it would lose its relevance. The same word, the *Jñāna*, has been used in *Nyāyasūtra* in transcendental context and according to which the *Jñāna* stands for the salvation.[39]

In *Īśa Upaniṣad* also the words *Vidyā* and *Avidyā* have been used in a relativistic context. According to *Īśa Upaniṣad*, those who worship *Avidyā* (rites) enter into blinding darkness. It has been further stated that the man who is aware of *Vidyā* and *Avidyā* together attains immortality through *Vidyā* (wisdom) by crossing over to death through *Avidyā*. Here the words *Vidyā* and *Avidyā* have been used in transcendental context.[40] It is evident that the orientalists were aware of the science and the philosophy of linguistics and semantics long before the Western philosophers and the linguists postulated the different theories of meaning and semantics. As the oriental tradition is rooted in monastic and mysticism, it has given more emphasis and importance to the moral and the spiritual aspects of human existence and being. And as a result, oriental philology and semantics are very much rooted in Ontological Mysticism.

According to Ontological Mystical tradition, life is not a mathematical formulation, it is a living and authentic creation of something new. Life is not futile and dead connection of cause and effect. Life moves on not by nullifying the past but by accepting it, in which the past takes a new birth in the form of future. The whole doctrine of rebirth is based on this book. Confucius says, "He who by reanimating the old can gain knowledge of the new is fit to be a teacher".

The world is only a complex within the self and my own body is complex within the world-complex. Schrodinger writes, "With equal certainty we must reject the world existing outside self, because both consists of the same empirical '*elements*', and in fact that to which the term 'world' is applied consists entirely of the elements which also belong to self."[41]

Schrodinger further writes, "We do not belong to this material world that science constructs for us. We are not in it; we are outside. We are only spectators. The reason why we believe that we are in it, that we belong to the picture, is that our bodies are in the picture. Our bodies belong to it, not only my own body, but of those friends, also of my dog and cat and horse and of all other people and animals. And this is my only means of communicating with them."[42] Further he raised the issue that "whence came I, whither go I". Science doesn't have any answer to such transcendental problems. Science is profoundly ignorant of the cosmic world of unity and being which has been conceived by Greek philosopher Parmenides. We are all a form and modification of that being and existence. We are essentially by nature and reality a cosmic being. This has been the vision and the discovery of the oriental seers and mystics. *Chāndogya Upaniṣad* says, "All that is *Brahman*. (This) is born from, dissolves in, and exists in That. Therefore, one should meditate by becoming calm. Because a person is identified with (his) belief, (therefore) just as the belief a man has in this world, so does he become after departing from here, therefore, one should save his thought and conviction in accordance with all that is *Brahman*."[43]

According to monastic and mystical tradition (cosmic consciousness) is the only truth and reality. The whole cosmos emanates from the ultimate reality and the whole cosmos exists in it and again merges into it. The new cosmology speaks of the same truth. It would be wrong to believe that the life of the universe is 13.7 billion years. It could be applicable to this universe, but there are many universes, as I have already stated before that the creation has been started from the time immemorial and it would continue till infinity. As there are innumerable universes and multi-galaxies, Milky Ways, etc., so, it would be applicable to this new findings of age of the universe as about 14 billion years may be applicable to this universe, but this is not the only universe which has been created out of the Big Bang. This is a continuous process.

According to Kashmir Śaivism, the entire creation is *Ābhāsa* manifestation of the ultimate reality. Creation is the result of self-movement (*Aspanda*) on the part of Śiva (cosmic consciousness) and *Śakti* (cosmic principles).

The world of waves and vibrations, things and beings is the self-manifestation of the non-dual cosmic consciousness. The supreme reality splits itself spontaneously into two: subject and object, and again coalesce into one undivided unity of transcendentality. The former is Illuminating (*Prakāśa*) and knowing entity, the latter is Veiling (*Vimarśa*) and activating creative entity. So long as the creative matrix (*Śakti*) remains merged in cosmic consciousness (Śiva) and does not get any scope for her activation, Śiva (cosmic consciousness) is unqualified and objectless. This theoretical dualism of Śiva (cosmic consciousness) and *Śakti* (cosmic principles) is symbolically represented by a grain of gram having two seeds closely joined and covered with a seed which is *māyā*. Creation starts only when they come apart. When cosmic principle or the creative matrix (*Śakti*) starts acting and reacting, differentiation starts. This differentiation between cosmic consciousness (Śiva) and creative matrix (*Śakti*) is the cause of the creative ideation (*Sṛṣṭi Kalpanā*). By differentiation is meant the objectivation of supreme subjectivity. *Bindū* (point), *Nāda* (*śabda*) and *kalā* (curvature) are the three phases of evolution. Involution is the process of crudification of cosmic consciousness which undergoes metamorphosis. Consciousness is transformed into crude matter. According to the variation in the degree of bondage of the creative matrix, consciousness has taken different forms, but the fundamental stuff is one and the same. When cosmic consciousness undergoes metamorphosis, the cosmic consciousness is called qualified consciousness. This qualified consciousness is called

Saguṇa Brahman. The creation is nothing, but the thought projection and metamorphosis of qualified consciousness. The creative matrix (*Śakti*) is *magna matter* who conceives, bears and nourishes the entire cosmos. Śiva is pure consciousness and *Śakti* is the activating principle. As the dynamic aspects of Śiva, the creative matrix ideates the world. The cosmos is nothing, but the creative ideation of the causal matrix.

Śiva (cosmic consciousness) and *Śakti* (creative matrix) coalesce into one undivided unity of transcendentality. The former is Illuminating (*Prakāśa*) and Witnessing entity, the latter Veiling (*Vimarśa*) and Activating entity.

Involution is a process of analysis, the one infinite self, and the one cosmic self is transformed into innumerable entity. In course of an analysis, the higher principles are involved in lower principles. The scientific explanation of the evolution and the creation of cosmos will be like this. After the formation of triangle of forces, sentient, mutative and static functional factors of creative matrix (inherent) in *Śakti*, the creative matrix, the three fundamental principles when they could not contain the state of equilibrium due to their belligerent nature, it burst from *bindū* (i.e., point). The *bindū* or point is both *Śūnyatā* (void) and *Guṇa*. In the void aspect of it, *bindū* or point is supreme *Brahman* or the ultimate transcendental reality. In its *Guṇa* aspect, it is *Śakti*, the creative matrix. As the result of constant clash amongst the three principles, it is, but logical that the balance would be disturbed and the triangle of forces would burst from one of the vertices. The point from which the triangle of forces bursts out is called *Bīja* (the seed of creation). When this seed of creation is expressed in metaphysical straight line, it is called *śabda* (*nāda*). It is dominated by the sentient principles. But due to the activation or domination of the static principles (*Tamo Guṇa*) the expression takes the form of a curvature which is known in Śaivism as *kalā* (curvature).

With the creation of the curvature and the waves and the vibrations the phenomenal world comes into being. In the scientific language, the universe is nothing, but a collection of different waves or curvatures. This bursting of the triangle of forces, is called the "Big Bang" in modern scientific terminology. In the Hindu philosophy, it is called *Sphoṭa*. Mādhavācārya, while enumerating the philosophy of Pāṇinī says, "The eternal word is called

Sphoṭa....."[44] *Sphoṭa* is nothing, but the bursting of the *Kāmabīja* (seed of the cosmos). It is the first sound. That is why it is said that in the beginning there was nothing but word and the word was God.

Bindū (point) is of the nature of Śiva (consciousness) and *Bīja* (the seed) of *Śakti* (creative matrix) and *Nāda* (word) represents the mutual relation with the ultimate reality, i.e., transcendentality. *Nāda* or *Śabda* is the first expression of creation.

Śabda Brahman is the cause of the manifest and differentiated word and meaning or the subtle and the crude objects. Without understanding the meaning and significance of *Sphoṭa* or the eternal word of creation, one cannot understand the significance of the *Brahman* (the reality). The enlightenment which is of the nature of supreme bliss is accomplished only after the proper understanding and significance of *nāda-bindū* (*śabda* and point).

When *Śakti* (cosmic principle) which is an operative principle becomes the creative principle, it is called *māyā*. *Māyā* is a causal matrix. It is the cause of physical manifestation. *Māyā* is the creative principle. It is a principle of obscuration and limitation. It limits the true nature of both the subject and object and the self and the universe. The reality is constituted of Śiva (cosmic consciousness) and *Śakti* (the creative matrix). It is the absolute and ultimate reality. *Śakti* has been conceived in Kashmir Śaivism as a liberator from the trammels of primeval ignorance. She is the beckon of light with whose help one can swim across the ocean of worldliness. And at the same time, she is basis of false universe (*Mithyā Jagadadiṣṭhāna*).[45]

Māyā is all pervasive because it is a causal matrix. It is subtle because it is incomprehensible to the intellect. It is eternal because it is the immanent aspect of the absolute. *Mālinīvijayottārā* says: "She is one, pervasive, undivided, the origin of the world, without beginning and the end, and it is also called the *Īśānī of Śiva*."[46] All creations are an unfolding and the manifestation of consciousness (*Citi*). Consciousness gets itself transformed into different forms and modifications. Śiva is consciousness force (*Citi Śakti*). Consciousness is the very cause of the universe which is the process of becoming perfect. Kurt F. Lei Decker says, "When the universe is in the process of becoming perfected means as much as when (all suchness) from *Sadāśiva* to the earth emerge".[47] We observe that the process of becoming perfected means mergence or reabsorption of the world process into Śiva. When all our loves and longings, aspirations and desires are directed into Him, we attain perfection by becoming one with Him. According to the *Śaivādvaita* School, the original cause of the world must be the unity of male and female principles as all beings are constituted of *he* and *she* parts. The *Śaivādvaita* systems form the basis of the *Sāṁkhya* conception *Tantra* and its commentator Kṣemarāja, *Śiva-tattva* is *Aprameya* "immeasurable"[48] and hence, He does not come within the purview of logical thinking and metaphysical speculation. *Śiva* (cosmic consciousness) is *Jñāna-tattva* and *Śakti* (creative principle) is *Kriyāśakti*. *Śakti* is a primordial force. She is the immanent principle of Śiva.[49] Śiva (cosmic consciousness) appears to have taken different forms. However, notwithstanding, the operation of the *Śakti* (creative principle), Śiva does not lose his transcendentality. Although *Śakti* (creative principle) exists at all levels of manifestation and unmanifestation, even in the state of *Paramaśiva*, the transcendentality of Śiva (cosmic consciousness) always remains uncontaminated. When *Śakti* (creative principle) is merged into Śiva (cosmic consciousness), She is called *Mūlaprakṛti*. *Śakti* or *Prakṛti* is a combination of three attributes or *Guṇas*, i.e., *Sattva* (sentient), *Rajaḥ* (mutative) and *Tamaḥ* (static). In the state of *Mūlaprakṛti*, all these three *Guṇas* remain in equilibrium and hence, *Śakti* (creative principle) is unmanifested. But the moment of equipoise is disturbed due to the belligerent nature of the three *Guṇas*, *Śakti* (creative principle) is transformed into *Māyā*, the creative matrix. This is why in Śaivism She is addressed as Cosmo form *Mahāmāyā*. The phenomenal world is the manifestation of her heterogeneous forms. It is nothing, but her playful motivation.

Evolution is a process of mental dilation. It is a movement from imperfection to perfection, from animality to divinity. It is the birth place of microcosm. It is a stream of consciousness. Involution is dominated by *Avidyā-Māyā* and evolution is guided by *Vidyā-Māyā*. The whole process of involution and evolution is known as *Brahma-Cakra* (eternal recurrence).

The philosophy and theory of evolution of Kashmir Śaivism have some similarity with *Sāṁkhya* system of Evolution. Both Kashmir Śaivism and *Sāṁkhya* systems hold the view that for the creation for the world active participation of both Śiva (*Puruṣa*) and *Śakti* (*Prakṛti*) is required. Unlike the *Vedānta*, both the systems profess that the world is neither real nor unreal. It is neither unreal like man's horn, nor real since it passes away. According to Kashmir Śaivism, the universe is neither real nor an illusion. It is a relative truth. However, Kashmir Śaivism, theory of evolution is nearer to the *Sāṁkhya* than the *Vedānta*. It stands in between *Sāṁkhya* and the *Vedānta*. It is real for the microcosm, but unreal from transcendental perspective. In the process of involution, Śiva (cosmic consciousness) is metamorphosed into crude physicality. In the process of evolution, the Crude physicality is transformed into the psychic being. Here Kashmir Śaivism agrees with the materialists that mind is the by-product of matter. But contrary to the materialistic thinkers Kashmir Śaivism holds that matter itself is nothing but the transformed and modified form of consciousness. However, the phenomenal world is not false appearance due to original Error. The world is neither *Māyā*, illusion nor reality. The cosmic consciousness has no externality.

According to Kashmir Śaivism, the entire creation is *Ābhāsa*. The phenomenal world is real in the sense that it is manifestation of *Parama Śiva*. Evolution is the result of self-movement (*Spanda*) on the part of Śiva-*Śakti*. The world of waves and vibrations, things and beings is the self-manifestation of non-dual Cosmic Consciousness. The Supreme Reality splits itself spontaneously into two sections—subject and object. *Māyā* is essentially identical with Cosmic Consciousness. She creates infinite forms, but never swerves from the essence. Gopinath Kaviraj states: "When the universe comes into being it does so as only an image within the unique self. The universe as such is varied, but underlying it is the pure and simple unity of the *Caitanya* revealing itself to the eye of diligent search (*Anusandhāna*). The manifestation of the universe, due to the Free Will (*Svātantra*) of the Absolute, is thus the process of *Ābhāsa* and for the initiation of this process nothing beyond the play of the will is needed...."[50] The world of appearance is real in the same way as an image is real, but it has no existence apart from the consciousness in which it is manifested. Its existence is only the existence of the Absolute.

All things of the universe are made of the same cosmic consciousness. The transcendental aspects of Śiva (cosmic consciousness) of ultimate reality are the fundamental stuff of the cosmos. *Śakti* (the creative matrix) is the cause of multiplicity. She is the *Vimarśa* (Veiling) aspects of reality. Śiva is the witnessing consciousness. *Śakti* is the binding principle.

The material cause and the efficient cause are the cardinal principles of creative idealism. Every object has these two causes. Over and above these, there is a conjunctive principle which acts as a catalytic agent between the material and efficient cause. Śiva is the material cause and *Śakti* is the vital force. As efficient cause, Śiva is primary and *Śakti* is the secondary factor. Śiva is consciousness force and all-pervading entity. *Śakti* is always merged in Śiva. She activated the process of creation when Śiva offers an opportunity and grants divine permission. Hence, the doer ship lies with Śiva. The ultimate reality which is called in Kashmir Śaivism, *Paramaśiva*, remains the fundamental stuff and supreme doer, the nucleus of all the nuclei, the soul of all the souls and life of life. He is described as one because he can be realised by making the mind apexed or one pointed. Only the apexed mind realizes the transcendental nature of the absolute in the state of deep meditation in which mind is dissolved into divine consciousness. This stage is called mystic oneness of Śiva and Śakti.

According to Śivādvaita School of Kashmir Śaivism, supreme reality is of the nature of pure consciousness, self-luminous and all-pervading. Its mystic experience is characterised by vividness, directness and bliss. Śiva is *Sat* (Being), *Śakti* is *Satī* (Being as power), Śiva is *Cit* (Consciousness), *Śakti* is *Citi* (Consciousness as force). Śiva is *Ānanda* (Bliss), *Śakti* is *Paramānanda Sandoharūpa* (Soul of bliss).

Śiva is *Brahman*, *Śakti* is *Brahmamayī*. Some say that Truth is *Advaita* (non-dual), some others speak of it as *Dvaita* (dual). But it is in the *Śaivādvaita* view *Dvaitādvaitavivarjītā*: neither the one nor the other. It is beyond dualism and non-dualism.

Thus the theory of evolution enunciated by Kashmir Śaivism is most logical and scientific. It solves to great extent all the intricacies of both science and philosophy. Kashmir Śaivism is essentially rooted in Ontological Mysticism and hence it is the meeting ground of both science and philosophy. In mystical experience, knowledge and wisdom become one. Monism and mysticism are true philosophy and science. Oneness with reality is the goal of both science and spirituality. Convergence of science and Ontological Mysticism will herald a new era of spiritual humanism. Spiritual humanism is the hope and the promise of mankind. Science and spirituality are integral form of human existence.

Rene Descartes observes, "The feebleness of human understanding and the arrogance that masks it is most apparent when we try to reduce the transcendent reality of God to the limits of human concepts. But the uncertainty of human knowledge is not limited to speculation about God. Our senses frequently deceive us: "Anybody can provide as many examples as he pleases of the ways our senses deceive or cheat us, since so many of their faults or deceptions are quite banal". Why should we, therefore, not doubt whether our thinking and acting are but another dream, our waking, and some other species of sleep?"[51] The Quantum Mechanics have made a ground breaking revelation and that the object has no existence independent of the observing mind. According to new experiments and revelation in science, the scientists have accepted the mysterious limitation between the subject and the object. We have no perception or of any object without its being modified or tinged by the observing mind. The element of mysticism in any discovery and observation has been accepted. Schrodinger writes, "On the other hand (and this is my second objection), the mere contention that every observation depends on both the subject and the object, which are inextricably interwoven—this contention is hardly new, it is almost as old as science itself. Protagoras and Democritus maintained that all our sensations, perceptions, and observations have a strong personal, subjective tinge and do not convey the nature of the thing-in-itself (the difference between them was that Protagoras dispensed with the thing-in-itself, to him our sensations were the only truth, while Democritus thought differently)."[52]

Pythagoras was a great mystic and is considered as the father of western mystic tradition. According to Pythagoras, philosophy is a means of spiritual purification. He talks about the destiny of soul with its possibility of rising and becoming one with the divine. Some scholars suggests that he incorporated the practice of Orphic mystery cult known for its raw emotional manifestation which he attempted to reform with his emphasis on knowledge and science as a path to salvation. However, it has been accepted by modern scholars that he was greatly influenced by Indian mystical traditions and some of the Pythagoreans lived a life of Indian mystics and they were the firm believer in rebirth and salvation. The concept of rebirth and *Nirvāṇa* (salvation) are the root concepts of ancient mystic traditions. Even the great psychologists Jung is considered as believer in the identity of soul and God.

Murray Stein writes, "With the theory of synchronicity, Jung went out on a limb. Here the psyche by itself would not support him. Nevertheless at the age of seventy five, he must have felt he has earned the right to indulge himself in this kind of cosmological speculation. He was ready to go into print with one of his wildest notions, the unity of self and being. Is this so different from saying that the self and God are one? He took the risk of sounding like a prophet or worse as a crank."[53]

Now, the search for truth and reality is becoming deeper and spiritual.

With the new discovery of science that has broken down the mysterious boundary between the subject and the object, between spirituality and science, there is a difference between the knowledge and wisdom. In Indian tradition, knowledge is termed as *Aparā-Jñāna* and wisdom as *Parā-Jñāna*. Knowledge is considered as bondage because it does not give the proper and the complete understanding of anything it has been accepted by Neil Bohr, Heisenberg and Schrodinger's that the object has no existence independent of the observing mind. This was a philosophical stand taken by Kant. According to Kant we cannot know thing in itself. According to Kant space and time are *a priori* categories of mental intuition, space being the form of external and the time that of internal sensibility or intuition. However, Kant's idea was not completely wrong but it required some modification. Bohr and Heisenberg have come out with a very original theory that we cannot make any factual statements about the physical objects. We cannot have complete and gapless description of physical objects. This has long been stated by Vedic seers that the reality is beyond the reach of speech and mind.[54] And it has been considered in Indian tradition, knowledge. The Kashmir Śaivism also believes that all our experiences have limitations of time (*kāla*) and *Niyati* (fate). Kant's theory deals with the epistemological problem. He has formulated his theory with reference to knowledge. On the other hand, Kashmir Śaivism and Vedānta have formulated the theory of epistemology on the foundation of Ontological Mysticism. According to Kashmir Śaivism, and *Vedānta* reality is unknown in common parlance but with the esoteric practice and meditation, reality is knowable. One can experience reality in the state of spiritual sublimity and divine effulgence. According to Kashmir Śaivism and *Vedānta*, to know is to become. Those who have the knowledge and the experience of *Brahman* (reality) becomes *Brahman*. And in this context the very second aphorism of *Śiva Sūtra* should be understood. According to *Śiva Sūtra's*, *sūtra* second that knowledge is bondage, here the knowledge has been used in the sense of the ignorance of once own real nature in reality, the real nature of self is cosmic consciousness. In the absence of this knowledge of the real nature of one's own being and existence, knowledge becomes bondage. The *Īśo Upaniṣad* has also the same opinion and it also believes that according to those who worship *Avidyā* (rites) enter into blinding darkness; but into greater darkness than that enter they who are engaged in *Vidyā* (knowledge) (*Īśo upaniṣad,* verse 9). The word *Vidyā* has been used in a different sense. According to Wittgenstein, the word does not have any fixed meaning; its meaning depends upon the uses. And the meaning of a word could be considered in a cultural context. And because of this there has been great confusion in understanding the word like *Vidyā* and *Jñāna* in Sanskrit semantics. The *Īśo Upaniṣad* and Kashmir Śaivism have used word *Jñāna* (knowledge) and *Vidyā* in the context of spirituality and Ontological Mysticism. Apart from without the proper cultural context it leads to many Sanskrit lexicons to misunderstanding and confusion. According to the mystic and the monastic Indian tradition the supreme goal of life is not only to acquire knowledge, but to become and to know the transcendental nature of his own existence and being. What has been the goal and the supreme end of life is now being considered by a great scientist like Heisenberg also as the *summum bonum* of life. He writes, "I do not think I am prejudiced against the importance that science has from the purely human point of view. I had expressed by the original title of these lectures, and I have explained in the introductory passages, that I consider science an integrating part of our endeavour to answer the one great philosophical question which embraces all others, the one that Plotinus expressed by his brief : who are we? And more than that: I consider this not only one of the tasks, but the task of science, the only one that really counts."[55]

Knowledge is a dialectical process and the wisdom is a *satori*. The scientific research and recent discovery have brought about great change and revolution in our perception of the universe and the mankind. In process of our scientific research universe reveals itself. However, the more we try to understand the scientific truth and reality it becomes more mysterious.

Life is a great enigma. The more we try to resolve, the more enigmatic it becomes. With all the monumental scientific discoveries, the modern era is only a mere blip on the timeline of human achievements. The new discoveries have posed some basic questions which are still unresolved. One of the big problems before scientific community is to understand the real nature and function of elementary particle interaction but the problem which is vexed and unresolved is why the elementary particles are what they are. The question of why does not belong to the domain of pure science. It comes within the purview and domain of Ontological Mysticism or spirituality. But the greatest problem that the seekers of truths are trying to understand and comprehend what has been raised by Plotinus and the whole community of Indian mystics (*Who am I?*) Lisa Randall also comes to the same conclusion and writes, "Understanding nature, life and the universe poses extraordinarily difficult problems. We all would like to better understand who we are, where we came from, and where we are going—and to focus on things larger than ourselves and more permanent than the latest gadget or fashion."[56]

The anthromorphic character of God is predominant feature of religion. Religion becomes theology and almost all the religious tradition the concept of personal God dominates. This has created much misunderstanding about the core concept of religion which is spirituality. The dross of anthromorphism is based on the egocentric cravings, desires and fears which are the greatest impediments in the path of salvation. However, it is the mystery of sublime and divine effulgence that guides our destiny because we are all the Whole of reality. Einstein writes, "The individual feels the futility of human desires and aims and the sublimity and marvellous order which reveal themselves both in nature and in the world of thought. Individual existence impresses him as a sort of prison and he wants to experience the universe as a single significant whole. The beginning of cosmic religious feelings already appear at an early stage of development, e.g., in many of the Psalms of David and in some of the Prophets. Buddhism, as we have learned especially from the wonderful writings of Schopenhauer, contains a much stronger element of this."[57] Now, the scientists are also coming to the conclusion that subject and object, God and the world belong to the same reality. The same elements compose both my mind and the phenomenal world. Subject and object are only one reality. Plurality is a misnomer. This has been expressed by *Upaniṣad 'tattvamasi'*, i.e., *thou art that*; I am the *Brahman*, I am this whole world because I am the reality. The world is an appearance. It is not real. This is the quintessential teachings of Kashmir Śaivism and *Vedānta*. Consciousness is by its very nature a *singular tantrum*. Science breaks down at the level of transcendentality. The propositions of natural science have their own limited validity. Science has failed to develop a world of a nature as a whole or about the essence of things because of its limitations. Science has even failed to reveal the inherent essence of natural phenomena.

As I have stated before that Kashmir Śaivism, *Advaita Vedānta*, Buddhism and Taoism are based on Ontological Mysticism. Ontological mysticism is the foundation of the non-dual systems of philosophy and modern science. Gauḍapāda is the founding father of non-dual system of *Vedānta*. *Māṇḍūkya Kārikā* is a treatise of non-dual system of *Vedānta* and it could be considered as the source of modern scientific thinking. There has been harmonious and happy blending of Buddhism, Taoism and non-dual Vedāntic systems. Professor S.N. Das Gupta in his celebrated work *'A History of Indian Philosophy'* has made observation regarding Gauḍapāda, "Gauḍapāda thus flourished after all great Buddhist teachers Aśvaghoṣa, Nāgārjuna, Asaṅga and Vasubandhu and I believe that there is sufficient evidence in his *Kārikās* for thinking that he was possibly himself a Buddhist and considered that the teachings of the *Upaniṣads* tallied, with those of Buddha."

Thus, at the beginning of the fourth chapter of his *Kārikā* he says that he adores that great man (*dvipadaṁ varam*) who by knowledge as wide as the sky realized (*sambuddha*) that all appearances (*Dharma*) were like the vacuous sky (*gaṅganopaman*). He thus goes on to say that he adores him who has dictated (*deśita*) that the touch of the untouch (*Asparśa Yoga*—probably referring to *Nirvāṇa*) was the goal that produced happiness to all beings and that he was neither in disagreement with the doctrine nor found any contradiction in it (*avivadaḥ aviruddhaśca*)..... In IV.19 of his *Kārikā*, he again says that the Buddha has shown that there is no coming into being in any way (*sarvathā buddhai-rajati paridipitaḥ*)."[58] Knowledge is a dialectical process. Hence, it is natural that a system of thoughts incorporates some of the basic ideas and thoughts of previous philosophical systems and those ideas are assimilated in a systematic way which gives birth to a new thought in the form of a new synthesis. Thus, it is no wonder that the great Buddhist truth of indefinable and unspeakable *Vijñāna* and *Śūnyatā* have been assimilated in Gauḍapāda's *Māṇḍūkya Kārikā* and it has been equated with *Ātman* or *Brahman* of *Upaniṣad*. This could be the new synthesis of Vedāntic thoughts in the form of Buddhist tradition and thinking. Prof. S.N. Das Gupta has tried to prove that Gauḍapāda might have been a Buddhist and his whole philosophical theory has been borrowed from the teachings of Buddha. I would not agree with Prof. Das Gupta that Gauḍapāda was a Buddhist but I do agree with Das Gupta that Gauḍapāda had incorporated some of the thoughts and ideas of the *Vijñānavāda* and *Śūnyavāda* in his *Māṇḍūkya Kārikā*. There is a great similarity between Nāgārjuna's doctrine of no origination and Gauḍapāda's theory of *Ajātivāda*. *Māṇḍūkya Kārikā* says, "There is no dissolution, no birth, none in bondage, none aspiring for wisdom, no seeker of liberation and none liberated. This is the absolute truth."[59]

According to both Nāgārjuna's doctrine of no origination and *Gauḍapāda's* theory of *Ajātivāda*, duality doesn't exist. There is non-dual reality which is called *Ātman* or *Brahman* in *Vedānta* and *Śūnyatā* (emptiness) in Buddhism. Both Buddhism and *Vedānta* while enumerating their philosophical systems have accepted the two truths, transcendental and empirical. From the transcendental point of view, the world doesn't exist. All is *Brahman*. Hence, there is no creation, no dissolution, no one in bondage and hence, there is no need of any method and means for the attainment of liberation. There is no seeker from the bondage as bondage doesn't exist. *Brahman* or emptiness is one without second; all that exist is verily the *Brahman* or emptiness. The birth and death, bondage and liberation could not be discussed as that which does not exist as the horns of a hare. In the Buddhist treatise of great value called *Vissudhi Magga*, it has been stated that there is path but no walker, there is *nirvāṇa* but no seeker, and there is misery but no miserable. The same truth and philosophy has been stated by J. Krishna Murthy in the following words, "The truth is pathless. There is a choiceless awareness." Gauḍapāda has given the most brilliant and far reaching exposure of Vedāntic thought in his *Māṇḍūkya Kārikā*. While expounding his philosophical system he has formulated Vedāntic thought and philosophy purely from the transcendental perspective. In summarising his whole philosophical system, he said that it is the repetition of the teachings of *Chāndogya Upaniṣad* that "All this is *Brahman*. Only the *Brahman* exists. There is no phenomenal world." From the Gauḍapāda point of view individual selves are all a piece from the very beginning and it is eternally inseparable and it is *Ātman*. The individual self is unborn and enlightened *Brahman*. The individual self is *Brahman* hence there is no need of any enlightenment, it is enlightened. Gauḍapāda rejects the theory of causation in the fourth chapter of *Kārikā* and propagates the doctrine of *Ajātivāda*. *Brahman* has never become the universe. There has never been any creation. The one does not become many as many do not exist. According to the doctrine of *Ajātivāda* or theory of no origination there is ultimate reality which could not be described and which is beyond the reach of mind and the senses. Gauḍapāda doesn't believe in the process of becoming and hence, its resultant exposition is that there is no creation. Śaṅkara introduced the concept of *Vivartavāda* to explain the world of appearance.

According to which *Brahman* appears as the phenomenal world without losing its essential nature and transcendentality. It is like a rope appearing as a snake. Gauḍapāda being an ardent believer in non-dual system of thought and propagator of *Ajātivāda* according to which the *Brahman* has never become the universe. And he outrightly rejects the causality of causation in the fourth chapter of *Māṇḍūkya Kārikā*. According to Gauḍapāda, as *Ātman* is the only reality and is always in the state of transcendentality he just rejects any form of worship and practice of meditation or the attainment of *Nirvāṇa*. Gauḍapāda says, "The *Jīva* betaking itself to devotion (*upāsanā*) thinks itself to be related to the *Brahman* that is supposed to have manifested Himself. He is said to be of narrow intellect because he thinks that before creation all was of the nature of the unborn (Reality)."[60] According to Gauḍapāda, it would be futile exercise to indulge in any kind of devotional practices to attain liberation. In the second chapter Gauḍapāda has dealt in detail about the concept of illusion. According to which the whole theory of dualism that includes the object and the act of worshipping and mediating is illusory because only the attributeless non-dual *Brahman* is the ultimate reality. It would be wrong on the part of the individual self or a devotee to think that by practicing meditation and other rituals he would regain his lost glory and spiritual sublimity of *Brahman*. Only the fools and the narrow minded intellect indulge in such kind of devotional practices and thinking that he or she would regain the real nature of *Brahman* which he was before the birth. The *Kena Upaniṣad* also supports this kind of stand. According to *Talavakara* (*Kena*) "That which is not uttered by speech, that by which speech is revealed, know that alone to be *Brahman*, and not what people worship as an object."[61] The *Avadhūta Gītā* which is also considered a text of the school of *Vedānta* representing the real form of *Advaita* and non-dualism is in full agreement with Gauḍapāda and it observes, "The wise, my child, give up all meditations; they give up all good and evil deeds and drink the nectar of renunciation. I am free from disease—my form has been extinguished."[62] Further *Avadhūta Gītā* states, "In thy mind there is neither the meditation, nor the object of meditation. Thou hast no *Samādhi*. There is no region outside thee, nor is there any substance or time. I am the nectar of Knowledge, homogeneous Existence, like the Sky (formless)."[63] Reality is neither devoid (*śūnya*) nor is non-void (*aśūnya*). Reality is a cosmic consciousness. It is neither pure nor of impure nature, neither form nor formless. Reality is of the form of its own nature. The purity and impurity, the virtue and the sin, bad and good are all rooted in dualistic nature of things and beings. But the cosmic consciousness which constitutes ultimate reality is beyond any kind of dualism, subject or object, virtue or vice, etc. It is beyond also transcendental and relative states. Reality does not come within the purview of the domain of our knowledge and hence there could not be versification. The cosmic consciousness lives and has its being in the consciousness of homogeneous being. The philosophers and the rationalists only prattle about Truth and Reality. And hence there is no need of any kind of religious prostration, worship, performance of rituals for the attainment of enlightenment and liberation because self is ever luminous, pure cosmic consciousness and state of liberation (*tūrya*). *Avadhūta Gītā* rejects all kinds of religious practices and performance of rituals in the strongest possible condemnation. It says, "By making pilgrimage to Thee Thy all-pervasiveness has been destroyed by me. With my meditation Thy transcendence of the mind has been destroyed by me. Thy transcendence of speech has been destroyed by me by my singing Thy praise. Ever forgive me these three sins."[64] This is a pure form of non-dual philosophical school. In the state of ultimate reality (cosmic consciousness) there is no difference between cause and effect. Reality is one indivisible and all comprehensive absolute. We cannot make any differentiation between self and not-self, the world and God, *Puruṣa* and *Prakṛti*. According to this system of thought there has been no creation. The world is not a modification of the *Brahman*.

Māṇḍūkya Kārikā says that, "The immortal cannot become mortal, nor can the mortal ever become immortal. For, it is never possible for a thing to change its nature."[65] *Māṇḍūkya Kārikā* further says, "The unreal cannot be born either really or through *Māyā*. For the son of a barren woman is neither in reality nor in illusion."[66]

From the Gauḍapāda's philosophical perspective, the introduction of the concept of *Māyā* does not explain the existence of the phenomenal world rather it creates confusion and contradiction in propagating the teachings of *Vedānta* as a system of *Advaita*. It loses its purity and fervour of non-dual system of *Vedānta*.

Māṇḍūkya Kārikā and *Avadhūta Gītā* have enunciated the non-dual school of thought from the transcendental point of view, but when we discuss the nature and reality from empirical point of view, the world is a relative truth. It is a modification of Spinoza's substance, the *Vedāntic Brahman*, the Buddhist's *Śūnyatā* (emptiness) and Taoist's Tao. There is a creation. I have already discussed in previous chapters and explained the nature of world as a modification of cosmic consciousness. Buddhism and *Vedānta* have discussed the truth from transcendental and empirical points of view. The whole philosophical and the scientific formulations are based on Ontological Mysticism. From one perspective there is a *Brahman* and from the other there is a world. Both the scientific and the spiritual perspectives are required for understanding truth and nature. The question of, Who am I? is not a heuristic hypothesis. Reality, existence, being, *Brahman* or God are not empty words. These are pregnant with deep metaphysical and scientific import. Schrodinger writes, "Hence this life of yours which you are living is not merely a piece of the entire existence, but is in a certain sense, the whole; only this whole is not so constituted that it can be surveyed in one single glance. This, as we know, is what the Brāhmins express in that sacred, mystic formula which is yet really so simple and so clear: *Tat tvam asi*, this is you. Or, again, in such words as 'I am in the east and in the west, I am below and above, I am this whole world'."[67]

I am in complete agreement with the observation of Schrodinger, "Briefly stated, it is the view that all of us living beings belong together in as much as we are all in reality sides or aspects of one single being which may perhaps in Western terminology be called God while in the *Upaniṣads* its name is *Brahman*. A comparison used in Hinduism is of the many almost identical images which a many-faceted diamonds makes of some *one* object such as the sun. We have already conceded that we are here dealing not with something logically deducible, but with mystical metaphysics—just like the acceptance of a real object-world (usually called an external world, but it includes one's own abode)."[68]

For proper understanding and comprehension of Ontological Mysticism, one will have to equip oneself with proper frame of mind, cultivated by mystical and moral discipline of non-attachment, discrimination and the longing for the realisation of truth in its wholeness. Without proper understanding the study of philosophy and science in a dilettante fashion will land him in confusion and contradiction. The path of spirituality and ontological mysticism is like walking on the razor's edge. The Upaniṣadic seers have rightly stated "Arise, awake, and learn by approaching the excellent ones. The wise ones describe that path to be impassable as a razor's edge, which when sharpened, is difficult to tread on."[69]

From the Ontological mystical perspective, ultimate reality is one and homogeneous being and existence. It is cosmic consciousness. There is only one consciousness. World and reality are constituted of this cosmic consciousness. It is beyond the reach of both philosophy and science. Neither exact science is really possible nor can any philosophical knowledge comprehend the nature of reality. It is mystical and metaphysical.

References

1. *Philosophy and Ethics, The Philosophy of Civilization,* Albert Schweitzer. A & C Black Ltd., 4, 526 Soho Square, London, W. 1, 1929, pp. 2-3.
2. *Quantum Questions, Mystical Writings of the World's Greatest Physicists,* Ken Wilber, p. 123.
3. *Ibid.*, p. 126.
4. *Ibid., The Mechanism Demands Mysticism,* p. 129.
5. *Science and Humanism: Physics in our Times.* Erwin Schrodinger, Cambridge, At The University Press, 1952, pp. 50-51.
6. *Physics and Philosophy: The Revolution in Modern Science,* Werner Heisenberg, p. 55.
7. *Ibid.*, p. 24.
8. *Quantum Questions, Mystical writings of the World's Greatest Physicists.* Ken Wilber, In the *Mind of Some Eternal Spirit,* p. 135.
9. *Knocking on Heavens Door,* Lisa Randall, Harper Colin Publishers, p. 412.
10. *Science and Humanism: Physics of Our Time,* Erwin Schrodinger, 1952, p. 51.
11. *Pure Rationalist has No Place Here, Quantum Questions,* p. 163.
12. *Science and Humanism, Physics of Our Time, Form not substance—The Fundamental Concept,* Erwin Schrodinger, 1952, p. 18.
13. *Muṇḍakopaniṣad,* Chapter II-2-9, p. 96.
14. *My View of the World,* Erwin Schrodinger, pp. 66-67.
15. *Science and Religion. Quantum Questions,* pp. 112-113.
16. *The Roots of Consciousness,* Jeffrey Mishlone, Marlow & Company, 1993. *Consciousness: A Hyperspace View,* p. 376.
17. *Ibid.*, pp. 410-411.
18. *My View of the World,* Erwin Schrodinger, p. 64.
19. *Ibid.*, p. 83.
20. *The Roots of Consciousness,* Jeffrey Mishlone, Marlow & Company 1993. *Consciousness: A Hyperspace View,* pp. 41-42.
21. *Meditations and Other Metaphysical Writings,* Rene Descartes. Complete Essays, p. 669.
22. *Ibid.*, p. 674.
23. *Quantum Questions, Cosmic Religious Feeling,* p. 104.
24. *Ibid., The Mystic Vision,* p. 96.
25. *Ibid., The I That is God,* p. 93.
26. *The Tao of Physics.*
27. *Civilization and Ethics, The Philosophy of Civilization.* Part II, Albert Schweitzer. A. 2C Black Ltd., 4, 526 Soho Square London, W. 1. 1921, pp. 1-2.

28. *The Decline of the West*, Oswald Spengler. An Abridged Edition Helmut Werner, Oxford University Press, New York, Oxford 1991. Preface to Present Edition, p. XIV.
29. India's Contribution to World Thought and Culture, Vivekananda Kendra Prakashan Trust, 5, Singarachari Street, Triplicane, Chennai – 600 006, Oct. 1970, p. xv (Arnold Toynbee on Sri Ramakrishna).
30. *Indian Thoughts and its Development*, Albert Schweitzer, pp. 12-13.
31. *What Psychical Research has Accomplished*, In Gardner Murphy and Robert O. Ballon (Eds.) William James on Psychical Research, London. Chatto and Windus, 1961.
32. *Philosophic III*, pp. 38-39.
33. Karl Jaspers.
34. *Ibid.*, p. 104.
35. *Ibid.*, *The I That is GOD*, p. 93.
36. *Ibid.*, p. 98.
37. *My Views of the World, The Doctrine of Reality*, p. 101.
38. *Śiva Sūtra*. Chapter I, *Sūtra* II.
39. *Jñānatā Mukti*. *Nyāya Sūtra*.
40. *Īśa Upaniṣad*, Verse 11.
41. *My Views of the World, The Doctrine of Reality*, p. 12.
42. *Quantum Questions, Why not Talk Physics?* pp. 83-84.
43. *Chāndogya Upaniṣad*, III.14. I.
44. *The Sarva-Darśana Saṅgraha*, p. 220.
45. *Lalitā Sahasranāma*, verse 10.2.
46. सा चैका व्यापिनीरूपा निष्कला जगतानिधिः।

    अनाधन्ता शिवेशानी व्ययहीना च कथ्यते।

    Mālinīvijayottara Ch.1 Vir. 26 Kashmir Sanskrit Texts and Studies, Shrinagar, 1922.
47. *Pratyabhijñāhṛdayam*, p. 20.
48. *Aprameyan tato Jñeyaṁ śivatattvaṁ varānane. Svacchandatabtram* 10, 674; Vol. V, Part B, (ed. Kashmir Series of Texts and Studies, 1993), p. 281.
49. *Śaktiḥ sa śivasya śaktiḥ. Ānandasūtram* verse 2, p. 3.
50. *Tr:pūra-Rahasyam*, p.11.
51. *Meditations and Other Metaphysical Writings*, Rene Descartes. The Complete Essays, p. 669.
52. *Science and Humanism, Physics in our Time*. Erwin Schrodinger. Cambridge, At the University Press, 1952, p. 52.
53. *Jung's Map of the Soul*, Murray Stein. Open Coat, Chicago and La Salle Illinois 1998, p. 204.
54. यतो वाचो निर्वतन्ते अप्राप्य मनसा सह।

    Tattirīya Upaniṣad, 11.4.1
55. *Science and Humanism, Physics in Our Times*. Erwin Schrodinger, p. 51.
56. *Knocking on Heaven's Door,* Lisa Randall, p. 412.

57. *Quantum Questions, Cosmic Religious Feelings*, p. 104.
58. *A History of Indian Philosophy*, Prof. S.N. Das Gupta, pp. 423-29.
59. *Māṇḍūkya Kārikā*, Chapter II, Verse 32.
60. *Māṇḍūkya Kārikā*, Chapter III, *Advaita Prakaraṇas,* Verse 1.
61. *Kena Upaniṣad*, Chapter I, Verse 5.
62. *Avadhūta Gītā*, Chapter IV, Verse 24.
63. *Ibid.*, Chapter III, Verse 41.
64. *Ibid.*, Chapter VIII, Verse 1.
65. *Māṇḍūkya Kārikā*, Chapter IV, *Alataśānti*. Verse 7.
66. *Ibid.*, Chapter III, *Advaita Parakaraṇas*. Verse 28.
67. *My View of the World*, Erwin Schrodinger, pp. 21-22.
68. *Ibid.*, p. 95.
69. *Kaṭha Upaniṣad* I. iii. 15, Verse 14.

Bibliography

Books

Abhinavagupta Tantrāloka, (1921-38), 12 vols. Kashmir Sanskrit Texts and Studies, Vols. 27-39, Kashmir Government Publication, Srinagar.

Albert Einstein, (2011), *Relativity, The Special and the General Theory*, Mahaveer Publishers, New Delhi.

Albert Einstein. Copyright 1954, 1982, *Ideas and Opinions*, Crown Publishers, Inc.

Albert Schweitzer (1921), *Civilization and Ethics, The Philosophy of Civilization. Part II*. A. 2C Black Ltd. 4, 526 Soho Square London, W. 1.

Albert Schweitzer (1929), *Philosophy and Ethics, The Philosophy of Civilization*, A & C Black Ltd. 4, 526 Soho Square, London, W. 1.

Albert Schweitzer. (1936), *Indian Thoughts and its Development*. Hodder and Stranghton Ltd., London.

Alex Vilenkin (2006), *Many Worlds in One, The Search For Other Universes*. Hill and Wang Publications, New York.

Alexander Berzin, (1997), *Taking the Kālacakra Initiation*, Snow Lion Publication, Ithaca, New York.

Ānanda Sūtram, p. 1. Ananda Nagar, Purulia (W. Bengal).

Aṣṭābakra Saṁhitā (2010), Advaita Ashrama, 5, Dehi Entally Road, Kolkata.

Arnold Benz. (2000), *Future of the Universe*, Continuum, New York, London.

Arthur Stanley Eddington, *New Pathways in Science*, Cambridge University Press.

Arthur Stanley, *Science and the Unseen World*, Eddington Cambridge University Press.

Arthur Stanley, *The Nature of the Physical World*, Eddington, Cambridge University Press.

Avadhūta Gītā, (1984), Datatreya Avadhuta, Advaita Ashrama Publication Department, 5 Dehi Entally Road, Kolkata.

Avalon Arthur (Sir John Woodroffe), (1953), *Mahānirvāṇa Tantra* (the Great Liberation), 3rd edn., Ganesh & Co., Madras.

Ayer, A.J. (1952), *Language, Truth and Logic*, Dover Publications. Inc., New York.

Banerjee, Biswanath, (1985, rept. 1993), *Sri Kālacakratantra-Raja*, New Asia Printers, Calcutta.

Basham, A.L., *The Wonder That Was India*, Sidgwick and Jackson, London.

Besant, Annie, (1927), *Brahma Vidyā*, Theosophical Publishing House, Adyar, Madras.

Bhaskara, (1916), *Śiva Sūtra Vārtika*, Kashmir Sanskrit Texts and Studies, Srinagar.

Bhattacharya, Benayatosh, *An Introduction to Buddhist Esoterism*, Chowkhamba Sanskrit Series, Varanasi.

Bhattacharya, Benoytosh (ed.), (1931), *Guhyasamāja Tantra*, Oriental Institute, Baroda.

Bhattacharya, Benoytosh (ed.), (1952-58), *Sādhanāmālā*, 2 Vols., Gaekward Oriental Series, XXVI & XLI, Baroda.

Bhattacharya, Dinesh Chandra (1956), *The Cultural Heritage of India* (2nd edition), Vols. I-IV, pp. 211-12. Ramakrishna Mission Institute of Culture, Calcutta.

Bhattacharya, Dinesh Chandra (1969), *The Cultural Heritage of India*, Vol. III. Post-Sankara Advaita.

Bhattacharya, Surendranath (1969), *The Philosophy of Sankara. The Cultural Heritage of India*, Vol. III.

Bloomsbury T&T Clark (January 1, 2000), *Encyclopaedia of Religion and Ethics*.

Book of East.

Brown (2010), *Sex Worship and Symbolism of Primitive Races*, Kessinger Publishing, LLC (September 10).

Brown, W. Norman (ed.), (1958), *Saundaryalaharī*, Harvard Oriental Series, vol. 43, Cambridge, Massachusetts.

Śakti and Śākta, Ganesh & Co., Madras.

Capra Fritjof (1984), *The Tao of Physics*. Bantam Books, New York.

Chāndogya Upaniṣad.

Chatterjee, J.C. (1962), *Kashmir Śaivism*, Research & Publication Department, Srinagar.

Christopher Toumey, (1994), *God's Own Scientist: Creationist in a Secular World*, New Brunswick, N.J.: Rutgers University Press.

Cooper, J.C. (1976), *Taoism, The Way of The Mystic*. The Aquarian Press, Wellingborough, Northamptonshire.

Cornford, C., *From Religion to Philosophy, A Study in the Origins of Western Speculation* (1 April, 2004), Dover Publications Inc.

Cowell & Mitra, (1932), *Prinicpal Upanishads*, 3 vols., Theosophical Publishing House, Adyar, Madras.

CRC Childers Dictionary of Pali Language.

Dasgupta, S.B. (1958), *An Introduction to Tantric Buddhism*, University of Calcutta.

Dhammapada, Oxford University Press.

Dumpier, Sir William Cecil, (1961), *A History of Science and its Relations with Philosophy and Religion*, Cambridge University Press.

Eliade, Mircea, (1954), *Le Yoga: Immortaliteet*, Paris. English version (trans.), W.R. Trask, 1958. *Yogi: Immortality and Freedom*, Bolligm Series Panthoen Inc., New York.

Encyclopaedia Britannica. Encyclopedia Britannica Inc.

Encyclopaedia of Indian Literature, Sahitya Akademi, New Delhi.

Encyclopaedia of Science and Technology, (2007), McGraw Hill, 10th Edition. New York.

Eranos Tanrbuch, *Zur Bedeutungdes Indischen Indeschen Tantra-Yogo*, Vol. I, Zurich, 9-94.

Ervin Schrodinger. (1983), *My Views of the World*, Ox Bow Press, Woodbridge, Connecticut.

Erwin Schrodinger (1952), *Science and Humanism, Physics in our Times*. Cambridge University Press.

Erwin Schrodinger (1952). *Science and Humanism*. Cambridge, University Press.

Erwin Schrodinger (1958), *Mind and Matter*. Cambridge University Press.

Erwin Schrodinger, *Nature and the Greeks*, Cambridge University Press.

*Ethics by Spinoza (*1989), J. M. Dent & Sons, London. Every man's Library.

Farquhar, J.N., (1928), *Religious Literature of India*, Motilal Banarsidass, Delhi.

Galileo Galilei, (1953), *Dialogue Concerning Two Chief World Systems: Ptolemaic and Copernican*. Berkeley and Los Angles: University of California Press.

Galileo, (1632). *Science and Religion: Opposing Viewpoints*, (ed.) Janelle Rohr (1988) (Greenhaven Press).

Gardner Murphy and Robert O. Ballon (1961) (Eds.), *What Psychical Research has Accomplished*, In *William James on Psychical Research*, London. Chatto & Windus.

Garfield, Jay L. (1995), *The Fundamental Wisdom of the Middle Way*. Nāgārjuna's *Mūlamādhyamakākārikā*, Translation and Commentary. New York, Oxford University Press.

Geoffrey Red Mound (2008), *Science and Spiritual Traditions*, Green Wood Press, Westport Connecticut, London.

Geshe Dhargyey (ed.), (1999), *Kālacakra Tantra, Rite of Imitation*, Library of Tibetan Works and Archives, Dharmashala.

Gill, H.S. (2005), *Signification in Language and Culture*. Indian Institute of Advanced Studies, Shimla.

Gupta, Prof. S.N. Das (2000), *A History of Indian Philosophy*, Motilal Banarsidass.

Harper Perennial (1994), *Tao Te Ching*. Compact edition (January 1).

Herrlee G. Creel (1970), *What is Taoism? and Other Studies in Chinese Cultural History*. The University of Chicago Press, Chicago and London.

Īśa Upaniṣad.

If Science is Conscious of its Limits. Quantum Question (1984). Shambhala Publications, Inc.

International Encyclopaedia of Social Sciences. (2007), MacMillan Reference USA; 2 edition ((November 9).

Introduction to B.S., The System of Sankara, according to Sir Charles Eliot, "in Consistency, thoroughness and profundity, holds the first place in Indian philosophy". (*Hinduism and Buddhism*, Vol. II, p. 208).

Jeffrey Mishlone, (1993), *The Roots of Consciousness*, Marlow & Company.

Joachim Kohler (2000), *Who Was Friedrich Nietzsche, Thoughts in a Centenary Year*. Inter Nationes. Bonn.

John Lippitt and James Urpeth (eds.), (2000), See the Essay. "Nature and the Human "Redivinized": Mahayana Buddhist Themes in Thus Spoke Zarathustra", *Nietzsche and the Divine* (Manchester: Clinamen Press).

Kaṭho Upaniṣad.

Kaviraj, Dr. Gopinath (ed.), (1965), *Tripura Rahasyam*, Saraswati Granthamala, vol. 15, Varanasi.

Kaviraj, Gopinath (1963), *Bhāratīya Saṁskrti Aur Sādhanā*, Bihar Rashtrabhasha Parisad, Patna.

Kaviraj, M.M. Gopinath (2002), *Sanātan Sādhan Ki Gupt Dhārā*, II edition, Vishvavidyalaya Prakashan, Varanasi.

Kegan Paul Trench, (1908), *Mādhavācārya, The Sarva-Darśana-Saṁgraha*, Trubner & Co. Ltd., Dryden House, Gerrard Street, London.

Ken Wilber (1984), *Quantum Questions, Mystical Writings of the World's Greatest Physicists*. Shambhala Publications, Inc.

Ken Wilber, (1984), Cosmic Religious Feelings. Quantum Questions, *the Mystic Writings of the World's Greatest Physicists*. Shambhala Publications, Boston, Massachusetts.

Kitty Ferguson (1992), *Quest for a Theory of Everything*, Stephan Hawking, Bantom Books, Great Britain.

Kṣemarāja, Svacchanda Tantram, (1921-25), 6 vols., Kashmir Sanskrit Texts and Studies, Srinagar.

Kulārṇava Tantra, (1965), Ganesh & Co., Madras.

L. Gardet, "*La Mention du nom divin* (dhikr) *dans la mystique musulmane*," Revue Thomiste, LII (1952), 642-79; LIII (1953).

Lama Angarika Govind in an article on *Mantra* in the Stepping Stones, Vol. II, No. I, published from Kalimpong. p. 21, SI. 40.

Leidecker, Kurt, F. (ed.) (1938), *Pratyābhijñahṛdayam* (The Scent of Recognition), Adyar Library, Madras.

Lisa Randall. (2011), *Knocking on Heaven's Door*. Harper Collins Publisher. New York.

Living Zen, (1994), Grove Press (January 11).

Louis de Broglie (1939), *Matter and Light: The New Physics*, Trans. W.H. Johnston (New York: Norton).

Louis de Broglie, (Copyright 1955), *From Physics and Microphysics*, translated by Martin Davidson, by Pantheon Books, Inc. Division of Random House, Inc.

Mādhyamikā Kārikās of Nagarjuna. Ed. by L. de La V. Roussin.

Māṇḍūkya-kārikā II. 32.

Mahābhārata.

Majjhima Nikāya, Translated by Chalmon.

Majumdar, R.C. (1958), *An Advanced History of India*, MacMillan, London.

Malalasekera, G.P. (1972), *Encyclopaedia of Buddhism*, Published by the Government of Sri Lanka, Government Press, Caylon.

Manjit Kumar (2008), *Quantum, Einstein, Bohr and the Great Debate About the Nature of Reality*, Hachette UK Company.

Marquis De Laplace (1951), *A Philosophical Essay on Probabilities*, Dover Publications, Inc. New York.

Marshall, Sir John, (1931), *Mohenjo-daro and the Indus Valley Civilization*, 41, Great Russell Street, London.

Max Kaltenmark (1969), *Lao Tzu and Taoism.* Translated by the French; by Roger Greaves. Stanford University Press. Stanford, California.

Max Müller, F. (Ed.), *Atharva Veda, Sacred Books of the East*, Vol. XXIX, Motilal Banarsidass, Delhi.

Max Müller, F. (1891), *The Sacred Books of the East.* Vol. XXXIX, Oxford. At the Clarendon Press.

Mercia Eliade (1958), *Yoga Immortality and Freedom.* Translated by the French Willard R. Trask. Bollingen Foundation Inc.

Meridan, (1958), *The Philosophies of India*, New York.

Mishlove, Jeffrey (1993) *Consciousness: 'A Hyper Space View' (Appendix)*, The Roots of Consciousness, Marlow & Company.

Mitra, Rajender Lal (edited), *Lalitavistara.*

Mookherjee, Satkari (2006), *The Buddhist Philosophy of Universal Flux.* Motilal Banarsidass Publishers.

Moreno, M.M. (1945), "*Misticamusulmana e mistica Indiana,*" AnnaliLateranensi, X, 102-212, especially pp. 140 ff.

Mūṇḍaka Upaniṣad.

Murray Stein (1998), *Jung's Map of the Soul.* Open Coat, Chicago and La Salle Illinois.

Murti, T.R.V. (1960), *The Central Philosophy of Buddhism*, George Allen & Unwin Ltd., Ruskin House, Museum Street, London.

Nietzsche, F., *Human, Are Too Human.*

Nietzsche, Friedrich, (1954), *Thus Spoke Zarathustra.* Translated by Walter Kaufmann. The Vikcing Press, New York.

Nietzsche, Friedrich (2005), *Thus Spoke Zarathustra, A Book for Everyone and Nobody*, Translated by Graham Parkes. Oxford University Press.

Nirvāṇa Śatakam.

Nyāya Sūtra.

Okakuro-Kakuzo, *The Book of Tea* (published by Fox Duffield, New York).

Oswald Spengler (1991), The Decline of the West. An abridged edition Helmut Werner, Oxford University Press, New York, Oxford. Preface to Present Edition, p. XIV.

Pande, G.C. (1993). *Studies in Mahāyāna*, Central Institute of higher Tibetan Studies, Saranath, Varanasi.

Paratriṁsika.

Patañjali Yoga Sūtra.

Pears, D.F. (1960), *Logical Atomism : Russell and Wittgenstein.* The Revolution in Philosophy: London, MacMillan & Co. Limited.

Philosophy of Gorakh Nath.

Physics and Beyond, Werner Heisenberg, George Allen & Unwin, London.

Piggot, (1950), *Pre-Historic India,* Harmondsworth.

Prajñāpāramitā Piṇḍārthatacchabdyyam Nirdeśa of Diṅnāga, quoted in Haribhadra's *Abhisamayalaṅkārāloka* twice.

Pratyagatmananda, Swami, (1966), *Jayasūtram,* Bharatiya Vidya Prakashan, Varanasi.

Radhakrishnan, S., (1940), *Eastern Religion and Western Thought,* Oxford University Press.

Radhakrishnan, S. (1999), *Indian Philosophy,* Volume 1, Oxford University Press.

Rene Descartes (1998), *Meditation and Other Metaphysical Writings.* The Complete Essays, Penguin Books, London.

Rene Descartes (1998), Replies to the Penultimate counter-objections. *Meditations and Other Metaphysical Writings,* Penguin Books, London.

Russell, Bertrand (1972), *The History of Western Philosophy,* A Touch Stone Book, London.

Sankaracarya (1956), *Vivekacūḍāmani,* Ramakrishna Mission Institute of Culture, Calcutta.

Sarkar, S.C. (1948), 'A Tibetan Account of Nāgārjuna', *The Sino-Indian Journal,* December.

Sastri, Haraprasad (Ed.) (1927), *Advayavarja Saṁgraha,* Gaekward Oriental Series, No. XL, Baroda.

See Thomas H. Brobjer (2005), *Nietzsche's Knowledge of Philosophy* (Urban, III: University of Illinois Press), cha. 6. For Nietzsche's Japanophile friend, see my '*Nietzsche and East-Asian Thought*'. W II: 26[317]; B3 Jan. 1888; BGE 56.

Sharma, D.S. (1956), *Hinduism Through the Ages,* Bharatiya Vidya Bhavan, Bombay.

Shastri, Madhusudan Kaul (1921), *Īśvarapratyabhijña,* 2 vols., Kashmir Sanskrit Texts and Studies, Srinagar.

Simon and Schuster, (1986). *The Making of the Atomic Bomb,* Quoted for Example in *Richard Rhodes.*

Singh, Jai Deva (2008), *The Yoga of Supreme Identity.* Motilal Banarsidass Publishers.

Singh, Jaidev (1979), *Śiva Sūtra. The Yoga of Supreme Identity,* Motilal Banarsidass Publishers Pvt. Ltd., Delhi.

Singh, Lalan Prasad (2010), *Buddhist Tantra, A Philosphical Reflection and Religious Investigation,* Concept Publishing Company Pvt. Ltd.

Singh, Lalan Prasad (2010), *Tantra It's Mystic and Scientific Basis.* Concept Publication Company Pvt. Ltd., New Delhi.

Sir John Marshall, (1931), *Mohenjo-Daro and the Indus Civilization.* Arthur Probsthain, 41, Great Russell Street, London.

Snellgrove, D.L. (1959), *The Hevajra Tantra: A Critical Study*, Part I, Introduction and translation, London Oriental Series, Oxford University Press, London.

Sri Ramanasramam (2011), *The Mystery Beyond the Trinity, Tripūra Rahasya.* Tiruvannanmalai. Chapter XVII.

Stace, W.T. (2012). *A Critical History of Greek Philosophy*, Khosla Publishing House, Daryaganj, New Delhi.

Stebbing, L. Susan, *Philosophy and the Physicists*, Dover Publications Inc., New York.

Stephen Hawking & Leonard Mlodinow (2010), *A Briefer History of Time*, Bantam Press, London.

Stephen Hawking & Leonard Mlodinow. (2010), *The Grand Design*, Bantam Press, London.

Suzuki, D.T. (1950), *Essays in Zen Buddhism* (Second Series), Buddhist Society, London, Rider and Company.

Suzuki, D.T., (1957), *Studies in Zen*, Buddhist Society, Rider-London, Second Impression.

Suzuki , D.T., (1968), *On Indian Mahayana Buddhism*, Harper & Row.

Suzuki, D.T., *The Essence of Buddhism.*

Swami Muktananda (1999), *Pratyabhijñahṛdayam* 2, Nothing exists that is not Śiva. A Siddha Yoga Meditation Publication. Chitshakti Publications, Chennai.

Swami Vivekananda, (1984), *Conquering the Internal Nature, Rāja Yoga.* Advaita Ashrama Publications 2012. 5 Dehi Entally Road, Kolkata.

Swamy Iyer, K.A. Krishna, *Philosophy of the Advaita.*

Taittirīya Upaniṣad.

Tantras – Studies on their Religion and Literature, (1963), p. 2. Punthi Pustak, Calcutta.

Tantric Texts, (1992), Vol. IX, p. 60, Luzac & Co., Great Russell Street, London.

The Aspiration towards Spirit, Quantum Questions, Ken Wilber.

The Garland of Letters. Ganesh & Co., Madras.

The New Encyclopaedia Britannica, (1976), Encyclopaedia Britannica Inc., U.S.A.

The Revolution in Philosophy (1960), MacMillan & Co. Ltd., London.

The Sarva Darśana Saṁgraha.

The Serpent Power.

Thomas Cleary, (1993), *The Essential Tao*, Translated and Presented. Harper San Francisco. Tao Te Ching.

Tony Rothman & George Sudarshan (1998), *Doubt and Certainty*, Srishti Publishers and Distributors for Centre for Philosophy & Foundation of Science, Greater Kailash II, New Delhi.

Tractatus Logico-Philosophicus, Wittgenstein, Routledge Taylor & Francis Group.

Trevor Leggett, (1990), *Śaṅkara on the Yoga Sūtra*, A Full Translation of the Newly Discovered Text. Motilal Banarsidass Publishers Private Ltd., New Delhi.

Trevor Leggett, (1992), *Śaṅkara on the Yoga Sūtras*, Motilal Banarsidass Publishers Private Ltd, Delhi.

Tripūra Rahasyam, (1965), Sarasvati Bhavan Grathamala, Vol. 15, Varanasi.

Tucci, G., (1949), *Teoria Praticadel Mandala.* Casa Editrice Astrolabia, Roma.

Uber Grenzen (1971), *Scientific and Religious Truths*, Werner Heisenberg, Schritte, R. Piper & Co., Verlag, English Edition Across the Frontiers, Harper & Row, 1974.

Underhill, Evelyn (1960), *Mysticism*, University Paperbacks, Methuen & Co. Ltd., 36, Essex Street Strand, London.

Vivekananda, Swami (1962), *Rāja-Yoga*, Advaita Ashram, Entally Road, Calcutta.

Wall, (2004), *Sex and Sex Worship*, Kessinger Publishing, LLC (October 15).

Washington Post, 25th September, 2011. *Faster than Light: Revolution or error.* Particles burst Einstein's Speed Limit by Brian Vastag.

Wellington, A.C., (1960), *The Mathematical Theory of Relativity*, University Press, Cambridge.

Werner Heisenberg, (1952), *Positivism, Metaphysics and Religion* from Physics and Beyond, Translated from the German by Arnold Pomerans, Harper & Row, Publishers, Inc.

Werner Heisenberg (2002), *Physics and Philosophy, The Revolution in Modern Science.* Harper Perennial Modern Thought Publishers, New York.

What is Life? Erwin Schrodinger. Cambridge University Press.

Where is Science going? Max Planck, George Allen & Unwin, London.

Wilkerson, T.E. (1976), *Kant's Critique of Pure Reason*, Oxford University Press, London.

William James (1961), "What Psychological Research has Accomplished", In Gardner Murphy and Robert O. Ballon (edited). *William James on Psychological Research*, London; Chatto and Windus.

Yoga Vāśiṣṭha Sāra Saṅgraha (2012), Central Chinmaya Mission Trust, Mumbai.

Yoginī Hṛdaya, (1963), Sarasvati Bhavan Granthamala, Varanasi.

Zen A Way of Life.

Zukav, Gary (1979), *The Dancing Wu Li Masters, An Overview of the New Physics.* Perennial Classics, New York.

Journals

Journal of Asiatic Society of Bengal (1883).

Journal of the Asiatic Society of Bengal, Proceedings (1921).

Index